普通高等院校英语专业"十四五"规划系列精品教材

英美文学简明教程
（上册　英国文学）
（第3版）

An Introductory Course Book of English and American Literatures
（Volume One　English Literature）
（The 3rd Edition）

主　　编　　张　文　　张伯香
参编人员　　江宝珠　　路　璐　　张秀芳
　　　　　　孙　灵　　周厚银　　万　欣

华中科技大学出版社
中国·武汉

内 容 提 要

本书广泛比较了国内外现有同类教材,吸收了近几年国内外英国文学研究的最新成果,按照选取适合学生阅读又具代表性的常见作品为原则,并结合编者自己多年的教学和研究体会,以英国文学发展的历史为顺序,编选了各个历史时期主要作家的代表作品。在体裁上,注意了诗歌、小说、戏剧与散文的适当比例。每章的内容包括历史文化背景、作者简介、作品选读、注释和思考题等。与其他同类书相比,本书扩大了入选作者,调整了选读作品,增加了学习思考题,从而使教材内容更加充实,语言叙述更加简明,选读作品的难度也相对降低,这将有利于学生的理解与掌握。本书为普通高等院校英语专业教材,也可供独立学院、教育学院、广播电视大学、成人高等教育及社会上英语自学者学习使用。(本书为授课教师提供 ppt 课件,免费索取请洽 QQ:3307902061)

图书在版编目(CIP)数据

英美文学简明教程.上册,英国文学/张文,张伯香主编.—3 版.—武汉:华中科技大学出版社,2020.8(2024.8 重印)
 ISBN 978-7-5680-4422-6

Ⅰ.①英… Ⅱ.①张… ②张… Ⅲ.①英语-阅读教学-高等学校-教材 ②文学史-英国 Ⅳ.①H319.37

中国版本图书馆 CIP 数据核字(2020)第 144253 号

英美文学简明教程(上册 英国文学)(第 3 版)　　　　　张　文　张伯香　主编
Yingmei Wenxue Jianming Jiaocheng (Shangce　Yingguo Wenxue)(Di-3 Ban)

策划编辑:刘　平
责任编辑:刘　平
责任校对:封力煊
封面设计:刘　卉
责任监印:周治超
出版发行:华中科技大学出版社(中国·武汉)　　电话:(027)81321913
　　　　　武汉市东湖新技术开发区华工科技园　　邮编:430223
录　　排:华中科技大学惠友文印中心
印　　刷:武汉市籍缘印刷厂
开　　本:787mm×1092mm　1/16
印　　张:20.25
字　　数:653 千字
版　　次:2024 年 8 月第 3 版第 5 次印刷
定　　价:49.80 元

本书若有印装质量问题,请向出版社营销中心调换
全国免费服务热线:400-6679-118　　竭诚为您服务
版权所有　侵权必究

第3版前言

《英美文学简明教程》(上下)是一套用英语撰写的高校英语专业本科生教材。其编写目的在于通过阅读和分析英美文学作品,促进学生语言基本功和人文素质的提高,增强学生对西方文学及文化的了解,从而培养学生阅读、理解、欣赏英语文学原著的能力,掌握文学批评的基本知识和方法。

本教材选择了英美文学历史上各个时期主要作家的代表作品,包括诗歌、戏剧、小说、散文等,并对各个历史断代的主要历史背景、文学思潮、文学流派,以及具体作家的文学生涯、创作思想、艺术特色及其代表作品的主题、人物、结构、语言等作了简明扼要的介绍和评价。

本教材自2009年面世以来,多次重印。不少高校将它作为英语专业本科生文学课教材和硕士研究生入学考试参考书;许多自学考试英语专业本科生、英语专业函授本科生以及报考英美文学专业研究生的同学对本教材也表现出了极大的兴趣;同时,好些读者还给编者发来热情洋溢的信件,表达他们对使用教材后的感受和意见。为了更好地满足广大读者的需要,2013年我们在保留教材原有优点的基础上,对其进行了修订,扩大了入选作者的数量,调整了选读作品,增加了学习思考题,从而使教材内容更加充实,语言叙述更加简明。为方便教师备课和学生自学,我们又于2015年编写出版了《英美文学简明教程学习指南》。

随着改革开放的逐步深入和科学技术的飞速发展,教材也要与时俱进,富有时代气息,要有利于学生创新能力和人文素质的培养。为此,我们决定对这套文学教材进行第三次修订。这次修订的重点是利用二维码链接,将原《英美文学简明教程学习指南》的内容融入教材中,让学生根据个人的兴趣、爱好,利用手机扫码功能,进一步了解英美作家与作品知识,既不增加教材分量,又能满足学生自主学习的需求。

《英美文学简明教程》(第3版)的问世与华中科技大学出版社领导的关心与支持密不可分,更是出版社责任编辑辛勤劳动的结晶。在此,我谨代表所有编者向他们表示诚挚的谢意。

参加《英美文学简明教程》(第3版)上册编写工作的有江宝珠、路璐、张秀芳、孙灵、周厚银、万欣等老师,参加下册编写工作的有罗城、孙平、徐莉红、向菁、陈娃、柯倩等老师,他们在选材、撰稿、注释、校对等方面做了大量的工作。全书的内容设计、章节安排、文字修改和通读定稿都由主编负责。由于多人执笔,风格难以统一,各种错误也在所难免,敬请广大读者批评指正。

张伯香

2020年4月于珞珈山

Contents

Chapter 1　The Old and Medieval Period ······ 1

　1.1　An Introduction ······ 1

　1.2　Geoffrey Chaucer ······ 2

　1.3　Folk Ballads ······ 8

Chapter 2　The Renaissance Period ······ 14

　2.1　An Introduction ······ 14

　2.2　Edmund Spenser ······ 17

　2.3　Christopher Marlowe ······ 21

　2.4　Walter Raleigh ······ 29

　2.5　William Shakespeare ······ 31

　2.6　Francis Bacon ······ 43

　2.7　John Donne ······ 45

　2.8　George Herbert ······ 49

　2.9　Andrew Marvell ······ 51

　2.10　Ben Jonson ······ 53

　2.11　Robert Herrick ······ 55

　2.12　John Milton ······ 57

Chapter 3　The Neoclassical Period ······ 65

　3.1　An Introduction ······ 65

　3.2　John Dryden ······ 67

　3.3　John Bunyan ······ 70

　3.4　Jonathan Swift ······ 75

　3.5　Alexander Pope ······ 82

　3.6　Daniel Defoe ······ 87

　3.7　Henry Fielding ······ 92

　3.8　Samuel Johnson ······ 98

- 3.9 Thomas Gray ... 101
- 3.10 Robert Burns ... 105
- 3.11 William Blake ... 107
- 3.12 Richard Brinsley Sheridan ... 111

Chapter 4 The Romantic Period ... 123
- 4.1 An Introduction ... 123
- 4.2 William Wordsworth ... 126
- 4.3 Samuel Taylor Coleridge ... 130
- 4.4 George Gordon Byron ... 133
- 4.5 Percy Bysshe Shelley ... 137
- 4.6 John Keats ... 144
- 4.7 Jane Austen ... 149

Chapter 5 The Victorian Period ... 156
- 5.1 An Introduction ... 156
- 5.2 Charles Dickens ... 158
- 5.3 Alfred Tennyson ... 166
- 5.4 Robert Browning ... 170
- 5.5 Elizabeth Barrett Browning ... 176
- 5.6 Charlotte Brontë ... 178
- 5.7 Emily Brontë ... 187
- 5.8 Matthew Arnold ... 196
- 5.9 Gerard Manley Hopkins ... 199
- 5.10 Thomas Hardy ... 201

Chapter 6 The Modern Period ... 211
- 6.1 An Introduction ... 211
- 6.2 George Bernard Shaw ... 216
- 6.3 Alfred Edward Housman ... 224
- 6.4 John Galsworthy ... 226
- 6.5 William Butler Yeats ... 234
- 6.6 T. S. Eliot ... 238
- 6.7 James Joyce ... 247
- 6.8 D. H. Lawrence ... 254
- 6.9 William Golding ... 261
- 6.10 Samuel Beckett ... 266
- 6.11 Dylan Thomas ... 276
- 6.12 Ted Hughes ... 278

  6.13 Seamus Heaney ··· 280

Appendix Ⅰ Sample Test Paper ··· 283

Appendix Ⅱ A Brief Introduction to the Study of Literature ························· 291

Acknowledgments ··· 315

Chapter 1　The Old and Medieval Period

1.1　An Introduction

  Since historical times, the English race has shaped itself out of several distinct peoples that had successively occupied or conquered the island of Great Britain. The earliest inhabitants of the island were the Celts. Then for over three hundred years, from the first century A. D. to the beginning of the fifth, the island became a Roman province. In the middle of the fifth century, the Jutes, Angles and Saxons from the shores of the North Sea came in large bands with the purpose of permanent settlement. The Norman-French arrived six centuries later at the time of the Norman invasion. The Anglo-Saxons brought to England the Germanic language and culture, while the Normans brought a fresh wave of Mediterranean civilization, which includes Greek culture, Roman law and the Christian religion. It is the cultural influences of these conquests that provided the source for the rise and growth of English literature.

  The period of Old English literature extends from about 450 to 1066, the year of the Norman conquest of England. The Germanic tribes from Northern Europe brought with them not only the Anglo-Saxon language, but also a specific poetic tradition which is both bold and strong, mournful and elegiac in spirit. Generally speaking, the Old English poetry that has survived can be divided into two groups: the religious group and the secular one. The poetry of the religious group is mainly on biblical themes. *Genesis A*, *Genesis B* and *Exodus* are poems based on the Old Testament; whereas *The Dream of the Rood* comes from the New Testament. In this poem, Christ is portrayed as the young warrior striding to embrace death and victory, while the rood (cross) itself takes on the burden of his suffering. In addition to these religious compositions, Old English poets produced the national epic poem, *Beowulf*, and a number of more or less lyrical poems of shorter length, which do not contain specific Christian doctrines but evoke the Anglo-Saxon sense of the harshness of circumstance and the sadness of the human lot. *The Wanderer*, *Deor*, *The Seafarer* and *The Wife's Complaint* are among the most beautiful in this secular group. The harsh climate of North Sea strongly affected the tone or mood of the poets. The life is sorrowful, and the speakers are fatalistic, though at the same time courageous and determined.

  The Norman Conquest brought England more than a change of rulers. Politically, a feudalist system was established in England; religiously, the Rome-backed Catholic Church had a much stronger control over the country; and great changes also took place in languages. After the conquest, three languages co-existed in England: French became the official language used by the king and the Norman lords; Latin became the principal tongue of church affairs and in universities; and Old English was spoken only by the common English people. Thus, Britain was opened up to the whole European continent.

With the Norman Conquest, the medieval period of English literature started. In the early part of the period, i.e. from 1066 up to the mid-14th century, there was not much to say about literature in English. It was almost a barren period in literary creation. But in the second half of the 14th century, English literature started to flourish with the appearance of writers like Geoffrey Chaucer, William Langland, John Gower and others. In comparison with Old English literature, Middle English literature deals with a wider range of subjects; and it is uttered by more voices and is presented in a greater diversity of styles, tones and genres. Popular folk literature also occupies an important place in this period. Its presentation of life is not only accurate but also lively and colorful, though the originality of thought is often absent in the literary works of this period. Besides, Medieval English literature strongly reflects the principles of the medieval Christian doctrines, which were primarily concerned with the issue of personal salvation.

Romance, which uses narrative verse or prose to sing knightly adventures or other heroic deeds, is a popular literary form in the medieval period. It has developed the characteristic medieval patterns of the quest, the test, the meeting with the evil giant and the encounter with the beautiful beloved. The hero is usually the knight who sets out on a journey to accomplish some missions — to protect the church, to attack infidelity, to rescue a maiden, to meet a challenge, or to obey a knightly command. There is often a liberal use of the improbable, sometimes even supernatural, things in romance such as mysteries and fantasies. Romantic love is an important part of the plot in romance. Characterization is standardized so that heroes, heroines and wicked stewards can be easily moved from one romance to another. While the structure is loose and episodic, the language is simple and straightforward. The importance of the romance itself can be seen as a means of showing medieval aristocratic men and women in relation to their idealized view of the world. If the epic reflects a heroic age, the romance reflects a chivalric one.

Among the three great Medieval English poets, the author of *Sir Gawain* and the *Green Knight* is the one who produced the best romance of the period; while William Langland is a more realistic writer who dealt with the religious and social issues of his day in *Piers Plowman*. However, it is Chaucer alone who, for the first time in English literature, presented to us a comprehensive realistic picture of the English society of his time and created a whole gallery of vivid characters from all walks of life in his masterpiece, *The Canterbury Tales*.

1.2 Geoffrey Chaucer

1.2.1 About the Author

Geoffrey Chaucer (ca. 1343-1400) was born into a middle-class family of a wealthy wine merchant around the year 1343. In 1357 and 1358 he was a page to the wife of

Chapter 1 The Old and Medieval Period

Lionel, Duke of Clarence. As a young man, he fought for King Edward Ⅲ, and was captured and ransomed later. He married in 1366, and pursued a public life, eventually holding jobs as Italian diplomat, customs official, and a Justice of the Peace. Chaucer's varied experiences gave him a broad opportunity to find much to write about, and he wrote through his entire lifetime. His early writings followed French trends, but his later ones were greatly influenced by Italian authors, notably Boccaccio and
Petrarch. He began *The Canterbury Tales* in 1373 and was occupied by it on and off for the rest of his life. *The Canterbury Tales* was his most famous but unfinished work. It is unique for its variety, humor, grace and realism. Because of this, Chaucer became the first great poet of the English nation and gave strong influences over the development of English literature. He died in London and was buried in Westminster Abbey.

The influence of Renaissance was already felt in the field of English literature when Chaucer was learning from the great Italian writers in the last part of the 14th century. In his works, Chaucer affirmed man's right to pursue earthly happiness and opposed asceticism; he praised man's energy, intellect, quick wit and love of life; he exposed and satirized the social vices, including religious abuses. It can thus be said that though essentially still a medieval writer, Chaucer bore marks of humanism and anticipated a new era to come.

1.2.2 Excerpts from the General Prologue[1] of *The Canterbury Tales*

When in April the sweet showers fall
And pierce the drought of March to the root[2], and all
The veins are bathed in liquor of such power[3]
As brings about the engendering of the flower[4],
When also Zephyrus[5] with his sweet breath
Exhales an air in every grove and heath
Upon the tender shoots, and the young sun
His half-course in the sign of the Ram has run[6],
And the small fowls are making melody
That sleep away the night with open eye
(So nature pricks them and their heart engages)
Then people long to go on pilgrimages
And palmers[7] long to seek the stranger strands
Of far-off saints, hallowed in sundry lands[8],
And specially, from every shire's end

In England, down to Canterbury they wend[9]
To seek the holy blissful martyr[10], quick
To give his help to them when they were sick.
 It happened in that season that one day
In Southwark[11], at The Tabard[12], as I lay
Ready to go on pilgrimage and start
For Canterbury, most devout at heart,
At night there came into that hostelry[13]
Some nine and twenty in a company
Of sundry folk happening then to fall
In fellowship, and they were pilgrims all
That towards Canterbury meant to ride.
The rooms and stables of the inn were wide[14],
They made us easy, all was of the best.
And shortly, when the sun had gone to rest,
By speaking to them all upon the trip
I soon was of them in fellowship
And promised to rise early and take the way
To Canterbury, as you heard me say.
 But nonetheless, while I have time and space,
Before my story takes a further pace[15],
It seems a reasonable thing to say
What their condition[16] was, the full array[17]
Of each of them, as it appeared to me,
According to profession and degree[18],
And what apparel[19] they were riding in;
And at a Knight I therefore will begin.

   *   *   *

 There also was a Nun, a Prioress[20];
Her way of smiling was simple and coy[21].
Her greatest oath was only "By St. Loy!"[22]
And she was known as Madam Eglantyne,
And well she sang a service[23], with a fine
Intoning through her nose, as was most seemly,
And she spoke daintily in French, extremely,
After the school of Stratford-atte-Bowe[24];
French in the Paris style she did not know.
At meat her manners were well taught withal;
No morsel from her lips did she let fall,

Nor dipped her fingers in the sauce too deep;
But she could carry a morsel up and keep
The smallest drop from falling on her breast.
For courtliness[25] she had a special zest.
And she would wipe her upper lip so clean
That not a trace of grease was to be seen
Upon the cup when she had drunk; to eat,
She reached a hand sedately for the meat.
She certainly was very entertaining,
Pleasant and friendly in her ways, and straining
To counterfeit a courtly kind of grace,
A stately bearing fitting to her place,
And to seem dignified in all her dealings.
As for her sympathies and tender feelings,
She was so charitably solicitous.
She used to weep if she but saw a mouse
Caught in a trap, if it were dead or bleeding.
And she had little dogs she would be feeding
With roasted flesh, or milk, or fine white bread.
And bitterly she wept if one were dead
Or someone took a stick and made it smart;
She was all sentiment and tender heart.
Her veil was gathered in a seemly way,
Her nose was elegant, her eyes glass-gray;
Her mouth was very small, but soft and red,
Her forehead, certainly, was fair of spread,
Almost a span[26] across the brows, I own;
She was indeed by no means undergrown.
Her cloak, I noticed, had a graceful charm.
She wore a coral trinket on her arm,
A set of beads, the gaudies[27] tricked[28] in green,
Whence hung a golden brooch of brightest sheen
On which there first was graven a crowned A,
And lower, *Amor vincit omnia*[29].

        *   *   *

A worthy *woman* from beside Bath city
Was with us, somewhat deaf, which was a pity.
In making cloth she showed so great a bent[30]
She bettered those of Ypres and of Ghent[31]

In all the parish not a dame dared stir
Towards the altar steps in front of her
And if indeed they did, so wrath was she
As to be quite put out of charity[32].
Her kerchiefs were of finely woven ground[33];
I dared have sworn they weighed a good ten pound,
The ones she wore on Sunday, on her head.
Her hose were of the finest scarlet red
And gartered tight; her shoes were soft and new.
Bold was her face, handsome, and red in hue.
A worthy woman all her life, what's more
She'd had five husbands, all at the church door,
Apart from other company in youth[34];
No need just now to speak of that, forsooth[35].
And she had thrice been to Jerusalem,
Seen many strange rivers and passed over them;
She'd been to Rome and also to Boulogne,
Saint James of Compostella and Cologne[36],
And she was skilled in wandering by the way.
She had gap-teeth, set widely, truth to say.
Easily on an ambling horse she sat
Well wimpled up, and on her head a hat
As broad's is a buckler or a shield;
She had a flowing mantle that concealed
Large hips, her heels spurred sharply under that.
In company she liked to laugh and chat
And knew the remedies for love's mischances,
An art in which she knew the oldest dances[37].

Notes

1. In this modern English translation, Chaucer's original metrical form, the heroic couplet, is used.
2. **pierce the drought of March to the root**: The gentle spring rain penetrates the very roots of the plants. Here drought of March refers to the general situation on the European continent, not specifically to Britain, for March in Britain is not very dry.
3. **The veins are bathed in liquor of such power**: Spring rain provides enough water for every rib of the leaves, thus endowing the plants with its power.
4. **the engendering of the flower**: the budding of the flower. Here, engendering means springing up.

Chapter 1　The Old and Medieval Period

5. **Zephyrus**: the west wind (personified).
6. **the young sun /His half-course in the sign of the Ram has run**: The sun is young because it has run only half way through the Ram, which is the first sign of the Zodiac. The sun runs through the sign of the Ram annually from March 21st to April 21st.
7. **palmers**: pilgrims, so called because they carried palms to show that they had been to Jerusalem.
8. **the stranger strands/ Of far-off saints, hallowed in sundry lands**: the foreign shores where there were the distant shrines of the saints, which were considered as holy places in different countries.
9. **wend**: (archaic) go.
10. **the holy blissful martyr**: Here it refers to Thomas à Becket who in his lifetime was Chancellor of Britain and Archbishop of Canterbury. He resisted the efforts of King Henry II to deprive the church courts of part of their power. As a result of the quarrel, four of Henry's knights rode to Canterbury and murdered Thomas in the cathedral. Thomas was later considered a martyr and worshipped as a saint. His tomb at Canterbury became one of the most famous shrines in England.
11. **Southwark**: a suburb of London.
12. **The Tabard**: an inn at Southwark.
13. **hostelry**: an inn, a lodging house.
14. **wide**: spacious.
15. **Before my story takes a further pace**: Before I proceed with my story.
16. **condition**: social status, position.
17. **the full array**: the complete outfit (dress and appearance).
18. **degree**: rank.
19. **apparel**: clothing.
20. **Prioress**: a nun corresponding in rank to a prior (i.e. the superior of a convent).
21. **coy**: The word carries two slightly different meanings: (1) "shrinking from contact or familiarity", (2) "marked by cute, coquettish or artful playfulness".
22. **"By St. Loy!"**: a very mild oath. St. Loy was a well-known French goldsmith in the 6th century.
23. **sang a service**: sang hymns in a church service.
24. **Stratford-atte-Bowe**: a monastery near London. Chaucer is making fun of the prioress by describing her speaking of French with a strong local accent.
25. **courtliness**: courtly behaviour, refined manners adopted by courtiers and ladies of the court.
26. **a span**: the maximum distance between the tips of the thumb and the little finger.
27. **gaudies**: A gaud is a large bead placed between every ten beads in a rosary to mark a division in a prayer.

28. **tricked**: decorated.
29. ***Amor vincit omnia***: (Latin) Love conquers all.
30. **a bent**: a natural skill.
31. **Ypres and Ghent**: cities in Belgium known for clothmaking in Chaucer's time.
32. **put out of charity**: to lose temper.
33. **ground**: texture.
34. **Apart from other company in youth**: not including other lovers she had in her youth.
35. **forsooth**: (archaic) truly, no doubt.
36. **Boulogne, / Saint James of Compostella and Cologne**: Boulogne, a seaside city in France; Compostella, a city in Spain; Cologne, a city in Germany. In Chaucer's time, the shrines of these places attracted many pilgrims.
37. **An art in which she knew the oldest dances**: She got to know all the old tricks of the art (of love).

Study Questions

1. What is the "framing device" that Chaucer uses for his collection of stories?
2. Study lines 1-18 of the "General Prologue". What seems to be the motives offered for the pilgrimage? In what ways are the season and the nature images important factors?
3. Based on Prioress's portrait, can you give a possible reason why she is undertaking this pilgrimage?
4. What details does the narrator use in describing the Prioress, and in what order?
5. Why does the Wife of Bath go on pilgrimage?
6. How does Chaucer reveal his attitude toward the Wife of Bath?

Essay Topics

1. Please name and define five specific methods of characterization Chaucer uses in the "General Prologue". In what additional ways are the pilgrims characterized?
2. Do you think the Prioress is portrayed by Chaucer as a perfect lady or a perfect nun? Why?

1.3 Folk Ballads

The folk ballad is a popular literary form; it comes from unlettered people rather than from professional minstrels or scholarly poets. As the main form of medieval folk literature, the folk ballad has an oral tradition which makes it easier to remember and memorize. Therefore, all the stylistic features of the folk ballad have derived from their oral nature. The first is its simple language; the simplicity is reflected both in the verse form and the colloquial expressions. So far as the verse form is concerned, ballads are composed mainly in quatrains, which are known as the ballad stanza, rhyming *abcb*, with the first and third lines carrying 4 accented syllables and the second and fourth carrying 3. By making use of a simple, plain language or dialect of the common people with colloquial and, sometimes, idiomatic expressions in its narration or dialogues, the ballad leaves a strong dramatic effect to the reader. The second is its wonderful story which deals only with the culminating incident or climax of a plot. Most of the ballads have a romantic or tragic dimension, with a tragic incident, often a murder or an accidental death, as their subject. Like classical tragedy, ballads have an inevitability, which reflects the folk belief that people are lured into the fatally attractive traps just because all human life is shaped by fate. It is a common pattern of romantic tragic balladry that if one lover dies the other must follow suit. So usually the hero would die of his wound, and the heroine of her sorrow. The third is its dominant mood or tone, either tragic like "Sir Patrick Spens", which tells a story of treachery, or comic like "Get up and Bar the Door", which presents a funny scene of the domestic life. Furthermore, to strengthen the dramatic effect of the narration, ballads also make full use of hyperbole; actions and events are much exaggerated. This hyperbolic style partly comes from a desire to astonish, for the poor folk would be delighted to hear of the larger-than-life exploits of ballad people. Music has an important formative influence on ballads, too. Another impressive feature of the ballad is the use of refrains and other kinds of repetitions. Poetically the refrains are decorative; musically they are absolutely essential. Through refrains and repetitions, the narration is lent a quality of liturgy, or of incantation. Magic or supernatural force, the perpetual presence of impossibility, is a rich narrative source of balladry. In the ballad world, things happen suddenly and without warning; only the help of magic or supernatural force can overcome the fatal powers of destruction. Love, adventure, courageous feats of daring, and sudden disaster are frequent topics of folk ballads.

1.3.1 "The Three Ravens"[1]

There were three ravens sat on a tree,
   Down a down, hey down, hey down,
They were three ravens sat on a tree,
   With a down.

There were three ravens sat on a tree,
They were as black as black might be,
   With a down, derry, derry, derry down, down.

The one of them said to his mate.
Where shall we our breakfast take?

Down in yonder green field
There lies a knight slain under his shield.

His hounds they lie down at his feet,
So well they can their master keep[2].

His hawks they fly so eagerly,[3]
There's no fowl[4] dare him come nigh.

Down there comes a fallow doe[5],
As great with young as she might go.

She lifted up his bloody head,
And kissed his wounds that were so red.

She got him up upon her back,
And carried him to earthen lake[6].

She buried him before the prime[7];
She was dead herself ere evensong[8] time.

God send every gentleman
Such hawks, such hounds, and such lemman[9].

Notes

1. Instead of the regular ballad form, this ballad basically consists of 11 two-lined stanzas. The second and the fourth lines in the first stanza and the third line in the second stanza are tunes sung by the ballad singer to attract the listener's attention.
2. **So well they can their master keep**: So well do they keep guard over their master.
3. **His hawks they fly so eagerly**: The hawks he bred fly so fiercely.
4. **no fowl**: no bird.
5. **fallow doe**: reddish brown female deer. Here the doe is alluding to the knight's mistress.
6. **earthen lake**: pit.
7. **prime**: the first hour of the morning.
8. **evensong**: the service of evening prayer in the church.
9. **lemman**: mistress.

Study Questions

1. What happens in this ballad?
2. What is the mood of this ballad?
3. What is its theme?

1.3.2 "Get Up and Bar the Door"

It fell about the Martinmas¹ time,
   And a gay time it was then,
When our good wife got puddings to make,
   And she's boild them in the pan.

The wind sae cauld² blew south and north,
   And blew into the floor;
Quoth our goodman to our goodwife,
   "Gae³ out and bar the door."

"My hand is in my hussyfskap⁴,
   Goodman, as ye may see;
An it shoud nae⁵ be barrd this hundred year,
   It's no be barrd for me."

They made a paction⁶ tween them twa⁷,
   They made it firm and sure,
That the first word whaeer⁸ shoud speak,
   Shoud rise and bar the door.

Then by there came two gentlemen,
   At twelve o'clock at night,
And they could neither see house nor hall,
   Nor coal nor candle-light.

"Now whether is this a rich man's house,
   Or whether is it a poor?"
But neer a word wad ane⁹ o them speak,
   For barring of the door.

And first they ate the white puddings,

　　　　And then they ate the black;
Tho muckle[10] thought the goodwife to herself,
　　　　Yet neer a word she spake.

Then said the one unto the other,
　　　　"Here, man, tak ye my knife;
Do ye tak aff the auld man's beard,
　　　　And I'll kiss the goodwife."

"But there's nae water in the house,
　　　　And what shall we do then?"
"What ails thee at the pudding-broo,[11]
　　　　That boils into the pan?"

O up then started our goodman,
An angry man was he:
"Will ye kiss my wife before my een,
And scad[12] me wi pudding-bree?"

Then up and started our goodwife,
Gied[13] three skips on the floor:
"Goodman, you've spoken the foremost word,
Get up and bar the door."

Notes
1. **Martinmas**: November 11, the feast of St. Martin.
2. **sae**: so; **cauld**: cold.
3. **gae**: go.
4. **hussyfskap**: housewifery.
5. **shoud nae**: should not.
6. **paction**: compact.
7. **twa**: two.
8. **whaeer**: whoever.
9. **wad**: would; **ane**: one (of the husband and the wife).
10. **muckle**: much.
11. **What ails thee**: "Why don't you use…"; **pudding-broo**: pudding-broth.
12. **scad**: scald.
13. **gied**: gave.

Chapter 1　The Old and Medieval Period

Study Questions

1. What is the mood of this ballad?
2. What can you learn from this ballad?
3. How is the story told?

Chapter 2 The Renaissance Period

2.1 An Introduction

Generally, Renaissance refers to the period between the 14th and mid-17th century. It first started in Italy with the flowering of painting, sculpture and literature. From Italy the movement went to embrace the rest of Europe. The Renaissance, which means rebirth or revival, is actually a movement stimulated by a series of historical events, such as the rediscovery of ancient Roman and Greek culture, the new discoveries in geography and astrology, the religious reformation and the economic expansion. The Renaissance, therefore, in essence, is a historical period in which the European humanist thinkers and scholars made attempts to get rid of those old feudalist ideas in medieval Europe, to introduce new ideas that expressed the interests of the rising bourgeoisie, and to recover the purity of the early Christianity from the corruption of the Roman Catholic Church.

The Renaissance was slow in reaching England not only because of England's separation from the Continent but also because of its domestic unrest. The century and a half following the death of Chaucer is the most volcanic period of English history. The war-like nobles seized the power of England and turned it into self-destruction. The Wars of the Roses are examples to show how the energy of England was violently destroying itself. The frightful reign of Richard Ⅲ marked the end of civil wars, making possible a new growth of English national feelings under the popular Tudors. With Henry Ⅷ's encouragement, the Oxford reformers, scholars and humanists introduced classical literature to England. Education, based upon the classics and the Bible, was revitalized; literature, already much read during the 15th century, became even more popular. Thus began the English Renaissance, which was perhaps England's Golden Age, especially in literature. Among the literary giants were Philip Sidney, Edmund Spenser, Christopher Marlowe, William Shakespeare, Ben Jonson, Francis Bacon and John Donne. The English Renaissance had no sharp break with the past. Attitudes and feelings which had been characteristic of the 14th and 15th centuries persisted well down into the era of Humanism and Reformation.

Humanism is the essence of the Renaissance. But in the medieval society, people as individuals were largely subordinated to the feudalist rule without any freedom and independence; and in medieval theology, people's relationships to the world were largely reduced to a problem of adapting to or avoiding the circumstances of earthly life in an effort to prepare their souls for a heavenly life. However, Renaissance humanists found in the classics a justification to exalt human nature and came to see that human beings were glorious creatures capable of individual development in the direction of perfection, and that the world they inhabited was theirs not to despise but to question, explore and enjoy. Thus, by emphasizing the dignity of human beings and the importance of the present life, they voiced their beliefs that man did not only have the right to enjoy the beauty of his life, but also had the ability to perfect himself and to perform wonders. Humanism began to take hold in England when the Dutch scholar Desiderius Erasmus (1466-1536) came to teach the classical learning, first at Oxford and then at Cambridge. Thomas More, Christopher Marlowe and William Shakespeare are the best representatives of the English humanists.

Another important part of this Renaissance movement was the religious reformation, which was initiated by Martin Luther (1483-1546), a German Protestant. Luther believed that every true Christian was his own priest and was entitled to interpret the Bible for himself. Encouraged by Luther's preaching, reformers from northern Europe vitalized the Protestant movement. The colorful and dramatic rituals of the Catholic Church were simplified. Indulgences, pilgrimages and other practices were condemned. In the early stage of the continental reformation, Henry VIII was regarded as a faithful son of the Catholic Church and named "Defender of the Faith" by the Pope. Only his need for a legitimate male heir, and hence a new wife, led him to cut ties with Rome. But the common English people had long been dissatisfied with the corruption of the church and inspired by the reformers' ideas from the Continent. So they welcomed and supported Henry's decision of breaking away from Rome. When Henry VIII declared himself through the approval of the Parliament as the Supreme Head of the Church of England in 1534, the Reformation in England was in its full swing. One of the major results was the fact that the Bible in English was placed in every church and services were held in English instead of Latin so that people could understand. In the brief reign of Henry's son Edward VI the reform of the church's doctrine and teaching was carried out. But after Mary ascended the throne, there was a violent swing to Catholicism. However, by the middle of Elizabeth's reign, Protestantism had been firmly established with a certain extent of compromise between Catholicism and Protestantism. The religious reformation was actually a reflection of the class struggle waged by the new rising bourgeoisie against the feudal class and its ideology.

Strong national feeling in the time of the Tudors gave a great incentive to the cultural development in England. English schools and universities were established in place of the old monasteries. With classical culture and the Italian humanistic ideas coming into England, the English Renaissance began flourishing. One of the men who made a great contribution in this respect was William Caxton for he was the first person who introduced printing into England. Thus, for the first time in history it was possible for a book or an idea to reach the whole nation in a speedy way. With the introduction of printing, an age of translation came into being. Lots and lots of continental literary works both ancient and modern were translated and printed in English. As a result, the introduction of printing led to a commercial market for literature and provided numerous books for the English people to read, thus making everything ready for the appearance of the great Elizabethan writers.

The early stage of the English Renaissance was one of imitation and assimilation. Academies after the Italian type were founded. And Petrarch was regarded as the fountainhead of literature by the English writers. Wyatt and Surrey began engraving the forms and graces of Italian poetry upon the native stock. While the former introduced the Italian sonnet into England, the latter brought in blank verse. Sidney followed with the sestina and *terza rima*. And Marlowe gave new vigor to the blank verse with his "mighty lines". Poetry, which was regarded as a concentrated exercise of the mind, of craftsmanship, and of learning, came into a great boom. Spenser's *The Shepherd's Calendar* showed how the pastoral convention could be adapted to a variety of subjects, moral or heroic, and how the rules of decorum, or fitness of style to subject, could be applied through variations in the diction and metrical scheme. In "The Passionate Shepherd to His Love", Marlowe spoke with a voice so innocent that it would be very difficult for us to connect it with the voice in his tragedies. But the poetry written by John Donne, George Herbert and others like them (who were later labeled as the metaphysical poets by Dryden and Johnson) represented a sharp break from the poetry by their predecessors and most of their contemporaries.

The Elizabethan drama, in its totality, is the real mainstream of the English Renaissance. It could be dated back to the Middle Ages. Interludes and morality plays thriving in the medieval period continued to be popular down to Shakespeare's time. But the development of the drama into a sophisticated art form required another influence — the Greek and Roman classics. Lively, vivid native English materials were put into the regular form of the Latin comedies of Plautus and Terence. Tragedies were in the style of Seneca. The fusion of classical form with English content brought about the possibility of a mature and artistic drama. The most famous dramatists in the Renaissance England are Christopher Marlowe, William Shakespeare and Ben Jonson, who wrote plays with such universal qualities of greatness. By imitating the romances of Italy and Spain, embracing the mysteries of German legend, and combining the fictions of poetic fancy with the facts of daily life, they made a vivid depiction of the sharp conflicts between feudalism and the rising bourgeoisie in a transitional period. And with humors of the moment, abstractions of philosophical speculation, and intense vitality, this extraordinary drama, with Shakespeare as the master, left a monument of the Renaissance unrivaled for pure creative power by any other product of that epoch.

Francis Bacon (1561-1626), the first important English essayist, is best known for his essays which greatly influenced the development of this literary form. He was also the founder of modern science in England. His writings paved the way for the use of scientific method. Thus, he is undoubtedly one of the representatives of the English Renaissance.

2.2 Edmund Spenser

2.2.1 About the Author

Edmund Spenser (1552-1599) was born in London to a poor family and was educated at Cambridge on a scholarship. He studied philosophy, rhetoric, Italian, French, Latin and Greek to prepare himself as a poet. He left Cambridge in 1576 and served as personal secretary to several prominent men, including the earl of Leicester. Later he met Sir Philip Sidney and started a friendship with him. In 1580, through Leicester's influence, Spenser was made secretary to Lord Grey of Wilton, the queen's deputy in Ireland. He spent the rest of  his life there holding various posts in the government except for two visits to England. In 1598 a fierce Irish rebellion forced Spenser to abandon his Kilcolman Castle. Spenser never recovered from the shock of this frightful experience. He returned to England heartbroken, and in the following year he died in an inn at Westminster.

Spenser's most ambitious poetic achievement is *The Faerie Queene*, set in the mythical world of King Arthur and his knights. Spenser had planned to write twelve books for this great poem, but he completed only six. According to his own explanation, his principal intention is "to fashion a gentleman in virtuous and gentle discipline". Each book has a hero knight who performs noble deeds for a glorious fairy queen whom Spenser intentionally associates with Queen Elizabeth Ⅰ. The knight in each book represents a different moral virtue: justice, courtesy and so on. The hero of heroes, who possesses all of these virtues, is Arthur, and he is to play a role in each of the twelve major adventures, which has its own individual hero. The recurring appearances of Arthur serve as a unifying element for the poem as a whole. Another character contributing to the unity of the work is Gloriana, the Fairy Queen. It is from her court and at her bidding that each of the heroes sets out on his particular adventure. Prince Arthur's great mission is his search for the Fairy Queen, whom he has fallen in love with through a love vision. Obstacles the knights encounter in the poem stand for evils and temptations that must be overcome. And the reader will find that all these would happen in an enchanted world of dragons, giants, witches and other marvels.

2.2.2 "Sonnet 75"

One day I wrote her name upon the strand[1],
But came the waves and washed it away;
Agayne I wrote it with a second hand,
But came the tyde, and made my paynes his pray[2].

"Vayne man," sayd she, "that doest in vaine assay[3],
A mortal thing so to immortalize,
For I my selve shall lyke to this decay,
And eek[4] my name bee wyped out lykewize."
"Not so," quod[5] I, "let baser things devize[6],
To dy in dust, but you shall live by fame:
My verse your vertues rare shall eternize[7],
And in the heavens wryte your glorious name.
Where whenas death shall all the world subdew,
Our love shall live, and later life renew."

Notes

1. **strand**: seashore.
2. **pray**: prey.
3. **assay**: try.
4. **eek**: also.
5. **quod**: said.
6. **devize**: contrive.
7. **eternize**: to make eternal.

Study Questions

1. What is the thematic significance of the waves and the tide?
2. Is Spenser's "Sonnet 75" more like an Italian sonnet or an English sonnet?
3. Why does the speaker say that their love will live after death has "subdued" all the world?

2.2.3 An Excerpt from Canto I, Book I of *The Faerie Queene*[1]

1

A Gentle Knight was pricking on the plaine,
    Ycladd[2] in mightie armes and silver shielde,
    Wherein old dints of deepe wounds did remaine,
    The cruell markes of many a bloudy fielde;
    Yet armes till that time did he never wield:[3]
    His angry steede did chide his foming bitt,
    As much disdayning to the curbe to yield:[4]
    Full jolly knight he seemed, and faire did sitt,
As one for knightly giusts[5] and fierce encounters fitt.

And on his brest a bloudie Crosse he bore,
The deare rememberance of his dying Lord,
For whose sweete sake that glorious badge he wore,
And dead as living ever him ado'd:[6]
Upon his shield the like was also scor'd,
For soveraine hope, which in his helpe he had:[7]
Right faithfull true he was in deede and word,
But of his cheere did seeme too solemne sad,[8]
Yet nothing did he dread, but ever was ydrad.[9]

Upon a great adventure he was bond,
That greatest *Gloriana* to him gave,
That greatest Glorious Queene of *Faerie* lond,
To winne him worship, and her grace to have,
Which of all earthly things he most did crave;
And ever as he rode, his heart did yearn[10]
To prove his puissance[11] in battle brave
Upon his foe, and his new force to learn;
Upon his foe, a Dragon horrible and stearne.[12]

A lovely Lady rode him faire beside,
Upon a lowly Asse more white than snow,
Yet she much whiter,[13] but the same did hide
Under a vele, that wimpled was full low,[14]
And over all a black stole she did throw,
As one that inly mourned:[15] so was she sad,
And heavie sat upon her palfrey[16] slow:
Seemed in heart some hidden care she had,
And by her in a line a milke white lambe she lad.[17]

So pure and innocent, as that same lambe,[18]
She was in life and every vertuous lore,
And by descent from royall lynage came
Of ancient Kings and Queenes, that had of yore
Their scepters stretcht from east to westerne shore,
And all the world in their subjection held;
Till that infernall feend with foule uprore
Forwasted all their land,[19] and them expeld:
Whom to avenge, she had this Knight from far compeld.[20]

Behind her farre away a Dwarfe did lag,
That lasie seemed in being ever last,
Or wearied with bearing of her bag
Of needments[21] at his backe. Thus as they past,
The day with cloudes was suddeine overcast,
And angry Jove[22] an hideous storme of raine
Did poure into his Lemans lap[23] so fast,
That everie wight to shrowd it did constrain,[24]
And this faire couple eke to shroud themselves were fain.[25]

Enforst to seeke some covert nigh at hand,
A shadie grove not far away they spide,[26]
That promist ayde the tempest to withstand:
Whose loftie trees yclad with sommers pride
Did spred so broad, that heavens light did hide,
Not perceable with power of any starre:
And all within were pathes and alleies wide,
With footing worne, and leading inward farre:
Faire harbour that them seemes; so in they entred arre.[27]

Notes

1. The poem is written in the stanza invented by the poet himself, the Spenserian stanza, i. e., a stanza of nine lines, with the first eight lines in iambic pentameter and the last line in iambic hexameter, rhyming *ababbcbcc*.
2. **ycladd**: clad.
3. **Yet armes till that time did he never wield**: i. e., the knight had never fought in the battle field, so the weapon was new to him.
4. **His angry steede did chide his foming bitt, /As much disdayning to the curbe to yield**: His horse, foaming with anger, ground the mouth-piece of the bridle as if too proud to yield to its master's control.
5. **giust**: same as joust, meaning: the encounter of two knights on horseback at a tournament.
6. **And dead as living ever him ador'd**: And always adored him (Jesus Christ) dead as if alive.
7. **Upon his shield the like was also scor'd, /For soveraine hope, which in his helpe he had**: Upon his shield there was also the mark of a Cross, as a sign of supreme hope which he received with the help of the Lord.
8. **But of his cheere did seeme too solemne sad**: But in countenance and bearing he

seemed too solemnly grave. cheere = countenance.
9. **ydrad**: dreaded.
10. **his hart did earne**: his heart did yearn.
11. **puissance**: strength, power.
12. **stearne**: stern.
13. **Yet she much whiter**: here signifying the surpassing purity and spotlessness of Virgin Una.
14. **Under a vele, that wimpled was full low**: Her veil was plaited in folds, falling to cover her face.
15. **As one that inly mourned**: as one who felt sorrowful at heart.
16. **palfrey**: a saddle-horse, esp. for a lady, here referring to Una's ass.
17. **lad**: old form for "led".
18. **as that same lambe**: referring to the Lamb of God, i.e., Jesus Christ.
19. **Forwasted all their land**: here referring to the dragon devastating the country.
20. **compeld**: old form for "compelled", summoned.
21. **needments**: things needed.
22. **Jove**: Jupiter, king of gods in Roman mythology.
23. **his Lemans lap**: his sweetheart's lap; Lemans: old form for sweetheart, here referring to earth.
24. **That everie wight to shrowd it did constrain**: that every person was forced to take shelter. wight = person, human being.
25. **fain**: glad.
26. **spide**: spied.
27. **Faire harbour that them seemes; so in they entered arre**: It seems to them to be a fair shelter and so they enter it.

Study Questions
1. What more than anything else on earth does the knight want?
2. What do we learn about the Lady (stanzas 4-5)?
3. What can you anticipate when they were forced to take shelter in the forest?

2.3　Christopher Marlowe

2.3.1　About the Author

　　Christopher Marlowe (1564-1593) was the son of a Canterbury shoemaker. Scholarships took him first to the King's School, and then Cambridge. His play, *Tamburlaine*, written before he left Cambridge, turned out to be a sweeping success on the stage. When he came to London in 1584, his mind was surging with the ideals of Renaissance, which later found expression in *Dr. Faustus*. He became an actor and led a tempestuous life in the following six years since his first great success. On May 30,

1593, Marlowe was killed in a quarrel over a tavern bill in Deptford.

As the most gifted of the "University Wits", Marlowe wrote six plays within his short lifetime. Among them the most important are: *Tamburlaine* (1587-1588), *The Jew of Malta* (1590?) and *Dr. Faustus* (1592-1593). Marlowe's non-dramatic poetry includes *Hero and Leander*, "The Passionate Shepherd to His Love", and a verse translation of *Ovid's Amores*.

Dr. Faustus is a play based on the German legend of a magician aspiring for knowledge and finally meeting his tragic end as a result of selling his soul to the Devil. The play's dominant moral is human rather than religious. It celebrates the human passion for knowledge, power and happiness; it also reveals man's frustration in realizing the high aspirations in a hostile moral order. The confinement to time is the cruelest fact of man's condition.

Marlowe's greatest achievement lies in that he perfected the blank verse and made it the principal medium of English drama. To achieve this, Marlowe employed hyperbole as his major figure of speech which indicates the poetic energy and intensity conveyed through the verse. Marlowe's second achievement is his creation of the Renaissance hero for English drama. Such a hero is always individualistic and full of ambition, facing bravely the challenge from both gods and men.

Though Marlowe is masterful in handling blank verse and creating dramatic effects, he is not so strong in dramatic construction, and compared with Shakespeare, his women characters are rather pale. But his brilliant achievement as a whole raised him to an eminence as the pioneer of English drama.

2.3.2 "The Passionate Shepherd to His Love"

Come live with me and be my love,
And we will all the pleasures prove[1]
That valleys, groves, hills, and fields,
Woods, or steepy mountain yields.

And we will sit upon the rocks,
Seeing the shepherds feed their flocks,
By shallow rivers to whose falls
Melodious birds sing madrigals[2].

And I will make thee beds of roses

And a thousand fragrant posies,
A cap of flowers, and a kirtle[3]
Embroidered all with leaves of myrtle;

A gown made of the finest wool
Which from our pretty lambs we pull;
Fair lined slippers for the cold,
With buckles of the purest gold;

A belt of straw and ivy buds,
With coral clasps and amber studs:
And if these pleasures may thee move,
Come live with me, and be my love.

The shepherds' swains[4] shall dance and sing
For thy delight each May morning:
If these delights thy mind may move,
Then live with me and be my love.

Notes
1. **prove**: experience, test.
2. **madrigal**: a short love lyric that can be set to music.
3. **kirtle**: a long dress worn by women.
4. **swains**: country youths.

Study Questions
1. What images are used in this poem? Are the images literal, or figurative?
2. Name three promises that the shepherd has made for his love. Why would he make these promises?
3. What ideas are implied by the total impression of the whole poem?

2.3.3 An Excerpt from Act 5 of *Dr. Faustus*

Scene 2

[*Thunder. Enter Lucifer, Beelzebub, and Mephistophilis.*]

LUC. Thus from infernal Dis[1] do we ascend
   To view the subjects of our monarchy,
   Those souls which sin seals the black sons of hell.
   'Mong which as chief, Faustus, we come to thee,
   Bringing with us lasting damnation

To wait upon thy soul; the time is come

　　　Which makes it forfeit.

MEPH. And this gloomy night

　　　Here in this room will wretched Faustus be.

BEL. And here we'll stay

　　　To mark him how he doth demean himself.

MEPH. How should he but in desperate lunacy?

　　　Fond worldling, now his heart-blood dries with grief,

　　　His conscience kills it, and his laboring brain

　　　Begets a world of idle fantasies

　　　To overreach the devil, but all in vain.

　　　His store of pleasures must be sauced with pain.

　　　He and his servant Wagner are at hand;

　　　Both come from drawing Faustus' latest will.

　　　See where they come.

　　　　　[*Enter Faustus and Wagner.*]

FAUST. Say, Wagner, thou hast perused my will;

　　　How dost thou like it?

WAG. Sir, so wondrous well

　　　As in all humble duty I do yield

　　　My life and lasting service for your love.

　　　　　[*Enter the Scholars.*]

FAUST. Gramercies, Wagner. Welcome, gentlemen.

1 SCH. Now, worthy Faustus, methinks your looks are changed.

FAUST. Ah, gentlemen!

2 SCH. What ails Faustus?

FAUST. Ah, my sweet chamber-fellow, had I lived with thee, then had I lived still, but now must die eternally. Look, sirs! Comes he not? Comes he not?

1 SCH. O my dear Faustus, what imports this fear?

2 SCH. Is all our pleasure turned to melancholy?

3 SCH. He is not well with being over-solitary.

2 SCH. If it be so, we'll have physicians, and Faustus shall be cured.

3 SCH. 'Tis but a surfeit,² sir; fear nothing.

FAUST. A surfeit of deadly sin that hath damned both body and soul.

2 SCH. Yet, Faustus, look up to heaven: remember God's mercies

　　　Are infinite.

FAUST. But Faustus' offense can ne'er be pardoned; the Serpent that tempted Eve may be saved, but not Faustus. Ah, gentlemen, hear with patience, and tremble not at my speeches. Though my heart pants and quivers to remember that I have been a student here these thirty years, O would I had never seen Wittenberg, never read book! And what wonders I have done all Germany can witness, yea, all the world, for which Faustus hath lost both Germany and the world, yea heaven itself — heaven the seat of God, the throne of the blessed, the kingdom of joy, and must remain in hell forever, hell, ah hell, forever! Sweet friends, what shall, become of Faustus, being in hell forever?

3 SCH. Yet, Faustus, call on God.

FAUST. On God, whom Faustus hath abjured? On God, whom Faustus hath blasphemed? Ah, my God, I would weep, but the devil draws in my tears! Gush forth, blood, instead of tears, yea, life and soul! O he stays my tongue; I would lift up my hands but, see, they hold 'em, they hold 'em!

All. Who, Faustus?

FAUST. Why, Lucifer and Mephistophilis.
Ah Gentlemen, I gave them my soul for my cunning.

All. God forbid!

FAUST. God forbade it indeed, but Faustus hath done it: for the vain pleasure of four-and-twenty years hath Faustus lost eternal joy and felicity. I writ them a bill with mine own blood; the date is expired, this is the time, and he will fetch me.

1 SCH. Why did not Faustus tell us of this before, that divines might have prayed for thee?

FAUST. Oft have I thought to have done so, but the devil threatened to tear me in pieces if I named God, to fetch both body and soul if I once gave ear to divinity; and now 'ts too late. Gentlemen, away, lest you perish with me!

2 SCH. O what may we do to save Faustaus?

FAUST. Talk not of me, but save yourselves and depart.

3 SCH. God will strengthen me: I will stay with Faustus.

1 SCH. Tempt not God, sweet friend, but let us into the next room, and there pray for him.

FAUST. Aye, pray for me, pray for me! And what noise soever ye hear, come not unto me, for nothing can rescue me.

2 SCH. Pray thou, and we will pray that God may have mercy upon thee.

FAUST. Gentlemen, farewell. If I live till morning, I'll visit you; if not, Faustus is gone to hell.

All. Faustus, farewell. [*Exeunt Scholars.*]

MEPH. Aye Faustus, now thou hast no hope of heaven;
Therefore despair, think only upon hell,
For that must be thy mansion, there to dwell.

FAUST. O, thou bewitching fiend, 'twas thy temptation
Hath robbed me of eternal happiness.

MEPH. I do confess it, Faustus, and rejoice.
'Twas I, that when thou wer't i'the way to heaven
Damned up thy passage; when thou tookest the book
To view the scriptures, then I turned the leaves
And led thine eye.
What, weep'st thou? 'tis too late. Despair, farewell!
Fools that will laugh on earth must weep in hell. [*Exit.*]

[*Enter the Good Angel, and the Evil Angel at several doors.*]

G. ANG. Ah Faustus, if thou hadst given ear to me,
Innumerable joys had followed thee,
But thou didst love the world.

B. ANG. Gave ear to me,
And now must taste hell's pains perpetually.

G. ANG. O what will all thy riches, pleasures, pomps,
Avail thee now?

B. ANG. Nothing but vex thee more,
To want in hell, that had on earth such store.

[*Music while the throne descends.*[3]]

G. ANG. O, thou hast lost celestial happiness,
Pleasures unspeakable, bliss without end.
Hadst thou affected sweet divinity
Hell or the devil, had had no power on thee.
Hadst thou kept on that way, Faustus, behold,
In what resplendent glory thou hadst sit
In yonder throne, like those bright shining saints,
And triumphed over hell; that hast thou lost.
And now, poor soul, must thy good angel leave thee;
The jaws of hell are open to receive thee.

[*Exit. Hell is discovered.*]

B. ANG. Now Faustus, let thine eyes with horror stare
Into that vast perpetual torture-house.
There are the furies tossing damned souls

Chapter 2　The Renaissance Period

　　　On burning forks; their bodies broil in lead.
　　　There are live quarters[4] broiling on the coals
　　　That ne'er can die. This ever-burning chair
　　　Is for o'er-tortured souls to rest them in;
　　　These that are fed with sops of flaming fire
　　　Were gluttons, and loved only delicates
　　　And laughed to see the poor starve at their gates.
　　　But yet all these are nothing; thou shalt see
　　　Ten thousand tortures that more horrid be.
FAUST. O, I have seen enough to torture me.
B. ANG. Nay, thou must feel them, taste the smart of all;
　　　He that loves pleasure must for pleasure fall.
　　　And so I leave thee, Faustus, till anon;
　　　Then wilt thou tumble in confusion.[5]
　　　　　[*Exit. The clock strikes eleven.*]
FAUST. Ah, Faustus,
　　　Now hast thou but one bare hour to live
　　　And then thou must be damned perpetually!
　　　Stand still, you ever-moving spheres of heaven,
　　　That time may cease, and midnight never come;
　　　Fair Nature's eye, rise, rise again and make
　　　Perpetual day; or let this hour be but
　　　A year, a month, a week, a natural day,
　　　That Faustus may repent, and save his soul!
　　　O lente lente currite noctis equi.[6]
　　　The stars move still, time runs, the clock will strike,
　　　The devil will come, and Faustus must be damned.
　　　O, I'll leap up to my God! Who pulls me down?
　　　See, see where Christ's blood streams in the firmament! —
　　　One drop would save my soule — half a drop! Ah, my Christ!
　　　Rend not my heart for naming of my Christ;
　　　Yet will I call on him — O, spare me, Lucifer!
　　　Where is it now? 'Tis gone; and see where God
　　　Stretcheth out his arm and bends his ireful brows.
　　　Mountains and hills, come, come, and fall on me
　　　And hide me from the heavy wrath of God,
　　　No, no?
　　　Then will I headlong run into the earth.
　　　Earth, gape! O no, it will not harbor me.

You stars that reigned at my nativity,
Whose influence hath allotted death and hell,
Now draw up Faustus like a foggy mist
Into the entrails of yon laboring cloud
That when you vomit forth into the air,
My limbs may issue from your smoky mouths,
So that my soul may but ascend to heaven.[7]

   [*The watch strikes.*]

Ah, half the hour is past; 'twill all be past anon.
O God,
If thou wilt not have mercy on my soul,
Yet for Christ's sake, whose blood hath ransomed me
Impose some end to my incessant pain:
Let Faustus live in hell a thousand years,
A hundred thousand, and at last be saved!
O, no end is limited to damned souls!
Why wert thou not a creature wanting soul?
Or why is this immortal that thou hast?
Ah, Pythagoras' *metempsychosis*[8]— were that true,
This soul should fly from me, and I be changed
Unto some brutish beast. All beasts are happy,
For when they die
Their souls are soon dissolved in elements,
But mine must live still[9] to be plagued in hell.
Curst be the parents that engendered me!
No, Faustus, curse thyself, curse Lucifer
That hath deprived thee of the joys of heaven.
   [*The clock striketh twelve.*]
It strikes, it strikes! Now, body, turn to air
Or Lucifer will bear thee quick[10] to hell!
   [*Thunder and lightning.*]
O soul, be changed to little water drops,
And fall into the *ocean*, ne'er be found.
My God, my God, look not so fierce on me!
[*Enter Devils.*]
Adders and serpents, let me breathe a while!
Ugly hell, gape not — come not, Lucifer —
I'll burn my books — ah, Mephistophilis.
   [*Exeunt Devils with Faustus.*]

Notes

1. **Dis**: the underworld.
2. **surfeit**: indigestion, the effects of overindulgence.
3. **the throne descends**: A throne suspended by ropes descended to the stage near the end of many Elizabethan plays and was an expected theatrical display. Here the throne clearly symbolizes heaven, as the next speech shows.
4. **quarters**: bodies.
5. **confusion**: destruction, perdition.
6. **O lente lente currrite** *noctis* **equi**: "Slowly, slowly run, O horses of the night," adapted from a line in Ovid's *Amores*.
7. **You stars... but ascend to heaven**: The seven lines here tell about how Faustus begs his natal stars to draw him up into the cloud, where his body may be compacted into a thunderstone and fall to earth, so that his soul, thus purified, may ascend to heaven.
8. **Pythagoras' metempsychosis**: Pythagoras' doctrine of the transmigration of souls.
9. **still**: always.
10. **quick**: alive.

Study Questions

1. The quest for forbidden knowledge usually leads the hero to corruption and fall. How does Faustus' quest degrade him?
2. What is Faustus' agony during the final scene of the play?
3. Of all the things that Faustus desires, what does he desire most?
4. What kind of relationship exists between Faustus and Mephistophilis?
5. What is the significance of the Good Angel and the Bad Angel?

Essay Topics

1. In what ways does Dr. Faustus epitomize Renaissance attitudes about knowledge and learning?
2. How is Dr. Faustus representative of the spirit of the Renaissance?
3. Double characters are often used to represent opposing qualities within the hero. How do double characters externalize the conflict between repentance and defiance in Faustus' soul? What does the conflict between double characters tell us about human nature?

2.4 Walter Raleigh

Sir Walter Raleigh (1552-1618) may be taken as the great typical figure of the age of Elizabeth. Courtier and statesman, soldier and sailor, scientist and man of letters, he

 engaged in almost all the main lines of public activity in his time, and was distinguished in them all. He organized expeditions to the new world, popularized tobacco, and found time to write poetry as well. His verse, usually fragment or formally flawed, bears the impress of a mind tortured and with much powerful imagination.

James Ⅰ, Elizabeth's successor, feared and distrusted Raleigh. During James's reign Raleigh was charged with treason and was convicted and sentenced to death. He was imprisoned instead in the Tower of London, where for twelve years he lived with his family and servants and wrote his *History of the World*. After a failed quest to South America for gold that was to buy his release, Raleigh was executed in 1618.

Much of Raleigh's poetry has been lost, but one gem that has survived is "The Nymph's Reply to the Shepherd." In it Raleigh's speaker, a young woman, replies to Marlowe's famous "the Passionate Shepherd to His Love".

2.4.1 "The Nymph's Reply to the Shepherd"

If all the world and love were young,
And truth in every shepherd's tongue,
These pretty pleasures might me move
To live with thee and be thy love.

Time drives the flocks from field to fold[1]
When rivers rage and rocks grow cold,
And Philomel[2] becometh dumb;
The rest complains of cares to come.

The flowers do fade, and wanton[3] fields
To wayward winter reckoning yields;
A honey tongue, a heart of gall,[4]
Is fancy's spring, but sorrow's fall.

Thy gowns, thy shoes, thy beds of roses,
Thy cap, thy kirtle,[5] and thy posies
Soon break, soon wither, soon forgotten,
In folly ripe, in reason rotten.

Thy belt of straw and ivy buds,
Thy coral clasps and amber studs,
All these in me no means can move
To come to thee and be thy love.

But could youth last and love still breed,[6]
Had joys no date[7] nor age no need,
Then these delights my mind might move
To live with thee and be thy love.

Notes

1. **fold**: enclosure or pen for sheep.
2. **Philomel**: According to Greek myth, the princess Philomel's tongue was cut out to prevent her from revealing a scandal. Later the gods turned Philomela into a nightingale.
3. **wanton**: here, profuse or ample.
4. **gall**: bitterness.
5. **kirtle**: skirt, outer petticoat.
6. **still breed**: always thrive.
7. **date**: ending.

Study Questions

1. What is the Nymph's attitude towards love? Are there any differences in their attitude towards love between the Shepherd and the Nymph?
2. According to the last stanza, what would make the nymph accept the shepherd's offer?
3. What do all the predictions in stanza 3 and 4 have in common? Basically, why does the speaker find the shepherd's offer unimpressive?
4. How are the views expressed in the first and last stanzas similar? Is the speaker saying there is a possibility she will accept the shepherd's offer, or is her answer a definite "no"? Explain.

Essay Topics

Write an essay to discuss what Raleigh's poem adds to Marlowe's poem "The Passionate Shepherd to His Love," and defend your thesis with examples from the two poems.

2.5 William Shakespeare

2.5.1 About the Author

Not much is known about Shakespeare's early life. William Shakespeare (1564-

1616) was born probably on April 23, 1564 into a merchant's family at Stratford-on-Avon. He spent his childhood in that beautiful market town and attended the Stratford Grammar School. His real teachers were nature and its people that surrounded him. Shakespeare left Stratford for London in 1586 or 1587. There he worked both as actor and playwright. Shakespeare established himself so well as a playwright that Robert Greene, one of the "University Wits", resentfully declared him to be "an upstart crow".

As the precise dates of many of Shakespeare's plays are still in doubt, critics hold different views on the division of his dramatic career. But generally the four-period division is accepted. The first period was one of the apprenticeship. Shakespeare wrote five history plays — *Henry Ⅳ*, Parts Ⅰ, Ⅱ and Ⅲ, *Richard Ⅲ*, and *Titus Andronicus*; and four comedies — *The Comedy of Errors*, *The Two Gentlemen of Verona*, *The Taming of the Shrew*, and *Love's Labour's Lost*.

In the second period, Shakespeare's style and approach became highly individualized. By constructing complex patterns of plots and characters, he made subtle comments on a variety of human foibles. In this period he wrote five histories — *Richard Ⅱ*, *King John*, *Henry Ⅳ*, Parts Ⅰ and Ⅱ, and *Henry V*; six comedies — *A Midsummer Night's Dream*, *The Merchant of Venice*, *Much Ado About Nothing*, *As You Like It*, *Twelfth Night*, and *The Merry Wives of Windsor*; and two tragedies — *Romeo and Juliet* and *Julius Caesar*.

Shakespeare's third period includes his greatest tragedies and his so-called dark comedies. The tragedies — *Hamlet*, *Othello*, *King Lear*, *Macbeth*, *Antony and Cleopatra*, *Troilus and Cressida*, and *Coriolanus*. The comedies are — *All's Well That Ends Well* and *Measure for Measure*.

The last period of Shakespeare's work includes his principal romantic tragicomedies — *Pericles*, *Cymbeline*, *The Winter's Tale* and *The Tempest*; and his two final plays — *Henry Ⅷ* and *The Two Noble Kinsmen*.

Shakespeare did not confine his genius merely to the theater. In 1593 and 1594, he published two narrative poems, *Venus and Adonis* and *The Rape of Lucrece*. He also wrote 154 sonnets, which were published in 1609. Shakespeare wrote his sonnets in the popular English form of three quatrains and a couplet. The couplet usually ties the sonnet to one of the general themes of the series, leaving the quatrains free to develop the poetic intensity which makes the separate sonnets memorable.

Shakespeare, as a humanist of the time, was shocked by the feudal tyranny and disunity and internal struggle for power at the court which led to civil wars. In his plays, he did not hesitate to describe the cruelty and anti-natural character of the civil wars, but he did not go all the way against the feudal rule. In his dramatic creation, especially in his histories or tragedies, he affirmed the importance of the feudal system to uphold social order. "The King's government must be carried on", but carried on for the good of the nation, not for the pleasure of the King.

Shakespeare is against religious persecution and racial discrimination, against social inequality and the corrupting influence of gold and money. In *King Lear*, Shakespeare has not only made a profound analysis of the social crisis in which evils can be seen everywhere, but also criticized the bourgeois egoism. He has shown us the twofold effects exerted by the feudalist corruption and the bourgeois egoism, which have gradually corroded the ordered society. On the other hand, there is also a limit to his sympathy for the downtrodden. He fears anarchy, hates rebellion and despises democracy. Thus, he finds no way to solve social problems. In the end, the only thing he can do as a humanist is to escape from reality to seek comfort in his dreams.

Shakespeare has accepted the Renaissance views on literature. He holds that literature should be a combination of beauty, goodness and truth, and should reflect nature and reality. Based on this consideration, he has claimed through the mouth of Hamlet that the "end" of dramatic creation is to give faithful reflection of the social realities of the time. Shakespeare also states that literary works, which have truly reflected nature and reality, can reach immortality. We can find quite a few examples in which Shakespeare sings the immortality of poetry in his sonnets.

Shakespeare's major characters are neither merely individual ones nor type ones; they are individuals representing certain types. Each character has his or her own personalities; meanwhile, they may share features with others. By employing a psychoanalytical approach, Shakespeare succeeds in exploring the characters' inner mind. The soliloquies in his plays fully reveal the inner conflict of his characters. Shakespeare also portrays his characters in pairs. Contrasts are frequently used to bring vividness to his characters.

Also well-known is the adroit plot construction of his plays. Shakespeare seldom invents his own plots; instead, he borrows them from some old plays or storybooks, or from ancient Greek and Roman sources. In order to make the play more lively and compact, he would shorten the time and intensify the plot. There are usually several threads running through the play, thus providing the story with suspense and apprehension.

Irony is a good means of dramatic presentation. It makes the characters who are ignorant of the truth do certain ridiculous things. There is so much fun that the audience are immediately amused. Disguise is also an important device to create dramatic irony, usually with woman disguised as man.

Lastly, to understand Shakespeare, it is necessary to study the subtlest of his instruments — the language. Shakespeare can write skillfully in different poetic forms, like the sonnet, the blank verse and the rhymed couplet. His blank verse is especially beautiful and mighty. He has an amazing wealth of vocabulary and idioms. He is known to have used a very large number of different words. His coinage of new words and distortion of the meaning of the old ones also create striking effects on the reader. Shakespeare's influence on later writers is immeasurable. Almost all English writers after him have been benefited from him either in artistic point of view, in literary form or in language.

2.5.2 "Sonnet 18"

Shall I compare thee to a summer's day[1]?
Thou art more lovely and more temperate;
Rough winds do shake the darling buds of May,
And summer's lease[2] hath all too short a date[3];
Sometime too hot the eye of heaven shines
And often is his gold complexion dimmed;
And every fair from fair[4] sometimes declines,
By chance or nature's changing course untrimmed[5];
But thy eternal summer shall not fade,
Nor lose possession of that fair thou ow'st[6];
Nor shall death brag thou wander'st in his shade,
When in eternal lines[7] to time thou grow'st:
So long as men can breathe, or eyes can see,
So long lives this, and this gives life to thee.

Notes

1. **a summer's day**: Here it may refer to a period or the season of summer.
2. **lease**: allotted time.
3. **date**: duration.
4. **fair from fair**: beautiful thing from beauty.
5. **untrimmed**: stripped of beauty.
6. **thou ow'st**: you possess.
7. **lines**: lines of poetry.

Study Questions

1. What images does Shakespeare use in order to strengthen the theme?
2. How does Shakespeare use the final couplet for effect?
3. What is the value or significance of the poem's theme? Is it topical or universal in its application?

Essay Topics

Write an essay to compare and contrast Shakespeare's "Sonnet 18" with Spenser's "Sonnet 75".

2.5.3 "Sonnet 73"

That time of year thou mayst in me behold
When yellow leaves, or none, or few, do hang
Upon those boughs which shake against the cold,
Bare ruined choirs[1], where late sweet birds sang.
In me thou seest the twilight of such day
As after sunset fadeth in the west;
Which by and by black night doth take away,
Death's second self[2] that seals up all in rest.
In me thou seest the glowing of such fire,
That on the ashes of his youth doth lie,
As the deathbed whereon it must expire,
Consumed with that which it was nourished by.[3]
   This thou perceiv'st, which makes thy love more strong,
   To love that well, which thou must leave ere long.

Notes

1. **choirs**: choir lofts; parts of church interiors occupied by choirs.
2. **Death's second self**: that is, night.
3. **Consumed with that which it was nourished by**: choked by the ashes of the wood that previously fueled its flame.

Study Questions

1. How does the speaker take the image in lines 1-2 and expand it in lines 3-4?
2. What do all the images in lines 1-12 symbolize?
3. What ideas do the descriptive details in this poem suggest?

Essay Topics

1. Analyze Shakespeare's use of nature imagery in relation to love.
2. The tone in this sonnet is different from "Sonnet 18". Compare the use of language to convey tone and meaning.

2.5.4 An Excerpt from Act IV of *The Merchant of Venice*

Scene 1. Venice. A Court of Justice.

[*Enter Portia, (Dr. Balthasar)*]

DUKE Give me your hand. Come you from old Bellario?

PORTIA (Dr. BALTHASAR) I did, my lord.

DUKE You are welcome: take your place.
Are you acquainted with the difference[1]
That holds this present question in the court?

PORTIA I am informed thoroughly of the cause.
Which is the merchant here, and which the Jew?

DUKE Antonio and old Shylock, both stand forth.

PORTIA Is your name Shylock?

SHYLOCK Shylock is my name.

PORTIA Of a strange nature is the suit you follow;
Yet in such rule that the Venetian law
Cannot impugn[2] you as you do proceed.
You stand within his danger, do you not?[3]

ANTONIO Ay, so he says.

PORTIA Do you confess the bond?

ANTONIO I do.

PORTIA Then must the Jew be merciful.

SHYLOCK On what compulsion must I? Tell me that.

PORTIA The quality of mercy is not strained,
It droppeth as the gentle rain from heaven
Upon the place beneath. It is twice blessed;—
It blesseth him that gives, and him that takes.
'Tis mightiest in the mightiest[4]: it becomes
The throned monarch better than his crown.
His sceptre shows the force of temporal power,
The attribute to awe and majesty,
Wherein doth sit the dread and fear of kings;
But mercy is above this sceptred sway,
It is enthroned in the hearts of kings,
It is an attribute to God himself;
And earthly power doth then show likest God's
When mercy seasons justice. Therefore, Jew,
Though justice be thy plea, consider this,
That, in the course of justice, none of us
Should see salvation. We do pray for mercy;
And that same prayer doth teach us all to render
The deeds of mercy. I have spoke thus much

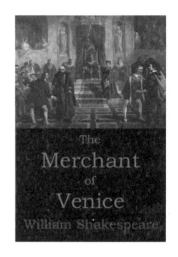

Chapter 2 The Renaissance Period

　　To mitigate[5] the justice of thy plea;
　　Which if thou follow, this strict court of Venice
　　Must needs give sentence 'gainst the merchant there.
SHYLOCK　My deeds upon my head![6] I crave the law,
　　The penalty and forfeit of my bond.
PORTIA　Is he not able to discharge the money?
BASSANIO　Yes, here I tender it for him in the court;
　　Yea, twice the sum. If that will not suffice,
　　I will be bound to pay it ten times o'er,
　　On forfeit of my hands, my head, my heart.
　　If this will not suffice, it must appear
　　That malice bears down truth[7]. And I beseech you,
　　Wrest once the law to your authority:
　　To do a great right, do a little wrong,
　　And curb this cruel devil of his will.
PORTIA　It must not be. There is no power in Venice
　　Can alter a decree established.
　　'Twill be recorded for a precedent,
　　And many an error by the same example,
　　Will rush into the state. It cannot be.
SHYLOCK　A Daniel[8] come to judgment! Yea, a Daniel!
　　O wise young judge, how I do honor thee!
PORTIA　I pray you let me look upon the bond.
SHYLOCK　Here 'tis, most reverend doctor; here it is.
PORTIA　Shylock, there's thrice thy money offered thee.
SHYLOCK　An oath, an oath, I have an oath in heaven.
　　Shall I lay perjury upon my soul?
　　No, not for Venice.
PORTIA　Why, this bond is forfeit;
　　And lawfully by this the Jew may claim
　　A pound of flesh, to be by him cut off
　　Nearest the merchant's heart. Be merciful:
　　Take thrice thy money. Bid me tear the bond.
SHYLOCK　When it is paid, according to the tenor[9],
　　It doth appear you are a worthy judge;
　　You know the law, your exposition
　　Hath been most sound. I charge you by the law,
　　Whereof you are a well-deserving pillar,
　　Proceed to judgment. By my soul I swear

There is no power in the tongue of man

To alter me. I stay here on my bond.

ANTONIO　Most heartily I do beseech the court

To give the judgment.

PORTIA　Why then thus it is:

You must prepare your bosom for his knife.

SHYLOCK　O noble judge! O excellent young man!

PORTIA　For the intent and purpose of the law

Hath full relation[10] to the penalty,

Which here appeareth due upon the bond.

SHYLOCK　'Tis very true! O wise and upright judge!

How much more elder art thou than thy looks.

PORTIA　Therefore lay bare your bosom.

SHYLOCK　Ay, his breast:

So says the bond: — doth it not, noble judge? —

"Nearest his heart." Those are the very words.

PORTIA　It is so. Are there balance here to weigh

The flesh?

SHYLOCK　I have them ready.

PORTIA　Have by some surgeon, Shylock, on your charge,

To stop his wounds, lest he do bleed to death.

SHYLOCK　Is it so nominated in the bond?

PORTIA　It is not so expressed; but what of that?

'Twere good you do so much for charity.

SHYLOCK　I cannot find it: 'tis not in the bond.

PORTIA　You, merchant, have you any thing to say?

ANTONIO　But little: I am armed and well prepared.

Give me your hand, Bassanio: fare you well!

Grieve not that I am fall'n to this for you;

For herein Fortune shows herself more kind

Than is her custom. It is still her use[11]

To let the wretched man outlive his wealth,

To view with hollow eye and wrinkled brow

An age of poverty; from which lingering penance

Of such a misery doth she cut me off.

Commend me to your honourable wife:

Tell her the process of Antonio's end.

Say how I loved you, speak me fair in death;

And, when the tale is told, bid her be judge

Whether Bassanio had not once a love.
Repent but you that you shall lose your friend,
And he repents not that he pays your debt;
For if the Jew do cut but deep enough,
I'll pay it instantly with all my heart[12].

BASSANIO Antonio, I am married to a wife
Which is as dear to me as life itself;
But life itself, my wife, and all the world,
Are not with me esteemed above thy life.
I would lose all, ay, sacrifice them all
Here to the devil, to deliver you.

PORTIA Your wife would give you little thanks for that,
If she were by, to hear you make the offer.

GRATIANO I have a wife, who I protest, I love.
I would she were in heaven, so she could
Entreat some power to change this currish Jew.

NERISSA [aside] 'Tis well you offer it behind her back;
The wish would make else an unquiet house[13].

SHYLOCK These be the Christian husbands. I have a daughter;
Would any of the stock of Barrabas[14]
Had been her husband rather than a Christian! —
We trifle time; I pray thee pursue sentence.

PORTIA A pound of that same merchant's flesh is thine.
The court awards it, and the law doth give it.

SHYLOCK Most rightful judge!

PORTIA And you must cut this flesh from off his breast.
The law allows it, and the court awards it.

SHYLOCK Most learned judge! A sentence! Come, prepare!

PORTIA Tarry a little; there is something else.
This bond doth give thee here no jot of blood.
The words expressly are "a pound of flesh."
Take then thy bond, take thou thy pound of flesh;
But, in the cutting it, if thou dost shed
One drop of Christian blood, thy lands and goods
Are, by the laws of Venice, confiscate
Unto the state of Venice.

GRATIANO O upright judge! Mark Jew! O learned judge!

SHYLOCK Is that the law?

PORTIA Thyself shalt see the act;

For as thou urgest justice, be assured
　　Thou shalt have justice more than thou desir'st.
GRATIANO　O learned judge! Mark Jew: a learned judge!
SHYLOCK　I take this offer, then: pay the bond thrice,
　　And let the Christian go.
BASSANIO　Here is the money.
PORTIA　Soft.
　　The Jew shall have all justice. Soft, no haste.
　　He shall have nothing but the penalty.
GRATIANO　O Jew, an upright judge, a learned judge!
PORTIA　Therefore prepare thee to cut off the flesh.
　　Shed thou no blood; nor cut thou less nor more
　　But just a pound of flesh. If thou tak'st more
　　Or less than a just pound, be it but so much
　　As makes it light or heavy in the substance,
　　Or the division of the twentieth part
　　Of one poor scruple[15], nay, if the scale do turn
　　But in the estimation of a hair[16],
　　Thou diest and all thy goods are confiscate.
GRATIANO　A second Daniel, a Daniel, Jew!
　　Now, infidel, I have you on the hip.
PORTIA　Why doth the Jew pause? Take thy forfeiture.
SHYLOCK　Give me my principal, and let me go.
BASSANIO　I have it ready for thee: here it is.
PORTIA　He hath refused it in the open court.
　　He shall have merely justice and his bond.
GRATIANO　A Daniel, still say I, a second Daniel!
　　I thank thee, Jew, for teaching me that word.
SHYLOCK　Shall I not have barely my principal?
PORTIA　Thou shalt have nothing but the forfeiture,
　　To be so taken at thy peril, Jew.
SHYLOCK　Why, then the devil give him good of it!
　　I'll stay no longer question.
PORTIA　Tarry, Jew:
　　The law hath yet another hold on you,
　　It is enacted in the laws of Venice,
　　If it be proved against an alien
　　That by direct, or indirect attempts
　　He seek the life of any citizen,

        The party 'gainst the which he doth contrive
        Shall seize one half his goods; the other half
        Comes to the privy coffer of the state[17];
        And the offender's life lies in the mercy
        Of the Duke only, 'gainst all other voice;
        In which predicament, I say, thou stand'st.
        For it appears by manifest proceeding,
        That indirectly, and directly too,
        Thou hast contrived against the very life
        Of the defendant; and thou hast incurred
        The danger formerly by me rehearsed[18].
        Down, therefore, and beg mercy of the Duke.

GRATIANO Beg that thou mayst have leave to hang thyself.
        And yet, thy wealth being forfeit to the state,
        Thou hast not left the value of a cord;
        Therefore thou must be hanged at the state's charge.

DUKE That thou shalt see the difference of our spirit,
        I pardon thee thy life before thou ask it.
        For half thy wealth, it is Antonio's;
        The other half comes to the general state,
        Which humbleness may drive unto a fine[19].

PORTIA Ay, for the state, not for Antonio.

SHYLOCK Nay, take my life and all, pardon not that!
        You take my house, when you do take the prop
        That doth sustain my house. You take my life
        When you do take the means whereby I live.

PORTIA What mercy can you render him, Antonio?

GRATIANO A halter gratis[20]: nothing else, for God's sake.

ANTONIO So please my lord the Duke and all the court
        To quit[21] the fine for one half of his goods,
        I am content; so he will let me have
        The other half in use[22], to render it,
        Upon his death, unto the gentleman
        That lately stole his daughter:
        Two things provided more, that, for this favor,
        He presently become a Christian[23];
        The other, that he do record a gift,
        Here in the court, of all he dies possessed.
        Unto his son Lorenzo, and his daughter.

DUKE   He shall do this, or else I do recant[24]
   The pardon that I late pronounced here.
PORTIA   Art thou contented, Jew? What dost thou say?
SHYLOCK   I am content.

Notes

1. **difference**: focus of the dispute.
2. **impugn**: to oppose.
3. **You stand within his danger, do you not**: This sentence is addressed to Antonio. "within his danger" means in his power.
4. **'Tis mightiest in the mightiest**: It is the greatest thing in the greatest person.
5. **mitigate**: to make less severe.
6. **My deeds upon my head**: To let me responsible for what I do!
7. **malice bears down truth**: malice crushes honesty.
8. **a Daniel**: an upright judge in the Bible.
9. **tenor**: the general purport of the bond.
10. **full relation**: fully applies to.
11. **use**: habit.
12. **with all my heart**: sincerely. There is a pun on the word "heart", as it may literally refer to Antonio's body organ.
13. **would make else an unquiet house**: would otherwise cause a quarrel between husband and wife.
14. **any of the stock of Barrabas**: any descendant of Barrabas, a well-known Jewish bandit in the time of Christ.
15. **scruple**: a small weight.
16. **in the estimation of a hair**: by the difference of the weight of a hair.
17. **the privy coffer of the state**: the secret treasury of the state.
18. **formerly by me rehearsed**: previously described by me.
19. **Which humbleness may drive unto a fine**: your humble beg for mercy may reduce your penalty from confiscating half of your property to a fine.
20. **a halter gratis**: a rope to hang him, free of charge.
21. **quit**: remit.
22. **in use**: in trust.
23. **He presently become a Christian**: Notice, the Christian treatment is not so lenient as supposed. For the Jew, to be forced to give up their religious belief would be worse than to take away their life.
24. **recant**: cancel, withdraw.

Study Questions

1. Why does Portia, disguised as the lawyer, initially conclude that Shylock's bond must be adhered to?
2. How do the Christians treat the Jews?
3. Is Shylock in any way a sympathetic character? Why or why not?
4. Would the Elizabethans think it just and proper for Shylock to be forced to convert to Christianity? Why? Does this kind of religious arrogance still exist today? Explain.

Essay Topics

1. How does Shakespeare handle the racial/religious conflicts in the play?
2. Do you think Shylock's hatred for the Christians can be justified? Why or why not?

2.6 Francis Bacon

2.6.1 About the Author

Francis Bacon (1561-1626) was born in London. His father was the Lord Keeper of the Great Seal under Queen Elizabeth Ⅰ. Thus, Bacon had a fortunate heritage and background. He studied at Cambridge and Gray's Inn, entered Parliament, and gradually established his reputation. At the height of his career, under King James, he became Lord Keeper and then Lord Chancellor of England. But he was later accused of taking bribes in office. He admitted accepting presents but defended the justice of his act. After a token imprisonment, Bacon retired in disgrace to spend the last five years of his life.

Although Bacon's career was successful, his real interests lay in science. He wrote some very important philosophical works. The best is The Advancement of Learning (1605), in which Bacon emphasized the belief that people are the servants and interpreters of nature, that truth is not derived from authority, and that knowledge is the fruit of experience. Novum Organum (1620), an enlarged Latin version of The Advancement of Learning, is a successful treatise on methodology, which greatly influenced the acceptance of accurate observation and experimentation in science. In the second part of the book, Bacon suggests the inductive reasoning, i. e. proceeding from the particular to the general, in place of the Aristotelian method, the deductive reasoning, i. e. proceeding from the general to the particular. Because it added significantly to the improvement of scientific hypotheses, this method was a fundamental advancement of the scientific method.

Bacon's Essays, his chief contributions to literature were published at various times between 1597 and 1625. They are famous for brevity, compactness and powerfulness. Yet there is an obvious stylistic change in the Essays. The sentences in the first edition are charged and crowded with symmetries. They are composed in a rather affected way. However, the final edition not only enlarges the range of theme, but also brings forth the looser and more persuasive style. The essays are well-arranged and enriched by Biblical allusions, metaphors and cadence.

2.6.2 "Of Studies" from *Essays*

Studies serve for delight, for ornament, and for ability. Their chief use for delight, is in privateness and retiring[1]; for ornament, is in discourse; and for ability, is in the judgment and disposition of business. For expert men[2] can execute, and perhaps judge of particulars, one by one; but the general counsels, and the plots marshalling of affairs come best from those that are learned. To spend too much time in studies is sloth[3]; to use them too much for ornament is affectation; to make judgment wholly by their rules is the humor[4] of a scholar. They perfect nature, and are perfected by experience: for natural abilities are like natural plants that need pruning[5] by study; and studies themselves do give forth directions too much at large, except they be bounded in by experience. Crafty men contemn[6] studies, simple men admire them, and wise men use them, for they teach not their own use, but that is a wisdom without them, and above them, won by observation. Read not to contradict and confute, nor to believe and take for granted, nor to find talk and discourse, but to weigh and consider. Some books are to be tasted, others to be swallowed, and some few to be chewed and digested; that is, some books are to be read only in parts; others to be read, but not curiously[7]; and some few to be read wholly, and with diligence and attention. Some books also may be read by deputy, and extracts made of them by others, but that would be only in the less important arguments, and the meaner sort of books; else distilled books are like common distilled waters, flashy things[8]. Reading maketh a full man, conference[9] a ready man, and writing a exact man. And therefore, if a man write little, he had need have a great memory; if he confer little, he had need have a present wit[10]; and if he read little, he had need have much cunning, to seem to know that[11] he doth not. Histories make men wise; poets, witty; the mathematics, subtle; natural philosophy[12], deep; moral, grave; logic and rhetoric, able to contend. *Abeunt studia in mores*[13]. Nay, there is no stond[14] or impediment in the wit but may be wrought out by fit studies, like as diseases of the body may have appropriate exercises. Bowling is good for the stone and reins[15], shooting[16] for the lungs and breast, gentle walking for the stomach, riding for the head, and the like. So if a man's wit be wandering, let him study the mathematics; for in demonstrations, if his wit be called away never[17] so little, he must begin again. If his wit be not apt to distinguish or find differences, let him study the Schoolmen[18], for they are *cumini sectores*[19]. If he be not apt to beat over matters[20] and to call up one thing to prove and illustrate another, let him study the lawyers' cases. So every defect of the mind may have a special receipt[21].

Notes

1. **privateness and retiring**: private life and seclusion.
2. **expert men**: men of experience.
3. **sloth**: laziness; idleness.
4. **humor**: (archaic) temperament; here peculiar character.
5. **pruning**: cultivating.
6. **contemn**: condemn.
7. **curiously**: with great care.
8. **distilled waters, flashy things**: infusions of herbs, etc., used as home remedies — without real value.
9. **conference**: conversations, meetings.
10. **present wit**: lively intelligence.
11. **that**: that which.
12. **natural philosophy**: science.
13. *Abeunt studia in mores*: "Studies culminate in manners" (Ovid, *Heroides*).
14. **stond**: obstacle.
15. **stone and reins**: gall bladder and kidneys.
16. **shooting**: archery.
17. **never**: ever.
18. **Schoolmen**: scholastic philosophers.
19. **cumini sectores**: (Latin) "dividers of cumin seeds", i.e., hairsplitters.
20. **beat over matters**: to discuss a subject thoroughly.
21. **receipt**: cure; prescription.

Study Questions

1. What is Bacon's attitude toward study and learning?
2. Do you agree with Bacon that "Some books are to be tasted, others to be swallowed, and some few to be chewed and digested"? Why or why not?
3. What writing techniques does Bacon employ to convey the essay's themes and ideas?

2.7 John Donne

2.7.1 About the Author

John Donne (1572-1631) was born into a prosperous merchant family. He studied both at Oxford and Cambridge, but left without taking a degree because of his Roman Catholic background. In 1591, Donne began his legal studies at the Inns of Court in London, where he spent much of his time studying law, languages, literature and

theology.

Upon completing his studies, Donne became private secretary to Sir Thomas Egerton, the eminent Lord Keeper of the Great Seal. His great prospects of the worldly success were ruined by his secret marriage with Lady Egerton's niece, Ann More, in 1601. For over ten years then on, Donne had been working hard, fighting against poverty. Donne's conversion to Anglicanism was a gradual process. In 1615, after a final attempt at secular preferment, John Donne entered the Anglican Church and took orders. Donne took his new vocation seriously and performed his holy duties exceptionally well, acquiring a great reputation as an impressive deliverer of insightful sermons. After his wife's death in 1617, Donne devoted all his time and efforts to his priestly duties, writing sermons and religious poems. Donne was appointed the Dean of St. Paul's in 1621 and kept that post until his death.

John Donne is the leading figure of the "metaphysical school". His poems give a more inherently theatrical impression by exhibiting a seemingly unfocused diversity of experiences and attitudes, and a free range of feelings and moods. The mode is dynamic rather than static with ingenuity of speech, vividness of imagery and vitality of rhythms. His poetry shows a notable contrast to the other Elizabethan lyric poems which are pure, serene, tuneful and smooth-running. The most striking feature of Donne's poetry is precisely its tang of reality, in the sense that it seems to reflect life in a real rather than a poetical world.

2.7.2 "Valediction Forbidding Mourning"

As virtuous men pass mildly away,
   And whisper to their souls to go,
While some of their sad friends do say,
   "The breath goes now", and some say No;

So let us melt[1], and make no noise,
   No tear-floods nor sigh-tempests move;
'Twere profanation[2] of our joys
   To tell the laity[3] our love.

Moving of the earth brings harm and fears:
   Men recon what it did and meant;
But trepidation of the spheres,

Chapter 2　The Renaissance Period

　　Though greater far, is innocent. [4]

Dull sublunary[5] lovers' love
　　(Whose soul is sense[6]) cannot admit
Absence, because it doth remove
　　Those things which elemented it[7].

But we, by a love so much refined
　　That ourselves know not what it is,
Inter-assured[8] of the mind
　　Care less eyes, lips, and hands to miss.

Our two souls, therefore, which are one,
　　Though I must go, endure not yet
A breach, but an expansion,
　　Like gold to airy thinness beat[9].

If they be two, they are two so
　　As stiff twin compasses[10] are two;
Thy soul, the fixed foot, makes no show
　　To move, but doth if the other do.

And though it in the centre sit,
　　Yet, when the other far doth roam,
It leans and hearkens after it
　　And grows erect as that comes home.

Such wilt thou be to me, who must
　　Like the other foot obliquely run;
Thy firmness makes my circle just[11],
　　And makes me end where I begun.

Notes
1. **melt**: part, change state. This line may also refer to the quietness with which pure gold melts.
2. **profanation**: debasement; violation.
3. **laity**: layman, non-clergy. Here, the speaker is implying he and his beloved are like priest and priestess as opposed to the laity.
4. **Moving... is innocent**: Earthquakes are harmful and dangerous, whereas the much

greater movements of the celestial spheres are harmless.
5. **sublunary**: under the moon, or earthly. Everything under the moon's sphere, including the earth, was considered subject to change; all beyond that sphere was permanent and perfect.
6. **Whose soul is sense**: Whose essence is the senses, not the mind.
7. **which elemented it**: which constituted its essential nature.
8. **inter-assured**: mutually assured.
9. **Like gold to airy thinness beat**: Gold leaf is made by beating gold into tissue-thin pieces. Baser metals would break up under the beating. "airy" in this line refers to the buoyancy of gold leaf.
10. **twin compasses**: the two legs of a geometrical compass.
11. **just**: true; accurate.

Study Questions
1. What, if anything, is startling about the speaker's comparing himself and his beloved to the two feet of a compass? Why?
2. Why should the parting of the lovers not be a cause for mourning?
3. Look at the figurative language of the poem — metaphors, similes, analogies, personification. How do these images add to the meaning of the poem or intensify the effect of the poem?

2.7.3 "Death Be Not Proud"[1]

Death, be not proud, though some have called thee
Mighty and dreadful, for thou art not so;
For those whom thou think'st, thou dost overthrow,
Die not, poor Death, nor yet canst thou kill me.
From rest and sleep, which but thy pictures[2] be,
Much pleasure; then from thee, much more must flow,
And soonest our best men with thee do go,
Rest of their bones, and soul's delivery.[3]
Thou art slave to fate, chance, kings, and desperate men,
And dost with poison, war, and sickness dwell,
And poppy[4], or charms can make us sleep as well,
And better than thy stroke; why swell'st[5] thou then?
One short sleep past, we wake eternally,
And death shall be no more; Death, thou shalt die.

Notes
1. This is a sonnet written in the Petrarchan pattern, with 14 lines of iambic pentameter

rhyming abba abba cddc ee.
2. **pictures**: images.
3. **And... delivery**: Our best men die willingly, in order to rest their bones and free their souls.
4. **poppy**: opium.
5. **swell'st**: swell with pride.

Study Questions

1. What is the relationship of sleep and Death in this sonnet?
2. What standard portrait of Death is the speaker negating in this poem? Instead, what does the speaker think about the dominion of Death?
3. What does the poet achieve by personifying Death?

Essay Topics

1. To what extent does Donne's poetry express Christian humanist values?
2. What are the basic characteristics of metaphysical poetry?

2.8 George Herbert

2.8.1 About the Author

George Herbert (1593-1633) was born in Wales into a wealthy family. He received his education at Westminster School and Trinity College, Cambridge. It was during this time that Herbert wrote his first known poems. In them, he declared that love of God was a more worthy subject for poetry than love of women. After taking his degrees with distinction, Herbert was elected a major fellow of Trinity. In 1618 he was appointed Reader in Rhetoric at Cambridge, and in 1620 he was elected public orator. In 1626 he took holy orders within the Church of England and became a  country parson. He devotedly served the local community as a rector at Bremerton outside of Salisbury for the rest of his relatively short life. He served faithfully as a parish priest, diligently visiting his parishioners and bringing them the sacraments when they were ill, and food and clothing when they were in want. His spontaneous generosity and good will won him the affection of his parishioners.

Throughout this time Herbert continued to privately compose poetry, but it wasn't until he was on his deathbed that he sent his unpublished poems to a friend, telling him to publish them only if he thought they might help "any dejected poor soul". The manuscript was first published as The Temple the year when Herbert died. It was immediately influential in both British poetry and spirituality, inspiring other spiritual poets, like Henry Vaughan and Richard Crashaw.

Herbert's devotional poems combine a homely familiarity with religious experience and a reverent sense of its magnificence. His poems are marked by quietness of tone, precision of language, metrical versatility, and the use of conceits that was favored by the metaphysical school of poets. His poems include almost every known form of song and poem, but they also reflect Herbert's concern with speech — conversational, persuasive, proverbial. Carefully arranged in related sequences, the poems explore and celebrate the ways of God's love as Herbert discovered them within the fluctuations of his own experience.

2.8.2 "Virtue"

Sweet day, so cool, so calm, so bright,
The bridal of the earth and sky;
The dew shall weep thy fall tonight;
   For thou must die.

Sweet rose, whose hue, angry and brave[1],
Bids the rash gazer wipe his eye;
Thy root is ever in its grave,
   And thou must die.

Sweet spring, full of sweet days and roses,
A box where sweets[2] compacted lie;
My music shows ye have your closes[3],
   And all must die.

Only a sweet and virtuous soul,
Like seasoned timber, never gives;
But though the whole world turn to coal[4],
   Then chiefly lives.

Notes
1. **angry and brave**: having the hue of anger, red; brave: splendid.
2. **sweets**: perfumes.
3. **closes**: concluding cadences. The expression shows that Herbert intended his poem to be sung.
4. **turn to coal**: be reduced to a cinder at the Last Judgment.

Study Questions

1. What metaphors does Herbert use in this poem?
2. How does the third stanza logically summarize the preceding two stanzas in imagery?
3. With what thought does he conclude the poem?

2.9 Andrew Marvell

2.9.1 About the Author

Andrew Marvell (1621-1678), the son of a vicar, was born in Winestead, Yorkshire. He was educated at the grammar school in Hull, and at Trinity College, Cambridge. After leaving university he worked as a clerk, traveled abroad, and returned to serve as tutor to Lord Fairfax's daughter in Yorkshire. In September, 1657, Marvell was appointed assistant to John Milton, Latin Secretary for the Commonwealth. Starting in 1659, Marvell was elected M. P. for his hometown of Hull, and he continued to represent it until his death.

Marvell is the only Puritan among these metaphysical poets. As a humanist, a wit, and a high-minded patriot, he could praise Cromwell without defaming Charles, and was able to help secure the safety of Milton. He campaigned for religious toleration and became a satirist against the court poetry. But Marvell is not a professional writer in the way Jonson had been. He launches his poems quietly. His poetry includes love lyrics, pastorals, and religious poems. Typically, he mixes dialectical argument with sensuous evocation and hints of hidden meaning or allegory in a rich and suggestive manner. It is often difficult to determine precisely what he means, or what his attitude to the subject is. His apparent lightness and even rhythms stand him apart from Donne, but the depth of his concerns justifies placing him in the same school of poetry.

In his exquisite love poem, "To his Coy Mistress," Marvell, by juxtaposing passion and logic, brings to its highest point one of the great themes of Renaissance classicism: the seizing of erotic pleasure before the onset of inevitable death. The poet begins with a cool and reasonable proposition; the poem gathers speed from that quiet beginning and rushes to the cruelly real resolution. Image follows image with precise brevity, each extending and enriching the idea.

2.9.2 "To His Coy Mistress"

Had we but world enough, and time,
This coyness, lady, were no crime.

We would sit down, and think which way
To walk, and pass our long love's day.
Thou by the Indian Ganges' side
Shouldst rubies find; I by the tide
Of Humber would complain.[1] I would
Love you ten years before the Flood,
And you should, if you please, refuse
Till the conversion of the Jews.[2]
My vegetable love should grow
Vaster than empires and more slow;
An hundred years should go to praise
Thine eyes, and on thy forehead gaze;
Two hundred to adore each breast,
But thirty thousand to the rest;
An age at least to every part
And the last age should show your heart.
For, lady, you deserve this state,[3]
Nor would I love at lower rate.
   But at my back I always hear
Time's winged chariot hurrying near;
And yonder all before us lie
Deserts of vast eternity.
Thy beauty shall no more be found.
Nor, in thy marble vault, shall sound
My echoing song; then worms shall try
That long-preserved virginity,
And your quaint honor turn to dust,
And into ashes all my lust:
The grave's a fine and private place,
But none, I think, do there embrace.
   Now therefore, while the youthful hue
Sits on thy skin like morning dew,
And while thy willing soul transpires
At every pore with instant fires,[4]
Now let us sport us while we may,
And now, like amorous birds of prey,
Rather at once our time devour
Than languish in his slow-chapped[5] power.
Let us roll all our strength and all

Chapter 2　The Renaissance Period

Our sweetness up into one ball,
And tear our pleasures with rough strife
Thorough the iron gates of life:
Thus, though we cannot make our sun
Stand still, yet we will make him run. [6]

Notes

1. **complain**: Compared to the gorgeous Oriental Ganges, the Humber (which flows past Marvell's home town of Hull) is a muddy estuary, where one is more likely to encounter herring-boats and coal scows than rubies. "Complain" implies ditties of plaintive, unavailing love.
2. **the conversion of the Jews**: According to popular chronology, the Jews were to be converted just before the Last Judgment.
3. **state**: dignity.
4. **instant fires**: immediate, present enthusiasm. "Transpires": breathes forth.
5. **slow-chapped**: slow-jawed. Time is envisaged as slowly chewing up the world and its people.
6. In the final lines, lover and mistress triumphantly reverse the field, eating time avidly instead of being eaten by it, forcing the sun to race them instead of vainly imploring it to stand still.

Study Questions

1. What is the dramatic situation of this poem?
2. How does time influence the speaker's relationship with his lover?
3. What is the logical relationship of the three stanzas? How convincing is the argument? Do the frequent exaggerations undermine the logic, or make it work?
4. What does the speaker offer as the logical conclusion to be drawn from the ideas presented in the first two stanzas?

2.10　Ben Jonson

2.10.1　About the Author

Ben Jonson (1572-1637) was probably born in London, about a month after the death of his father. He attended the free parish school when he was very young. Then he received a brief education at Westminster School, where he was introduced to the humanist culture which dominated English thought at the time. After working as a bricklayer for his stepfather and serving as a soldier, he became an actor and a playwright. In 1598 he was tried for killing another actor in a duel, but escaped execution by claiming right of clergy.

Jonson was an excellent playwright. Since 1598, he produced fourteen comedies and

 two tragedies, not including his masques. His play, *Every Man in His Humor*, was performed in 1598 by the Lord Chamberlain's *Men at the Globe* with William Shakespeare in the cast. This play is a model of what is called the "comedy of humors", in which each character's action is ruled by a whim or affectation. Jonson gained fame when he wrote *Volpone, or the Fox in* 1606. In this play, Volpone, as a man governed by an overwhelming love of money for its own sake, plays upon the avarice of the other men to increase his wealth by pretending to be at the point of death. Sickened by the greed which was becoming a predominant feature of the economic system, Jonson was no longer simply drawing an amusing picture of Elizabethan times, but flatly assailing the morals of the age. Jonson's plays, written along classical lines, are marked by a pungent and uncompromising satire, by a liveliness of action, and by numerous humor characters, whose single passion or oddity overshadows all their other traits. He was a moralist who sought to improve the ways of men by portraying human foibles and passions through exaggeration and distortion.

Jonson also wrote a large number of poems, almost all of them written in response to particular events in the poet's experience. Most of his poetry was written in short lyric forms, which he handled with great skill. Jonson's poetic style tends to be simple and unadorned yet highly polished. With his great learning, his ability and his commanding position as poet laureate, Jonson set himself squarely against his contemporaries and the romantic tendency of the age. For twenty-five years he was the literary dictator of London, the chief of all the wits that gathered nightly at the old Devil Tavern. His major contribution to poetry was to adapt the poetic form that had been used by the classic writers of ancient Rome.

2.10.2 "Song — To Celia"

Drink to me only with thine eyes,
   And I will pledge[1] with mine;
Or leave a kiss but in the cup,
   And I'll not look for wine.
The thirst that from the soul doth rise
   Doth ask a drink divine:
But might I of Jove's[2] nectar[3] sup,
   I would not change for thine.

I sent thee late[4] a rosy wreath,

Not so much honoring thee,
As giving it a hope that there
　　It could not withered be.
But thou thereon did'st only breathe,
　　And sent'st back to me;
Since when it grows and smells, I swear,
　　Not of itself, but thee.

Notes

1. **pledge**: to drink a toast.
2. **Jove's**: Jupiter's, referring to the Roman ruler of the gods.
3. **nectar**: the drink of the gods.
4. **late**: recently.

Study Questions

1. What images are used to intensify the effect of the poem?
2. What methods does the poet employ to realize his theme?

2.11　Robert Herrick

2.11.1　About the Author

　　Robert Herrick (1591-1674) was born into a middle-class family. As the son of a prosperous goldsmith, Robert received his education at Trinity Hall, Cambridge. After graduation in 1620, he took holy orders and commenced duties in a parish in Devon. The solitude there oppressed him at first: the village was dull and remote, and he felt very bitterly that he was cut off from all literary and social associations; but soon the quiet existence in Devonshire soothed and delighted him. He was pleased with the rural and semi-pagan customs that survived in the village. Indeed, the charm of much of his poetry derives from his sophisticated treatment of simple country pleasures. As a Royalist he was forced to give up the parish in 1647, but the restoration of Charles Ⅱ brought him back to Devon, where he lived out his last years quietly.

　　Herrick was a disciple of Ben Jonson. His lyrics show considerable classical influence; but his greatness rests on his simplicity, his sensuousness, his care for design and detail, and his management of words and rhythms. He wrote on a number of themes, often on the attributes of young women, but also on rural life, religious themes and, in his later life, on his approaching death. Herrick's directness of speech is accompanied by an equally clear and simple presentment of his thought; we have, perhaps, no poet who writes more consistently and earnestly with his eye upon his subject.

2.11.2 "To the Virgins, to Make Much of Time"[1]

Gather ye rosebuds while ye may,
    Old time is still a-flying;
And this same flower that smiles today,
    Tomorrow will be dying.

The glorious lamp of heaven[2], the sun,
    The higher he's a-getting,
The sooner will his race be run,
    And nearer he's to setting.

That age is best which is the first,
    When youth and blood are warmer;
But being spent, the worse, and worst[3]
    Times still succeed the former.

Then be not coy, but use[4] your time,
    And while ye may, go marry;
For having lost but once your prime[5],
    You may forever tarry[6].

Notes
1. This poem is written in quatrains of iambic tetrameter alternating with iambic trimeter. The rhyme scheme is *abab*.
2. **lamp of heaven**: the sun.
3. **best, worse,** and **worst**: referring to the three stages of one's life — the youth, the middle age, and the old age.
4. **use**: to enjoy.
5. **prime**: the best part of one's life.
6. **tarry**: to stay in a place, linger.

Study Questions
1. What is compared to the flower in the first stanza?
2. What implied meaning does the central image in the second stanza carry?
3. What is the best stage of life? And what is the worst?

4. What conclusion can you draw from the last stanza?

2.12 John Milton

2.12.1 About the Author

John Milton (1608-1674) was born in Cheapside, London. From 1618 to 1620, he was privately tutored at home. He then attended St. Paul's School and Cambridge University. Upon leaving Cambridge in 1632 with a master's degree, Milton retired to Horton, his father's rural retreat, where he undertook to give himself a liberal education by wide reading. In 1638, he embarked on a European journey which was to last nearly fifteen months. The experience brought him into contact with the major thinkers of the day, especially in Italy. In this early period he wrote some short poems, such as the ode "On the Morning of Christ's Nativity" (1629), the sonnet "On Shakespeare" (1630), "L'Allegro" and "Il Penseroso" (both probably 1631), and the elegy *Lycidas* (1637).

With the coming of the English Civil War and the Commonwealth, Milton's life changed completely as his attentions shifted from private to public concerns. He believed wholeheartedly in the Puritan cause, and set aside his poetry to write pamphlets in defense of various aspects of liberty as he saw it. The most famous prose work he wrote in this period was *Areopagitica* (1644), an impassioned plea for freedom of the press in which Milton demands "the liberty to know, to utter, and to argue freely according to conscience, above all liberties". In 1649 he accepted an invitation to become Cromwell's Latin secretary for foreign affairs. While in this post he wrote several tracts in Latin defending the Commonwealth government against foreign criticism for having executed the king.

After 1660, with the monarchy restored, Milton suffered considerable persecution. He became blind, deserted, ruined and broken-hearted. He retired to private life and returned to his true vocation — the writing of poetry. Although isolated and embittered, he fulfilled the tasks he had set for himself. The three great poems, *Paradise Lost* (1667), *Paradise Regained* (1671), and *Samson Agonistes* (1671), appeared one after another. Among the three, the first is the greatest, indeed the only generally acknowledged epic in English literature since *Beowulf*; and the last one is the most perfect example of the verse drama after the Greek style in English.

2.12.2 An Excerpt from Book I of *Paradise Lost*

Of Man's first disobedience, and the fruit[1]
Of that forbidden tree, whose mortal taste

Brought death into the world, and all our woe,
With loss of Eden, till one greater Man[2]
Restore us, and regain the blissful seat,
Sing, Heavenly Muse, that, on the secret top
Of Oreb, or of Sinai, didst inspire
That shepherd who first taught the chosen seed[3]
In the beginning how the Heavens and Earth
Rose out of Chaos: or, if Sion hill[4]
Delight thee more, and Siloa's brook[5] that flowed
Fast[6] by the oracle of God, I thence
Invoke thy aid to my adventurous song,
That with no middle flight intends to soar
Above th' Aonian mount[7], while it pursues
Things unattempted yet in prose or rhyme.
And chiefly thou, O Spirit[8], that dost prefer
Before all temples th' upright heart and pure,
Instruct me, for thou know'st; thou from the first
Wast present, and, with mighty wings outspread,
Dovelike sat'st brooding[9] on the vast abyss,
And mad'st it pregnant: what in me is dark
Illumine; what is low, raise and support;
That, to the height of this great argument[10],
I may assert[11] Eternal Providence,
And justify the ways of God to men.

Say first, (for Heaven hides nothing from thy view,
Nor the deep tract of Hell), say first what cause
Moved our grand[12] parents, in that happy state,
Favored of Heaven so highly, to fall off
From their Creator, and transgress his will
For one restraint, lords of the world besides?
Who first seduced them to that foul revolt?

Th' infernal Serpent; he it was, whose guile,
Stirred up with envy and revenge, deceived
The mother of mankind, what time his pride
Had cast him out from Heaven, with all his host
Of rebel angels, by whose aid aspiring
To set himself in glory above his peers[13],
He trusted to have equaled the Most High,
If he opposed; and with ambitious aim

Against the throne and monarchy of God
Raised impious war in Heaven and battle proud
With vain attempt. Him the Almighty Power
Hurled headlong flaming from th' ethereal sky
With hideous ruin and combustion down
To bottomless perdition, there to dwell
In adamantine chains and penal fire,
Who durst defy th' Omnipotent to arms.
   Nine times the space that measures day and night
To mortal men, he with his horrid crew
Lay vanquished, rolling in the fiery gulf
Confounded though immortal. But his doom
Reserved him to more wrath; for now the thought
Both of lost happiness and lasting pain
Torments him; round he throws his baleful[14] eyes,
That witnessed huge affliction and dismay
Mixed with obdurate pride and steadfast hate.
At once, as far as angels ken[15], he views
The dismal situation waste and wild:
A dungeon horrible, on all sides round
As one great furnace flamed; yet from those flames
No light[16], but rather darkness visible
Served only to discover sights of woe,
Regions of sorrow, doleful shades, where peace
And rest can never dwell, hope never comes
That comes to all[17], but torture without end
Still urges[18], and a fiery deluge, fed
With ever-burning sulphur unconsumed:
Such place Eternal Justice had prepared
For those rebellious; here their prison ordained
In utter darkness, and their portion set
As far removed from God and light of Heaven
As from the center[19] thrice to th' utmost pole.
O how unlike the place from whence they fell!
There the companions of his fall, o'erwhelmed
With floods and whirlwinds of tempestuous fire,
He soon discerns; and weltering by his side
One next himself in power, and next in crime,
Long after known in Palestine, and named

Beelzebub[20]. To whom th' archenemy,
And thence in Heaven called Satan, with bold words
Breaking the horrid silence thus began:
"If thou beest he — but O how fallen! how changed
From him, who in the happy realms of light
Clothed with transcendent brightness didst outshine
Myriads, though bright! if he whom mutual league,
United thoughts and counsels, equal hope
And hazard in the glorious enterprise,
Joined with me once, now misery hath joined
In equal ruin: into what pit thou seest
From what height fallen, so much the stronger proved
He with his thunder[21]: and till then who knew
The force of those dire arms? Yet not for those,
Nor what the potent Victor in his rage
Can else inflict, do I repent or change,
Though changed in outward luster, that fixed mind
And high disdain, from sense of injured merit,
That with the Mightiest raised me to contend,
And to the fierce contention brought along
Innumerable force of spirits armed,
That durst dislike his reign, and me preferring,
His utmost power with adverse power opposed
In dubious battle on the plains of Heaven,
And shook his throne. What though the field be lost?
All is not lost: the unconquerable will,
And study[22] of revenge, immortal hate,
And courage never to submit or yield:
And what is else not to be overcome?
That glory never shall his wrath or might
Extort from me. To bow and sue for grace
With suppliant knee, and deify his power
Who from the terror of this arm so late
Doubted his empire — that were low indeed,
That were an ignominy and shame beneath
This downfall; since by fate the strength of gods
And this empyreal substance cannot fail[23];
Since, through experience of this great event,
In arms not worse, in foresight much advanced,

We may with more successful hope resolve
To wage by force or guile eternal war,
Irreconcilable to our grand Foe,
Who now triumphs, and in th' excess of joy
Sole reigning holds the tyranny of Heaven."
...
Whereto with speedy words th' arch-fiend replied:
"Fall'n Cherub, to be weak is miserable,
Doing or suffering[24]: but of this be sure,
To do aught good never will be our task,
But ever to do ill our sole delight,
As being the contrary to his high will
Whom we resist. If then his providence
Out of our evil seek to bring forth good,
Our labor must be to pervert that end,
And out of good still to find means of evil;
Which oft times may succeed, so as perhaps
Shall grieve him, if I fail not[25], and disturb
His inmost counsels from their destined aim.
But see! the angry Victor hath recalled
His ministers of vengeance and pursuit
Back to the gates of Heaven; the sulphurous hail,
Shot after us in storm, o'erblown hath laid
The fiery surge that from the precipice
Of Heaven received us falling; and the thunder,
Winged with red lightning and impetuous rage,
Perhaps hath spent his shafts, and ceases now
To bellow through the vast and boundless deep.
Let us not slip th' occasion, whether scorn
Or satiate fury yield it from our Foe.
Seest thou yon dreary plain, forlorn and wild,
The seat of desolation, void of light.
Save what the glimmering of these livid flames
Casts pale and dreadful? Thither let us tend
From off the tossing of these fiery waves;
There rest, if any rest can harbor there,
And reassembling our afflicted powers[26],
Consult how we may henceforth most offend
Our enemy, our own loss how repair,

> How overcome this dire calamity,
>
> What reinforcement we may gain from hope,
>
> If not, what resolution from despair."

Notes

1. **fruit**: both "fruit" and "result", just as "mortal" in the next line can mean both "human" and "fatal".
2. **greater Man**: Christ.
3. **Heavenly Muse... chosen seed**: The poet is asking for inspiration from the spirit that inspired Moses ("That shepherd"), who taught the Israelites ("the chosen seed") the laws as God pronounced them on Oreb, or Sinai, a mountain in the Holy Land. Moses is also traditionally regarded as the author of the first five books of the Bible, including Genesis, on which *Paradise Lost* is based.
4. **Sion hill**: a hill in Jerusalem on which stood the Temple ("the oracle of God").
5. **Siloa's brook**: a stream near Jerusalem.
6. **Fast**: Close.
7. **Aonian mount**: Mount Helicon. In Greek mythology, the home of the classical Muses. Milton has chosen a more exalted theme than the writers of the classical epics.
8. **Spirit**: Holy Spirit.
9. **with mighty wings outspread, /Dovelike sat'st brooding**: A composite of phrases and ideas from Genesis 1.2 ("And the earth was without form, and void; and darkness was upon the face of the deep. And the Spirit of God moved upon the face of the waters"), and Luke 3.22 ("and the Holy Ghost descended in a bodily shape like a dove upon him"). Milton's mind as he wrote was impregnated with expressions from the King James Bible, only a few of which can be indicated in the notes.
10. **argument**: subject matter; theme.
11. **assert**: defend; champion.
12. **grand**: first in importance, by implication, in time also.
13. **peers**: his equals. The sentence mimics Satan's action, piling clause loosely upon clause, and building ever higher, till "with vain attempt" brings the whole structure crashing down. It is a dramatic entry into "the midst of things", where epics begin. Book 6 will recount more largely the war in Heaven, in the full narrative form which Aeneas used to tell Dido of the last days of Troy (*Aeneid* 2).
14. **baleful**: malignant, as well as suffering.
15. **as far as angels ken**: as far as angels can see.
16. **No light**: Here omitting the verb conveys abruptly the paradox: fire without light.
17. **hope never comes /That comes to all**: The phrase echoes an expression in Dante ("All hope abandon, ye who enter here"), but Milton expresses it as a logical absurdity.

Hope comes to "all" but not to Hell-dwellers; they are not included in "all".

18. **urges**: afflicts; presses.
19. **As from the center**: the earth. Milton makes use in Paradise Lost of two images of the cosmos: (1) the earth is the center of the created cosmos of ten concentric spheres; but (2) the earth and the whole created cosmos are a mere appendage, hanging from Heaven by a golden chain, in the larger, aboriginal and less shapely cosmos. In the present passage, the fall from Heaven to Hell (through the aboriginal universe) is described as thrice as far as the distance (in the created universe) from the center (earth) to the outmost sphere.
20. **Beelzebub**: a Phoenician deity, or Baal (the name means "Lord of flies"); traditionally, prince of devils and enemy of Jehovah. The Phoenician Baal, a sun god, had many aspects and so many names; most Baals were nature deities. But in the poem's time scheme all this lies in the future; Beelzebub's angelic name, whatever it was, has been erased from the Book of Life, and as he has not yet got another one, he must be called by the name he will have later on.
21. **he with his thunder**: God with his thunderbolts.
22. **study**: pursuit.
23. **by fate the strength of gods /And this empyreal substance cannot fail**: The essence of Satan's fault is this claim to the position of a god, subject to fate but to nothing else. His substance is "empyreal" (heavenly, from the empyrean), and cannot be destroyed; but, as he learns in the poem, it can be confounded by God's greater power and weakened by its own corruption and self-contradictions. fail: cease to exist.
24. **doing or suffering**: Whether one is active or passive.
25. **if I fail not**: unless I'm mistaken.
26. **afflicted powers**: stricken armies.

Study Questions

1. How does Satan feel about being in Hell according to the poem?
2. Satan considers himself the equal to God in reason. How, then, does Satan explain his defeat?
3. How does Satan see himself?
4. How is Satan's pride as tragic as it is heroic?

Essay Topics

1. To what extent is Milton's Satan a heroic figure?
2. How does Milton portray Satan?

2.12.3 "When I Consider How My Light Is Spent"

When I consider how my light is spent
　　Ere[1] half my days in this dark world and wide,
　　And that one talent which is death to hide[2]
　　Lodg'd with me useless, though my soul more bent
To serve therewith my Maker, and present
　　My true account, lest he returning chide,
　　"Doth God exact day-labour, light denied?"
　　I fondly[3] ask. But Patience, to prevent
That murmur, soon replies: "God doth not need
　　Either man's work or His own gifts; who best
　　Bear his mild yoke, they serve him best. His state
Is kingly: thousands[4] at His bidding speed,
　　And post[5] o'er land and ocean without rest;
　　They also serve who only stand and wait."

Notes

1. **Ere**: before.
2. **And that one talent which is death to hide**: The parable of the talents (Matthew 25) loomed large in Puritan minds, and particularly in Milton's. The servants who put their master's money (talents of gold and silver) out to earn interest while he was away were called "good and faithful;" while one who simply returned what he had been given was deprived of everything and cast into outer darkness. Usury, which under Catholic theology had been a deadly sin, changed its meaning for the Puritans; it became a metaphor, and sometimes more than a metaphor, for "working out one's salvation."
3. **fondly**: foolishly.
4. **thousands**: that is, thousands of angels.
5. **post**: hasten.

Study Questions

1. Examine Milton's choice of language, imagery, simile and metaphor. How do they contribute to his themes?
2. Does the speaker find consolation? Explain.
3. What are the major thematic concerns in this sonnet?

Chapter 3 The Neoclassical Period

3.1 An Introduction

The Neoclassical period, which covered the time from 1660 to 1798, was one of political and military unrest. Of the great events, there were the Restoration of King Charles II in 1660, the Great Plague of 1665 which took 70 000 lives in London alone, the Great London Fire which destroyed a large part of the city, and the Glorious Revolution in which King James II was replaced by his Protestant daughter Mary and her Dutch husband William in 1688. In this period, England was also involved in a series of commercial wars against the Dutch, French, Austrians, Spanish, and eventually its own American colonists over the profitable trade opportunities with the New World and with the South Seas. Besides, there was constant strife between the monarch and the parliament between the two big parties, the Tories and the Whigs, over the control of the parliament and government, between opposing religious sects such as the Roman Catholicism, the Anglican Church and the Dissenters, and between the ruling class and the laboring poor. In short, it was an age full of conflicts and divergence of values.

This period also saw the fast development of England as a nation. At home, Acts of Enclosure were putting more land into fewer privileged rich landowners and forcing thousands of small farmers and tenants off land to become wage laborers in industrial towns. Abroad, the Afro-Caribbean slave trade and colonialist expansion into India, Australia, and the Far East provided England with both immense wealth and a vast market. The coming together of the free labor from home and the large capital gathered or plundered from the colonies provided the essential conditions for the Industrial Revolution. So, towards the middle of the eighteenth century, England had become the first powerful capitalist country in the world.

Along with the fast economic development, the English bourgeois class, who were mainly composed of traders, merchants, manufacturers and other adventurers such as slave traders and colonists, also grew rapidly. They were people who had known poverty and hardship, and many of them had obtained their present social status through hard work. They believed in self-restraint, self-reliance and hard work. To work, to economize and to accumulate wealth constituted the whole meaning of their life. This aspect of social life is best found in the realistic novels of the century.

This was also an age of Enlightenment, which was conventionally seen as a European intellectual movement exalting reason and the scientific method. The enlighteners held that through the exercise of reason human beings could clear away the darkness of ignorance, intolerance and prejudice, and move towards a more just and better life. John Locke, the most influential philosopher of the age, analyzed logically how our minds function (1690), argued for religious toleration (1689), and maintained that government was justified not by divine right but by a "social contract". If the people's natural rights were not respected, the contract was broken and the government failed its function. This belief provided theory for the French Revolution of 1789 and the American War of Independence in 1776. At the same time, the enlighteners also advocated universal education. They believed that human beings were limited, dualistic, imperfect, and yet capable of rationality and perfection through education. If the masses were well educated, they thought, there would be great chance for a democratic and equal human society.

In the field of literature, the Enlightenment Movement brought about a revival of interest in the old classical works. This tendency is known as Neoclassicism. According to the Neoclassicists, all forms of literature were to be modeled after the classical works of ancient Greek and Roman writers and those of the contemporary French ones. To a certain extent Neoclassicism represented a reaction against the optimistic, exuberant, and enthusiastic Renaissance view of man as a being fundamentally good and possessed of an infinite potential for spiritual and intellectual growth. Neoclassicists, by contrast, saw man as an imperfect being, inherently sinful, whose potential was limited. They also believed that the artistic ideals should be order, logic, restrained emotion and accuracy, and that literature should be judged in terms of its service to humanity. This belief led them to seek proportion, unity, harmony and grace in literary expressions, in an effort to delight, instruct and correct human beings, primarily as social animals.

The Neoclassical period witnessed the flourish of English poetry in the classical style from Restoration to about the second half of the 18th century, climaxing with John Dryden, Alexander Pope and Samuel Johnson. Much attention was given to the wit, form and art of poetry. Mock epic, romance, satire and epigram were popular forms adopted by poets of the time. Besides the elegant poetic structure and diction, the Neoclassical poetry was also noted for its seriousness and earnestness in tone and constant didacticism.

The 18th century was, however, predominated by a newly rising literary form — the modern English novel, which, contrary to the traditional romance of aristocrats, gives a realistic presentation of life of the common people. This English novel was a product of several differing literary traditions, among which were the French romance, the Spanish picaresque tale, and such earlier prose models in English as John Lyly's *Euphues* (1578), Sir Philip Sidney's *Arcadia* (1590) and John Bunyan's *Pilgrim's Progress* (1684). The authors of these works collectively helped pave the way for the rising of the English novel. Literary historians have generally considered *Robinson Crusoe* the first successful English novel and Defoe as one of the originators of realistic fiction in the eighteenth century. The other important novelists are: Samuel Richardson, Henry

Fielding, Laurence Sterne, Tobias George Smollett, and Oliver Goldsmith.

From the middle part to the end of the 18th century, there was also an apparent shift of interest from the classic literary tradition to originality and imagination, from society to individual, and from the didactic to the confessional, inspirational and prophetic. Gothic novels, mostly stories of mystery and horror which took place in some haunted or decaying Middle Age castles, were turned out in large numbers by both male and female writers. Eulogizing or lamenting lyrics by nature poets like James Thomson, William Collins, and William Cowper, and by such sentimentalists as the "Graveyard School" were widely read. The romantic poems of William Blake and Robert Burns, the Scottish peasant poet, also joined in, paving the way for the flourish of Romanticism early the next century.

In the theatrical world, Richard Brinsley Sheridan was the leading figure among a host of playwrights. Of the witty and satiric prose, those written by Joseph Addison, Richard Steele and Jonathan Swift, are especially worth studying. Swift's *A Modest Proposal* is generally regarded as the best model of satire, not only of the period but also in the whole English literary history.

3.2 John Dryden

3.2.1 About the Author

John Dryden (1631-1700) was born into a Puritan family in Aldwinkle, Northamptonshire. He received a classical education at Westminster School and Trinity College, Cambridge. He then moved to London in 1657 to start his career as a professional writer. His first important poem, *Heroic Stanzas* (1659), was written in memory of Cromwell. After the Restoration, however, Dryden became a Royalist and celebrated the return of King Charles II in two poems, *Astraea Redux* (1660) and *Panegyric on the Coronation* (1661). In 1662 Dryden began to write plays as a

source of income. During the next 20 years, he became the most prominent dramatist in England, written altogether 27 plays. One of his later tragedies in blank verse, *All for Love or The World Well Lost* (a version of Shakespeare's *Antony and Cleopatra*) is considered his greatest play and one of the masterpieces of Restoration tragedy.

Dryden's reputation grew quickly. In 1668, only ten years after his move to London, he was appointed Poet Laureate of England. In 1681 he wrote his first and greatest political satire, *Absalom and Achitophel*, a masterful allegory in heroic couplets. It employs biblical characters and incidents to glorify the Tories and criticize the Whigs. In 1668, Dryden began a fruitful period of both critical and dramatic writing. His first major critical work was *An Essay of Dramatic Poesy* (1668), followed by *A Defence of an*

Essay (1668), and *Essay of Heroic Plays* (1672).

Dryden's contribution to English literature, besides his poems and plays, was his improving of the English prose in the Elizabethan age. He invented a prose style that is clear, straightforward, terse, forceful, easy and simple and yet dignified, fluent in vocabulary, varied, and of pleasing rhythm.

3.2.2 An Excerpt from *An Essay of Dramatic Poesy*

To begin, then, with Shakespeare[1], he was the man who of all modern, and perhaps ancient poets, had the largest and most comprehensive soul. All the images of Nature were still[2] present to him, and he drew them, not laboriously, but luckily[3]; when he describes anything, you more than see it, you feel it too. Those who accuse him to have wanted[4] learning, give him the greater commendation: he was naturally learned; he needed not the spectacles of books to read Nature[5]; he looked inwards, and found her there. I cannot say he is everywhere alike[6]; were he so, I should do him injury to compare him with the greatest of mankind. He is many times flat, insipid[7]; his comic wit degenerating into clenches[8], his serious swelling into bombast[9]. But he is always great, when some great occasion is presented to him; no man can say he ever had a fit subject for his wit and did not then raise himself as high above the rest of poets,

Quantum lenta solent inter viburna cupressi. [10]

The consideration of this made Mr. Hales of Eaton[11] say, that there was no subject of which any poet ever writ, but he would produce it much better treated of in Shakespeare; and however others are now generally preferred before him, yet the age wherein he lived, which had contemporaries with him Fletcher[12] and Jonson[13], never equaled them to him in their esteem: and in the last king's court[14], when Ben's reputation[15] was at highest, Sir John Suckling[16], and with him the greater part of the courtiers, set our Shakespeare far above him...

As for Jonson, to whose character I am now arrived, if we look upon him while he was himself[17] (for his last plays were but his dotages[18]), I think him the most learned and judicious writer which any theatre ever had. He was a most severe judge of himself, as well as others. One cannot say he wanted wit, but rather that he was frugal of it. In his works you find little to retrench or alter. Wit, and language, and humor also in some measure, we had before him[19]; but something of art was wanting to the Drama, till he came. He managed his strength to more advantage than any who preceded him. You seldom find him making love in any of his scenes, or endeavoring to move the passions; his genius was too sullen and saturnine[20] to do it gracefully, especially when he knew he came after those who had performed both to such an height. Humor was his proper sphere[21], and in that he delighted most to represent mechanic people[22]. He was deeply conversant in the ancients[23], both Greek and Latin, and he borrowed boldly from them: there is scarce a poet or historian among the Roman authors of those times whom he has

Chapter 3 The Neoclassical Period

not translated[24] in *Sejanus* and *Catiline*[25]. But he has done his robberies so openly, that one may see he fears not to be taxed[26] by any law. He invades authors like a monarch; and what would be theft in other poets is only victory in him. With the spoils of these writers he so represents old Rome to us, in its rites, ceremonies, and customs, that if one of their poets had written either of his tragedies, we had seen less of it than in him. If there was any fault in his language, 'twas that he weaved it too closely and laboriously, in his serious plays: perhaps too, he did a little too much Romanize our tongue[27], leaving the words which he translated almost as much Latin as he found them: wherein, though he learnedly followed the idiom of their language, he did not enough comply with the idiom of ours. If I would compare him with Shakespeare, I must acknowledge him the more correct poet, but Shakespeare the greater wit. Shakespeare was the Homer[28], or father of our dramatic poets; Jonson was the Virgil[29], the pattern of elaborate writing; I admire him, but I love Shakespeare. To conclude of him; as he has given us the most correct plays, so in the precepts which he has laid down in his *Discoveries*[30], we have as many and profitable rules for perfecting the stage, as any wherewith the French can furnish us.

Notes

1. **To begin, then, with Shakespeare**: The whole excerpt given here is part of a speech by Neander, whose views have generally been supposed to represent those of the author.
2. **still**: ever; always.
3. **luckily**: happily.
4. **wanted**: lacked.
5. **Nature**: the external world of reality.
6. **I cannot say he is everywhere alike**: I cannot say that he achieves a similar degree of excellence in all his works.
7. **insipid**: lifeless; dull.
8. **clenches**: (or clinches) referring to puns that play upon words.
9. **his serious swelling into bombast**: his serious thoughts expanding into extravagant language.
10. *Quantum lenta solent inter viburna cupressi*: (Latin) As the cypresses are wont to tower above the yielding osiers (a line quoted from the ancient Roman poet Virgil's *Eclogues*, I, 26).
11. **Mr. Hales of Eaton**: referring to John Hales (1584-1656), a fellow of Eton.
12. **Fletcher**: John Fletcher (1579-1625), English dramatist.
13. **Jonson**: Ben Jonson (1572-1637), English dramatist and poet.
14. **in the last king's court**: referring to the court of King Charles I.
15. **Ben's reputation**: the reputation of Ben Jonson.
16. **Sir John Suckling** (1609-1642): English poet.

17. **while he was himself**: when he attained to his usual level of achievement.
18. **his dotages**: his works written in old age when he was in his decline.
19. **we had before him**: we had before his time.
20. **saturnine**: heavy.
21. **Humor was his proper sphere**: i. e., he was especially adept in portraying "humors" or characteristic temperaments of the characters in his drama.
22. **mechanic people**: artisans.
23. **deeply conversant in the ancients**: very well acquainted with the writers of ancient Greece and Rome.
24. **translated**: carried over, transferred, here meaning borrowed boldly and directly (from "the Roman authors of those times").
25. *Sejanus* **and** *Catiline*: *Sejanus* is a tragedy by Ben Jonson, based on the story of the rise and fall of Sejanus, the favourite of the emperor Tiberius, in ancient Roman history. It was first produced in 1603. *Catiline* is a tragedy also by Ben Jonson, based on the story of the struggle between Catiline and Cicero in ancient Roman history. It was first acted in 1611.
26. **taxed**: accused.
27. **Romanize our tongue**: to introduce linguistic elements of Latin (the language of the ancient Romans) into English.
28. **Homer**: a great Greek epic poet, born between 1050 B. C. and 850 B. C.
29. **Virgil**: a great Roman poet (70 B. C. -19 B. C.).
30. *Discoveries*: the full title being *Timber, or Discoveries Made upon Men and Matte* (1640), a book of literary criticism by Ben Jonson.

Study Questions

1. Why does Dryden say that Shakespeare "was naturally learned"?
2. What strong and weak points does Shakespeare show in his drama according to John Dryden?
3. What strong and weak points does Jonson show in his drama according to John Dryden?
4. Who does Dryden value more when he says that he "admires" Jonson but "loves" Shakespeare?

3.3 John Bunyan

3.3.1 About the Author

John Bunyan (1628-1688) was born into a poor tinker's family in Bedfordshire. He received very little formal education. When he was still a little boy, he took up his father's trade and had the least promise of becoming a writer. But the boy had a profound imagination. His marriage in 1647 with a Christian woman led him to the Lord.

He joined a Non-conformist church and began to preach, by the roadside or on the village green, telling people of his vision and interpretation of God's doctrine. However, he was thrown into prison in 1660 for preaching without receiving permission from the Established Church. He remained in prison for 12 years because he refused to take a vow to give up preaching. He was imprisoned again in 1675 on charge of the same offence. It was during this second term in prison that he wrote *The Pilgrim's Progress*, which was published in 1678 after his release. His other works include *Grace Abounding to the Chief of Sinners*
(1666), *The Life and Death of Mr. Badman* (1680), *The Holy War* (1682) and *The Pilgrim's Progress*, Part Ⅱ (1684). He died in 1688 from a bad fever.

Like most working men at the time, Bunyan had a deep hatred for the corrupted, hypocritical rich who accumulated their wealth "by hook and by crook". As a stout Puritan, he had made a conscientious study of the Bible and firmly believed in salvation through spiritual struggle.

Bunyan's style was modeled after that of the English Bible. With his concrete and living language as well as carefully observed and vividly presented details, he made it possible for the reader of the least education to share the pleasure of reading his work and to relive the experience of his characters.

3.3.2 "The Vanity Fair": An Excerpt from *The Pilgrim's Progress*

Then I saw in my dream, that when they were got out of the wilderness, they presently saw a town before them, and the name of that town is Vanity; and at the town there is a fair kept, called Vanity Fair. It is kept all the year long. It beareth[1] the name of Vanity Fair, because the town where it is kept is lighter than vanity, and also because all that is there sold, or that cometh thither[2], is vanity; as is the saying of the wise, "All that cometh is vanity."[3]

This fair is no new-erected business but a thing of ancient standing. I will show you the original of it.

Almost five thousand years ago there were pilgrims walking to the Celestial City[4], as these two honest persons are; and Beelzebub, Apollyon, and Legion[5], with their companions, perceiving by the path that the pilgrims made, that their way to the city lay through this town of Vanity, they contrived here to set up a fair; a fair wherein should be sold all sorts of vanity, and that it should last all the year long. Therefore, at this fair are all such merchandise sold as houses, lands, trades, places, honors, preferments, titles, countries, kingdoms, lusts, pleasures; and delights of all sorts, as harlots, wives, husbands, children, masters, servants, lives, blood, bodies, souls, silver, gold, pearls, precious stones, and what not.

And moreover, at this fair there is at all times to be seen jugglings, cheats, games, plays, fools, apes[6], knaves, and rogues, and that of every kind.

Here are to be seen, too, and that for nothing, thefts, murders, adulteries, false-swearers, and that of a blood-red color.

And, as in other fairs of less moment[7], there are the several rows and streets under their proper names, where such and such wares are vended[8]; so here, likewise, you have the proper places, rows, streets, (namely, countries and kingdoms,) where the wares of this fair are soonest to be found. Here is the Britain Row, the French Row, the Italian Row, the Spanish Row, the German Row, where several sorts of vanities are to be sold. But, as in other fairs, some one commodity is as the chief of all the fair; so the ware of Rome and her merchandise[9] is greatly promoted in this fair; only our English nation, with some others, have taken a dislike thereat[10].

Now, as I said, the way to the Celestial City lies just through this town, where this lusty[11] fair is kept; and he that will go to the city, and yet not go through this town, "must needs[12] go out of the world". The Prince of princes[13] himself, when here, went through this town to his own country, and that upon a fair-day too[14]; yea, and, as I think, it was Beelzebub, the chief lord of this fair, that invited him to buy of his vanities, yea, would have made him lord of the fair, would he but have done him reverence as he went through the town. Yea, because he was such a person of honor, Beelzebub had[15] him from street to street, and showed him all the kingdoms of the world in a little time, that he might, if possible, allure that Blessed One[16] to cheapen[17] and buy some of his vanities; but he had no mind to the merchandise, and therefore left the town, without laying out so much as one farthing upon these vanities. This fair, therefore, is an ancient thing, of long standing, and a very great fair.

Now, these pilgrims, as I said, must needs go through this fair. Well, so they did; but behold, even as they entered into the fair, all the people in the fair were moved; and the town itself, as it were, in a hubbub[18] about them, and that for several reasons:

First, The Pilgrims were clothed with such kind of raiment[19] as was diverse from the raiment of any that traded in that fair. The people, therefore, of the fair made a great gazing upon them: some said they were fools; some, they were Bedlams[20]; and some, they were outlandish[21] men.

Secondly, and as they wondered at their apparel, so they did likewise at their speech; for few could understand what they said. They naturally spoke the language of Canaan[22]; but they that kept the fair were the men of this world: so that from one end of the fair to the other, they seemed barbarians each to the other[23].

Chapter 3　The Neoclassical Period

　　Thirdly, But that which did not a little amuse the merchandisers was, that these pilgrims set very light by[24] all their wares. They cared not so much as to look upon them; and if they called upon them to buy, they would put their fingers in their ears, and cry, "Turn away mine eyes from beholding vanity, " and look upward, signifying that their trade and traffic[25] was in heaven.

　　One chanced, mockingly, beholding the carriage of the men, to say unto them, "What will ye buy?" But they, looking gravely upon him, said, "We buy the truth. " At that there was an occasion taken[26] to despise the men the more; some mocking, some taunting, some speaking reproachfully, and some calling upon others to smite[27] them. At last, things came to an hubbub and great stir in the fair, insomuch that all order was confounded[28]. Now was word presently brought to the great one of the fair, who quickly came down, and deputed[29] some of his most trusty friends to take those men into examination about whom the fair was almost overturned. So the men were brought to examination; and they that sat upon[30] them asked them whence[31] they came, whither[32] they went, and what they did there in such an unusual garb. The men told them they were pilgrims and strangers in the world, and that they were going to their own country, which was the heavenly Jerusalem, and that they had given no occasion to the men of the town, nor yet to the merchandisers, thus to abuse them[33], and to let them in their journey, except it was for that, when one asked them what they would buy, they said they would buy the truth. But they that were appointed to examine them did not believe them to be any other than bedlams and mad, or else such as came to put all things into a confusion in the fair. Therefore they took them and beat them, and besmeared[34] them with dirt, and then put them into the cage, that they might be made a spectacle[35] to all the men of the fair. There, therefore, they lay for some time, and were made the objects of any man's sport, or malice, or revenge; the great one of the fair laughing still at all that befell them. But the men being patient, and "not rendering railing for railing, but contrariwise blessing, " and giving good words for bad, and kindness for injuries done, some men in the fair, that were more observing and less prejudiced than the rest, began to check and blame the baser sort for their continual abuses done by them to the MEN. They, therefore, in an angry manner let fly at them again, counting them as bad as the men in the cage, and telling them that they seemed confederates[36], and should be made partakers of their misfortunes. The others replied that, for aught they could see, the men were quiet and sober, and intended nobody any harm; and that there were many that traded in their fair that were more worthy to be put into the cage, yea, and pillory too, than were the men that they had abused. Thus, after divers words had passed on both sides, (the men behaving themselves all the while very wisely and soberly before them,) they fell to some blows among themselves, and did harm one to another. Then were these two poor men brought before their examiners again, and were charged as being guilty of the late hubbub that had been in the fair. So they beat them pitifully, and hanged irons upon them, and led them in chains up and down the fair, for an example and terror to others, lest any should speak in their behalf, or join themselves unto them. But Christian and Faithful behaved themselves yet more wisely, and received the ignominy and shame that was cast upon them with so much meekness and patience, that it won to their side (though but few in comparison of the rest) several of the men in the fair. This put the other party yet into a greater rage, insomuch that[37] they concluded the death of these two MEN. Wherefore they threatened that neither cage nor irons should serve their turn, but that they should die for the abuse they had done, and for deluding the men of the fair.

Then were they remanded to the cage again, until further order should be taken with them. So they put them in, and made their feet fast in the stocks.

Notes

1. **beareth**: bears. "th" is used to indicate third person single in ancient English.
2. **cometh thither**: comes there.
3. From Bible Eccl. 11:8; see also 1:2-14; 2:11-17; Isa. 40:17.
4. **the Celestial City**: the heavenly city the pilgrims are going to.
5. **Beelzebub, Apollyon, and Legion**: *Beelzebub*, a "prince of demons" according to the Bible, is the fallen angel next to Satan in power and crime as described in Milton's *Paradise Lost*. *Appollyon*, a friend against god, who is described early in the book. *Legion*, referring to all those followers of Satan.
6. **ape**: a person who copies the behavior of others.
7. **of less moment**: of less importance.
8. **vended**: offered for sale.
9. **the ware of Rome and her merchandise**: the usage and temporal power of the Roman Catholic Church.
10. **thereat**: at or for that.
11. **lusty**: merry.
12. **must need**: must necessarily.
13. **The Prince of princes**: Jesus Christ.
14. **and that upon a fair-day too**: This alludes to the temptation of Jesus in the wilderness.
15. **had**: led.
16. **that Blessed One**: Jesus Christ.
17. **to cheapen**: to make something become lower in price.
18. **hubbub**: a mixture of loud noises.
19. **raiment**: clothing; garments.
20. **Bedlams**: lunatics from Bethlehem Hospital, the insane asylum in London.
21. **outlandish**: strange.

22. **the language of Canaan**: Canaan is the Promised Land, which was ultimately conquered by the children of Israel and settled by them, hence the pilgrims speak the language of the Bible and of true religion. Dissenters were notorious for their habitual use of biblical language.
23. **barbarians each to the other**: barbarians to each other. Barbarians, the Greeks and Romans designated all those who spoke a foreign language as barbarians.
24. **set very light by**: to treat as of little importance.
25. **trade and traffic**: business.
26. **an occasion taken**: a chance made use of.
27. **smite**: to strike hard.
28. **confounded**: confused and deeply troubled.
29. **deputed**: entrusted.
30. **sat upon**: judged; questioned.
31. **whence**: from where.
32. **whither**: to what place.
33. **thus to abuse them**: to abuse them thus, to treat them in such a rough manner.
34. **besmeared**: smeared, made dirty.
35. **be made a spectacle**: be made an object of public shame, disrespect and laugh.
36. **confederates**: members of a confederacy; allies.
37. **insomuch that**: with the result that; so.

Study Questions

1. Why is the market called "Vanity Fair"?
2. What did people in the fair do to Christian and his friend?
3. What does this episode symbolize?

Essay Topics

1. Explain the various elements of allegory in *The Pilgrim's Progress*.
2. Do you think *The Pilgrim's Progress is* still important to the modern reader? Why or why not?

3.4 Jonathan Swift

3.4.1 About the Author

Jonathan Swift (1667-1745) was born into an English family in Dublin. His father died before his birth. His uncle then provided him with education. Swift studied at the Kilkenny Grammar School and Trinity College, Dublin. After graduation, he obtained a position as secretary to retired diplomat Sir William Temple at his home in Moor Park, Surrey. While working there, Swift got to know many politically influential people of the day, and was allowed a free use of Temple's vast library, which helped him to grow

intellectually. He also met and tutored Esther Johnson, the daughter of Temple's housekeeper. They formed a profound and lasting affectionate friendship as shown in Swift's journals to "Stella".

In his early years, Swift intended to work in the Church. From 1699 to 1701 he served at different clerical posts in Ireland. In 1704 he published two powerful satires on corruption in religion and learning, *The Battle of the Books and A Tale of a Tub*. In 1710 Swift tried to start a political career among Whigs but changed his party and took over the Tory journal *The Examiner*. He then produced a number of pamphlets, in all of which he ably defended the policies of the Tory administration. From 1713 to 1742 Swift was the dean of St. Patrick's Cathedral in Dublin. During this period, he was interested in Irish affairs, and attained extraordinary popularity by his *Drapier's Letters*, directed against the introduction of "Wood's halfpence". His most well-known essay during this time was "A Modest Proposal", a classic satirical work in which Swift outlined a plan to sell the children of the Irish poor as food the English rich. It is believed that Swift began to write his most famous work, *Gulliver's Travels*, in 1721 and finished it in 1725. It is an allegorical attack on the vanity and hypocrisy of contemporary courts, statesmen and political parties. However, the work is so imaginatively, wittily and simply written that it became and has remained a favorite children's book.

Swift is one of the greatest writers of satiric prose. No reader of his can escape being impressed by the great simplicity, directness and vigor of his style. Simple and concrete diction, uncomplicated syntax, economy and conciseness of language mark all his writings.

3.4.2 An Excerpt from Chapter 3, Part I of *Gulliver's Travels*

My gentleness and good behavior had gained so far on the Emperor and his court, and indeed upon the army and people in general, that I began to conceive hopes of getting my liberty in a short time. I took all possible methods to cultivate this favorable disposition[1]. The natives came by degrees to be less apprehensive of any danger from me. I would sometimes lie down, and let five or six of them dance on my hand. And at last the boys and girls would venture to come and play at hide-and-seek in my hair. I had now made a good progress in understanding and speaking their language. The Emperor had a mind one day to entertain me with several of the country shows; wherein they exceed all nations I have

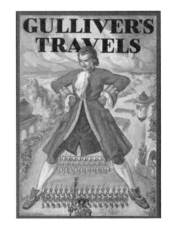

Chapter 3　The Neoclassical Period

known, both for dexterity and magnificence. I was diverted with none so much as that of the rope-dancers, performed upon a slender white thread, extended about two foot, and twelve inches from the ground. Upon which I shall desire liberty[2], with the reader's patience, to enlarge a little.

This diversion is only practiced by those persons, who are candidates for great employments, and high favor, at court. They are trained in this art from their youth, and are not always of noble birth or liberal education. When a great office is vacant either by death or disgrace (which often happens) five or six of those candidates petition the Emperor to entertain his Majesty and the court with a dance on the rope; and whoever jumps the highest without falling, succeeds in the office. Very often the chief ministers themselves are commanded to show their skill, and to convince the Emperor that they have not lost their faculty. Flimnap, the Treasurer, is allowed to cut a caper[3] on the strait rope, at least an inch higher than any other lord in the whole empire. I have seen him do the summerset[4] several times together upon a trencher fixed on the rope, which is no thicker than a common packthread in England. My friend Reldresal, Principal Secretary for Private Affairs, is, in my opinion, if I am not partial, the second after the Treasurer; the rest of the great officers are much upon a par.

These diversions are often attended with fatal accidents, whereof great numbers are on record. I myself have seen two or three candidates break a limb. But the danger is much greater when the ministers themselves are commanded to show their dexterity; for, by contending to excel themselves and their fellows, they strain so far, that there is hardly one of them who hath not received a fall; and some of them two or three. I was assured, that a year or two before my arrival, Flimnap would have infallibly broke his neck, if one of the King's cushions, that accidentally lay on the ground, had not weakened the force of his fall.

There is likewise another diversion, which is only shown before the Emperor and Empress, and first minister, upon particular occasions. The Emperor lays on a table three fine silken threads of six inches long. One is blue, the other red, and the third green. These threads are proposed as prizes for those persons whom the Emperor hath a mind to distinguish by a peculiar mark of his favor. The ceremony is performed in his Majesty's great chamber of state, where the candidates are to undergo a trial of dexterity very different from the former, and such as I have not observed the least resemblance of in any other country of the old or the new world. The Emperor holds a stick in his hands, both ends parallel to the horizon, while the candidates, advancing one by one, sometimes leap over the stick, sometimes creep under it backwards and forwards several times, according as the stick is advanced or depressed. Sometimes the Emperor holds one end of the stick, and his first minister the other; sometimes the minister has it entirely to himself. Whoever performs his part with most agility, and holds out the longest in *leaping and creeping*, is rewarded with the blue-colored silk; the red is given to the next, and the green to the third, which they all wear girt twice round about the middle[5]; and you see few great persons about this court who are not adorned with one of these girdles.

  The horses of the army, and those of the royal stables, having been daily led before me, were no longer shy, but would come up to my very feet, without starting. The riders would leap them over my hand as I held it on the ground; and one of the Emperor's huntsmen, upon a large courser[6], took[7], my foot, shoe and all; which was indeed a prodigious leap. I had the good fortune to divert the Emperor one day after a very extraordinary manner. I desired he would order several sticks of two foot high, and the thickness of an ordinary cane, to be brought me; whereupon his Majesty commanded the master of his woods to give directions accordingly; and the next morning six woodmen arrived with as many carriages, drawn by eight horses to each. I took nine of these sticks, and fixing them firmly in the ground in a quadrangular figure, two foot and a half square, I took four other sticks, and tied them parallel at each corner, about two foot from the ground; then I fastened my handkerchief to the nine sticks that stood erect, and extended it on all sides till it was as tight as the top of a drum; and the four parallel sticks, rising about five inches higher than the handkerchief, served as ledges on each side. When I had finished my work, I desired the Emperor to let a troop of his best horse, twenty-four in number, come and exercise upon this plain. His Majesty approved of the proposal, and I took them up one by one in my hands, ready-mounted[8] and armed, with the proper officers to exercise them. As soon as they got into order, they divided into two parties, performed mock skirmishes, discharged blunt arrows, drew their swords, fled and pursued, attacked and retired; and in short discovered the best military discipline I ever beheld. The parallel sticks secured them and their horses from falling over the stage; and the Emperor was so much delighted, that he ordered this entertainment to be repeated several days; and once was pleased to be lifted up, and give the word of command; and, with great difficulty, persuaded even the Empress herself to let me hold her in her close chair[9] within two yards of the stage, from whence she was able to take a full view of the whole performance. It was my good fortune that no ill accident happened in these entertainments, only once a fiery horse that belonged to one of the captains pawing with his hoof struck a hole in my handkerchief, and his foot slipping, he overthrew his rider and himself; but I immediately relieved them both; for covering the hole with one hand, I set down the troop with the other, in the same manner as I took them up. The horse that fell was strained in the left shoulder, but the rider got no hurt, and I repaired my handkerchief as well as I could; however, I would not trust to the strength of it any more in such dangerous enterprises.

  About two or three days before I was set at liberty, as I was entertaining the court with these kinds of feats, there arrived an express to inform his Majesty that some of his subjects, riding near the place where I was first taken up, had seen a great black

Chapter 3　The Neoclassical Period

　　substance lying on the ground, very oddly shaped, extending its edges round as wide as his Majesty's bedchamber, and rising up in the middle as high as a man; that it was no living creature, as they at first apprehended, for it lay on the grass without motion, and some of them had walked round it several times; that by mounting upon each other's shoulders, they had got to the top, which was flat and even; and stamping upon it they found it was hollow within; that they humbly conceived it might be something belonging to the Man-Mountain, and if his Majesty pleased, they would undertake to bring it with only five horses. I presently knew what they meant; and was glad at heart to receive this intelligence[10]. It seems upon my first reaching the shore after our shipwreck, I was in such confusion, that before I came to the place where I went to sleep, my hat, which I had fastened with a string to my head while I was rowing, and had stuck on all the time I was swimming, fell off after I came to land; the string, as I conjecture, breaking by some accident which I never observed, but thought my hat had been lost at sea. I entreated his Imperial Majesty to give orders it might be brought to me as soon as possible, describing to him the use and the nature of it: and the next day the wagoners arrived with it, but not in a very good condition; they had bored two holes in the brim, within an inch and half of the edge, and fastened two hooks in the holes; these hooks were tied by a long cord to the harness, and thus my hat was dragged along for above half an English mile: but the ground in that country being extremely smooth and level, it received less damage than I expected.

　　Two days after this adventure, the Emperor, having ordered that part of his army which quarters in and about his metropolis to be in a readiness, took a fancy of diverting himself in a very singular manner. He desired I would stand like a colossus, with my legs as far asunder as I conveniently could. He then commanded his general (who was an old experienced leader, and a great patron of mine) to draw up the troops in close order, and march them under me; the foot[11] by twenty-four in a breast[12], and the horse by sixteen, with drums beating, colors[13] flying, and pikes advanced. This body consisted of three thousand foot, and a thousand horse. His Majesty gave orders, upon pain of death[14], that every soldier in his march should observe the strictest decency with regard to my person; which, however, could not prevent some of the younger officers from turning up their eyes as they passed under me. And, to confess the truth, my breeches were at that time in so ill a condition, that they afforded some opportunities for laughter and admiration.

　　I had sent so many memorials and petitions for my liberty, that his Majesty at length mentioned the matter first in the cabinet, and then in a full council; where it was opposed by none, except Skyresh Bolgolam[15], who was pleased, without any provocation, to be my mortal enemy. But it was carried against him by the whole board, and confirmed by the Emperor. That minister was Galbet, or Admiral of the Realm; very much in his master's confidence, and a person well versed in affairs, but of a morose and sour complexion. However he was at length persuaded to comply; but prevailed that the articles and conditions upon which I should be set free, and to which I must swear, should be drawn up by himself. These articles were brought to me by Skyresh Bolgolam in person, attended by two under-secretaries, and several persons of distinction. After they were read, I was demanded to swear to the performance of them; first in the manner of my own country, and afterwards in the method prescribed by their laws; which was to hold my right foot in my left hand, to place the middle finger of my right hand on the crown of my head, and my thumb on the tip of my right ear. But because the reader may perhaps be curious to have some idea of the style and manner of expression peculiar to that people, as well as to know the articles upon which I recovered my liberty, I have made a translation of the whole instrument, word for word, as near as I was able, which I here offer to the public.

GOLBASTO MOMAREN EVLAME GURDILO SHEFIN MULLY ULLY GUE, most mighty Emperor of Lilliput, delight and terror of the universe, whose dominions extend five thousand blustrugs (about twelve miles in circumference) to the extremities of the globe; Monarch of all Monarchs; taller than the sons of men; whose feet press down to the center, and whose head strikes against the sun; at whose nod the princes of the earth shake their knees; pleasant as the spring, comfortable as the summer, fruitful as autumn, dreadful as winter. His most sublime Majesty proposeth to the Man-Mountain[16], lately arrived at our celestial dominions, the following articles, which by a solemn oath he shall be obliged to perform.

First, The Man-Mountain shall not depart from our dominions, without our license under our great seal.

Secondly, He shall not presume to come into our metropolis, without our express order[17]; at which time the inhabitants shall have two hours warning, to keep within their doors.

Thirdly, The said Man-Mountain shall confine his walks to our principal high roads; and not offer to walk or lie down in a meadow, or field of corn.

Fourthly, As he walks the said roads, he shall take the uttermost care not to trample upon the bodies of any of our loving subjects, their horses, or carriages, nor take any of our said subjects into his hands, without their own consent.

Fifthly, If an express require extraordinary dispatch, the Man-Mountain shall be obliged to carry in his pocket the messenger and horse, a six days' journey once in every moon, and return the said messenger back (if so required) safe to our Imperial Presence.

Sixthly, He shall be our ally against our enemies in the island of Blefuscu, and do his utmost to destroy their fleet, which is now preparing to invade us.

Seventhly, That the said Man-Mountain shall, at his times of leisure, be aiding and assisting to our workmen, in helping to raise certain great stones, towards covering the wall of the principal park, and other our royal buildings.

Eighthly, That the said Man-Mountain shall, in two moons' time, deliver in an exact survey of the circumference of our dominions by a computation of his own paces round the coast.

Lastly, That upon his solemn oath to observe all the above articles, the said Man-Mountain shall have a daily allowance[18] of meat and drink sufficient for the support of 1 728 of our subjects; with free access to our Royal Person, and other marks of our favor[19]. Given at our palace at Belfaborac the twelfth day of the ninety-first moon of our reign.

I swore and subscribed to these articles with great cheerfulness and content, although some of them were not so honorable as I could have wished; which proceeded wholly from the malice of Skyresh Bolgolam the High Admiral: whereupon my chains were immediately unlocked, and I was at full liberty: the Emperor himself in person did me the honor to be by at the whole ceremony. I made my acknowledgments by prostrating myself at his Majesty's feet: but he commanded me to rise; and after many gracious expressions, which, to avoid the censure of vanity, I shall not repeat, he added, that he hoped that I should prove a useful servant, and well deserve all the favors he had already conferred upon me, or might do for the future.

The reader may please to observe, that in the last article for the recovery of my liberty, the Emperor stipulates to allow me a quantity of meat and drink, sufficient for the support of 1 728 Lilliputians. Some time after, asking a friend at court how they came to fix on that determinate number, he told me, that his Majesty's mathematicians, having taken the height of my body by the help of a quadrant, and finding it to exceed theirs in the proportion of twelve to one, they concluded from the similarity of their bodies, that mine must contain at least 1 728 of theirs, and consequently would require as much food as was necessary to support that number of Lilliputians. By which, the reader may conceive an idea of the ingenuity of that people, as well as the prudent and exact economy of so great a prince.

Notes

1. **cultivate this favorable disposition**: to encourage and develop a general tendency of character.
2. **desire liberty**: beg leave or permission.
3. **cut a caper**: to jump about in a joyful manner.
4. **summerset**: somersault.
5. **wear girt twice round about the middle**: to wear girdle which goes twice round the waist.
6. **courser**: a swift horse.
7. **took**: jump over.

8. **ready-mounted**: be placed on the horse in advance.
9. **close chair**: an enclosed or sedan chair.
10. **intelligence**: news.
11. **the foot**: the foot soldier; infantry.
12. **in a breast**: in a rank (in which the members stand side by side).
13. **colors**: the official flags of the army.
14. **upon pain of death**: with the punishment of death.
15. **Skyresh Bolgolam**: here it indicates the earl of Nottingham, an enemy of Swift.
16. **Man-Mountain**: it refers to Gulliver.
17. **express order**: urgent order.
18. **allowance**: something provided regularly, provision.
19. **marks of our favor**: persons of importance.

Study Questions

1. What are the major political practices satirized in Chapter 3, Part I?
2. How do you see the Lilliputian Emperor?
3. What aspects of human nature does Swift seem to be satirizing through Gulliver's huge size in Lilliput?
4. Do you think Swift's technique of ridicule is more or less effective than simple, direct criticism? Why?

Essay Topics

1. What does Gulliver discover about human nature? Draw your own conclusion to this question and support it with examples from personal or current events.
2. On the basis of *Gulliver's Travels*, discuss Swift's notions of a good and just government.

3.5 Alexander Pope

3.5.1 About the Author

Alexander Pope (1688-1744) was born into a Roman Catholic family in London. Between 1696 and 1700 Pope was tutored at home by a priest, and then enrolled in two Catholic schools, but he was largely self-educated. During his later childhood he suffered from a severe illness of tuberculosis that ruined his health. He developed a hunchback, which resulted in a disfigured body. Because of his constant sickness and the family religion, he was not able to go to university or hold any public office like many of his contemporaries. However, he was very industrious. He spent some eight or nine years in arduous and

enthusiastic discipline, reading, studying and experimenting in order to achieve his literary success.

Pope made his name as a great poet with the publication of *An Essay on Criticism* in 1711. The poem was written in heroic couplets outlining critical tastes and standards based on neoclassical doctrines. The next year, he published *The Rape of the Lock*, which immediately made Pope famous as a poet. The story is based on an actual episode in which a young man attempted to cut a lock of hair from a young lady, thus breaking up the friendship between the two families. Pope was told to write something to restore peace but he chose to use the mock epic form to ridicule the trivial incident, to emphasize the pettiness of the quarrel and to satirize the foolish, meaningless life of the lords and ladies in the eighteenth century England. *The Dunciad* (1728-1743) is a scathing satire on dunces and literary hacks in which Pope viciously attacked his enemies. But the poem is not confined to personal attack. It also exposed and satirized, in general, the dullness that was reflected in the corruptness of government, social morals, education and even religion. In 1734, Pope published his most ambitious work, *An Essay on Man*, which was a poetic summary of current philosophical speculations.

As a successful author, pope embarked, between 1715 and 1720, on his verse translation of Homer's *Iliad* with the purpose of securing his financial future. He also produced an edition of Shakespeare's works in 1725. It is said that Pope was the first Englishman to make a living from his pen, free from the shackles of patronage and flattery.

Pope is without doubt one of the greatest poets of the English language. Strongly advocating Neoclassicism, he developed a satiric, concise, smooth, graceful and well-balanced style and finally brought to its last perfection the heroic couplet Dryden had successfully used in his plays.

3.5.2 "Ode on Solitude[1]"

Happy the man, whose wish and care
A few paternal[2] acres bound,
Content to breathe his native air,
In his own ground.

Whose herds with milk, whose fields with bread,
Whose flocks supply him with attire[3],
Whose trees in summer yield[4] him shade,
In winter fire.

Blest! who can unconcern'dly find
Hours, days, and years slide[5] soft away,

In health of body, peace of mind,
Quiet by day,

Sound sleep by night; study and ease
Together mix'd; sweet recreation,
And innocence, which most does please,
With meditation.

Thus let me live, unseen, unknown;
Thus unlamented[6] let me dye;
Steal from the world, and not a stone
Tell where I lye.

Notes

1. The hint for this poem was taken from Horace's well-known Epode 2, which praises the simplicity and innocence of country life, a favorite literary theme in Pope's time.
2. **paternal**: fatherly.
3. **attire**: clothing.
4. **yield**: to give.
5. **slide**: to move somewhere quietly without being noticed.
6. **unlamented**: not being feeling sad.

Study Questions

1. What function does repetition play in this poem?
2. What images does the poet use to realize his theme?
3. What does the poet celebrate in this poem?

3.5.3 An excerpt from *An Essay on Criticism*

Some to conceit[1] alone their taste confine,
And glittering thoughts struck out at every line;
Pleased with a work where nothing's just or fit,
One glaring chaos and wild heap of wit.
Poets like painters, thus unskilled to trace
The naked nature and the living grace,[2]
With gold and jewels cover every part,
And hide with ornaments their want of art.[3]
  True wit is Nature to advantage dressed,[4]
What oft was thought, but ne'er so well expressed;

Something, whose truth convinced at sight we find,
That gives us back the image of our mind.[5]
As shades more sweetly recommend the light,[6]
So modest plainness sets off sprightly wit;
For works may have more wit than does them good,
As bodies perish through excess of blood.

 Others for language all their care express,[7]
And value books, as women men, for dress.
Their praise is still — the style is excellent;
The sense they humbly take upon content.[8]
Words are like leaves; and where they most abound,
Much fruit of sense beneath is rarely found.[9]
False eloquence, like the prismatic glass,[10]
Its gaudy colors spreads on every place;
The face of Nature we no more survey,
All glares alike, without distinction gay.
But true expression, like the unchanging sun,
Clears, and improves whate'er it shines upon,
It gilds all objects, but it alters none.
Expression is the dress of thought, and still
Appears more decent as more suitable.[11]
A vile conceit in pompous words expressed
Is like a clown[12] in regal purple[13] dressed:
For different styles with different subjects sort,
As several garbs with country, town, and court.
Some by old words to fame have made pretence,
Ancients in phrase, mere moderns in their sense.[14]
Such labored nothings,[15] in so strange a style,
Amaze the unlearn'd, and make the learned smile.
Unlucky as Fungoso[16] in the play,
These sparks[17] with awkward vanity display
What the fine gentleman wore yesterday;
And but so mimic ancient wits at best,
As apes our grandsires in their doublets dressed.[18]
In words as fashions the same rule will hold,
Alike fantastic if too new or old:[19]
Be not the first by whom the new are tried,
Nor yet the last to lay the old aside.

Notes

1. **conceit**: pointed wit, ingenuity and extravagance, or affectation in the use of figures, especially similes and metaphors.
2. **to trace/ The naked nature and the living grace**: to portray (in their paintings or writings) nature in its plainness and the beautiful objects from real life.
3. **want of art**: lack of artistic skill or talent.
4. **dressed**: adorned or decorated.
5. **Something, whose truth convinced at sight we find, /That gives us back the image of our mind**: True wit, whose truth is constantly convinced when we see it brings back to our mind what we have only an imperfect image or notion of.
6. **As shades more sweetly recommend the light**: The light looks brighter if seen against the background of shade or darkness.
7. **Others for language all their care express**: Other people show all their interest in the language of the poem.
8. **content**: mere acquiescence.
9. **where they most abound, / Much fruit of sense beneath is rarely found**: Where/ When too many words are used, they seldom express much sense.
10. **prismatic glass**: a very up-to-date scientific reference. Newton's Optics, which treated of the prism and the spectrum, had been published in 1704, though his theories had been known earlier.
11. **Appears more decent as more suitable**: The more suitable the expression is, the more decent it appears.
12. **clown**: fool, a position one held at an old royal court, whose function was to keep the king amused and who was usually dressed in silly-looking patterned clothes.
13. **regal purple**: the color supposedly to be dressed in only by the royal members.
14. **Ancients in phrase, mere moderns in their sense**: (They are) ancients when judged by their language but mere moderns judged by the ideas they express.
15. **labored nothings**: elaborate but meaningless expressions.
16. **Fungoso**: a character in Ben Jonson's *Every man Out of His Humour*, a man who is depicted as one "that follows the fashion far off like a spy. He buys clothes to imitate a spruce courtier, but fails, for the fashion changes so fast that his money is thrown away."
17. **sparks**: (a contemptuous term) men of fashion.
18. **in their doublets dressed**: dressed in the doublets of our grandfathers. *Doublet*: a tightly-fit dress for men.
19. **Alike fantastic if too new or old**: They are both absurd whether the words used are too new or too old for the ideas.

Study Questions

1. What is a conceit?
2. What is Pope's definition of true wit?
3. What metaphor dominates Pope's discussion of wit?
4. Do you think more wit will make a better literary work? Why or why not?
5. What metaphor dominates Pope's discussion of language?
6. What is the metaphorical relationship between thought and expression?

3.6 Daniel Defoe

3.6.1 About the Author

Daniel Defoe (1660-1731) was born in London. His father was a poor, but hard-working butcher. As a son from a dissenter's family, Defoe was unable to attend traditional schools such as Oxford and Cambridge; instead, he had to attend a dissenting institution, where he studied science and humanities, preparing to become a Presbyterian minister. Though he gave up this plan later on, his Protestant values endured throughout his life despite discrimination and persecution. By the time he was a young man in his 20s, Defoe became a successful merchant in London. Visiting Holland, France and Spain on business, Defoe developed a life-long taste for travel. Throughout his life, Defoe's business underwent many ups and downs, but he was never beaten. His quick mind, abundant energy and never-failing enthusiasm always brought him back on his feet after a fall.

Defoe also had a passion for politics. He wrote quite a number of pamphlets on the current political issues. His "The Shortest Way with Dissenters" (1702) brought him into jail and made him go through public exposure in the pillory, while his "The True-Born Englishman" (1701) won him friendship from the king. He worked, at different times, as a government agent, both for the Whigs and the Tories, and was among the best informed political and economic pamphleteers of the time.

Defoe began writing novels late in life, around the age of sixty. He published his first novel, *Robinson Crusoe*, in 1719, attracting a large number of middle-class readers. In the following years, he wrote four other novels: *Captain Singleton* (1720), *Moll Flanders* (1722), *Colonel Jack* (1722) and *Roxana* (1724).

Robinson Crusoe, as a story of unprecedented adventure in a distant and unknown region, speaks thrillingly to the universal human sense of romance. The book records how a plain Englishman overcame all kinds of difficulties in a deserted island through the plain virtues of courage, patience, perseverance and mechanical ingenuity. It makes a strong appeal to the instinct for practical, every-day realism which is the controlling quality of the English middle class. Further, it directly addresses the dissenting conscience in its emphasis on religion and morality.

Stylistically, Defoe was a great innovator. He used the simple, direct, fact-based style of the middle classes. There is nothing artificial in his language; everything is easy, colloquial and mostly vernacular. His influence in helping to shape modern journalism and modern every-day English style was not only large, but also revolutionary.

3.6.2　An Excerpt from Chapter 4 of *Robinson Crusoe*

A little afternoon I found the sea very calm, and the tyde[1] ebbed so far out that I could come within a quarter of a mile of the ship; and here I found a fresh renewing of my grief, for I saw evidently, that if we had kept on board, we had been all safe, that is to say, we had all got safe on shore, and I had not been so miserable as to be left entirely destitute of all comfort and company, as I now was; this fore'd tears from my eyes again, but as there was little relief in that, I resolved, if possible, to get to the ship, so I pulled off my clothes, for the weather was hot to extremity, and took the water, but when I came to the ship, my difficulty was still greater to know how to get on board, for as she lay aground, and high out of the water, there was nothing within my reach to lay hold of. I swam round her twice, and the second time I spy'd a small piece of a rope, which I wondered I did not see at first, hang down by the fore-chains so low, as that with great difficulty I got hold of it, and by the help of that rope, got up into the forecastle of the ship. Here I found that the ship was bulged, and had a great deal of water in her hold, but that she lay so on the side of a bank of hard sand, or rather earth, that her stern lay lifted up upon the bank, and her head low almost to the water; by this means all her quarter was free, and all that was in that part was dry; for you may be sure my first work was to search and to see what was spoiled and what was free; and first I found that all the ship's provisions were dry and untouched by the water, and being very well disposed to eat, I went to the bread-room and filled my pockets with bisket, and eat it as I went about other things, for I had no time to lose; I also found some rum in the great cabin, of which I took a large dram, and which I had indeed need enough of to

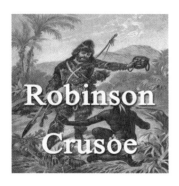

spirit me for what was before me. Now I wanted nothing but a boat to furnish myself with many things which I foresaw would be very necessary to me.

It was in vain to sit still and wish for what was not to be had, and this extremity roused my application[2]. We had several spare yards, and two or three large spars of wood, and a spare top-mast or two in the ship; I resolved to fall to work[3] with these, and I flung as many of them over board as I could manage for their weight, tying every

Chapter 3 The Neoclassical Period

one with a rope that they might not drive away; when this was done I went down the ship's side, and pulling them to me, I ty'd four of them fast together at both ends as well as I could, in the form of a raft, and laying two or three short pieces of plank upon them crossways, I found I could walk upon it very well, but that it was not able to bear any great weight, the pieces being too light; so I went to work, and with the carpenter's saw I cut a spare topmast into three lengths, and added them to my raft, with a great deal of labor and pains; but hope of furnishing myself with necessaries encouraged me to go beyond what I should have been able to have done upon another occasion.

My raft was now strong enough to bear any reasonable weight; my next care was what to load it with, and how to preserve what I laid upon it from the surf of the sea, but I was not long considering this. I first laid all the planks or boards upon it that I could get, and having considered well what I most wanted, I first got three of the seamen's chests, which I had broken open and empty'd, and lowered them down upon my raft; the first of these I filled with provision, viz. bread, rice, three Dutch cheeses, five pieces of dry'd goat's flesh, which we lived much upon, and a little remainder of European corn which had been laid by for some fowls which we brought to sea with us, but the fowls were killed; there had been some barley and wheat together, but, to my great disappointment, I found afterwards that the rats had eaten or spoiled it all; as for liquors, I found several cases of bottles belonging to our skipper, in which were some cordial waters, and in all about five or six gallons of rack; these I stowed by themselves, there being no need to put them into the chest, nor no room for them. While I was doing this, I found the tyde began to flow, tho' very calm, and I had the mortification to see my coat, shirt, and waistcoat which I had left on shore upon the sand, swim away; as for my breeches, which were only linen and open knee'd, I swam on board in them and my stockings. However, this put me upon rummaging for clothes, of which I found enough, but took no more than I wanted for present use, for I had other things which my eye was more upon[4], as first tools to work with on shore, and it was after long searching that I found out the carpenter's chest, which was indeed a very useful prize to me, and much more valuable than a ship loading of gold would have been at that time; I got it down to my raft, even whole as it was, without losing time to look into it, for I knew in general what it contained.

My next care was for some ammunition and arms; there were two very good fowling-pieces[5] in the great cabin, and two pistols; these I secured first, with some powder-horns, and a small bag of shot, and two old rusty swords; I knew there were three barrels of powder in the ship, but knew not where our gunner had stowed them, but with much search I found them, two of them dry and good, the third had taken water; those two I got to my raft, with the arms; and now I thought myself pretty well freighted, and began to think how I should get to shore with them, having neither sail, oar, or rudder, and the least cap full of wind would have overset all my navigation[6].

89

I had three encouragements: 1. a smooth calm sea; 2. the tide rising, and setting in to the shore; 3. what little wind there was blew me towards the land; and thus, having found two or three broken oars belonging to the boat, and besides the tools which were in the chest, I found two saws, an axe, and a hammer, and with this cargo I put to sea. For a mile, or thereabouts, my raft went very well, only that I found it drive a little distant from the place where I had landed before, by which I perceived that there was some indraft of the water[7], and consequently I hoped to find some creek or river there, which I might make use of as a port to get to land with my cargo.

As I imagined, so it was, there appeared before me a little opening of the land, and I found a strong current of the tide set into it, so I guided my raft as well as I could to keep in the middle of the stream. But here I had like to have suffered a second shipwreck[8], which, if I had, I think verily would have broke my heart, for knowing nothing of the coast, my raft run aground at one end of it upon a shoal, and not being aground at the other end, it wanted but a little that all my cargo had slip'd off towards that end that was a-float, and so fallen into the water. I did my utmost by setting my back against the chests to keep them in their places, but could not thrust off the raft with all my strength, neither durst I stir from the posture I was in, but holding up the chests with all my might, stood in that manner near half an hour, in which time the rising of the water brought me a little more upon a level, and a little after, the water still rising, my raft floated again, and I thrust her off with the oar I had into the channel, and then driving up higher, I at length found myself in the mouth of a little river, with land on both sides, and a strong current or tide running up. I looked on both sides for a proper place to get to shore, for I was not willing to be driven too high up the river, hoping in time to see some ship at sea, and therefore resolved to place myself as near the coast as I could.

At length I spy'd a little cove on the right shore of the creek, to which with great pain and difficulty I guided my raft, and at last got so near, as that, reaching ground with my oar, I could thrust her directly in; but here I had like to have dipt all my cargo in the sea again; for that shore lying pretty steep, that is to say sloping, there was no place to land, but where one end of my float, if it run on shore, would lie so high, and the other sink lower as before, that it would endanger my cargo again. All that I could do was to wait till the tide was at the highest, keeping the raft with my oar like an anchor to hold the side of it fast to the shore, near a flat piece of ground, which I expected the water would flow over; and so it did. As soon as I found water enough, for my raft drew about a foot of water, I thrust her on upon that flat piece of ground, and there fastened or moored her by sticking my two broken oars into the ground, one on one side near one end, and one on the other side near the other end; and thus I lay 'till the water ebbed away, and left my raft and all my cargo safe on shore.

My next work was to view the country, and seek a proper place for my habitation,

Chapter 3   The Neoclassical Period

and where to stow my goods to secure them from whatever might happen; where I was, I yet knew not, whether on the continent or on an island, whether inhabited or not inhabited, whether in danger of wild beasts or not. There was a hill not above a mile from me, which rose up very steep and high, and which seemed to overtop some other hills, which lay as in a ridge from it northward; I took out one of the fowling pieces, and one of the pistols, and an horn of powder, and thus armed I traveled for discovery up to the top of that hill, there after I had with great labor and difficulty get to the top, I saw my fate to my great affliction, viz. that I was in an island environed every way with the sea, no land to be seen, except some rocks which lay a great way off, and two small islands less than this, which lay about three leagues to the west.

I found also that the island I was in was barren, and, as I saw good reason to believe, uninhabited, except by wild beasts, of whom however I saw none, yet I saw abundance of fowls, but knew not their kinds, neither when I killed them could I tell what was fit for food, and what not; at my coming back, I shot at a great bird which I saw sitting upon a tree on the side of a great wood. I believe it was the first gun that had been fired there since the creation of the world; I had no sooner fired, but from all the parts of the wood there arose an innumerable number of fowls of many sorts, making a confused screaming, and crying every one according to his usual note; but not one of them of any kind that I knew. As for the creature I killed, I took it to be a kind of a hawk, its color and beak resembling it, but had no talons or claws more than common; its flesh was carrion, and fit for nothing.

Contented with this discovery, I came back to my raft, and fell to work to bring my cargo on shore, which took me up the rest of that day, and what to do with myself at night I knew not, nor indeed where to rest; for I was afraid to lie down on the ground, not knowing but some wild beast might devour me, tho', as I afterwards found, there was really no need for those fears.

However, as well as I could, I barricaded myself round with the chests and boards that I had brought on shore, and made a kind of a hut for that night's lodging; as for food, I yet saw not which way to supply myself, except that I had seen two or three creatures like hares run out of the wood where I shot the fowl.

Notes
1. **tyde**: tide. The spelling of some words in this novel is different from nowadays.
2. **this extremity roused my application**: this extreme hardship stirred me up to do something.
3. **fall to work**: to begin to work.
4. **which my eye was more upon**: upon which I looked with greater attention.
5. **fowling-pieces**: light guns used for shooting fowls.
6. **overset all my navigation**: upset all my attempts to sail the raft.

7. **some indraft of the water**: some inward flow of water.
8. **I had like to have suffered a second shipwreck**: I nearly suffered from a second shipwreck ("I had like" (archaic) = it was likely for me).

Study Questions

1. What did Robinson Crusoe discover when he came back to the wrecked ship?
2. Describe Crusoe's behavior immediately after the shipwreck.
3. What makes Crusoe think that he could manage to sail his raft to a safe port?
4. What qualities in Robinson Crusoe's character strike you most?

Essay Topics

1. What kind of man is Robinson Crusoe? Cite examples from the selected reading to illustrate your idea.
2. Why does Daniel Defoe use such great details in his description?

3.7 Henry Fielding

3.7.1 About the Author

Henry Fielding (1707-1754) was born in a genteel family, which was closely allied to the aristocracy. He studied at Eton College (1719-1724), where he learned to love ancient Greek and Roman literature. In 1728 he went to the University of Leiden in the Netherlands, to enlarge his knowledge of classical literature. After returning to England,

he devoted himself to writing for the stage. During the next dozen years he produced a number of farces, burlesques and light plays, ridiculing the society and politics of the time. His career as a dramatist ended abruptly in 1737 when the government passed the Licensing Act. He then took up law and was admitted to the Bar at the Middle Temple in 1740. He was made justice of the peace for the city of Westminster in 1748 and for the county of Middlesex in 1749. But his legal profession did not bring him enough to maintain his family, so he became editor of a paper called *The Champion*.

After reading *Pamela* (1740) by Samuel Richardson, he was disgusted by the morality of its contents and produced a parody entitled *Shamela* (1741). *Joseph Andrews* (1742) was also supposed to be a parody of *Pamela* and it set out just like that. But after a number of chapters, Fielding found himself considering all the forces working on humans, and in the end he created what he called "a comic epic poem in prose". The success of *Joseph Andrews* caused Fielding to write more novels in the same style, such as *The History of Jonathan Wild the Great* (1743), *The History of Tom Jones*, a

Foundling (1749) and *The History of Amelia* (1751).

Among Fielding's novels, the best known is *Tom Jones*, which established his reputation as a founder of the English novel. While Samuel Richardson is seen as the psychological realist of the early novel, Fielding is the humorist, the inventor of the authorial narrative voice of scope and breadth. The structures of his novel are always well planned and often imitations of the classics. The characters, each indispensable to the development of the plot, are true to life. His writings are also noted for dramatic dialogues and other devices such as suspense, coincidence and unexpectedness. His language style is easy, unlabored and familiar, but extremely vivid and vigorous.

3.7.2 An Excerpt from Chapter 2, Book III of *Tom Jones*

The hero of this great history appears with very bad omens. A little tale of so low a kind that some may think it not worth their notice. A word or two concerning a squire, and more relating to a gamekeeper and a schoolmaster.

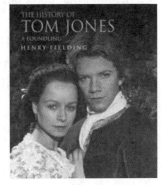

As we determined, when we first sat down to write this history, to flatter no man, but to guide our pen throughout by the directions of truth[1], we are obliged to bring our hero on the stage in a much more disadvantageous manner than we could wish; and to declare honestly, even at his first appearance, that it was the universal opinion of all Mr. Allworthy's family that he was certainly born to be hanged.

Indeed, I am sorry to say there was too much reason for this conjecture; the lad having from his earliest years discovered a propensity[2] to many vices, and especially to one which hath as direct a tendency as any other to that fate[3] which we have just now observed to have been prophetically denounced against him: he had been already convicted of three robberies[4], viz., of robbing an orchard, of stealing a duck out of a farmer's yard, and of picking Master Blifil's pocket of a ball.

The vices of this young man were, moreover, heightened by the disadvantageous light in which they appeared when opposed to the virtues of Master Blifil, his companion[5]; a youth of so different a cast from little Jones, that not only the family but all the neighborhood resounded his praises. He was, indeed, a lad of a remarkable disposition: sober, discreet, and pious beyond his age; qualities which gained him the love of every one who knew him; while Tom Jones was universally disliked; and many expressed their wonder that Mr. Allworthy would suffer such a lad to be educated with his nephew, lest the morals of the latter should be corrupted by his example.

An incident which happened about this time will set the characters of these two lads more fairly before the discerning reader than is in the power of the longest dissertation.

Tom Jones, who, bad as he is, must serve for the hero of this history, had only one friend among all the servants of the family; for as to Mrs. Wilkins[6], she had long since given him up, and was perfectly reconciled to her mistress[7]. This friend was the gamekeeper, a fellow of a loose kind of disposition, and who was thought not to entertain much stricter notions concerning the difference of *meum* and *tuum* than the young gentleman himself[8]. And hence this friendship gave occasion to many sarcastic remarks among the domestics, most of which were either proverbs before, or at least are become so now[9]; and, indeed, the wit of them all may be comprised in that short Latin proverb, *Noscitur a socio*; which, I think, is thus expressed in English, "You may know him by the company he keeps."

To say the truth, some of that atrocious wickedness in Jones, of which we have just mentioned three examples, might perhaps be derived from the encouragement he had received from this fellow who, in two or three instances, had been what the law calls an accessory after the fact[10]: for the whole duck, and great part of the apples, were converted to the use of the gamekeeper and his family; though, as Jones alone was discovered, the poor lad bore not only the whole smart, but the whole blame; both which fell again to his lot on the following occasion.

Contiguous to Mr. Allworthy's estate was the manor of one of those gentlemen who are called preservers of the game[11]. This species of men, from the great severity with which they revenge the death of a hare or partridge, might be thought to cultivate the same superstition with the Bannians in India[12]; many of whom, we are told, dedicate their whole lives to the preservation and protection of certain animals; was it not that[13] our English Bannians, while they preserve them from other enemies, will most unmercifully slaughter whole horse-loads themselves; so that they stand clearly acquitted[14] of any such heathenish superstition[15].

I have, indeed, a much better opinion of this kind of men than is entertained by some, as I take them to answer the order of Nature[16], and the good purposes for which they were ordained[17], in a more ample manner than many others. Now, as Horace[18] tells us that there are a set of human beings

Fruges consumere nati,

"Born to consumethe fruits of the earth;" so I make no manner of doubt but that there are others

Feras consumere nati,

"Born to consume the beasts of the field;" or, as it is commonly called, the game; and none, I believe, will deny but that those squires fulfill this end of their creation[19].

Little Jones went one day a shooting with the gamekeeper; when happening to spring a covey of partridges near the border of that manor over which Fortune, to fulfill the wise purposes of Nature, had planted one of the game consumers, the birds flew into it, and were marked[20] (as it is called) by the two sportsmen, in some furze bushes, about two or three hundred paces beyond Mr. Allworthy's dominions.

Chapter 3 The Neoclassical Period

Mr. Allworthy had given the fellow strict orders, on pain of forfeiting his place[21], never to trespass on any of his neighbors; no more on those who were less rigid in this matter than on the lord of this manor. With regard to others, indeed, these orders had not been always very scrupulously kept; but as the disposition of the gentleman with whom the partridges had taken sanctuary was well known, the gamekeeper had never yet attempted to invade his territories. Nor had he done it now, had not the younger sportsman, who was excessively eager to pursue the flying game, over-persuaded him; but Jones being very importunate, the other, who was himself keen enough after the sport, yielded to his persuasions, entered the manor, and shot one of the partridges.

The gentleman himself was at that time on horse-back, at a little distance from them; and hearing the gun go off, he immediately made towards the place, and discovered poor Tom; for the gamekeeper had leapt into the thickest part of the furze-brake, where he had happily concealed himself.

The gentleman having searched the lad, and found the partridge upon him, denounced great vengeance[22], swearing he would acquaint Mr. Allworthy. He was as good as his word; for he rode immediately to his house, and complained of the trespass on his manor in as high terms and as bitter language as if his house had been broken open, and the most valuable furniture stole out of it. He added, that some other person was in his company, though he could not discover him; for that two guns had been discharged almost in the same instant. And, says he, "We have found only this partridge, but the Lord knows what mischief they have done."

At his return home, Tom was presently convened before Mr. Allworthy. He owned the fact, and alleged no other excuse but what was really true, viz., that the covey was originally sprung in Mr. Allworthy's own manor.

Tom was then interrogated who was with him, which Mr. Allworthy declared he was resolved to know, acquainting the culprit with the circumstance of the two guns, which had been deposed by the squire and both his servants; but Tom stoutly persisted in asserting that he was alone; yet, to say the truth, he hesitated a little at first, which would have confirmed Mr. Allworthy's belief, had what the squire and his servants said wanted any further confirmation.

The gamekeeper, being a suspected person, was now sent for, and the question put to him; but he, relying on the promise which Tom had made him, to take all upon himself, very resolutely denied being in company with the young gentleman, or indeed having seen him the whole afternoon.

Mr. Allworthy then turned towards Tom, with more than usual anger in his countenance, and advised him to confess who was with him; repeating, that he was resolved to know. The lad, however, still maintained his resolution, and was dismissed with much wrath by Mr. Allworthy, who told him he should have to the next morning to consider of it, when he should be questioned by another person, and in another manner.

Poor Jones spent a very melancholy night; and the more so, as he was without his usual companion; for Master Blifil was gone abroad on a visit with his mother. Fear of the punishment he was to suffer was on this occasion his least evil; his chief anxiety being, lest his constancy should fail him, and he should be brought to betray the gamekeeper, whose ruin he knew must now be the consequence.

Nor did the gamekeeper pass his time much better. He had the same apprehensions with the youth; for whose honor he had likewise a much tenderer regard than for his skin[23].

In the morning, when Tom attended the reverend Mr. Thwackum, the person to whom Mr. Allworthy had committed the instruction of the two boys, he had the same questions put to him by that gentleman which he been asked the evening before, to which he returned the same answers. The consequence of this was, so severe a whipping, that it possibly fell little short of[24] the torture with which confessions are in some countries extorted from criminals.

Tom bore his punishment with great resolution; and though his master asked him, between every stroke, whether he would not confess, he was contented to be flead[25] rather than betray his friend, or break the promise he had made.

The gamekeeper was now relieved from his anxiety, and Mr. Allworthy himself began to be concerned at Tom's sufferings: for besides that[26] Mr. Thwackum, being highly enraged that he was not able to make the boy say what he himself pleased, had carried his severity much beyond the good man's intention, this latter began now to suspect that the squire had been mistaken; which his extreme eagerness and anger seemed to make probable; and as for what the servants had said in confirmation of their master's account, he laid no great stress upon that. Now, as cruelty and injustice were two ideas of which Mr. Allworthy could by no means support the consciousness[27] a single moment, he sent for Tom, and after many kind and friendly exhortations, said, "I am convinced, my dear child, that my suspicions have wronged you; I am sorry that you have been so severely punished on this account." And at last gave him a little horse to make him amends; again repeating his sorrow for what had past.

Tom's guilt now flew in his face more than any severity could make it. He could more easily bear the lashes of Thwackum, than the generosity of Allworthy. The tears burst from his eyes, and he fell upon his knees, crying, "Oh, sir, you are too good to me. Indeed you are. Indeed I don't deserve it." And at that very instant, from the fullness of his heart[28], had almost betrayed the secret; but the good genius[29] of the gamekeeper suggested to him what might be the consequence to the poor fellow, and this consideration sealed his lips.

Thwackum did all he could to persuade Allworthy from showing any compassion or kindness to the boy, saying, "He had persisted in an untruth;" and gave some hints, that a second whipping might probably bring the matter to light.

Chapter 3 The Neoclassical Period

But Mr. Allworthy absolutely refused to consent to the experiment. He said, the boy had suffered enough already for concealing the truth, even if he was guilty, seeing that he could have no motive but a mistaken point of honor for so doing.

"Honor!" cried Thwackum, with some warmth, "mere stubbornness and obstinacy! Can honor teach any one to tell a lie, or can any honor exist independent of religion?"

This discourse happened at table when dinner was just ended; and there were present Mr. Allworthy, Mr. Thwackum and a third gentleman who now entered into the debate, and whom, before we proceed any further, we shall briefly introduce to our reader's acquaintance.

Notes
1. **by the directions of truth**: according to truth.
2. **propensity**: natural inclination or bent.
3. **that fate**: the fate to be hanged, as mentioned in the above paragraph.
4. **be convicted of three robberies**: be guilty of three robberies.
5. **The vices of this young man were, moreover, heightened by the disadvantageous light in which they appeared when opposed to the virtues of Master Blifil, his companion**: The young man seemed to be more wicked in comparison with Blifil.
6. **Mrs. Wilkins**: a woman servant of Mr. Allworthy.
7. **perfectly reconciled to her mistress**: completely agreed with her mistress.
8. **not to entertain much stricter notions concerning the difference of meum and tuum than the young gentleman himself**: to fail to distinguish one's property from that of others. *meum* (Latin) means "mine"; *tuum* (Latin) means "yours".
9. **are become so now**: have become so now.
10. **an accessory after the fact**: an accessory after certain wicked thing is done.
11. **preservers of the game**: protectors of animals.
12. **the Bannians in India**: a caste in India, most of them were merchants who do not eat meat.
13. **was it not that**: if it was not that.
14. **they stand clearly acquitted**: they discharge themselves completely from.
15. **such heathenish superstition**: the superstition of the Bannian's protection of wild animals.
16. **to answer the order of Nature**: to follow the law of Nature.
17. **they were ordained**: they were destined by the Deity or their fate.
18. **Horace**: a Roman poet.
19. **those squires fulfill this end of their creation**: those squires are born to consume the beasts of the field.
20. **marked**: noticed.
21. **on pain of forfeiting his place**: punishment will be ejection from his place.

22. **denounced great vengeance**: declared great revenge.
23. **for whose honor he had likewise a much tenderer regard than for his skin**: the gamekeeper showed more concern on Tom's promise than his skin pain.
24. **fell little short of**: was inferior to.
25. **to be flead**: to be flayed.
26. **besides that**: besides the fact that.
27. **of which Mr. Allworthy could by no means support the consciousness**: Mr. Allworthy could not let the two ideas come to his mind at the same time.
28. **from the fullness of his heart**: because of the gratefulness and shame he feels.
29. **genius**: attendant spirit.

Study Questions

1. How is Tom described by the narrator?
2. Who is Tom's only friend among the servants?
3. Why is Allworthy angry with Tom?
4. What human nature does Fielding try to praise through Tom's behavior?
5. What is the author's attitude towards Tom?

Essay Topics

1. The author has employed a series of contrasts to build his narrative. Write an essay on these contrasts and comparisons, citing examples from the selected reading to illustrate your idea.
2. How does Fielding characterize Tom and Blifil in this novel?

3.8 Samuel Johnson

3.8.1 About the Author

Samuel Johnson (1709-1784) was the son of a bookseller in Lichfield. He attended the local school, but his real education was informal, conducted primarily through his reading and studying the classics at his father's bookshop, which influenced his style greatly. In 1728 he entered Pembroke College at Oxford to study languages and law but had to leave in 1731 due to financial problems. The death of his father in 1731 plunged

him into a distressingly painful struggle for existence. In 1735 he married Elizabeth Porter, a widow 20 years his senior, and remained devoted to her until her death in 1752.

The years between 1737 and 1755 were very difficult for Johnson: he did translations, wrote poems, essays and accounts of parliamentary debates for the book-sellers and edited magazines, but earned no more than enough to maintain a meager living. It was only after the publication of his *Dictionary* that his financial status took a turn for the better. In 1762 the government gave him a special pension which freed him from the burden of "writing for a living". So during the last twenty years of his life he wrote as little as he decently could and enjoyed a pleasant and easy life, sort of as a literary authority, talking about and commenting on literature and literary men in his famous Literary Club.

Johnson was an energetic and versatile writer. He had a hand in all the different branches of literary activities. He was a poet, dramatist, prose romancer, biographer, essayist, critic, lexicographer and publicist. His chief works include poems: "London" (1738), and "The Vanity of Human Wishes" (1749); a romance: *The History of Rascals, Prince of Abyssinia* (1759); a tragedy: *Irene* (1749); and literary criticism as found in the preface to his edition of Shakespeare and in his comments on 52 poets in *The Lives of Poets* (1779-1781).

Johnson was the last great Neoclassicist enlightener in the second half of the eighteenth century. Beneath the rough surface Johnson was a man not only of very vigorous intellect and great learning, but of sincere piety, a very warm heart, unusual sympathy and kindness, and the most unselfish, though eccentric, generosity. In much of his writing, the most conspicuous things are power and strong effective exposition. He often uses short sentences, whether or not in contrast to his long ones, with full consciousness of their value; when he will take the trouble, no one can express ideas with clearer and more forceful brevity; and in a very large part of his work his style carries the finely tonic qualities of his clear and vigorous mind.

3.8.2 *To the Right Honorable the Earl of Chesterfield*

February 7, 1775

My Lord,

I have been lately informed by the proprietor of The World[1] that two papers in which my *Dictionary* is recommended to the public were written by your Lordship. To be so distinguished is an honor which, being very little accustomed to favors from the great, I know not well how to receive, or in what terms[2] to acknowledge.

When upon some slight encouragement I first visited your Lordship, I was overpowered like the rest of mankind by the enchantment of your address[3], and could not forbear to wish that I might boast myself "*le vainqueur du vainqueur de la terre*"[4]; that I might obtain that regard for which I saw the world contending[5]; but I found my attendance so little encouraged that neither pride nor modesty would suffer[6] me to continue it. When I had once addressed your Lordship in public, I had exhausted all the art of pleasing which a retired and uncourtly scholar can possess. I had done all that I could; and no man is well pleased to have his all neglected, be it ever so little[7].

Seven years, my Lord, have now passed since I waited in your outward rooms or was repulsed[8] from your door, during which time I have been pushing on my work through difficulties of which it is useless to complain, and have brought it at last to the verge of publication without one act of assistance, one word of encouragement, or one smile of favor. Such treatment I did not expect, for I never had a patron before.

The shepherd in Virgil grew at last acquainted with Love, and found him a native of the rocks.[9]

Is not a patron, my Lord, one who looks with unconcern on a man struggling for life in the water and, when he has reached ground, encumbers him with help? The notice which you have been pleased to take of my labors, had it been early, had been kind; but it has been delayed till I am indifferent and cannot enjoy it; till I am solitary and cannot impart it; till I am known and do not want it. I hope it is no very cynical asperity[10] not to confess obligations where no benefit has been received, or to be unwilling that the public should consider me as owing that to a patron which Providence has enabled me to do for myself.

Having carried on my work thus far with so little obligation to any favorer of learning, I shall not be disappointed though I should conclude it, if less be possible, with less[11]; for I have been long wakened from that dream of hope in which I once boasted myself with so much exultation, my Lord,

your Lordship's most humble,

most obedient servant,

Sam: Johnson

Notes

1. **the proprietor of The World**: the owner of the newspaper, The World, in which Lord Chesterfield had praised Johnson.
2. **terms**: language, a particular way of expression.
3. **address**: conversation.
4. **le vainqueur du vainqueur de la terre**: French for "the conqueror of the conqueror of the earth".
5. **contending**: competing for.
6. **suffer**: allow; permit.
7. **be it ever so little**: even if it should be so little.
8. **repulsed**: rejected.
9. **The shepherd in Virgil grew at last acquainted with Love, and found him a native of the rocks**. In a work by Virgil (70 B.C.-19 B.C.), a shepherd complains that love was born among jagged rocks.
10. **asperity**: roughness of manner or temper.
11. **if less be possible, with less**: (I would like to carry on my work) with less obligations (help) if less (help) is possible, i.e. I no longer need anybody's help.

Study Questions

1. Why did Johnson first visit Lord Chesterfield? How was he received?
2. What is Johnson's definition of a patron, according to paragraph 5?
3. How did Johnson feel about the notice Lord Chesterfield had taken of his work?
4. What appears to be the real purpose of Johnson's letter?

3.9 Thomas Gray

3.9.1 About the Author

Thomas Gray (1716-1771) was born into a lower middle class family in London. He was the only child in his family of eight to survive infancy. At the age of eight, he was sent to Eton College, where he displayed imagination and emotion for the love of literature. In 1734 he entered Peterhouse College, Cambridge and was deeply interested in literature and history. After leaving Cambridge, he made a grand tour of France and Italy with his friend Horace Walpole between 1739 and 1741. He also had several tours of the Lake District and Scotland in his life. In October of 1742, Gray returned to Peterhouse College, Cambridge, where he remained for the rest of his life. He got his bachelor's degree in law in 1743 but never made any attempt to go into practice. In 1768 he was made professor of History and Modern Languages at Cambridge.

During his career, Gray devoted himself to the study of the classics, of the Celtic and Iceland poetry. He was primarily a scholar and perhaps the most learned man of his time. He was familiar with the literature and history not only of the ancient world but of all the important modern nations of Western Europe. His work shows, however, considerable variety, including real appreciation for Nature, as in the "Ode on the Spring" (1742), delightful quiet humor, as in the "Ode on a Favorite Cat" (1748), rather conventional moralizing, as in the "Ode on a Distant Prospect of Eton College" (1747), and magnificent expression of the fundamental human emotions, as in his masterpiece, "Elegy Written in a Country Churchyard".

Gray was always reluctant to publish his works. Unlike other poets, he did not want the world's applause. Even after achieving recognition as a poet, he refused to give public lectures. He was the extreme type of the academic poet. He wrote with sincerity, honesty and integrity. He wrote of true thoughts, feelings, inspirations and experience. Every word he wrote reflected upon his emotion. His works were written about peacefulness, passiveness, thoughts of joy, of nostalgia, and most importantly, of innocence. His subject matter and attitude were anticipations of the Romantic Movement, but his perfection of the form reflected a neoclassical element.

3.9.2 An Excerpt from "Elegy Written in a Country Churchyard"

The curfew[1] tolls the knell[2] of parting day,
 The lowing[3] herd winds slowly o'er the lea[4],
The plowman homeward plods his weary way,
 And leaves the world to darkness and to me.
Now fades the glimmering landscape on the sight[5],
 And all the air a solemn stillness holds,
Save where the beetle wheels his droning[6] flight,
 And drowsy tinklings lull the distant folds[7];

Save that from yonder ivy-mantled tower
 The moping owl does to the moon complain
Of such, as wandering near her secret bower[8],
 Molest her ancient solitary reign.

Beneath those rugged elms, that yew-tree's shade,
 Where heaves the turf in many a moldering[9] heap,
Each in his narrow cell for ever laid,
 The rude[10] forefathers of the hamlet sleep.

The breezy call of incense-breathing Morn[11],
 The swallow twittering[12] from the straw-built shed,
The cock's shrill clarion[13], or the echoing horn,
 No more shall rouse them from their lowly bed.

For them no more the blazing hearth shall burn,
 Or busy housewife ply her evening care;
No children run to lisp their Sire's return,
 Or climb his knees the envied kiss to share.

Oft did the harvest to their sickle yield,
 Their furrow oft the stubborn glebe[14] has broke;
How jocund did they drive their team afield!
 How bowed the woods beneath their sturdy stoke!

Let not Ambition[15] mock their useful toil,
 Their homely joys and destiny obscure;
Nor Grandeur[16] hear with a disdainful smile

The short and simple annals of the poor.

The boast of heraldry[17], the pomp of power,
   And all that beauty, all that wealth e'er gave,
Awaits alike the inevitable hour,
   The paths of glory lead but to the grave.[18]

Nor you, ye proud, impute to these the fault,
   If memory o'er their tomb no trophies[19] raise,
Where, through the long-drawn aisle and fretted[20] vault
   The pealing anthem swells the note of praise.

Can storied urn[21] or animated bust[22]
   Back to its mansion call the fleeting breath?
Can honor's voice provoke[23] the silent dust,
   Or Flattery soothe the dull cold ear of Death?

Perhaps in this neglected spot is laid,
   Some heart once pregnant with celestial fire[24];
Hands that the rod of empire might have swayed,
   Or waked to ecstasy the living lyre.

But knowledge to their eyes her ample page
   Rich with the spoils of time did ne'er unroll,
Chill penury repressed their noble rage,
   And froze the genial current of the soul.

Full many a gem of purest ray serene,
   The dark unfathomed caves of ocean bear:
Full many a flower is born to blush unseen,
   And waste its sweetness on the desert air.

Some village-Hampden[25], that with dauntless breast
   The little tyrant of his fields withstood;
Some mute inglorious Milton here may rest,
   Some Cromwell guiltless of his country's blood.

The applause of listening senates to command,
   The treats of pain and ruin to despise,

To scatter plenty o'er a smiling land,
   And read their history in a nation's eyes,[26]

Their lot forbade: nor circumscribed alone
   Their growing virtues, but their crimes confined;
Forbade to wade through slaughter to a throne,
   And shut the gates of mercy on mankind.[27]

Notes

1. **curfew**: a ringing bell that reminded people in English towns of Gray's time to put out fires and go to bed.
2. **knell**: a sad, mournful sound.
3. **lowing**: mooing.
4. **lea**: meadow; field of grass.
5. **sight**: eyesight, vision; the view.
6. **droning**: marked by buzzing or humming.
7. **folds**: small valleys; level land between rolling hills; creatures in the distance.
8. **bower**: an enclosure formed by the ivy.
9. **moldering**: crumbling; decaying.
10. **rude**: untaught; robust, sturdy.
11. **incense-breathing Morn**: fragrant smells of the morning.
12. **twittering**: that is, chirping, making a short, shrill sound.
13. **clarion**: trumpet sound; wakeup call; loud sound.
14. **glebe**: soil; land.
15. **Ambition**: In this personification, Ambition becomes a proud person that would poke fun at humble people whose deeds receive little notice.
16. **Grandeur**: In this personification, Grandeur becomes a proud person that would poke fun at humble people whose deeds receive little notice.
17. **heraldry**: noble birth.
18. **The paths of glory lead but to the grave**. This line repeats the anti-glory motif as expressed by Shakespeare (Glory is like a circle) and later expressed by Shelley in *Ozymandias*.
19. **trophies**: an ornamental or a symbolic group of figures depicting the achievements of the dead man.
20. **fretted**: decorated with interesting lines in relief.
21. **storied urn**: a funeral urn with an epitaph inscribed on it.
22. **animated bust**: life like statue showing only the head, neck and part of the trunk.
23. **provoke**: to call forth.
24. **Some heart once pregnant with celestial fire**: One of these persons might have had

what it takes to perform great tasks.
25. **village-Hampden:** Allusion to John Hampden (1594-1643) who refused to pay an unfair tax imposed by the king and later died in a battle in the English Civil Wars (1642-1651).
26. **The applause... eyes:** If these buried people had had a chance, they could have made politicians in a senate listen to them, comforted people threatened by pain and ruin, provided great bounty for their nation, and earned a place in history books.
27. **Their lot... mankind.** Because they were deprived of power, the buried people were also deprived of the temptation to commit wrongs, such as murdering their way to a throne and deny mercy to worthy people.

Study Questions
1. What is the tone of the poem?
2. Who or what is the speaker of the poem lamenting?
3. What is the speaker's relationship to those he writes about?
4. What truths common to all humankind Gray is expressing?

Essay Topics
1. Discuss the connection between the setting and the speaker's state of mind. Cite examples from the poem to illustrate your ideas.
2. How does the poem develop its theme through images and metaphors?

3.10 Robert Burns

3.10.1 About the Author

Robert Burns (1759-1796) was born into a poor peasant's family in Alloway, Scotland. He got very little formal education, for he often had to help with the heavy work of farming. However, he was encouraged in his self-education by his father, and his mother acquainted him with Scottish folk songs, legends and proverbs. By the time that he had reached manhood he had a good knowledge of English, a reading knowledge of French, and a fairly wide acquaintance with the masterpieces of English literature from the time of Shakespeare to his own day. Family financial worries forced Burns to work as a farm laborer, and it was while thus occupied that he met his first love, Nelly Kirkpatrick. She inspired him to try his hand at poetry. So in 1774, he wrote his first poem, *O Once I Loved*.

Burns published his first work, Poems *Chiefly in the Scottish Dialect* in 1786. The book was an instant success; and he was invited to visit Edinburgh where he was welcomed as the "Heaven-taught Plowman" by the leading literary figures. In 1788 he returned to farming and became a devoted father. Over the next few years, Robert turned his attention to the gathering and writing of Scottish songs, which were published as *The Scots Musical Museum* (1787) in six volumes. Burns also put his own poems to music he composed, or to traditional Scottish airs. In 1787 he made some enjoyable travels throughout the country. Then his physical conditions began to decline, for longtime hard work and undernourishment in his youth permanently injured his health, leading to the rheumatic heart disease from which he eventually died.

Burns was an outspoken champion of the republican cause when the French Revolution broke out. He was considered a pioneer in the Romantic, socialist, and liberalism movements. He was also a keen and discerning satirist who reserved his sharpest barbs for sham, hypocrisy and cruelty. The range of his subjects and emotions is quite wide — love, comradeship, married affection, reflective sentiment, vigorous patriotism and delightful humor.

3.10.2 "A Red, Red Rose"[1]

O, My Luve[2]'s like a red, red rose,
   That's newly sprung in June;
O, My Luve's like the melodie[3],
   That's sweetly played in tune[4].

As fair art thou, my bonie lass[5],
   So deep in luve am I;
And I will luve thee still, my dear,
   Till a' the seas gang dry[6].

Till a' the seas gang dry, my dear,
   And the rocks melt wi' the sun:
O I will luve thee still, my dear,
   While the sands o' life shall run.[7]

And fare thee weel[8], my only luve,
   And fare thee weel a while!
And I will come again, my luve,
   Though it were ten thousand mile.

Notes

1. This poem is in the metrical form of the ballad stanza. The rhyme falls on the second and fourth lines of each stanza. The first and third lines each have four feet while the

second and fourth each have three feet.
2. **Luve**: love. Here it refers to the young man's sweetheart.
3. **melodie**: melody.
4. **in tune**: in harmony.
5. **bonie lass**: pretty girl.
6. **Till a' the seas gang dry**. Till all the seas go dry.
7. **While the sands o' life shall run**. As long as I live. "sands" refers to the sand in the sand-glass, which was used for measuring the passage of time.
8. **fare thee weel**: farewell to you.

Study Questions
1. Why is the word "red" repeated in the first line?
2. What other similes does the speaker use to describe his love?
3. What images does the speaker use to show his strong love for his beloved?
4. What other themes does this poem carry beside the love theme?

3.11　William Blake

3.11.1　About the Author

William Blake (1757-1827) was born into a lower middle class family in London. He received little regular education as a child. When he was ten, his father sent him to a drawing school. At fourteen he was apprenticed to an engraver. After studies at the Royal Academy School, he started to produce watercolors and engrave illustrations for magazines. Throughout his life, he experienced mystical visions that provided him with the inspiration for many of his poems. He married Catherine Boucher in 1782. In 1784 he was able to set up his own shop to sell prints and drawings. In 1789 he published his *Songs of Innocence*, and the *Songs of Experience* was followed in 1794. *The Marriage of Heaven and Hell* (c. 1792), which was infused with mysticism and complex symbolism is an important land mark in his poetic career.

During his later time, Blake began to work on his "prophetic books", which included *The Book of Urizen* (1794), *The Song of Los* (1795), *Milton* (1802), *The Four Zoas* (1803) and *Jerusalem* (1804). In these works, Blake created a complex personal mythology and invented his own symbolic characters to express his lifelong concern with the struggle of the soul to free its natural energies from reason and organized religion.

Blake was a total non-conformist and anti-establishment thinker who asserted his conviction that the established church and state hinder rather than nurture human freedom and the sense of divine love. Like Thomas Paine, Blake remained unswervingly committed to the principles of equality, liberty and justice. He heartily supported the American Revolution in 1775 and the French Revolution in 1789.

Blake was largely misunderstood and ignored for being eccentric in his lifetime. However, W. B. Yeats, James Joyce and D. H. Lawrence, among others, found inspiration in his writings, and his poem Milton was put to music and became a kind of Christian anthem of the English in the twentieth century.

3.11.2 "The Chimney Sweeper" (from *Songs of Innocence*)

When my mother died I was very young,
And my father sold me while yet my tongue
Could scarcely cry "'weep! 'weep! 'weep! 'weep!"[1]
So your chimney I sweep, and in soot I sleep.

There's little Tom Dacre who cried when his head
That curl'd like a lamb's back, was shav'd, so I said,
"Hush, Tom! never mind it, for when your head's bare,
You know that the soot cannot spoil your white hair."

And so he was quiet, and that very night,
As Tom was a-sleeping he had such a sight!
That thousands of sweepers, Dick, Joe, Ned, and Jack,
Were all of them lock'd up in coffins of black,

And by came an angel who had a bright key,
And he open'd the coffins and set them all free;
Then down a green plain, leaping, laughing they run
And wash in a river, and shine in the sun;

Then naked and white, all their bags left behind,
They rise upon clouds, and sport in the wind,
And the angel told Tom, if he'd be a good boy,
He'd have God for his father, and never want joy.

And so Tom awoke; and we rose in the dark
And got with our bags and our brushes to work.
Tho'[2] the morning was cold, Tom was happy and warm;
So if all do their duty, they need not fear harm.

Notes

1. **'weep**: Here it means "sweep". It is the child's lisping attempt at the chimney sweeper's street cry.
2. **tho'**: though.

Study Questions

1. What kind of dream did Tom have one night?
2. How do you interpret Tom's dream?
3. Why was Tom happy and warm after the dream?
4. What role does religion play towards the boys according to this poem?

3.11.3 "The Chimney Sweeper" (from *Songs of Experience*)

A little black thing among the snow
Crying "'weep! 'weep!" in notes of woe!
"Where are thy father & mother? say?"
"They are both gone up to the church to pray.

"Because I was happy upon the heath,[1]
And smil'd among the winter's snow;
They cloth'd me in the clothes of death,[2]
And taught me to sing the notes of woe.

"And because I am happy & dance & sing
They think they have done me no injury,
And are gone to praise God & his Priest & King,
Who make up a heaven of our misery."

Notes

1. **heath**: uncultivated land covered with shrubs.
2. **clothes of death**: clothes in dark color.

Study Questions

1. Examine Blake's use of light and dark imagery. How does his imagery help to convey his themes and ideas?
2. What social/political point is Blake making in these two poems?
3. Pay attention to the differences between the voice of innocence and the voice of experience in the "Chimney Sweeper" poems. The situation is the same in each, but how do the poems differ?

3.11.4 "London"

I wander through each chartered[1] street,
Near where the chartered Thames does flow,
And mark in every face I meet
Marks of weakness, marks of woe.

In every cry of every Man,
In every infant's cry of fear,
In every voice, in every ban[2],
The mind forged manacles[3] I hear.

How the chimney sweeper's cry
Every blackening[4] Church appalls;
And the hapless[5] Soldier's sigh
Runs in blood down palace walls.

But most through midnight streets I hear
How the youthful Harlot[6]'s curse
Blasts[7] the new born Infant's tear,
And blights with plagues the Marriage hearse[8].

Notes
1. **chartered**: the rights of people were restricted by charters and corporations.
2. **ban**: curse.
3. **mind-forged manacles**: restraints forged for the mind.
4. **blackening**: the wall of the church was blackened by the smoke.
5. **hapless**: unlucky.
6. **Harlot**: prostitute.
7. **blasts**: destroys.
8. **And blights with plagues the Marriage hearse**: spoil the marriage hearse with decease. "hearse", the vehicle for carrying a coffin in a funeral.

Study Questions
1. What was the speaker seeing and hearing in London?
2. What sort of world did Blake describe in this poem?
3. What metaphors and images did Blake use in order to realize his theme of this poem?

Essay Topics
1. In what ways is Blake a social critic? Cite examples from his poems to illustrate your

ideas.
2. In what ways are Blake's poems symbolic? Cite examples from his poems to illustrate your ideas.

3.12 Richard Brinsley Sheridan

3.12.1 About the Author

Richard Brinsley Sheridan (1751-1816) was born in Dublin, Ireland. His father was a prominent actor and his mother a writer. The family moved to London when Sheridan was still a boy. At the age of eleven he was sent to Harrow school, after which he became a student of the Middle Temple, but was never called to the bar. In 1773 he married Miss Linley, an accomplished singer. Then he began writing for the theater and in 1776 became part owner and director of the Drury Lane Theatre. In 1775 he brought out *The Rivals*, a comedy, which is concerned with the differing attitudes of the characters, young and old, to love, marriage and money.

The School for Scandal (1777) is considered his masterpiece: a series of gossipy but polished, fast-paced scenes exposing contemporary foibles through the actions of the vigorously drawn characters. The play also demonstrates Sheridan's brilliant display of wit and humor that derive from the difference between the image the characters have of themselves and the picture they actually present to the world.

During the course of his political career, Sheridan served as a Member of Parliament in 1780, undersecretary for foreign affairs in 1782, secretary to the treasury in 1783, and treasurer of the navy in 1806. As an M. P. he was noted for his eloquent speeches made in opposition to the British war against the American colonies, in support of the new French Republic, and in denunciation of the British colonial administrator Warren Hastings. In 1809, Sheridan was financially ruined by the burning of the new Drury Lane Theatre. And his last years were spent in poverty and disgrace, and he was harassed by debt and disappointment.

3.12.2 An Excerpt from Act I of *The School for Scandal*

Scene I Lady Sneerwell's *Dressing-room*

Discovered Lady Sneerwell[1] *at her dressing table*; Snake *drinking chocolate.*

LDAY SNEER. The paragraphs,[2] you say, Mr. Snake, were all inserted?

SNAKE. They were, madam; and, as I copied them myself in a feigned hand, there can be no suspicion whence they came.

LDAY SNEER. Did you circulate the report of Lady Brittle's intrigue with Captain

Boastall?

SNAKE. That's in as fine a train³ as your ladyship could wish. In the common course of things, I think it must reach Mrs. Clackit's ears within four-and-twenty hours; and then, you know, the business is as good as done.

LDAY SNEER. Why, truly, Mrs. Clackit has a very pretty talent, and a great deal of industry.

SNAKE. True, madam, and has been tolerably successful in her day. To my knowledge she has been the cause of six matches being broken off, and three sons being disinherited; of four forced elopements, and as many close confinements; nine separate maintenances,⁴ and two divorces. Nay, I have more than once traced her causing a *tête-à-tête*⁵ in the *Town and County Magazine*, when the parties, perhaps, had never seen each other's face before in the course of their lives.

LDAY SNEER. She certainly has talents, but her manner is gross.

SNAKE. 'Tis very true. — She generally designs well, has a free tongue and a bold invention; but her coloring is too dark,⁶ and her outlines often extravagant. She wants that delicacy of tint, and mellowness of sneer, which distinguishes your ladyship's scandal.

LDAY SNEER. You are partial, Snake.

SNAKE. Not in the least — everybody allows that Lady Sneerwell can do more with a word or a look than many can with the most labored detail, even when they happen to have a little truth on their side to support it.

LDAY SNEER. Yes, my dear Snake; and I am no hypocrite to deny the satisfaction I reap from the success of my efforts. Wounded myself, in the early part of my life by the envenomed tongue of slander, I confess I have since known no pleasure equal to the reducing others to the level of my own injured reputation.

SNAKE. Nothing can be more natural. But, Lady Sneerwell, there is one affair in which you have lately employed me, wherein, I confess, I am at a loss to guess your motives.

LDAY SNEER. I conceive you mean with respect to my neighbor, Sir Peter Teazle, and his family?

SNAKE. I do. Here are two young men, to whom Sir Peter has acted as a kind of guardian⁷ since their father's death; the eldest possessing the most amiable character, and universally well spoken of — the youngest, the most dissipated and extravagant young fellow in the kingdom, without friends or character: the former an avowed admirer of your ladyship, and apparently your favorite; the latter attached to Maria, Sir Peter's ward, and confessedly beloved by her. Now, on the face of these circumstances, it is utterly unaccountable to me why you, the widow of a City knight,⁸ with a good jointure,⁹ should not close with the passion of a man of such character and expectations as Mr. Surface; and more so why you should be so uncommonly earnest to destroy the mutual attachment subsisting between his brother Charles and Maria.

LDAY SNEER. Then, at once to unravel this mystery, I must inform you that love has no share whatever in the intercourse between Mr. Surface and me.

SNAKE. No!

LDAY SNEER. His real attachment is to Maria, or her fortune; but finding in his brother a favored rival, he has been obliged to mask his pretensions,¹⁰ and profit by my assistance.

SNAKE. Yet still I am more puzzled why you should interest yourself in his success.

LDAY SNEER. Heavens! How dull you are! Cannot you surmise the weakness which I hitherto, through shame, have concealed even from you? Must I confess that Charles, that libertine, that extravagant, that bankrupt in fortune and reputation, that he it is for whom I'm thus anxious and malicious, and to gain whom I would sacrifice everything?

SNAKE. Now, indeed, your conduct appears consistent: but how came you and Mr. Surface so confidential?

LDAY SNEER. For our mutual interest. I have found him out a long time since. I know him to be artful, selfish, and malicious — in short, a sentimental knave;¹¹ while with Sir Peter, and indeed with all his acquaintance, he passes for a youthful miracle of prudence, good sense, and benevolence.

SNAKE. Yes; yet Sir Peter vows he has not his equal in England; and, above all, he praises him as a man of sentiment.

LDAY SNEER. True — and with the assistance of his sentiment and hypocrisy, he has brought Sir Peter entirely into his interest with regard to Maria; while poor Charles has no friend in the house, though, I fear, he has a powerful one in Maria's heart, against whom we must direct our schemes.

Enter SERVANT

SERV. Mr. Surface.

LDAY SNEER. Show him up. [*Exit Servant*] He generally calls about this time. I don't wonder at people giving him to me for a lover.

Enter JOSEPH SURFACE

JOSEPH S. My dear Lady Sneerwell, how do you do today? Mr. Snake, your most obedient.

LDAY SNEER. Snake has just been rallying¹² me on our mutual attachment, but I have informed him of our real views. You know how useful he has been to us; and, believe me, the confidence is not ill-placed.

JOSEPH S.　　Madam, it is impossible for me to suspect a man of Mr. Snake's sensibility and discernment.

LDAY SNEER.　　Well, well, no compliments now; but tell me when you saw your mistress, Maria — or, what is more material to me, your brother.

JOSEPH S.　　I have not seen either since I left you; but I can inform you that they never meet. Some of your stories have taken a good effect on Maria.

LDAY SNEER.　　Ah, my dear Snake! the merit of this belongs to you: but do your brother's distresses increase?

JOSEPH S.　　Every hour. I am told he has had another execution in the house yesterday. In short, his dissipation and extravagance exceed anything I have ever heard of.

LDAY SNEER.　　Poor Charles!

JOSEPH S.　　True, madam; notwithstanding his vices, one cannot help feeling for him. Aye, poor Charles, indeed! I'm sure I wish it were in my power to be of any essential service to him; for the man who does not share in the distresses of a brother, even though merited by his own misconduct, deserves —

LDAY SNEER.　　O Lud![13] you are going to be moral, and forget that you are among friends.

JOSEPH S.　　Egad,[14] that's true! — I'll keep that sentiment till I see Sir Peter. However, it is certainly a charity to rescue Maria from such a libertine, who if he is to be reclaimed, can be so only by a person of your ladyship's superior accomplishments and understanding.

SNAKE.　　I believe, Lady Sneerwell, here's company coming: I'll go and copy the letter I mentioned to you. — Mr. Surface, your most obedient.

JOSEPH S.　　Sir, your very devoted. [*Exit SNAKE*] — Lady Sneerwell, I am very sorry you have put any farther confidence in that fellow.

LDAY SNEER.　　Why so?

JOSEPH S.　　I have lately detected him in frequent conference with old Rowley, who was formerly my father's steward, and has never, you know, been a friend of mine.

LDAY SNEER.　　And do you think he would betray us?

JOSEPH S.　　Nothing more likely: — take my word for't, Lady Sneerwell, that fellow hasn't virtue enough to be faithful even to his own villainy. — Ah! Maria!

Enter MARIA

LDAY SNEER.　　Maria, my dear, how do you do? — What's the matter?

MARIA.　　Oh! there's that disagreeable lover of mine, Sir Benjamin Backbite, has just called at my guardian's, with his odious uncle, Crabtree; so I slipped out, and ran hither to avoid them.

LDAY SNEER.　　Is that all?

JOSEPH S. If my brother Charles had been of the party, madam, perhaps you would not have been so much alarmed.

LDAY SNEER. Nay, now you are severe; for I dare swear the truth of the matter is, Maria heard *you* were here. — But, my dear, what has Sir Benjamin done, that you should avoid him so?

MARIA. Oh, he has done nothing — but 'tis for what he has said: his conversation is a perpetual libel on all his acquaintance.

JOSEPH S. Aye, and the worst of it is, there is no advantage in not knowing him — for he'll abuse a stranger just as soon as his best friend; and his uncle's as bad.

LDAY SNEER. Nay, but we should make allowance[15] — Sir Benjamin is a wit and a poet.

MARIA. For my part, I confess, madam, wit loses its respect with me, when I see it in company with malice. — What do you think, Mr. Surface?

JOSEPH S. Certainly, madam; to smile at the jest[16] which plants a thorn in another's breast is to become a principal in the mischief.[17]

LDAY SNEER. Pshaw! — there's no possibility of being witty without a little ill nature: the malice of a good thing is the barb that makes it stick. — What's your opinion, Mr. Surface?

JOSEPH S. To be sure, madam; that conversation, where the spirit of raillery is suppressed, will ever appear tedious and insipid.

MARIA. Well, I'll not debate how far scandal may be allowable; but in a man, I am sure, it is always contemptible. We have pride, envy, rivalship, and a thousand motives to depreciate each other; but the male slanderer must have the cowardice of a woman before he can traduce[18] one.

Enter SERVANT

SERV. Madam, Mrs. Candour is below, and if your ladyship's at leisure, will leave her carriage.

LDAY SNEER. Beg her to walk in. — [*Exit SERVANT*] — Now, Maria, here is a character to your taste; for though Mrs. Candour is a little talkative, everybody allows her to be the best natured and best sort of woman.

MARIA. Yes, — with a very gross affectation[19] of good nature and benevolence, she does more mischief than the direct malice of old Crabtree.

JOSEPH S. I' faith[20] 'tis true, Lady Sneerwell: whenever I hear the current running against the characters of my friends, I never think them in such danger as when Candour undertakes their defense.

LDAY SNEER. Hush! — here she is!

Enter MRS. CANDOUR

MRS. CAN. My dear Lady Sneerwell, how have you been this century? — Mr. Surface, what news do you hear? — though indeed it is no matter, for I think one hears nothing else but scandal.

JOSEPH S. Just so, indeed, ma'am.

MRS. CAN. Oh, Maria! child, — what, is the whole affair off between you and Charles? His extravagance, I presume — the town talks of nothing else.

MARIA. I am very sorry, ma'am, the town has so little to do.

MRS. CAN. True, true, child: but there's no stopping people's tongues. I own I was hurt to hear it, as I indeed was to learn, from the same quarter, that your guardian, Sir Peter, and Lady Teazle have not agreed lately as well as could be wished.

MARIA. 'Tis strangely impertinent for people to busy themselves so.

MRS. CAN. Very true, child; — but what's to be done? People will talk — there's no preventing it. Why, it was but yesterday I was told that Miss Gadabout[21] had eloped with Sir Filigree Flirt. — But, Lord! there's no minding what one hears; though, to be sure, I had this from very good authority.

MARIA. Such reports are highly scandalous.

MRS. CAN. So they are, child — shameful, shameful! But the world is so censorious, no character escapes. — Lord, now who would have suspected your friend, Miss Prim,[22] of an indiscretion? Yet such is the ill-nature of people, that they say her uncle stopped her last week, just as she was stepping into the York Mail with her dancing-master.

MARIA. I'll answer for't there are no grounds for that report.

MRS. CAN. Ah, no foundation in the world, I dare swear; no more, probably, than for the story circulated last month, of Mrs. Festino's[23] affair with Colonel Cassino; — though, to be sure, that matter was never rightly cleared up.

JOSEPH S. The license of invention[24] some people take is monstrous indeed.

MARIA. 'Tis so, — but, in my opinion, those who report such things are equally culpable.[25]

MRS. CAN. To be sure they are; tale-bearers are as bad as the tale-makers — 'tis an old observation, and a very true one: but what's to be done, as I said before? how will you prevent people from talking? To-day, Mrs. Clackit assured me, Mr. and Mrs. Honeymoon were at last become mere man and wife, like the rest of their acquaintance. She likewise hinted that a certain widow, in the next street, had got rid of her dropsy[26] and recovered her shape in a most surprising manner. And at the same time Miss Tattle, who was by, affirmed that Lord Buffalo had discovered his lady at a house of no extraordinary fame;[27] and that Sir Harry Bouquet and Tom Saunter were to measure swords[28] on a similar provocation. — But, Lord, do you think I would report these things! — No, no! tale-bearers, as I said before, are just as bad as the tale-makers.

JOSEPH S. Ah! Mrs. Candour, if everybody had your forbearance and good-nature!

MRS. CAN. I confess, Mr. Surface, I cannot bear to hear people attacked behind their backs; and when ugly circumstances come out against our acquaintance, I own I always love to think the best. — By-the-by, I hope 'tis not true that your brother is absolutely ruined?

JOSEPH S.   I am afraid his circumstances are very bad indeed, ma'am.

MRS. CAN.   Ah! I heard so — but you must tell him to keep up his spirits; everybody almost is in the same way: Lord Spindle, Sir Thomas Splint, Captain Quinze,[29] and Mr. Nickit — all up, I hear, within this week; so, if Charles is undone, he'll find half his acquaintance ruined too, and that, you know, is a consolation.

JOSEPH S.   Doubtless, ma'am — a very great one.

Enter SERVANT

SERV.   Mr. Crabtree and Sir Benjamin Backbite.   [*Exit SERVANT*]

LDAY SNEER.   So, Maria, you see your lover pursues you; positively you shan't escape.

Enter CRABTREE *and* SIR BENJAMIN BACKBITE

CRABT.   Lady Sneerwell, I kiss your hand — Mrs. Candour, I don't believe you are acquainted with my nephew, Sir Benjamin Backbite? Egad! ma'am he has a pretty wit, and is a pretty poet too. Isn't he, Lady Sneerwell?

SIR BENJ. B.   Oh, fie, uncle!

CRABT.   Nay, egad, it's true; I back him at a rebus or a charade[30] against the best rhymer in the kingdom. — Has your ladyship heard the epigram he wrote last week on Lady Frizzle's[31] feather catching fire? — Do, Benjamin, repeat it, or the charade you made last night extempore[32] at Mrs. Drowzie's conversazione.[33] Come now; — your first is the name of a fish, your second a great naval commander, and —

SIR BENJ. B.   Uncle, now — pr'thee —

CRABT.   I'faith, ma'am't would surprise you to hear how ready he is at all these sorts of things.

LDAY SNEER.   I wonder, Sir Benjamin, you never publish any thing.

SIR BENJ. B.   To say truth, ma'am, 'tis very vulgar to print; and as my little productions are mostly satires and lampoons[34] on particular people, I find they circulate more by giving copies in confidence to the friends of the parties. However, I have some love elegies, which, when favored with this lady's smiles, I mean to give the public.   [*Pointing to MARIA*]

CRABT.   'Fore heaven, ma'am, they'll immortalize you! — you will be handed down to posterity, like Petrarch's Laura,[35] or Waller's Sacharissa.[36]

SIR BENJ. B.   Yes, madam, I think you will like them, when you shall see them on a beautiful quarto page, where a neat rivulet of text shall murmur through a meadow of margin. 'Fore Gad, they will be the most elegant things of their kind!

CRABT.   But, ladies, that's true — have you heard the news?

MRS. CAN.   What, sir, do you mean the report of —

CRABT.　　No, ma'am, that's not it. — Miss Nicely is going to be married to her own footman.

MRS. CAN.　　Impossible!

CRABT.　　Ask Sir Benjamin.

SIR BENJ. B.　　'Tis very true, ma'am: everything is fixed, and the wedding liveries[37] bespoke.

CRABT.　　Yes — and they do say there were pressing reasons for it.

LDAY SNEER.　　Why, I have heard something of this before.

MRS. CAN.　　It can't be — and I wonder any one should believe such a story of so prudent a lady as Miss Nicely.

SIR BENJ. B.　　O Lud! ma'am, that's the very reason 'twas believed at once. She has always been so cautious and so reserved, that everybody was sure there was some reason for it at bottom.

MRS. CAN.　　Why, to be sure, a tale of scandal is as fatal to the credit of a prudent lady of her stamp, as a fever is generally to those of the strongest constitutions. But there is a sort of puny sickly reputation, that is always ailing, yet will outlive the robuster characters of a hundred prudes.[38]

SIR BENJ. B.　　True, madam, — there are valetudinarians[39] in reputation as well as constitution; who, being conscious of their weak part, avoid the least breath of air, and supply their want of stamina[40] by care and circumspection.

MRS. CAN.　　Well, but this may be all a mistake. You know, Sir Benjamin, very trifling circumstances often give rise to the most injurious tales.

CRABT.　　That they do, I'll be sworn, ma'am. Did you ever hear how Miss Piper came to lose her lover and her character last summer at Tunbridge?[41] — Sir Benjamin, you remember it?

SIR BENJ. B.　　Oh, to be sure! — the most whimsical circumstance.

LDAY SNEER.　　How was it, pray?

CRABT.　　Why, one evening, at Mrs. Ponto's assembly, the conversation happened to turn on the difficulty of breeding Nova Scotia[42] sheep in this country. Says a young lady in company, I have known instances of it — for Miss Letitia Piper, a first cousin of mine, had a Nova Scotia sheep that produced her twins. — What! cries the Lady Dowager Dundizzy (who you know is as deaf as a post), has Miss Piper had twins? — This mistake, as you may imagine, threw the whole company into a fit of laughing. However, 'twas the next day everywhere reported, and in a few days believed by the whole town, that Miss Letitia Piper had actually been brought to bed of[43] a fine boy and a girl; and in less than a week there were some people who could name the father, and the farm-house where the babies were put to nurse.

LDAY SNEER.　　Strange, indeed!

CRABT.　　Matter of fact, I assure you. — O Lud! Mr. Surface, pray is it true that your uncle, Sir Oliver, is coming home?

JOSEPH S.   Not that I know of, indeed, sir.

CRABT.   He has been in the East Indies a long time. You can scarcely remember him, I believe? Sad comfort whenever he returns, to hear how your brother has gone on!

JOSEPH S.   Charles has been imprudent, sir, to be sure; but I hope no busy people have already prejudiced Sir Oliver against him. He may reform.

SIR BENJ. B.   To be sure he may: for my part, I never believed him to be so utterly void of principle as people say; and though he has lost all his friends, I am told nobody is better spoken of by the Jews.

CRABT.   That's true, egad, nephew. If the Old Jewry[44] was a ward, I believe Charles would be an alderman: — no man more popular there, 'fore Gad! I hear he pays as many annuities as the Irish tontine;[45] and that whenever he is sick, they have prayers for the recovery of his health in all the synagogues.

SIR BENJ. B.   Yet no man lives in greater splendor. They tell me, when he entertains his friends he will sit down to dinner with a dozen of his own securities; have a score of tradesmen waiting in the antechamber, and an officer behind every guest's chair.

JOSEPH S.   This may be entertainment to you, gentlemen, but you pay very little regard to the feelings of a brother.

MARIA.   [*Aside*] Their malice is intolerable! — [*Aloud*] Lady Sneer, I must wish you a good morning: I'm not very well.   [*Exit MARIA*]

MRS. CAN.   O dear! she changes color very much.

LDAY SNEER.   Do, Mrs. Candour, follow her: she may want your assistance.

MRS. CAN.   That I will, with all my soul, ma'am. Poor dear creature, who knows what her situation may be!   [*Exit MRS. CANDOUR*]

LDAY SNEER.   'Twas nothing but that she could not bear to hear Charles reflected on, notwithstanding their difference.

SIR BENJ. B.   The young lady's *penchant*[46] is obvious.

CRABT.   But, Benjamin, you must not give up the pursuit for that: — follow her, and put her into good humor. Repeat her some of your own verses. Come, I'll assist you.

SIR BENJ. B.   Mr. Surface, I did not mean to hurt you; but depend on't your brother is utterly undone.

CRABT.   O Lud, ay! undone as ever man was. Can't raise a guinea!

SIR BENJ. B.   Everything sold, I'm told, that was movable.

CRABT.   I have seen one that was at his house. Not a thing left but some empty bottles that were overlooked, and the family pictures, which I believe are framed in the wainscot[47] —

SIR BENJ. B.   And I'm very sorry, also, to hear some bad stories against him.

[*Going*]

CRABT.　Oh, he has done many mean things, that's certain.

　　SIR BENJ.　But, however, as he's your brother — [*Going*]

CRABT.　We'll tell you all another opportunity.　[*Exit CRABTREE and SIR BENJAMIN*]

LDAY SNEER.　Ha! ha! 'tis very hard for them to leave a subject they have not quite run down.

JOSEPH S.　And I believe the abuse was no more acceptable to your ladyship than to Maria.

LDAY SNEER.　I doubt her affections are farther engaged than we imagine. But the family are to be here this evening, so you may as well dine where you are, and we shall have an opportunity of observing farther; in the meantime, I'll go and plot mischief, and you shall study sentiment.　[*Exeunt.*]

Notes

1. **Lady Sneerwell**: The names of most characters in the play reveal the qualities of the persons.
2. **The paragraphs**: that is, the paragraphs of scandals.
3. **in as fine a train**: in as good order or arrangement.
4. **separate maintenances**: The husband and wife live separately, the livelihood of the wife being maintained by the husband.
5. *tête-à-tête*: a private interview.
6. **her coloring is too dark**: that she exaggerates too much.
7. **Sir Peter has acted as a kind of guardian**: Besides taking Maria as his ward, Sir Peter also acts as the guardian of Joseph and Charles Surface during their uncle's absence.
8. **a City knight**: a merchant in the City of London who was conferred the title of knight.
9. **jointure**: a sole estate limited to the wife, to take effect upon the death of her husband, for her own life at least.
10. **mask his pretensions**: hide his intention.
11. **a sentimental knave**: a dishonest and unprincipled man with affected emotions.
12. **rallying**: teasing, ridiculing.
13. **Lud**: Lord.
14. **Egad**: by God.
15. **make allowance**: to be lenient toward.
16. **jest**: a jeering remark with the intention to harm.
17. **a principal in the mischief**: a person directly responsible for the harm.
18. **traduce**: slander.
19. **gross affectation**: outrageously putting on manners that are not one's own.
20. **I' faith**: In faith.

21. **Gadabout**: go about, meaning one who easily changes one's mind.
22. **Prim**: easily shocked by something rude.
23. **Festino**: Italian for festival.
24. **license of invention**: the literary taken in inventing scandals.
25. **culpable**: guilty.
26. **got rid of her dropsy**: The implied meaning is that the widow must have had an abortion.
27. **a house of no extraordinary fame**: a place of bad reputation.
28. **to measure swords**: to be engaged in a duel.
29. **Quinze**: a card game.
30. **charade**: parlor game in which words to be guessed are acted in pantomine.
31. **Frizzle**: to fry, to scorch.
32. **extempore**: without time for preparation.
33. **conversazione**: a social gathering.
34. **lampoon**: a piece of writing that attacks a person with ridicule.
35. **Petrarch's Laura**: Petrarch (1304-1374), the Italian poet, who wrote many sonnets to his lover Laura.
36. **Waller's Sacharissa**: Edmund Waller (1608-1687), a 17th century poet, who wrote many poems to Lady Dorothy Sidney, whom he celebrated as "Sacharissa".
37. **liveries**: distinctive uniforms worn by male servants in a great household.
38. **prudes**: a person of extreme or exaggerated propriety concerning behavior or speech, one who is easily shocked by sexual matters.
39. **valetudinarians**: sickly persons.
40. **want of stamina**: lacking strength or staying power.
41. **Tunbridge**: a hot spring near London.
42. **Nova Scotia**: New Scotland, in the east of Canada.
43. **brought to bed of**: gave birth to.
44. **Old Jewry**: the living quarters of the Jews in London.
45. **tontine**: a financial scheme by which the subscribers to a loan or common fund receive each an annuity during his life, which increases as the number is diminished by death, till the last survivor enjoys the whole income.
46. *penchant*: inclination.
47. **wainscot**: wooden panel on the wall.

Study Questions

1. What personal qualities can you guess from the names of the characters such as Lady Sneerwell, Mr. Snake, Mrs. Candour, and Sir Benjamin Backbite?
2. What kind of man is Joseph Surface according to Lady Sneerwell's understanding?
3. What kind of man is Charles Surface, judging from the opinions of the other

characters?
4. What is your impression about all those characters appeared in the first scene?
5. What is your understanding of the author's attitude towards his characters?

Chapter 4   The Romantic Period

4.1   An Introduction

Romanticism is a broad artistic and literary movement that affected the whole of Europe (and America). It marked a partial reaction against the 18th-century rationalism and physical materialism in literature, philosophy, art, religion and politics. Just as it is difficult to lend a date to its beginning, so it is vain to ascribe the precise time of its ending. However, English Romanticism, as a historical phase of literature, is generally said to have begun in 1798 with the publication of Wordsworth and Coleridge's *Lyrical Ballads* and to have ended in 1832 with Sir Walter Scott's death and the passage of the first Reform Bill in the Parliament.

The romantic era can be considered as indicative of an age of crisis. In 1789 there broke out the epoch-making French Revolution, which aroused great sympathy and enthusiasm in the English liberals and radicals. Patriotic clubs and societies multiplied in England, all claiming liberty, equality and fraternity. The revolution also stimulated two influential books: one is Thomas Paine's *Rights of Man* (1791-1792), which justifies the revolution; the other is William Godwin's *Inquiry Concerning Political Justice* (1793), which was more important for its influence on Wordsworth, Shelley and other poets. Another important event was the full swing of English Industrial Revolution, with which the capitalist class came to dominate not only the means of production, but also trade and world market. Though England had increased its wealth by several times, it was only the rich who owned this wealth; the majority of the people were still poor, or even poorer. This cruel economic exploitation caused large-scale workers' disturbances in England; the desperation of the workers expressed itself in the popular outbreaks of machine-breaking known as the Luddite riots. However, the industrial capitalists made use of the workers' struggle to fight for their own supremacy in political power against the landed aristocrats. In 1832, the Reform Bill was enacted, which brought the industrial capitalists into power. But the sharp conflicts between capital and labor did not come to an end.

The Romantics, who were deeply immersed in the most violent phase of the transition from a decadent feudal to a capitalist economy, saw both the corruption and injustice of the feudal societies and the fundamental inhumanity of the economic, social and political forces of capitalism. They felt that the society denied people their essential human needs. So under the influence of the leading romantic thinkers like Kant, Goethe, Rousseau and others, they demonstrated a strong rejection of the dominant modes of thinking of the 18th-century writers and philosophers.

So far as its characteristics are concerned, Romanticism extolled the individual, celebrated the imagination, and glorified nature besides its usual emphasis over the features like the intuitive, the subjective, the irrational, the spontaneous, the visionary, the emotional, the exotic, the mysterious and the transcendental.

Rousseau established the cult of the individual and championed the freedom of the human spirit; his famous announcement was "I felt before I thought". Under his influence, the Romantics tend to place the individual at the center of art, making literature most valuable as an expression of his or her unique feelings and particular attitudes. Their chief emphasis was upon freedom of individual's self-expression: sincerity, spontaneity, and originality became the new standards in literature, replacing the decorous imitation of classical models favored by 18th-century Neoclassicism.

Imagination is defined by the Romantics as a dynamic, active power that creates all art. According to Coleridge, it is in solitude, in communion with the natural universe, that man can exercise this vital power of imagination. To contrast distinctly with the traditional arguments for the supremacy of reason, the Romantics elevate imagination to a position as the supreme faculty of the mind, which, accompanied by spontaneity, intuition and inspiration, "shapes" artistic works.

Nature is apprehended by the Romantics not only as an exemplar and source of vivid physical beauty but as a manifestation of spirit in the universe as well. Nature becomes the stage on which the human drama is played, the context in which man comes to understand his place in the universe, the transforming agent which harmonizes the individual soul with what the Transcendentalists would call the Over-Soul. Thus, the Romantics tend to show a deepened appreciation of nature, connecting it with a love for the remote, the strange, the mystery, the supernatural, and everything that creates wonder.

Romantics also tend to be nationalistic, defending the great poets and dramatists of their own national heritage against the advocates of classical rules who tended to glorify Rome and rational Italian and French neoclassical art as superior to the native traditions.

The Romantic period is an age of poetry. Blake, Wordsworth, Coleridge, Byron, Shelley and Keats are the major Romantic poets. Poetry has been traditionally regarded as an art governed by rules; but to the Romantics, poetry should be free from all rules. They would turn to the humble people and the common everyday life for subjects. Employing the commonplace, the natural, and the simple as their poetic materials, Romantic writers are always seeking for the absolute, the ideal through the transcendence of the actual. They have also made bold experiments in poetic language, versification and design, and constructed a variety of forms on original principles of organization and style; examples of such can be found in Blake's visionary prophetic poems, in Coleridge's mystic ballad, *The Ancient Mariner*, in Wordsworth's spiritual autobiography, *The Prelude*, and in Shelley's symbolic drama, *Prometheus Unbound*.

The Romantic period is also a great age of prose. With education greatly developed for the middle-class people, there was a rapid growth in the reading public and an increasing demand for reading materials. Thus, newspapers, magazines and periodicals run by private enterprises started to flourish in this period. *Edinburgh Review* (founded in 1802), *The Quarterly Review* (founded in 1809), *Blackwood's Magazine* (founded in 1817), *London Magazine* (founded in 1820), were among the most famous. They made literary comments on writers with high standards, which paved the way for the development of a new and valuable type of critical writings. Coleridge, Hazlitt, Lamb and De Quincey were the leading figures in this new development. Guided by rich knowledge of literature and a profound human sympathy, they read sympathetically the work of a new author, with the sole idea of finding what he had contributed or tried to contribute, to the magnificent total of the English literature. They also wrote familiar essays.

The two major novelists of the Romantic period are Jane Austen (1775-1817) and Walter Scott (1771-1832). Austen is of the 18t-century in her moral outlook, and in her prose style, though she is fully aware of the new strains of Romanticism. Her view of life is a totally realistic one. She has no sentimentality, no time for emotional excess. She honors the Augustan virtues of moderation, dignity, disciplined emotion and common sense. Not surprisingly she had in her day a small, select circle of admirers. But in the 20th century, she has become a popular classic and has been admired for her wit, her common-sense, her insight into characters and social relationships.

Walter Scott is the most popular novelist of his day. *Waverley* (1814), *Old Mortality* (1816), *The Heart of Midlothian* (1818), *Rob Roy* (1818), and *Ivanhoe* (1820) are among the most popular ones of his novels. In his depiction of Scotland, England, and the Continent from medieval times to the 18th century, he showed a keen sense of political and traditional forces and of their influence on the individual. He is the first major historical novelist, exerting a powerful literary influence both in Britain and on the Continent throughout the 19th century.

Gothic novel, type of romantic fiction that predominated in the late eighteenth century, was one phase of the Romantic Movement. Its principal elements are violence, horror and the supernatural which strongly appeal to the reader's emotion. With its descriptions of the dark, irrational side of human nature, the Gothic form has exerted a great influence over the writers of the Romantic period. Works like *The Mysteries of Udolpho* (1794) by Ann Radcliffe and *Frankenstein* (1818) by Mary Shelley are typical Gothic romance. Even poets like Blake, Coleridge, Shelley and Keats tend to use those fantastic, grotesque, savage and mysterious elements of Gothic fiction in their poetic works.

Besides poetry and prose, there are quite a number of writers who have tried their hand at poetic dramas in this period. This is partly because the lectures and criticism on Elizabethan drama given by Coleridge and Hazlitt have renewed interest in Shakespeare and led to the rediscovery of his contemporaries. Shelley's *Prometheus Unbound* and

The Cenci (1819), Byron's *Manfred* (1817), and Coleridge's *Remorse* (1813) are generally regarded as the best verse plays during this period. However, compared with the brilliant achievement in poetry and prose, drama in the Romantic period is less successful. There might be different reasons to explain this, but the chief one might be that none of these poets really understand the theater. Their plays are seldom if ever amongst the best of the stage plays, and they survive for readers, not for audience.

4.2 William Wordsworth

4.2.1 About the Author

William Wordsworth (1770-1850) was born at Cockermouth, Cumberland, in the Lake District. He was sent to Hawkshead Grammar School, near Windermere. During school vacation periods he frequently visited places noted for their scenic beauty, thus developing a keen love of nature as a youth. In 1787 he went up to St. John's College, Cambridge. While studying at Cambridge University, Wordsworth spent a summer holiday on a walking tour in Switzerland and France.

After receiving his degree in 1791 he returned to France, where he became an enthusiast for the ideals of the French Revolution. He also had an affair with Annette Vallon, who bore him an illegitimate daughter, Caroline, in 1792. In 1793 Wordsworth published *An Evening Walk* and *Descriptive Sketches*, which were written in the stylized idiom and vocabulary of the 18th century.

In 1795 the Wordsworths stayed in a cottage in Dorset, where they met Samuel Taylor Coleridge and Robert Southey. His friendship with Coleridge tended to confirm him in his resolution to devote himself to poetry; and a legacy of £ 900 from a friend freed him from financial worries. Together they collaborated on a book of poems entitled *Lyrical Ballads* (1798). Wordsworth wrote almost all the poems in the volume; Coleridge contributed the famous "Rime of the Ancient Mariner". Representing a revolt against the artificial classicism of contemporary English verse, *Lyrical Ballads* was greeted with hostility by most leading critics of the day.

In 1799, after a visit to Germany with Coleridge, Wordsworth and Dorothy settled at Dove Cottage in Grasmere in the Lake District. In 1802 Wordsworth married Mary Hutchinson, an old school friend. The union was evidently a happy one, and the couple had four children. In 1800, Wordsworth wrote a preface for the second edition of *Lyrical Ballads*, explaining his reasons for choosing to write as he had. For Wordsworth, poetry, which should be written in "the real language of men", is nevertheless "the spontaneous overflow of feelings: it takes its origin from emotion recollected in tranquility".

Wordsworth's greatest work, *The Prelude*, was completed in 1805, though it was not published until after his death. The purpose of *The Prelude* was to recapture and interpret, with detailed thoroughness, the whole range of experiences that had contributed to the shaping of his own mind. In 1842, he was given a government pension and the following year became poet laureate.

    Wordsworth is the leading figure of the English romantic poetry, the focal poetic voice of the period. He did much to restore simple diction to English poetry and to establish romanticism as the era's dominant literary movement. His verse celebrates the moral influence exerted by nature on human thought and feeling.

4.2.2 "I Wandered Lonely as a Cloud"[1]

I wandered lonely as a cloud
That floats on high o'er vales and hills,
When all at once I saw a crowd,
A host of[2] golden daffodils;
Beside the lake, beneath the trees,
Fluttering and dancing in the breeze.

Continuous[3] as the stars that shine
And twinkle on the milky way,
They stretched in never-ending line
Along the margin of a bay:
Ten thousand saw I at a glance,
Tossing their heads in sprightly[4] dance.

The waves beside them danced; but they
Outdid the sparkling waves in glee;
A poet could not but be gay
In such a jocund company;
I gazed — and gazed — but little thought
What wealth the show to me had brought:
For oft, when on my couch I lie
In vacant or in pensive mood[5],
They flash upon that inward eye
Which is the bliss of solitude;[6]
And then my heart with pleasure fills,
And dances with the daffodils.

Notes

1. Wordsworth wrote this beautiful poem of nature after he came across a long belt of

gold daffodils tossing, reeling and dancing along the waterside.
2. **a crowd, / a host of**: a large number of.
3. **continuous**: extending without break.
4. **sprightly**: lively, full of energy.
5. **In vacant or in pensive mood**: In a mood in which the mind is devoid of any thought or in a deeply thoughtful mood.
6. **They flash upon that inward eye/Which is the bliss of solitude**: When alone, the poet recalls the beautiful scene, which gives him great happiness.

Study Questions

1. What mood does the opening simile suggest, and what change in mood occurs later on?
2. What is the significance of close observation of individual details from nature in this poem?
3. What does this poem suggest about the powers of nature?
4. What role does memory play in this poem?

4.2.3 "Composed upon Westminster Bridge"

September 3, 1802[1]
Earth has not anything to show more fair:
Dull would he be of soul who could pass by
A sight so touching in its majesty;
This City now doth, like a garment, wear
The beauty of the morning; silent, bare,
Ships, towers, domes, theaters, and temples lie
Open unto the fields, and to the sky;
All bright and glittering in the smokeless air.
Never did sun more beautifully steep[2]
In his first splendor, valley, rock, or hill;
Ne'er saw I, never felt, a calm so deep!
The river glideth at his own sweet will[3]:
Dear God! the very houses seem asleep;
And all that mighty heart is lying still[4]!

Notes

1. The date of this experience was not Sept. 3, but July 31, 1802. Its occasion was a trip to France. The sonnet describes a vivid picture of a beautiful morning in London. It follows strictly the Italian form, with a clear division between the octave and the sestet; the rhyme scheme is abbaabba, cdcdcd.

2. **steep**: saturate.
3. **The river glideth at his own sweet will**: Wordsworth adds beauty to nature by treating it as a living thing.
4. **all that mighty heart is lying still**: What "mighty heart" refers to is ambiguous. Here it might refer to London.

Study Questions

1. At what time of day is London being described in this poem?
2. Which descriptive elements are presented objectively and which subjectively?
3. How is the simile "like a garment" developed?
4. What is the effect of personification in the poem and what does it suggest about the speaker's attitude toward an awakened London?

4.2.4 "She Dwelt Among the Untrodden Ways"[1]

She dwelt among the untrodden ways
   Beside the springs of Dove[2],
A maid whom there were none to praise
   And very few to love;

A violet by a mossy stone
   Half hidden from the eye!
— Fair as a star, when only one
   Is shining in the sky.

She lived unknown, and few could know
   When Lucy ceased to be;
But she is in her grave, and, oh,
   The difference to me!

Notes

1. This is one of the "Lucy poems", written in 1799.
2. The name of a river. There are several rivers by this name in England, including one in the Lake Country.

Study Questions

1. Who is the speaker of the poem?
2. What tone does the speaker use in this poem?
3. What do the "star" simile and "violet" metaphor imply about Lucy's qualities?

4.3 Samuel Taylor Coleridge

4.3.1 About the Author

Samuel Taylor Coleridge (1772-1834) was born in Devonshire, England. He was the youngest son of a clergyman. When he was nine years old, his father died. Then a year later, he was sent to a charity boarding school in London. In 1791, he went up to Jesus College, Cambridge, but left in 1794 without obtaining a degree. As a young man, Coleridge was quite a radical in politics and became a strong supporter of the French Revolution. He also joined Robert Southey in a utopian plan of establishing an ideal democratic community in America. Although nothing came of this plan, it led to Coleridge's marriage to Sara Fricker, which proved to be an unhappy one.

In 1797 Coleridge met Wordsworth for the first time and had begun what was to be a lifelong friendship with him. The two poets planned *Lyrical Ballads* (1798), which became a landmark in English poetry. Coleridge's principal contribution was *The Rime of the Ancient Mariner*, which tells of a sailor who kills an albatross and for that crime against nature endures terrible punishments.

Coleridge developed rheumatism early in life and suffered acute pain. To cure the pain, physicians freely prescribed opium for him. Coleridge became dependent on the drug, which gradually destroyed his health, happiness and poetic creativity. In 1816, Coleridge moved to London with the surgeon James Gillman in order to preserve his health. Despite a life filled with illness and depression, Coleridge did a prodigious amount of work. In addition to *The Rime of the Ancient Mariner*, Coleridge wrote "Kubla Khan", "Christabel" and some conversational poems, the best of which is "Frost at Midnight". Between 1808 and 1819 he gave his famous series of lectures on literature and philosophy; the lectures on Shakespeare were partly responsible for a renewed interest in the playwright. His *Biographia Literaria* (1817), a prose work of autobiographical memoirs and literary criticism, is considered one of his important works.

Coleridge was esteemed by some of his contemporaries and is generally recognized today as a lyrical poet and literary critic of the first rank. His poetic themes range from the supernatural to the domestic. His metaphysical anxiety, anticipating modern existentialism, has gained him reputation as an authentic visionary.

4.3.2 "Kubla Khan"[1]

In Xanadu[2] did Kubla Khan
A stately pleasure dome decree[3]:

Where Alph[4], the sacred river, ran
Through caverns measureless to man[5]
   Down to a sunless sea.
So twice five miles of fertile ground
With walls and towers were girdled round:
And there were gardens bright with sinuous rills[6],
Where blossomed many an incense-bearing tree;
And here were forests ancient as the hills,
Enfolding sunny spots of greenery.

But oh! that deep romantic[7] chasm which slanted
Down the green hill athwart a cedarn[8] cover!
A savage place! as holy and enchanted
As e'er beneath a waning moon was haunted
By woman wailing for her demon lover!
And from this chasm, with ceaseless turmoil seething,
As if this earth in fast thick pants were breathing,
A mighty fountain momently[9] was forced:
Amid whose swift half-intermitted burst
Huge fragments vaulted like rebounding hail,
Or chaffy grain beneath the thresher's flail:
And 'mid these dancing rocks at once and ever
It flung up momently the sacred river.
Five miles meandering with a mazy motion
Through wood and dale the sacred river ran,
Then reached the caverns measureless to man,
And sank in tumult to a lifeless ocean:
And 'mid this tumult Kubla heard from far
Ancestral voices prophesying war!
   The shadow of the dome of pleasure
   Floated midway on the waves;
   Where was heard the mingled measure
   From the fountain and the caves.
It was a miracle of rare device[10],
A sunny pleasure dome with caves of ice!
A damsel with a dulcimer[11]
   In a vision once I saw:
   It was an Abyssinian[12] maid,
   And on her dulcimer she played,

　　　　　　　　　Singing of Mount Abora[13].
　　　　　　Could I revive within me
　　　　　　Her symphony and song,
　　　　　　To such a deep delight 'twould win me
　　　　　　That with music loud and long,
　　　　　　I would build that dome in air,
　　　　　　That sunny dome! those caves of ice!
　　　　　　And all who heard should see them there,
　　　　　　And all should cry, Beware! Beware!
　　　　　　His flashing eyes, his floating hair!
　　　　　　Weave a circle round him thrice[14],
　　　　　　And close your eyes with holy dread,
　　　　　　For he on honeydew hath fed,
　　　　　　And drunk the milk of Paradise.

Notes

1. **Kubla Khan**: Mongol emperor, the founder of Yuan Dynasty.
2. **Xanadu**: Xamdu, the place in inner Mongolia where Kubla Khan ascended the throne.
3. **decree**: order to be built.
4. **Alph**: derived probably from the Greek river Alpheus, which flows into the Ionian Sea. Its waters were fabled to rise again in Sicily as the fountain of Arethusa; see Milton's *Lycidas*, lines 85 and 132.
5. **measureless to man**: too deep to be measured by man.
6. **sinuous rills**: small streams with many curves.
7. **romantic**: having imaginative appeal.
8. **athwart**: across; **cedarn**: poetic form of cedar.
9. **momently**: from moment to moment.
10. **device**: design.
11. **dulcimer**: musical instrument played by striking metal strings with two hammers.
12. **Abyssinian**: a place in the east Africa, now Ethiopia.
13. **Mount Abora**: probably Mount Amara in Milton's *Paradise Lost*. Abyssinian kings once sent their children there to avoid the outside disturbance.
14. **Weave a circle round him thrice**: a magic ritual, to protect the inspired poet from intrusion.

Study Questions

1. What are the distinctive details of the pleasure dome in Xanadu, as described in the first eleven lines?
2. What images in the second stanza does the poet use to emphasize that the world

outside the dome is "A savage place" (line 14)?
3. What vision is introduced (line 37)? What aspect of the vision does the speaker long to recover? What does he want to build?
4. What or whom do you suppose the damsel of the vision represents to the speaker?

4.4　George Gordon Byron

4.4.1　About the Author

George Gordon Byron (1788-1824) was born in London. When he was three years old, his father died, and he was taken by his mother to Aberdeen, where he was brought up in poverty and burdened with a clubfoot. To his Scottish upbringing he owed his love of mountains, his love and knowledge of the Bible. At the age of 10, he inherited his great uncle's title and became Lord Byron. He was sent to Harrow, one of England's most prestigious private schools, and then to Cambridge University. It was at Cambridge that Byron began to write poetry. In 1807 Byron published his first lyric poems entitled *Hours of Idleness* which was sharply attacked in the influential *Edinburgh Review*. Byron responded with a biting satire called "English Bards and Scotch Reviewers".

After graduating from Cambridge in 1809, he traveled in Portugal, Spain and the Near East for two years. His experiences of this journey inspired him to write the first two cantos of *Childe Harold's Pilgrimage* (1812). The poem presents a view of Europe colored by the violent sensibilities of its melancholic and passionate narrator, Childe Harold. The poem brought Byron instant success in England. As he said at the time, he awoke one morning and found himself famous. Byron married Anna Isabella Milbanke in 1815. From the start the marriage was doomed by the gulf between Byron and his unimaginative and humourless wife. But his breaking up with his wife caused such a scandal that he was forced to leave England in 1816.

The rest of his brief life was lived on the Continent, mostly in Italy. During his travels he befriended the poet Percy Bysshe Shelley with whom he developed a productive intellectual relationship. Byron, always an avid supporter of liberal causes and national independence, got involved with local politics in 1820, joining the Italian freedom fighters working for democracy. In 1823 Byron joined the Greek insurgents who had risen against the Ottoman Turks. However, in April, 1824, Byron died of marsh fever in Missolonghi before he saw any military action.

Don Juan is Byron's masterpiece, a great comic epic of the early 19th century. Byron puts into the poem his rich knowledge of the world and the wisdom gained from experience. Thus, *Don Juan* presents brilliant pictures of life in its various stages of love, joy, suffering, hatred and fear. Byron also invests in Juan the moral positives like courage, generosity and frankness, which, according to Byron, are virtues neglected by the modern society. In addition, though Don Juan is the central figure and all the threads of the story are woven around him, he and his adventures only provide the framework; the poet's true intention is to present a panoramic view of different types of society.

Byron's poetry, though much criticized by some critics on moral grounds, was immensely popular at home, and also abroad. Across Europe, patriots, poets, painters and musicians are all inspired by him and his poetry. Actually, Byron has enriched European literature with an abundance of ideas, images, artistic forms and innovations.

4.4.2 "Song for the Luddites[1]"

As the Liberty lads o'er the sea[2]
Bought their freedom, and cheaply, with blood,
　So we, boys, we
Will die fighting, or live free,
And down with all kings but King Ludd[3]!

When the web that we weave is complete,
And the shuttle exchanged for the sword,
　We will fling the winding sheet[4]
　O'er the despot at our feet[5],
And dye it deep in the gore he has pour'd[6].

Though black as his heart its hue,
Since his veins are corrupted to mud,
　Yet this is the dew
　Which the tree shall renew
Of Liberty,[7] planted by Ludd!

Notes

1. This is one of the two poems written by Byron to show his support of the Luddites who destroyed the machines in their protest against unemployment. The poet's great sympathy for the workers in their struggle against the capitalists is clearly shown.
2. **Liberty lads o'er the sea**: referring to the Americans who fought for their national independence in 1775-1781.
3. **King Ludd**: Referring to Ned Ludd, a Leicestershire workman who was said to have broken two frames in a Stockinger's house, in about 1779, and from whom the Luddites in their protest against unemployment in 1811-1816 took their name.

4. **the winding sheet**: the sheet used to wrap up the corpse.
5. **the despot at our feet**: Here it refers to the machine which the Luddites incorrectly considered to be the tyrant responsible for their unemployment.
6. **the gore he has pour'd**: the blood he (the despot) has shed.
7. **the tree shall renew/Of Liberty**: During the French Revolution (1789-1794) a symbolic procedure was established of planting trees of Liberty. Here Byron refers to this custom.

Study Questions

1. What is the circumstance of the poem?
2. What literary devices are employed in this poem and to what effect are they used?
3. How does Byron's rhyme scheme help convey his poem's themes?

4.4.3 "She Walks in Beauty[1]"

1

She walks in beauty, like the night
   Of cloudless climes and starry skies;
And all that's best of dark and bright
   Meet in her aspect and her eyes:
Thus mellowed to that tender light
   Which heaven to gaudy day denies.

2

One shade the more, one ray the less,
   Had half impaired the nameless grace
Which waves in every raven tress,
   Or softly lightens o'er her face,
Where thoughts serenely sweet express
   How pure, how dear their dwelling place.

3

And on that cheek, and o'er that brow,
   So soft, so calm, yet eloquent,
The smiles that win, the tints that glow,
   But tell of days in goodness spent,
A mind at peace with all below,
   A heart whose love is innocent!

Notes

   One of the lyrics in *Hebrew Melodies*, written to be set to adaptations of traditional Jewish tunes by the young musician Issac Nathan. Byron wrote the lines the morning after he had met his beautiful young cousin by marriage, Mrs. Robert John Wilmot, who wore a black mourning gown brightened with spangles.

Study Questions

1. How clearly does the poem picture its subject?
2. What do her eyes look like?
3. How are the woman's mind and heart reflected in her appearance?

4.4.4 "When We Two Parted[1]"

When we two parted
   In silence and tears,
Half broken-hearted
   To sever[2] for years,
Pale grew thy cheek and cold,
   Colder thy kiss;
Truly that hour foretold
   Sorrow to this.[3]

The dew of the morning
   Sunk chill on my brow —
It felt like the warning
   Of what I feel now.
Thy vows are all broken,
   And light[4] is thy fame;
I hear thy name spoken,
   And share in its shame.

They name thee before me,
   A knell to mine ear;
A shudder comes o'er me —
   Why wert[5] thou so dear?
They know not I knew thee,
   Who knew thee too well —
Long, long shall I rue[6] thee,
   Too deeply to tell.

In secret we met —
   In silence I grieve,

That thy heart could forget,
  Thy spirit deceive.
If I should meet thee
  After long years,
How should I greet thee? —
  With silence and tears.

Notes

1. The metrical movement of this poem is basically a combination of iambic and anapestic feet, with a rhyme scheme *ababcdcd*.
2. **sever**: separate.
3. **this**: this moment.
4. **light**: of small account.
5. **wert**: were.
6. **rue**: to be sorry for.

Study Questions

1. Who is the speaker? What does the poem reveal about the speaker's character?
2. By what particular event is the poem occasioned?
3. Is the speaker addressing a particular person? If so, who is that person, and why is the speaker interested in him or her?
4. What is your response to the poem on first reading?

4.5 Percy Bysshe Shelley

4.5.1 About the Author

Percy Bysshe Shelley (1792-1822) was born into a wealthy family near Horsham in Sussex. He was a delicate child, shy, sensitive, elflike, who wandered through the woods near his home. As a student in Eton, he was known for his radical views on politics and religion, earning the nickname "Mad Shelley". At 18, he attended Oxford University, where he read radical authors like Thomas Paine and William Godwin. A year later, he was expelled for publishing a pamphlet called *The Necessity of Atheism*. Shortly after his expulsion, Shelley eloped with Harriet Westbrook, a young girl of sixteen, and a marriage was soon followed. The pair spent the following two years traveling in England and Ireland, distributing pamphlets and speaking against political injustice. Three years later Shelley separated with his wife and fell in love with Mary Wollstonecraft Godwin. In December 1816,

Shelley married Mary just a few weeks after Harriet had drowned herself. In 1818, Shelley and Mary left England for good. In the following years, they lived a wandering life in Italy, where they saw much of Lord Byron. While on a short voyage along the Italian coast, Shelley's small sailboat was caught in a storm. He drowned on July 8, 1822.

Shelley was always interested in political and philosophic ideas. He was amongst the first of his class to consider the rights of the working man and the equality of the sexes. He drew no essential distinction between poetry and politics, and his works reflected the radical ideas and revolutionary optimism of the era. Throughout his life, his major creative effort was concentrated on producing a series of long poems and poetic dramas aimed at the main political and spiritual problems of his age. The best examples are: *Queen Mab* (1813), *The Revolt of Islam* (1818), *The Cenci* (1819), *Prometheus Unbound* (1819) and *Adonais* (1821). He also wrote sonnets, satires, odes, allegories and hymns. Shelley was a writer who moved with a sense of ulterior motive, a sense of greater design, a strong feeling for the historical moment, and overwhelming consciousness of his duty as an artist. His poetic quality was a delicate and ethereal lyricism unsurpassed in the literature of the world.

4.5.2 "A Song: 'Men of England'[1]"

Men of England, wherefore plough
For the lords who lay ye low?
Wherefore weave with toil and care
The rich robes your tyrants wear?

Wherefore feed and clothe and save
From the cradle to the grave
Those ungrateful drones[2] who would
Drain your sweat — nay, drink your blood?

Wherefore, Bees of England[3], forge
Many a weapon, chain, and scourge,
That these stingless drones may spoil
The forced produce of your toil[4]?

Have ye leisure, comfort, calm,
Shelter, food, love's gentle balm?
Or what is it ye buy so dear
With your pain and with your fear?[5]

The seed ye sow, another reaps;
The wealth ye find, another keeps;
The robes ye weave, another wears;
The arms ye forge, another bears.

Sow seed — but let no tyrant reap;
Find wealth — let no impostor heap;
Weave robes — let not the idler wear;
Forge arms — in your defense to bear.

Shrink to your cellars, holes, and cells —
In halls ye deck another dwells.
Why shake the chains ye wrought? when see
The steel ye tempered glance on ye[6].

With plough and spade and hoe and loom
Trace your grave and build your tomb
And weave your winding-sheet — till fair
England be your Sepulcher.[7]

Notes

1. This poem was written in 1819, the year of the Peterloo Massacre. It is unquestionably one of Shelley's greatest political lyrics. It is not only a war-cry calling upon all working people of England to rise up against their political oppressors, but also an address to point out to them the intolerable injustice of economic exploitation.
2. **drones**: male honey-bees that do not work. Here it refers to the parasitic class in human society.
3. **Bees of England**: referring here to the laboring people in England.
4. **The forced produce of your toil**: The products of your labor which are produced under compulsion.
5. **Or what is it ye buy so dear /With your pain and with your fear**? What is the recompense you obtain at the high price of your sufferings and anxieties?
6. **The steel ye tempered glance on ye**: The sword you forged is flashed in your face.
7. The last two stanzas of the poem are ironically addressed to those workers who submit passively to capitalist exploitation. They serve as a warning to the working people: if they give up their struggle they would be digging graves for themselves with their own hands. Compared to the preceding stanzas, these lines appear weak and ineffectual.

Study Questions

1. Who exactly are the "Men of England"?
2. How is the poet criticizing the upper class attitude towards the "Men of England"?
3. How does Shelley show his mounting anger?
4. What is the political message of the poem?

4.5.3 "Ozymandias[1]"

I met a traveller from an antique land
Who said: Two vast and trunkless legs of stone
Stand in the desert... Near them, on the sand,
Half sunk, a shattered visage lies, whose frown,
And wrinkled lip, and sneer of cold command,
Tell that its sculptor well those passions read
Which yet survive, stamped on these lifeless things.
The hand that mocked them[2] and the heart that fed:[3]
And on the pedestal these words appear:
"My name is Ozymandias, king of kings:
Look on my works, ye Mighty, and despair!"
Nothing beside remains. Round the decay
Of that colossal wreck, boundless and bare,
The lone and level sands stretch far away.

Notes

1. **Ozymandias**: the Greek name for Ramses Ⅱ, the pharaoh who ruled Egypt during the 13th century BC. During his rule Ramses Ⅱ conducted an extensive building program and was responsible for the largest statue in Egypt, which bore the inscription: "I am Ozymandias, king of kings; if anyone wishes to know what I am and where I lie, let him surpass me in some of my exploits." Ramses Ⅱ was also known as the pharaoh who oppressed the Israelites. Shelley — always an ardent challenger of oppression — depicts the ironical outcome of the pharaoh's legacy in this sonnet.
2. **The hand that mocked them**: The sculptor's hand that "mocked" (imitated and ridiculed) the ruler's passions.
3. **the heart that fed**: the king's heart which has "fed" his passions.

Study Questions

1. What form of irony is at work in this poem? How is the use of the word "despair" (line 11) itself ironic?
2. What figure of speech describes the poet's use of "hand" and "heart" (line 8)?
3. What are the connotations of the word "pedestal" (line 9)?

4. What idea or experience is the poet articulating in this poem?

4.5.4 "Ode to the West Wind"

I

O wild West Wind, thou breath of Autumn's being
Thou, from whose unseen presence the leaves dead
Are driven, like ghosts from an enchanter fleeing,

Yellow, and black, and pale, and hectic[1] red,
Pestilence-stricken multitudes:[2] O thou,
Who chariotest to their dark wintry bed

The wingèd seeds, where they lie cold and low,
Each like a corpse within its grave, until
Thine azure sister[3] of the Spring shall blow

Her clarion[4] o'er the dreaming earth, and fill
(Driving sweet buds like flocks to feed in air)
With living hues and odours plain and hill:

Wild Spirit, which art moving everywhere;
Destroyer and Preserver; hear, O hear!

II

Thou on whose stream, 'mid the steep sky's commotion,[5]
Loose clouds like earth's decaying leaves are shed,
Shook from the tangled boughs of Heaven and Ocean,[6]

Angels[7] of rain and lightning: there are spread
On the blue surface of thine aery surge,
Like the bright hair uplifted from the head

Of some fierce Mænad,[8] even from the dim verge
Of the horizon to the zenith's height,
The locks of the approaching storm. Thou Dirge

Of the dying year, to which this closing night
Will be the dome of a vast sepulcher,

Vaulted with all thy congregated might

Of vapours, from whose solid atmosphere
Black rain and fire and hail, will burst: O hear!

III

Thou who didst waken from his summer dreams
The blue Mediterranean, where he lay,
Lulled by the coil of his crystalline streams,[9]

Beside a Pumice[10] Isle in Baise's bay,[11]
And saw in sleep old palaces and towers
Quivering within the wave's intenser day,

All overgrown with azure moss and flowers
So sweet, the sense faints picturing them![12] Thou
For whose path the Atlantic's level powers

Cleave themselves into chasms, while far below
The sea-blooms and the oozy woods which wear
The sapless foliage of the ocean, know

Thy voice, and suddenly grow gray with fear,
And tremble and despoil themselves:[13] O hear!

IV

If I were a dead leaf thou mightest bear;
If I were a swift cloud to fly with thee;
A wave to pant beneath thy power, and share

The impulse of thy strength, only less free
Than thou, O Uncontrollable! If even
I were as in my boyhood, and could be

The comrade of thy wanderings over Heaven,
As then, when to outstrip thy skiey speed
Scarce seemed a vision; I would ne'er have striven

As thus with thee in prayer in my sore need.

Oh! lift me as a wave, a leaf, a cloud!
I fall upon the thorns of life! I bleed!

A heavy weight of hours has chained and bowed
One too like thee: tameless, and swift, and proud.

V

Make me thy lyre,[14] even as the forest is:
What if my leaves are falling like its own!
The tumult of thy mighty harmonies

Will take from both a deep, autumnal tone,
Sweet though in sadness. Be thou, Spirit fierce,
My spirit! Be thou me, impetuous one!

Drive my dead thoughts over the universe
Like withered leaves, to quicken a new birth!
And, by the incantation of this verse,

Scatter, as from an unextinguished hearth
Ashes and sparks, my words among mankind!
Be through my lips to unawakened Earth

The trumpet of a prophecy! O Wind,
If Winter comes, can Spring be far behind?

Notes

1. **hectic**: relating to the reddening of the face caused by the kind of fever which occurs in tuberculosis.
2. **Pestilence-stricken multitudes**: The leaves are like human beings hit by epidemic disease.
3. **thine azure sister**: refers to the west wind that will blow in the spring.
4. **clarion**: sound of a trumpet.
5. **'mid the steep sky's commotion**: in the midst of the great turbulence high up in the sky.
6. **tangled boughs of Heaven and Ocean**: a metaphorical representation of the manners in which the line between the sky and stormy sea is indistinguishable, the whole space from the horizon to the zenith being covered with trailing storm cloud.
7. **angels**: messengers, here it refers to the "clouds".

8. **Mænad**: a female worshiper of Dionysus (Bacchus), the Greek god of wine and vegetation. As vegetation god, he was fabled to die in autumn and to be reborn in spring.
9. **the coil of his crystalline streams**: The currents that flow in the Mediterranean Sea, sometimes with a visible difference in color.
10. **Pumice Isle**: an isle near Naples, Italy, formed by deposits of lava from a volcano.
11. **Baise's bay**: a favorite resort of the ancient Romans, near Naples.
12. **the sense faints picturing them**: seeing the images so beautiful one feel faint to describe them.
13. **And tremble and despoil themselves**: (Shelley's note) The vegetation at the bottom of the sea sympathizes with that of the land in the change of seasons.
14. **lyre**: refers to the Aeolian harp, a stringed instrument that produces musical sounds when the wind passes over it.

Study Questions
1. Whom and what is being addressed in this poem?
2. What does the speaker ask of the addressee at the very end of stanzas 1, 2, and 3?
3. What does wind signify in this ode? How is it used symbolically?
4. On what natural object does the wind's power show itself in stanza 1? In stanza 2? In stanza 3?
5. What is the speaker's present situation, as revealed in lines 54-56?
6. What does the speaker ask for in line 57?
7. Why is the west wind referred to as "Destroyer and preserver"?
8. How does the speaker in stanza 4 compare himself to the wind in terms of power and freedom?

4.6 John Keats

4.6.1 About the Author

John Keats (1795-1821) was born in London, and he was the first son of a livery-stable keeper. When Keats was eight years old, his father died. Later on, Keats was sent to a nearby school where his literary interests were encouraged by his teacher, Cowden Clarke. When he was fourteen, his mother died of tuberculosis. After he left school at the age of 16, Keats was apprenticed to a surgeon for four years. During this time his interest in poetry grew. He wrote his first poems in 1814 and passed his medical examinations in 1816. He became an enthusiastic disciple of the literary and political radical, Leigh Hunt and gave up his medical profession in favor of poetry. In 1817, Keats published his first book of poems, which was harshly criticized by the influential Blackwood's Magazine.

1818 was in many ways the most eventful year of his life: his brother George married and moved to America; in the summer, he went on a walking tour of the Lake district and Scotland with his friend Charles Brown; in the fall, he met Fanny Brawne, the great love of his life, while at the same time he was nursing his brother Tom, who died in December. During the following year, despite ill health and financial problems, he wrote an astonishing amount of poetry, including "The Eve of St Agnes", "La Belle Dame sans Merci", and his great odes. At the beginning of 1820 Keats started to show more pronounced signs of the deadly tuberculosis that had killed his mother and brother. In September of 1820 Keats sailed to Rome to seek a warm climate for the winter. He died there on February 23, 1821, and was buried in the Protestant cemetery.

Keats is one of the most important figures of the early nineteenth-century Romanticism. His poetry is distinctive for its sensual description, physical concreteness, colorful imagery, and closely-knit construction. The beauty of nature, the relation between imagination and creativity, the response of the passions to beauty and suffering, and the transience of human life in time always lie in the center of his poetic concerns. Thus, he is highly praised for his seriousness and thoughtfulness, for his dealing with difficult human conflicts and artistic issues, and for his impassioned mental pursuit of truth.

4.6.2 "To Autumn[1]"

1

Season of mists and mellow fruitfulness,
   Close bosom friend of the maturing sun;
Conspiring with him how to load and bless
   With fruit the vines that round the thatch-eaves run;
To bend with apples the moss'd cottage-trees,
   And fill all fruit with ripeness to the core;
     To swell the gourd, and plump the hazel shells
With a sweet kernel; to set budding more,
And still more, later flowers for the bees,
Until they think warm days will never cease,
   For Summer has o'er-brimm'd their clammy cells.

2

Who hath not seen thee oft amid thy store?
   Sometimes whoever seeks abroad may find
Thee sitting careless on a granary floor,

Thy hair soft-lifted by the winnowing[2] wind;
Or on a half-reap'd furrow sound asleep,
    Drows'd with the fume of poppies, while thy hook[3]
      Spares the next swath and all its twined flowers:
And sometimes like a gleaner thou dost keep
    Steady thy laden head across a brook;
    Or by a cider-press, with patient look,
      Thou watchest the last oozings hours by hours.

3

Where are the songs of spring? Ay, where are they?
    Think not of them, thou hast thy music too, —
While barred clouds bloom the soft-dying day,
    And touch the stubble-plains with rosy hue;
Then in a wailful choir the small gnats mourn
    Among the river sallows[4], borne aloft
      Or sinking as the light wind lives or dies;
And full-grown lambs loud bleat from hilly bourn[5];
    Hedge-crickets sing; and now with treble soft
    The red-breast whistles from a garden-croft[6];
      And gathering swallows twitter in the skies.

Notes

1. Two days after the poem was composed, Keats wrote to J. H. Reynolds: " I never liked stubble fields so much as now — Aye, better than the chilly green of the spring. Somehow a stubble plain looks warm — in the same way that some pictures look warm — this struck me so much in my Sunday's walk that I composed upon it."
2. **winnowing**: blowing; also, the fanning process by which the wheat chaff is separated from the grain.
3. **hook**: scythe.
4. **sallows**: willows.
5. **bourn**: region.
6. **croft**: A croft is an enclosed plot of farm land.

Study Questions

1. Please cite three instances in which the spirit of autumn is personified as a farm girl.
2. What sights are evoked at lines 25-26 to picture autumn's beauty? What autumn sounds are mentioned in the last seven lines of the final stanza?
3. What doe Keats suggest about autumn's beauty and about the cyclic pattern of nature?

4. What examples of tactile imagery — imagery that appeals to the sense of touch — do you find in this poem?

4.6.3 "Ode on a Grecian Urn[1]"

1

Thou still unravished bride of quietness,
   Thou foster-child of silence and slow time,
Sylvan historian,[2] who canst thus express
   A flowery tale more sweetly than our rhyme:
What leaf-fringed legend haunts about thy shape
    Of deities or mortals, or of both,
      In Tempe[3] or the dales of Arcady?[4]
    What men or gods are these? What maidens loth?[5]
What mad pursuit? What struggle to escape?
    What pipes and timbrels?[6] What wild ecstasy?

2

Heard melodies are sweet, but those unheard
   Are sweeter; therefore, ye soft pipes, play on;
Not to the sensual[7] ear, but, more endeared,
   Pipe to the spirit ditties of no tone:
Fair youth, beneath the trees, thou canst not leave
    Thy song, nor ever can those trees be bare;
      Bold Lover, never, never canst thou kiss,
Though winning near the goal — yet, do not grieve;
      She cannot fade, though thou hast not thy bliss,
    For ever wilt thou love, and she be fair!

3

Ah, happy, happy boughs! that cannot shed
   Your leaves, nor ever bid the spring adieu;[8]
And, happy melodist, unwearied,
   For ever piping songs for ever new;
More happy love! more happy, happy love!
    For ever warm and still to be enjoyed,
      For ever panting, and for ever young;
All breathing human passion far above,
    That leaves a heart high-sorrowful and cloyed,
      A burning forehead, and a parching tongue.[9]

4

Who are these coming to the sacrifice?
  To what green altar, O mysterious priest,
Lead'st thou that heifer[10] lowing at the skies,
  And all her silken flanks with garlands drest?
What little town by river or sea shore,
  Or mountain-built with peaceful citadel,[11]
    Is emptied of this folk, this pious morn?
And, little town, thy streets for evermore
  Will silent be; and not a soul to tell
    Why thou art desolate, can e'er return.

5

O Attic shape![12] Fair attitude! with brede[13]
  Of marble men and maidens overwrought,[14]
With forest branches and the trodden weed;
  Thou, silent form, dost tease us out of thought
As doth eternity: Cold Pastoral![15]
  When old age shall this generation waste,
    Thou shalt remain, in midst of other woe
Than ours, a friend to man, to whom thou say'st,
"Beauty is truth, truth beauty," — that is all
  Ye know on earth, and all ye need to know.

Notes

1. **Urn**: This urn, with its sculptured reliefs of Dionysian ecstasies, panting young lovers in flight and pursuit, a pastoral piper under spring foliage, and the quiet celebration of communal pieties, resembles parts of various vases, sculptures, and paintings; but it existed in all its particulars only in Keats's imagination. In the urn — which captures moments of intense experience in attitudes of grace and freezes them into marble immobility — Keats found the perfect correlative for his persistent concern with the longing for permanence in a world of change.
2. **Sylvan historian**: Sylvan means rustic, representing a woodland scene. Here "Sylvan historian" refers to the urn telling a pastoral tale.
3. **Tempe**: a beautiful valley in Greece, regarded as sacred to Apollo, the God of poetry.
4. **Arcady**: an ancient place in Greece, often used as a symbol of the pastoral ideal.
5. **loth**: unwilling.
6. **timbrels**: tambourines or similar instruments.
7. **sensual**: pertaining to the physical senses, in this case, hearing.
8. **nor ever bid the spring adieu**: Spring will forever stay with them; "adieu" means good

bye.

9. **All breathing human passion far above... and a parching tongue**: the young lovers on the urn and their love are far above the agony of human passion. Here "cloyed" means to annoy somebody because there is too much of it.
10. **heifer**: young cow.
11. **citadel**: fortress on high ground overlooking and protecting a town or city.
12. **Attic shape**: displaying the simple, graceful style characteristic of Attica, or Athens.
13. **brede**: a braided or inter-wound design.
14. **overwrought**: with the surface decorated.
15. **Cold Pastoral**: the pastoral scene is carried by the urn which lacks life and warmth.

Study Questions
1. Identify details of the scene that is described in stanzas 1 and 2?
2. What the other scene in stanza 4 is presented?
3. What does the speaker think about the changelessness of art, which is made clear by the piper who cannot sound his tune, by the trees that cannot shed their leaves, and by the lover who cannot kiss his beloved? How does actual human life compare to life as captured by art?
4. Explain the note of sadness introduced in stanza 4. How does the effect of art here contrast with the effect of art in stanza 2 and 3?

Essay Topics
1. Why art is so appealing to the speaker in spite of some negative qualities?
2. Why should we seek an ideal in spite of our human limitations?

4.7 Jane Austen

4.7.1 About the Author

Jane Austen (1775-1817) was born into a middle-class family in Hampshire, England. She was one of eight children of a clergyman and grew up in a close-knit family. Her father was a rector and a scholar with a good library. Jane had almost no formal education, but she had a wide reading in her father's library. She acquired a thorough knowledge of English eighteenth-century literature. She lived a quiet, retired and uneventful life, though she did move to several places like Bath, Southampton and Chawton. Her lifelong companion and confidant was her older and only sister, Cassandra, who, like her, never got married. She loved the country, enjoyed long country walks, and had many friends in Hampshire. She started to write novels for

family amusement when she was a child. Her works were later published anonymously due to the prejudice against women writers then. She died in Winchester in 1817.

Austen had two periods of busy and fruitful writing. The first lasted from 1795 to 1798. During this time she wrote the first versions of *Sense and Sensibility* (1811), *Pride and Prejudice* (1813), and *Northanger Abbey* (1818). Her second important period of writing lasted from 1811 to 1816, when her works first received public recognition and she deepened her mastery of her subjects and form. In this later period she revised and prepared her early works for publication, and wrote her last three completed novels: *Mansfield Park* (1814), *Emma*(1815) and *Persuasion* (1818).

As a novelist, Austen focused on middle-class provincial life. She depicted minor landed gentry, country clergymen and their families, in which marriage mainly determined women's social status. Her works combine romantic comedy with social satire and psychological insight. She considered it her duty to express in her works a discriminated and serious criticism of life, and to expose the follies and illusions of mankind. With her interest in heredity, education, economics and social forces, she touched upon the universal patterns of human behavior in her fictional world. In style, she upheld those traditional ideas of order, reason, proportion and gracefulness in novel writing.

4.7.2 An Excerpt from *Pride and Prejudice*

Chapter 1

It is a truth universally acknowledged, that a single man in possession of a good fortune must be in want of a wife.

However little known the feelings or views of such a man may be on his first entering a neighborhood, this truth is so well fixed in the minds of the surrounding families, that he is considered as the rightful property of some one or other of their daughters.

"My dear Mr. Bennet," said his lady[1] to him one day, "have you heard that Netherfield Park[2] is let at last?"

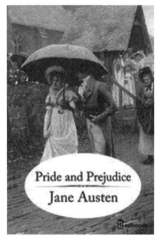

Mr. Bennet replied that he had not.

"But it is," returned she; "for Mrs. Long[3] has just been here, and she told me all about it."

Mr. Bennet made no answer.

"Do not you want to know who has taken it?" cried his wife impatiently.

"You want to tell me, and I have no objection to hearing it."

This was invitation enough.[4]

"Why, my dear, you must know. Mrs. Long says that Netherfield is taken by a young man of large fortune from the north of England; that he came down on Monday in a chaise and four[5] to see the place, and was so much delighted with it that he agreed with Mr. Morris[6] immediately; that he is to take possession before Michaelmas[7], and some of his servants are to be in the house by the end of next week."

"What is his name?"

"Bingley."

"Is he married or single?"

"Oh! single, my dear, to be sure! A single man of large fortune; four or five thousand a year[8]. What a fine thing for our girls!"

"How so? how can it affect them?"

"My dear Mr. Bennet," replied his wife, "how can you be so tiresome! You must know that I am thinking of his marrying one of them."

"Is that his design in settling here?"

"Design! nonsense, how can you talk so! But it is very likely that he *may* fall in love with one of them, and therefore you must visit him as soon as he comes."

"I see no occasion for that[9]. You and the girls may go, or you may send them by themselves, which perhaps will be still better; for, as you are as handsome as any of them, Mr. Bingley might like you the best of the party."

"My dear, you flatter me[10]. I certainly *have* had my share of beauty, but I do not pretend to be any thing extraordinary now. When a woman has five grown up daughters, she ought to give over thinking of her own beauty."

"In such cases, a woman has not often much beauty to think of."

"But, my dear, you must indeed go and see Mr. Bingley when he comes into the neighborhood."

"It is more than I engage for[11], I assure you."

"But consider your daughters. Only think what an establishment it would be for one of them. Sir William and Lady Lucas[12] are determined to go, merely on that account, for in general, you know, they visit no new comers. Indeed you must go, for it will be impossible for us to visit him, if you do not."

"You are over-scrupulous, surely. I dare say Mr. Bingley will be very glad to see you; and I will send a few lines by you to assure him of my hearty consent to his marrying which ever he chooses of the girls; though I must throw in a good word for my little Lizzy[13]."

"I desire you will do no such thing. Lizzy is not a bit better than the others; and I am sure she is not half so handsome as Jane, nor half so good humored as Lydia. But you are always giving *her* the preference."

"They have none of them much to recommend them," replied he; "they are all silly and ignorant like other girls; but Lizzy has something more of quickness than her sisters."

"Mr. Bennet, how can you abuse your own children in such a way? You take delight in vexing me. You have no compassion on my poor nerves."

"You mistake me, my dear. I have a high respect for your nerves. They are my old friends. I have heard you mention them with consideration these twenty years at least."

"Ah! you do not know what I suffer."

"But I hope you will get over it, and live to see many young men of four thousand a year come into the neighborhood."

"It will be no use to us if twenty such should come, since you will not visit them."

"Depend upon it[14], my dear, that when there are twenty I will visit them all."

Mr. Bennet was so odd a mixture of quick parts[15], sarcastic humor, reserve, and caprice, that the experience of three and twenty years had been insufficient to make his wife understand his character. *Her* mind was less difficult to develop. She was a woman of mean understanding, little information, and uncertain temper. When she was discontented, she fancied herself nervous. The business of her life was to get her daughters married; its solace was visiting and news[16].

Chapter 2

Mr. Bennet was among the earliest of those who waited on[17] Mr. Bingley. He had always intended to visit him, though to the last always assuring his wife that he should not go; and till the evening after the visit was paid, she had no knowledge of it. It was then disclosed in the following manner. Observing his second daughter employed in trimming a hat, he suddenly addressed her with,

"I hope Mr. Bingley will like it, Lizzy."

"We are not in a way to know what Mr. Bingley likes," said her mother resentfully, "since we are not to visit."

"But you forget, mama," said Elizabeth, "that we shall meet him at the assemblies[18], and that Mrs. Long has promised to introduce him."

"I do not believe Mrs. Long will do any such thing. She has two nieces of her own. She is a selfish, hypocritical woman, and I have no opinion of her."

"No more have I," said Mr. Bennet; "and I am glad to find that you do not depend on her serving you."

Mrs. Bennet deigned not to make any reply; but unable to contain herself, began scolding one of her daughters.

"Don't keep coughing so, Kitty[19], for heaven's sake! Have a little compassion on my nerves. You tear them to pieces."

"Kitty has no discretion in her coughs," said her father; "she times them ill[20]."

"I do not cough for my own amusement," replied Kitty fretfully.

"When is your next ball to be, Lizzy?"

"Tomorrow fortnight[21]."

"Aye, so it is, " cried her mother, "and Mrs. Long does not come back till the day before; so it will be impossible for her to introduce him, for she will not know him herself. "

"Then, my dear, you may have the advantage of your friend, and introduce Mr. Bingley to *her*. "

"Impossible, Mr. Bennet, impossible, when I am not acquainted with him myself; how can you be so teasing?"

"I honor your circumspection. A fortnight's acquaintance is certainly very little. One cannot know what a man really is by the end of a fortnight. But if we do not venture[22], somebody else will; and after all, Mrs. Long and her nieces must stand their chance; and therefore, as she will think it an act of kindness, if you decline the office, I will take it on myself. "

The girls stared at their father. Mrs. Bennet said only, "Nonsense, nonsense!"

"What can be the meaning of that emphatic exclamation?" cried he. "Do you consider the forms of introduction, and the stress that is laid on them, as nonsense? I cannot quite agree with you *there*. What you say, Mary? for you are a young lady of deep reflection I know, read great books and make extracts. "

Mary wished to say something very sensible, but knew not how.

"While Mary is adjusting her ideas, " he continued, "let us return to Mr. Bingley. "

"I am sick of Mr. Bingley, " cried his wife.

"I am sorry to hear *that*; but why did not you tell me so before? If I had known as much this morning[23], I certainly would not have called on him. It is very unlucky; but as I have actually paid the visit, we cannot escape the acquaintance now. "

The astonishment of the ladies was just what he wished; that of Mrs. Bennet perhaps surpassing the rest; though when the first tumult of joy was over, she began to declare that it was what she had expected all the while.

"How good it was in you, my dear Mr. Bennet! But I knew I should persuade you at last. I was sure you loved our girls too well to neglect such an acquaintance. Well, how pleased I am! and it is such a good joke, too, that you should have gone this morning, and never said a word about it till now. "

"Now, Kitty, you may cough as much as you choose, " said Mr. Bennet; and, as he spoke, he left the room, fatigued with the raptures of his wife.

"What an excellent father you have, girls, " said she, when the door was shut. "I do not know how you will ever make him amend for his kindness; or me either[24], for that matter. At our time of life, it is not so pleasant I can tell you, to be making new acquaintance every day; but for your sakes, we would do any thing. Lydia, my love, though you are the youngest, I dare say Mr. Bingley will dance with you at the next ball. "

"Oh!" said Lydia stoutly, "I am not afraid; for though I am the youngest, I'm the tallest."

The rest of the evening was spent in conjecturing how soon he would return Mr. Bennet's visit, and determining when they should ask him to dinner.

Notes

1. **his lady**: Here refers to Mrs. Bennet.
2. **Netherfield Park**: the name of a land estate in the neighborhood of the Bennets.
3. **Mrs. Long**: a neighbor of the Bennets.
4. **This was invitation enough**: This was enough to encourage Mrs. Bennet to tell.
5. **a chaise and four**: a light carriage driven by four horses.
6. **Mr. Morris**: the landlord of Netherfield Park.
7. **Michaelmas**: a festival celebrated on September 29th in honor of Michael, one of the seven archangels in Christian legend.
8. **four or five thousand a year**: Here it means an income of four or five thousand pounds a year.
9. **see no occasion for that**: see no reason or need for that.
10. **you flatter me**: a polite reply to a compliment. Here Mrs. Bennet does not see the ironical meaning in the remark of her husband.
11. **It is more than I engage for**: It is more than I promise to do.
12. **Sir William and Lady Lucas**: a neighboring couple.
13. **Lizzy**: (shortened form for Elizabeth) the second daughter of the Bennets.
14. **depend upon it**: There can be no doubt about it; you may be sure of it.
15. **quick parts**: Here "parts" in the plural form is used in the archaic sense of "abilities", "intelligence".
16. **Its solace was visiting and news**: The comfort of her life is to visit her neighbors and gossip with them about trivial things.
17. **waited on**: called on.
18. **the assemblies**: the balls; the dance parties.
19. **Kitty**: (shortened form for Catherine) the fourth daughter of the Bennets.
20. **she times them ill**: she coughs at the wrong time.
21. **Tomorrow fortnight**: the day after two weeks, i.e., fifteen days hence.
22. **But if we do not venture**: But if we do not venture to introduce Mr. Bingley to her.
23. **If I had known as much this morning**: If I had known this morning that you were sick of Mr. Bingley.
24. **or me either**: or make me amends either.

Study Questions

1. What does the opening sentence of the novel mean? What is the view of marriage that it suggests?

2. Why does Mrs. Bennet insist that her husband call on the new arrival immediately? Why does Mr. Bennet pretend to have no interest in doing so?
3. How do Mrs. Bennet and her daughters react when Mr. Bennet reveals that he has made their new neighbor's acquaintance?
4. How would you describe the marriage between Mr. and Mrs. Bennet after reading chapter one and two?

Essay Topics

1. What examples of humor do you find in *Pride and Prejudice*? What does this humor suggest about the tone of the novel?
2. How does Jane Austen use irony? Find examples in her novels.
3. Discuss the importance of dialogue to character development in the novel.
4. What was the political and social status of women during Jane Austen's time?

Chapter 5 The Victorian Period

5.1 An Introduction

The Victorian Age of English literature ran from 1837 when Queen Victoria took the throne, to 1901 when she died. It is an extremely diverse and contradictory age. On the one hand, it is a time of dramatic change, broad imperial expansion, great political reform and tremendous scientific progress; on the other hand, it is a time of cruel exploitation, social injustice and desperate poverty. While the wealth of the middle class increased, the lower class, thrown off their land and into the cities to form the great urban working class, lived ever more wretchedly. Just as John Morley said, it was an age of "paradise for the well-to-do, a purgatory for the able, and a hell for the poor".

In the early part of the period, the Industrial Revolution, by the introduction of coal and the steam engine, had created profound economic and social changes. Hundreds of thousands of workers had migrated to industrial towns, where they made up a new kind of working class. The result of this movement was the development of horrifying slums and cramped row housing in the overcrowded cities. The Reform Bill of 1832 extended voting rights to men of the middle class but didn't solve working-class problems. So in the 1830s and 1840s, workers started the Chartist Movement, asking for better life and working conditions and also the right to vote. Although the movement declined to an end in 1848, it did bring some improvement to the welfare of the working people.

The mid-Victorian period was one of economic prosperity and relative stability. Towards the mid-nineteenth century, the nation was well ahead of others, reaching its climax of development as a world power. It had completed its shift from a way of life based on the ownership of land to a modern urban economy based on trade and manufacturing. The middle-class life was characterized by prosperity and material progress. People as a whole were trying to live up to a national spirit of earnestness, respectability and modesty. Common sense and moral propriety, which were ignored by the Romanticists, again became the predominant preoccupation in literary works.

The later part of the Victorian Period witnessed the decline of British Empire and the decay of Victorian values. Abroad, Britain was confronted with growing threats to its military and economic preeminence. At home, the Irish question remained unsolved. Conditions of the working class were still bad, though, through the century. Three reform bills gradually gave the vote to most males over the age of twenty-one. Meanwhile, the inequality between men and women prevailed, stimulating a fight for women's equality and freedom, and for their educational and employment opportunities. Radical economic theory, developed by Karl Marx and his associates, gained great force in the second half of the century. In addition, the unsettling of religious belief by new advances in science, particularly the theory of evolution and the historical study of the Bible, drew people into considerations of problems of faith and truth.

The Victorian literature speaks for an age which witnessed greater changes than any that had gone before in all the conditions of life — material comforts, scientific knowledge, and, absolutely speaking, in intellectual and spiritual enlightenment. In this period, the novel became the most widely read and the most vital and challenging expression of progressive thought. Among the famous novelists of the time were Charles Dickens, William Makepeace Thackeray, the Brontë sisters, George Eliot, Mrs. Gaskell, Thomas Hardy and Anthony Trollope. Although writing from different points of view and with different techniques, they shared one thing in common, that is, they were all concerned about the fate of the common people. They were angry with the inhuman social institutions, the decaying social morality represented by the money-worship and utilitarianism, and the wide spread misery, poverty and injustice. Their truthful picture of life and strong criticism had done much in awakening public consciousness to the social problems and in the actual improvement of the society.

Besides the novels, the Victorian age was also a great one for non-fictional prose. Famous historians, critics, scientists and essayists abounded. Thomas Carlyle, Thomas Babington Macaulay, John Henry Newman, Matthew Arnold and John Ruskin are among the best. They brought English prose to a very high level in both prose art and literary criticism.

The poets of this period were mainly characterized by their experiment with new styles and new ways of expression. Its most representative poet was Alfred Tennyson, an independent thinker and a conservative liberal, who combined harmoniously classic perfection with romantic feeling in his poetic writings. Robert Browning, standing in striking artistic contrast to Tennyson — a contrast which perhaps serves to enhance the reputation of both, is the most thoroughly vigorous and dramatic of all the great poets. Other poets like Elizabeth Browning, Matthew Arnold, Edward Fitzgerald, Dante Gabriel Rossetti and his talented sister Christina, Gerald Manley Hopkin and Algernon Charles Swinburne all made their respective attempts at poetic innovations.

An art movement indicative of this period was the Pre-Raphaelites, which included William Holman Hunt, Dante Gabriel Rossetti, Christina Rossetti and John Everett Millais. Towards the end of the century, an Aestheticism and Decadence movement grew out of the French movement of the same name. The authors of this movement encouraged experimentation and advocated the theory of "art for art's sake", totally opposing "natural" norms of morality.

The nineteenth century was the age of a truly popular theatre. English playwrights produced a large number of plays, most of which were sentimental, melodramatic and dominated by a few very powerful actors, stars who often overwhelmed the works written for them. The sparkling, witty comedies of Oscar Wilde and those of W. S.

Gilbert and Sir Arthur Sullivan were perhaps the brightest dramatic achievements of this period.

5.2 Charles Dickens

5.2.1 About the Author

Charles Dickens (1812-1870) was born in Portsmouth, a son of a petty navy office clerk. The good fortune of being sent to school at the age of nine was short-lived because his father was imprisoned for bad debt. He was sent to work in Warren's blacking factory and endured appalling conditions as well as loneliness and despair. The hardship and suffering inflicted so early upon such a sensitive boy as Charles Dickens had left an everlasting bitter remembrance in his later life. In 1824-1827, Dickens studied at Wellington House Academy, London. At the age of fifteen, he left school and entered a lawyer's office. He taught himself shorthand to get an even better job later as a reporter in Parliament. The journalistic experience not only enabled him to get acquainted with some inside knowledge of the British legal and political system, and gave him a chance to meet people of all kinds, but also laid a good foundation for his coming literary career. While working for the *Morning Chronicle*, Dickens fell in love with and married Catherine Hogarth, daughter of the *Chronicle's* music critic.

From 1833 Dickens began to write occasional sketches of London life, which were later collected and published under the title *Sketches by Boz* (1836). Soon his first novel, *The Posthumous Papers of Pickwick Club*, appeared in monthly installments, which at once lifted him into a position of fame and fortune. After this success, Dickens embarked on a full-time career as a novelist, producing work of increasing complexity at an incredible rate. Besides the 17 novels he wrote, he was editor and owner of several newspapers and magazines. He also spent much time travelling and campaigning against many of the social evils with his pamphlets and other writings. In his last years, he did a lot of recitation of his own works before the public. In 1870, this man of great heart and vitality died of overwork, leaving his last novel unfinished.

Dickens is one of the greatest writers of the Victorian Age. His novels combine brutality with fairy-tale fantasy; sharp, realistic, concrete detail with romance, farce and melodrama; the ordinary with the strange. He attacks one or more specific social evils in each: debtor's prisons, workhouses, Yorkshire School, legal fraud, capital punishment, money-worship, envy and self-righteousness disguised as religion and justice. Dickens is also a master story-teller. With his first sentence, he engages the reader's attention and holds it to the end. The settings of his stories have an extraordinary vividness, a result of years' intimacy and rich imagination. His humor and wit seem inexhaustible. Character-portrayal is the most distinguishing feature of his works. Among a vast range of various characters, marked out by some peculiar physical trait, speech or manner, are both types and individuals. In language, he is often compared with Shakespeare for his deftness with the vernacular and large vocabulary with which he brings out many a wonderful verbal picture of man and scene.

5.2.2 An Excerpt from Chapter 8 of *Great Expectations*

For such reasons I was very glad when ten o'clock came and we started for Miss Havisham[1]'s; though I was not at all at my ease regarding the manner in which I should acquit myself[2] under that lady's roof. Within a quarter of an hour we came to Miss Havisham's house, which was of old brick, and dismal, and had a great many iron bars to it. Some of the windows had been walled up; of those that remained, all the lower were rustily barred. There was a courtyard in front, and that was barred; so, we had to wait, after ringing the bell, until some one should come to open it. While we waited at the gate, I peeped in (even then Mr. Pumblechook[3] said, "And fourteen[4]?" but I pretended not to hear him), and saw that at the side of the house there was a large brewery. No brewing was going on in it, and none seemed to have gone on for a long long time.

A window was raised, and a clear voice demanded, "What name?" To which my conductor replied, "Pumblechook." The voice returned, "Quite right," and the window was shut again, and a young lady came across the courtyard, with keys in her hand.

"This," said Mr. Pumblechook, "is Pip."

"This is Pip, is it?" returned the young lady, who was very pretty and seemed very proud; "come in, Pip."

Mr. Pumblechook was coming in also, when she stopped him with the gate.

"Oh!" she said. "Did you wish to see Miss Havisham?"

"If Miss Havisham wished to see me," returned Mr. Pumblechook, discomfited[5].

"Ah!" said the girl; "but you see she don't."

She said it so finally, and in such an indiscussible way, that Mr. Pumblechook, though in a condition of ruffled dignity, could not protest. But he eyed me severely — as if I had done anything to him! — and departed with the words reproachfully delivered: "Boy! Let your behavior here be a credit unto them[6] which brought you up by hand!" I was not free from apprehension that he would come back to propound through the gate, "And sixteen[7]?" But he didn't.

My young conductress locked the gate, and we went across the courtyard. It was paved and clean, but grass was growing in every crevice. The brewery buildings had a little lane of communication with it, and the wooden gates of that lane stood open, and all the brewery beyond, stood open, away to the high enclosing wall; and all was empty and disused. The cold wind seemed to blow colder there, than outside the gate; and it made a shrill noise in howling in and out at the open sides of the brewery, like the noise of wind in the rigging of a ship at sea.

She saw me looking at it, and she said, "You could drink without hurt all the strong beer that's brewed there now, boy."

"I should think I could, miss," said I, in a shy way.

"Better not try to brew beer there now, or it would turn out sour, boy; don't you think so?"

"It looks like it, miss."

"Not that anybody means to try," she added, "for that's all done with, and the place will stand as idle as it is, till it falls. As to strong beer, there's enough of it in the cellars already, to drown the Manor House[8]."

"Is that the name of this house, miss?"

"One of its names, boy."

"It has more than one, then, miss?"

"One more. Its other name was Satis, which is Greek, or Latin, or Hebrew, or all three — or all one to me — for enough."

"Enough House," said I; "that's a curious name, miss."

"Yes," she replied; "but it meant more than it said. It meant, when it was given, that whoever had this house, could want nothing else. They must have been easily satisfied in those days, I should think. But don't loiter[9], boy."

Though she called me "boy" so often, and with a carelessness that was far from complimentary, she was of about my own age. She seemed much older than I[10], of course, being a girl, and beautiful and self-possessed; and she was as scornful of me as if she had been one-and-twenty, and a queen.

We went into the house by a side door — the great front entrance had two chains across it outside — and the first thing I noticed was, that the passages were all dark, and that she had left a candle burning there. She took it up, and we went through more passages and up a staircase, and still it was all dark, and only the candle lighted us.

At last we came to the door of a room, and she said, "Go in."

I answered, more in shyness than politeness, "After you, miss."

To this, she returned: "Don't be ridiculous, boy; I am not going in." And scornfully walked away, and — what was worse — took the candle with her.

This was very uncomfortable, and I was half afraid. However, the only thing to be done being to knock at the door, I knocked, and was told from within to enter. I entered, therefore, and found myself in a pretty large room, well lighted with wax candles. No glimpse of daylight was to be seen in it. It was a dressing-room, as I supposed from the furniture, though much of it was of forms and uses then quite unknown to me. But prominent in it was a draped table with a gilded looking-glass, and that I made out at first sight to be a fine lady's dressing-table.

Whether I should have made out this object so soon, if there had been no fine lady sitting at it, I cannot say. In an arm-chair, with an elbow resting on the table and her head leaning on that hand, sat the strangest lady I have ever seen, or shall ever see.

She was dressed in rich materials — satins, and lace, and silks — all of white. Her shoes were white. And she had a long white veil dependent from her hair, and she had bridal flowers in her hair, but her hair was white. Some bright jewels sparkled on her neck and on her hands, and some other jewels lay sparkling on the table. Dresses, less splendid than the dress she wore, and half-packed trunks, were scattered about. She had not quite finished dressing, for she had but one shoe on — the other was on the table near her hand — her veil was but half arranged, her watch and chain were not put on, and some lace for her bosom lay with those trinkets, and with her handkerchief, and gloves, and some flowers, and a prayer-book, all confusedly heaped about the looking-glass.

It was not in the first few moments that I saw all these things, though I saw more of them in the first moment than might be supposed. But, I saw that everything within my view which ought to be white, had been white long ago, and had lost its luster[11], and was faded and yellow. I saw that the bride within the bridal dress had withered like the dress, and like the flowers, and had no brightness left but the brightness of her sunken eyes. I saw that the dress had been put upon the rounded figure of a young woman, and that the figure upon which it now hung loose, had shrunk to skin and bone. Once, I had been taken to see some ghastly waxwork at the Fair, representing I know not what impossible personage lying in state. Once, I had been taken to one of our old marsh churches to see a skeleton in the ashes of a rich dress, that had been dug out of a vault under the church pavement. Now, waxwork and skeleton seemed to have dark eyes that moved and looked at me. I should have cried out, if I could.

"Who is it?" said the lady at the table.

"Pip, ma'am."

"Pip?"

"Mr. Pumblechook's boy, ma'am. Come — to play."

"Come nearer; let me look at you. Come close."

It was when I stood before her, avoiding her eyes, that I took note of the surrounding objects in detail, and saw that her watch had stopped at twenty minutes to nine, and that a clock in the room had stopped at twenty minutes to nine.

"Look at me," said Miss Havisham. "You are not afraid of a woman who has never seen the sun[12] since you were born?"

I regret to state that I was not afraid of telling the enormous lie comprehended in the answer "No. "

"Do you know what I touch here?" she said, laying her hands, one upon the other, on her left side.

"Yes, ma'am. " (It made me think of the young man.)

"What do I touch?"

"Your heart. "

"Broken!"

She uttered the word with an eager look, and with strong emphasis, and with a weird smile that had a kind of boast in it. Afterwards, she kept her hands there for a little while, and slowly took them away as if they were heavy.

"I am tired, " said Miss Havisham. "I want diversion, and I have done with[13] men and women. Play. "

I think it will be conceded by my most disputatious reader, that she could hardly have directed an unfortunate boy to do anything in the wide world more difficult to be done under the circumstances.

"I sometimes have sick fancies, " she went on, "and I have a sick fancy that I want to see some play. There there!" with an impatient movement of the fingers of her right hand, "play, play, play!"

For a moment, with the fear of my sister's working me before my eyes, I had a desperate idea of starting round the room in the assumed character of Mr. Pumblechook's chaise cart. But, I felt myself so unequal to the performance that I gave it up, and stood looking at Miss Havisham in what I suppose she took for a dogged manner, inasmuch as she said, when we had taken a good look at each other:

"Are you sullen and obstinate?"

"No, ma'am, I am very sorry for you, and very sorry I can't play just now. If you complain of me I shall get into trouble with my sister, so I would do it if I could; but it's so new here, and so strange, and so fine — and melancholy — . " I stopped, fearing I might say too much, or had already said it, and we took another look at each other.

Before she spoke again, she turned her eyes from me, and looked at the dress she wore, and at the dressing-table, and finally at herself in the looking-glass.

"So new to him, " she muttered, "so old to me; so strange to him, so familiar to me; so melancholy to both of us! Call Estella. "

As she was still looking at the reflection of herself, I thought she was still talking to herself, and kept quiet.

"Call Estella, " she repeated, flashing a look at me. "You can do that. Call Estella. At the door. "

To stand in the dark in a mysterious passage of an unknown house, bawling[14] Estella to a scornful young lady neither visible nor responsive, and feeling it a dreadful liberty so to roar out her name, was almost as bad as playing to order. But, she answered at last, and her light came along the dark passage like a star.

Miss Havisham beckoned her to come close, and took up a jewel from the table, and tried its effect upon her fair young bosom and against her pretty brown hair. "Your own, one day, my dear, and you will use it well. Let me see you play cards with this boy."

"With this boy? Why, he is a common laboring-boy!"

I thought I overheard Miss Havisham answer — only it seemed so unlikely — "Well? You can break his heart."

"What do you play, boy?" asked Estella of myself, with the greatest disdain.

"Nothing but beggar-my-neighbor[15], miss."

"Beggar him," said Miss Havisham to Estella. So we sat down to cards.

It was then I began to understand that everything in the room had stopped, like the watch and the clock, a long time ago. I noticed that Miss Havisham put down the jewel exactly on the spot from which she had taken it up. As Estella dealt the cards, I glanced at the dressing-table again, and saw that the shoe upon it, once white, now yellow, had never been worn. I glanced down at the foot from which the shoe was absent, and saw that the silk stocking on it, once white, now yellow, had been trodden ragged. Without this arrest of everything, this standing still of all the pale decayed objects, not even the withered bridal dress on the collapsed form could have looked so like grave-clothes, or the long veil so like a shroud[16].

So she sat, corpselike, as we played at cards; the frillings and trimmings on her bridal dress, looking like earthy paper. I knew nothing then, of the discoveries that are occasionally made of bodies buried in ancient times, which fall to powder in the moment of being distinctly seen; but, I have often thought since, that she must have looked as if the admission of the natural light of day would have struck her to dust.

"He calls the knaves, Jacks[17], this boy!" said Estella with disdain, before our first game was out. "And what coarse hands he has! And what thick boots!"

I had never thought of being ashamed of my hands before; but I began to consider them a very indifferent pair. Her contempt for me was so strong, that it became infectious, and I caught it[18].

She won the game, and I dealt. I misdealt, as was only natural, when I knew she was lying in wait[19] for me to do wrong; and she denounced me for a stupid, clumsy laboring-boy.

"You say nothing of her," remarked Miss Havisham to me, as she looked on. "She says many hard things of you, but you say nothing of her. What do you think of her?"

"I don't like to say," I stammered.

"Tell me in my ear," said Miss Havisham, bending down.

"I think she is very proud," I replied, in a whisper.

"Anything else?"

"I think she is very pretty."

"Anything else?"

"I think she is very insulting." (She was looking at me then with a look of supreme aversion.)

"Anything else?"

"I think I should like to go home."

"And never see her again, though she is so pretty?"

"I am not sure that I shouldn't like to see her again, but I should like to go home now."

"You shall go soon," said Miss Havisham aloud, "Play the game out."

Saving for the one weird smile at first, I should have felt almost sure that Miss Havisham's face could not smile. It had dropped into a watchful and brooding expression — most likely when all the things about her had become transfixed[20] — and it looked as if nothing could ever lift it up again. Her chest had dropped, so that she stooped; and her voice had dropped, so that she spoke low, and with a dead lull upon her; altogether, she had the appearance of having dropped, body and soul, within and without, under the weight of a crushing blow.

I played the game to an end with Estella, and she beggared me. She threw the cards down on the table when she had won them all, as if she despised them for having been won of me.

"When shall I have you here again?" said Miss Havisham. "Let me think."

I was beginning to remind her that today was Wednesday, when she checked me with her former impatient movement of the fingers of her right hand.

"There, there! I know nothing of days of the week; I know nothing of weeks of the year. Come again after six days. You hear?"

"Yes, ma'am."

"Estella, take him down. Let him have something to eat, and let him roam and look about him while he eats. Go, Pip."

I followed the candle down, as I had followed the candle up, and she stood it in the place where we had found it. Until she opened the side entrance, I had fancied, without thinking about it, that it must necessarily be night-time. The rush of the daylight quite confounded me, and made me feel as if I had been in the candlelight of the strange room many hours.

"You are to wait here, you boy," said Estella, and disappeared and closed the door.

I took the opportunity of being alone in the courtyard, to look at my coarse hands and my common boots. My opinion of those accessories was not favorable. They had never troubled me before, but they troubled me now, as vulgar appendage[21]. I determined to ask Joe why he had ever taught me to call those picture-cards, Jacks, which ought to be called knaves. I wished Joe had been rather more genteelly brought

Chapter 5　The Victorian Period

up, and then I should have been so too.

　　She came back, with some bread and meat and a little mug of beer. She put the mug down on the stones of the yard, and gave me the bread and meat without looking at me, as insolently as if I were a dog in disgrace. I was so humiliated, hurt, spurned, offended, angry, sorry — I cannot hit upon the right name for the smart[22]— God knows what its name was — that tears started to my eyes. The moment they sprang there, the girl looked at me with a quick delight in having been the cause of them. This gave me power to keep them back and to look at her: so, she gave a contemptuous toss — but with a sense, I thought, of having made too sure that I was so wounded — and left me.

　　But, when she was gone, I looked about me for a place to hide my face in, and got behind one of the gates in the brewery-lane, and leaned my sleeve against the wall there, and leaned my forehead on it and cried. As I cried, I kicked the wall, and took a hard twist at my hair; so bitter were my feelings, and so sharp was the smart without a name, that needed counteraction.

Notes

1. **Havisham**: an eccentric old lady who lives in seclusion with her adopted daughter, Estella. She was deserted on her wedding day, and then made it her goal in life to get revenge on men. She lives in the past, wearing her yellowing wedding dress. All the clocks in her estate are stopped on the minute she found out her fiancee left her.
2. **acquit myself**: to do something, especially something difficult, well that you do for the first time in front of other people.
3. **Mr. Pumblechook**: Pip's pompous, arrogant uncle, a merchant obsessed with money. Pumblechook is responsible for arranging Pip's first meeting with Miss Havisham.
4. **And fourteen**: Mr. Pumblechook was fond of arithmetic and kept asking Pip about arithmetic questions in the early part of this chapter. Here he asked Pip an arithmetic question again. "And fourteen" means "and fourteen times nine".
5. **discomfited**: being made to feel slightly uncomfortable, annoyed or embarrassed.
6. **them**: here referring to Pip's elder sister and his other relatives, including Mr. Pumblechook.
7. **And sixteen**: And sixteen times nine.
8. **the Manor House**: a big old house with a large area of land around it. Here it refers to Miss Havisham's residence, which is called the Satis House.
9. **loiter**: to move or travel slowly, or to keep stopping when you should keep moving.
10. **She seemed much older than I**: She appeared to be much older than I, because of her superiority in manner and knowledge.
11. **luster**: the quality that makes something interesting or exciting.
12. **a woman who has never seen the sun**: a woman who has never been out of the house.

13. **have done with**: to finish dealing with someone, and never deal with them again.
14. **bawling**: shouting loudly.
15. **beggar-my-neighbor**: a card game in which the aim is to get all your opponent's cards.
16. **shroud**: cloth in which a dead person is wrapped for burial.
17. **He calls the knaves, Jacks**: In card games, both "knave" and "jack" refer to the card with a value between the ten and queen. However, upper-class people would call it "knave" and the lower-class people would call it "jack". The two names are now interchangeable, one hopes, at any level of society.
18. **Her contempt for me was so strong, that it became infectious, and I caught it**: Estella's contempt for Pip was so strong that it infected Pip and made him show contempt for himself.
19. **was lying in wait**: was remaining in hidden in a place and waiting for someone so that you can attack them.
20. **transfixed**: unable to move because you are very shocked, frightened etc.
21. **appendage**: something that is connected to a larger or more important thing.
22. **smart**: a feeling that you have when you are upset and offended by something.

Study Questions

1. In what detail does Pip describe Miss Havisham and her room?
2. What is Pip's impression about Estella?
3. How does Estella treat Pip?
4. What experiences have made Miss Havisham as she is? Is she a believable character?

Essay Topics

1. How is the theme of social class central to the novel?
2. Discuss Estella as an example of Dickens' social commentary. This discussion should include references to her parents as well as her upbringing under Miss Havisham.

5.3 Alfred Tennyson

5.3.1 About the Author

Alfred Tennyson (1809-1892) was born at Somersby, Lincolnshire, where his father was a learned clergyman. Tennyson attended school for only four years and received the rest of his education at home. He showed an early interest and talent in poetic composition. When he entered the Trinity College, Cambridge, he was drawn to a circle of brilliant young men, known as "the Apostles". They debated all the great issues of the day, and several of the members remained close personal friends throughout Tennyson's life. In his three years at Cambridge, Tennyson began his close friendship with Arthur Henry Hallam.

In 1831, following the death of his father, Tennyson left Cambridge without taking a degree. The next year he published *Poems*, which contained a variety of poems, beautiful in melody and rich in imagery. However, it received very harsh and hostile criticism. This, together with the death of his dearest friend, Hallam, threw the young poet into deep sorrow and gloom. For nearly ten years after that, Tennyson published almost nothing. During this time he devoted himself to reading and meditation. In 1842, Tennyson published his two-volume

Poems, which won an immediate success. In 1845, he received a government pension of ￡200 a year, which helped relieve his financial difficulties. For the success of his two poems, *The Princess* and *In Memoriam H. H.*, he was appointed as Poet Laureate in 1850, which finally established him as the most popular poet of the Victorian era.

In Memoriam is an elegy on the death of Hallam. As a poetic diary, the poem is an elaborate and powerful expression of the poet's philosophical and religious thoughts — his doubts about the meaning of life, the existence of the soul and the afterlife, and his faith in the power of love and the soul's instinct and immortality. Such doubts and beliefs were shared by most people in an age when the old Christian belief was challenged by new scientific discoveries; though to most readers today, the real attraction of the poem lies more in its profound feeling and artistic beauty than in the philosophical and religious reflections. Tennyson's poetic career is also marked out by *Idylls of the King* (1842-1885), his most ambitious work which took him over 30 years to complete. It is made up of 12 books, based on the Celtic legends of King Arthur and his *Knights of the Round Table*.

Tennyson is a real artist. He has a sensitive ear, an excellent choice and taste of words. He also has the natural power of linking visual pictures with musical expressions. His poetry is rich in poetic images and melodious language, and noted for its lyrical beauty and metrical charm. His works are not only the products of the creative imagination of a poetic genius but also the products of a long and rich English heritage.

5.3.2 "Break, Break, Break"[1]

Break, break, break,
   On thy cold gray stones, O Sea!
And I would[2] that my tongue could utter
   The thoughts that arise in me.
O, well for[3] the fisherman's boy,
   That he shouts with his sister at play!

O, well for the sailor lad,
   That he sings in his boat on the bay!
And the stately[4] ships go on
   To their haven[5] under the hill;
But O for the touch of a vanished hand[6],
   And the sound of a voice that is still[7]!
Break, break, break,
   At the foot of thy crags, O Sea!
But the tender grace of a day[8] that is dead
   Will never come back to me.

Notes

1. This short lyric is written in memory of Tennyson's best friend, Arthur Hallam, whose death has a life-long influence on the poet. Here, the poet's own feelings of sadness are contrasted with the carefree, innocent joys of the children and the unfeeling movement of the ship and the sea waves. The beauty of the lyric is to be found in the musical language and in the association of sound and images with feelings and emotions. The poem contains four quatrains, with combined iambic and anapestic feet. Most lines have three feet and some four. The rhyme scheme is *abcb*.
2. **I would**: I wish.
3. **O, well for**: O, it would be well for; in a double sense, that is, it is well for him, but not for me.
4. **stately**: the power of this adjective in its context is that the ships, though stately and dignified, are vulnerable.
5. **haven**: harbor.
6. **a vanished hand**: the hand of his friend who has vanished.
7. **a voice that is still**: the voice of his friend can no longer be heard.
8. **the tender grace of a day**: the loving kindness of the day when I was enjoying your company.

Study Questions

1. Why couldn't the speaker utter his thoughts that arise in him?
2. How does the speaker contrast himself with the fisherman's boy and the sailor lad?
3. Why do the pleasant sights often make the speaker sad?
4. What is the function of repetition used in this poem?

5.3.3 "Crossing the Bar"[1]

Sunset and evening star,[2]
   And one clear call for me!

And may there be no moaning of the bar[3],
    When I put out to sea,
But such a tide as moving seems asleep,
    Too full for sound and foam,
When that[4] which drew from out the boundless deep
    Turns again home.
Twilight and evening bell,
    And after that the dark!
And may there be no sadness of farewell,
    When I embark;
For though from out our bourne[5] of Time and Place
    The flood may bear me far,
I hope to see my Pilot[6] face to face
    When I have crossed the bar.

Notes

1. This poem was written in the later years of Tennyson's life. We can feel his fearlessness towards death, his faith in God and an afterlife. *Bar*, a bank of sand or stones under the water as in a river, parallel to the shore, at the entrance to a harbor. "Crossing the bar" means leaving this world and entering the next world.
2. **sunset**, **evening star**, **twilight**, **evening bell** are all images of the end of life.
3. **moaning of the bar**: mournful sound of the ocean beating on a sand bar at the mouth of a harbor.
4. **that**: Here it refers to the soul.
5. **bourne**: boundary.
6. **Pilot**: Here it refers to God.

Study Questions

1. With what hopes does the speaker bid the world farewell?
2. What does Tennyson actually mean by "crossing the bar"?
3. In what way does the poem express a consolation to those the speaker leaves behind?
4. How would you characterize the death that the speaker is wishing for?

5.3.4 *The Eagle*[1]

He clasps the crag with crooked hands;
Close to the sun in lonely lands,
Ringed with the azure world, he stands.

> The wrinkled sea beneath him crawls;
> He watches from his mountain walls,
> And like a thunderbolt he falls.

Notes

The stanza patterns in this poem are called a tercet. In the iambic rhythm there are six tetrametric lines. The poem has a rhyme scheme of *aaabbb*.

Study Questions

1. What is the interesting contrast between the two stanzas?
2. What is the theme of this poem?
3. What figures of speech are used in this poem?

5.4 Robert Browning

5.4.1 About the Author

Robert Browning (1812-1889) was born into a well-off family in Camberwell, south London. He was educated primarily through private tutoring, though he attended a boarding school and spent a short time at the University of London. Browning read widely as a youth, and began to write poetry while still quite young. He became a great admirer of the Romantic poets, especially Shelley. In 1833, young Browning published his first poetic work *Pauline*. However, it attracted little attention. From 1837 to 1846 Browning attempted to write verse drama for the stage, which led him to explore the dramatic monologue.

In 1845, Robert met Elizabeth Barrett, and a significant romance developed between them, leading to their secret marriage in 1846. The couple moved to Italy that same year and enjoyed remarkable happiness there. Mrs. Browning produced her best known book of love poetry — *Sonnets from the Portuguese* — while Mr. Browning presented to the world some of his best poems. After Elizabeth's death in 1861, the widower brought their son back to England and went on writing. His productivity and originality still remained powerful.

In 1868, he completed and published the long blank-verse poem The Ring and the Book, which told of a Roman murder and trial. It finally established his position as one of the greatest English poets. Browning died in 1889 and was buried in the Poet's Corner, Westminster Abbey, beside Tennyson.

Browning's fame today rests mainly on his dramatic monologues. In his poems, Browning would choose a dramatic moment or a crisis, in which his characters are made to talk about their lives, and about their minds and hearts. In "listening" to those one-sided talks, readers can form their own opinions and judgments about the speaker's personality and about what has really happened. For example, in "My Last Duchess", the Duke, as he talks about the portrait of his last Duchess, reveals bit by bit his own cruelty and possessiveness.

Browning's style owes much to his love of the seventeenth century poems of John Donne with their abrupt openings, colloquial phrasing and irregular rhythms. In general, his poems are not meant to entertain the readers with visual pleasures; they are supposed to keep them alert, thoughtful and enlightened.

5.4.2 "Meeting at Night[1]"

1

The gray sea and the long black land;
And the yellow half-moon large and low;
And the startled little waves that leap
In fiery ringlets from their sleep,
As I gain the cove with pushing prow,
And quench its speed I' the slushy sand.

2

Then a mile of warm sea-scented beach;
Three fields to cross till a farm appears;
A tap at the pane, the quick sharp scratch
And blue spurt of a lighted match,
And a voice less loud, through its joys and fears,
Than the two hearts beating each to each!

Notes

This poem and the one that follows it appeared originally under the single title *Night and Morning*. The speaker in both is a man. In this one, the man, a lover, describes the whereabouts of their meeting place.

Study Questions

1. This poem tells a story through a series of images. What is the story being told? How do the images work to tell that story?
2. Comment generally on the cinematic and dramatic qualities of the poem and how they complement each other.

5.4.3 "Home-Thoughts, from Abroad"

1

Oh, to be in England
Now that April's there,
And whoever wakes in England
Sees, some morning, unaware,
That the lowest boughs and the brushwood sheaf
Round the elm-tree bole[1] are in tiny leaf,
While the chaffinch[2] sings on the orchard bough
In England — now!

2

And after April, when May follows,
And the whitethroat builds, and all the swallows!
Hark, where my blossomed pear-tree in the hedge
Leans to the field and scatters on the clover
Blossoms and dewdrops — at the bent spray's edge —
That's the wise thrush[3]; he sings each song twice over,
Lest you should think he never could recapture
The first fine careless rapture!
And though the fields look rough with hoary dew,
All will be gay when noontide wakes anew
The buttercups, the little children's dower[4]
— Far brighter than this gaudy melon-flower[5]!

Notes
1. **bole**: tree trunk.
2. **the chaffinch**: a common small European bird.
3. **thrush**: a brown bird with spots on its front.
4. **dower**: endowment; gift.
5. **melon-flower**: large, trumpet-shaped yellow bloom from a melon plant (such as a cantaloupe or pumpkin). Browning contrasts this flower, which is native to a warm climate, with the smaller buttercups seen in early spring in England.

Study Questions
1. During what season does the poem take place? Where does the speaker want to be?
2. According to lines 3-6 what might someone in the speaker's homeland notice when he wakes one morning? What might he hear in line 7?
3. Where is the speaker? How do you know?
4. What picture of his present surroundings does the image in line 20 create? What

contrast between his homeland and present surroundings does the speaker suggest?

5.4.4 "My Last Duchess[1]"

FERRARA

That's my last Duchess painted on the wall,
Looking as if she were alive. I call
That piece of a wonder, now: Frà Pandolf's[2] hands
Worked busily a day, and there she stands.
Will't please you sit and look at her? I said
"Frà Pandolf" by design,[3] for never read
Strangers like you that pictured countenance,[4]
The depth and passion of its earnest glance,
But to myself they turned[5] (since none puts by
The curtain I have drawn for you, but I)
And seemed as they would ask me, if they durst,[6]
How such a glance came there; so, not the first
Are you to turn and ask thus. Sir, 't was not
Her husband's presence only, called[7] that spot
Of joy into the Duchess' cheek: perhaps
Frà Pandolf chanced to say "Her mantle laps
Over my lady's wrist too much,"[8] or "Paint
Must never hope to reproduce the faint
Half-flush that dies along her throat":[9] such stuff
Was courtesy,[10] she thought, and cause enough
For calling up that spot of joy. She had
A heart — how shall I say? — too soon made glad,
Too easily impressed; she liked whate'er
She looked on, and her looks went everywhere.
Sir, 't was all one![11] My favor at her breast,[12]
The dropping of the daylight in the West,
The bough of cherries some officious fool
Broke in the orchard for her, the white mule
She rode with round the terrace — all and each
Would draw from her alike the approving speech,
Or blush, at least. She thanked men — good! but thanked
Somehow — I know not how — as if she ranked
My gift of a nine-hundred-years-old name

With anybody's gift.[13] Who'd stoop to blame
This sort of trifling?[14] Even had you skill
In speech — (which I have not) — to make your will
Quite clear to such a one,[15] and say, "Just this
Or that in you disgusts me; here you miss,
Or there exceed the mark"[16] — and if she let
Herself be lessoned[17] so, nor plainly set
Her wits to yours,[18] forsooth,[19] and made excuse
— E'en then would be some stooping; and I choose
Never to stoop. Oh sir, she smiled, no doubt,
Whene'er I passed her; but who passed without
Much the same smile? This grew; I gave commands;[20]
Then all smiles stopped together.[21] There she stands
As if alive. Will't please you rise? We'll meet
The company below, then. I repeat,
The Count your master's known munificence[22]
Is ample warrant that no just pretense
Of mine[23] for dowry will be disallowed;[24]
Though his fair daughter's self, as I avowed
At starting, is my object. Nay, we'll go
Together down, sir. Notice Neptune,[25] though,
Taming a sea horse, thought a rarity,
Which Claus of Innsbruck[26] cast in bronze for me!

Notes

1. "My Last Duchess" is Browning's best-known dramatic monologue. The poem takes its sources from the life of Alfonso II, duke of Ferrara of the 16th-century Italy, whose first wife, Lucrezia, a young girl, died suspiciously in 1561 after three years of marriage. Not long after her death, the duke negotiated through an agent to marry a niece of the Count of Tyrol. This dramatic monologue is the duke's speech addressed to the agent who comes to negotiate the marriage. In his talk about his "last duchess," the duke reveals himself as a self-conceited, cruel and tyrannical man. The poem is written in heroic couplets, but with no regular metrical system. In reading, it sounds like blank verse.
2. **Frà Pandolf**: Brother Pandolf, an imaginary painter who painted the portrait of the Duchess ("frà" is an Italian word for "friar," meaning "brother").
3. **by design**: on purpose.
4. **for never read/Strangers like you that pictured countenance**: for strangers like you never looked at that face in the picture.

5. **But to myself they turned**: Strangers always turned to me.
6. **durst**: dare.
7. **called**: caused.
8. **"Her mantle laps/Over my lady's wrist too much"**: Her cloak covers up too much of my lady's wrist.
9. **the faint/Half-flush that dies along her throat**: the light reddish blush that gradually disappears along her throat.
10. **such stuff/Was courtesy**: such foolish words were regarded as acts of politeness and respect.
11. **'t was all one**: It was all the same.
12. **My favor at her breast**: the gift I gave her which she wore at her breast.
13. **she ranked/My gift of a nine-hundred-years-old name/With anybody's gift**: She regarded my gift, the title of the Duchess of Ferrara with a history of 900 years to be of the same value as the gifts given to her by some insignificant persons.
14. **Who'd stoop to blame/This sort of trifling**: Who would lower himself to find fault with this kind of trivial things? Notice the haughty and hypocritical tone of the Duke.
15. **such a one**: referring to the Duchess.
16. **here you miss, /Or there exceed the mark**: You have not done this quite enough, while you have overdone that.
17. **be lessoned**: be given a lesson.
18. **nor plainly set/Her wits to yours**: she didn't argue with you.
19. **forsooth**: indeed.
20. **This grew; I gave commands**: This kind of things grew worse and worse; I gave orders.
21. **Then all smiles stopped together**: Then she died.
22. **munificence**: bountifulness.
23. **just pretense/Of mine**: my well-grounded claim.
24. **disallowed**: refused (to give).
25. **Neptune**: the Roman god of the sea, whose chariot is often shown pulled by seahorses. The Duke is showing the statue of Neptune to the envoy as they are going downstairs to meet the others.
26. **Claus of Innsbruck**: Claus is an imaginary sculptor; Innsbruck is an Italian city, renowned for its sculpture, that Browning visited in 1838.

Study Questions

1. Who is the speaker in this poem? To whom is he speaking? What business or negotiation are they meeting to transact?
2. What happened to the "last" Duchess? Why? How do you know?
3. What was her character like? What is meant by "a heart too soon made glad"?

4. How would you characterize the Duke? What is generally revealed about him during the course of the poem?
5. What tone of voice do you imagine the speaker uses in these lines: "E'en then would be some stooping; and I choose/Never to stoop"?
6. What are the Duke's feelings about his late wife? How do you know? Do you think they are justified?
7. What is the Duke's motive for telling his listener all this?

Essay Topics

1. What is the Duke's opinion of the Duchess's personality? Do we as readers see her personality any differently?
2. In what way might the Duke's reference in the last three lines to the sea horse be related to his account of his marriage?
3. What report do you think the emissary should make to the Count about the proposed marriage of his daughter to the Duke?

5.5 Elizabeth Barrett Browning

5.5.1 About the Author

Elizabeth Barrett Browning (1806-1861) was born into a well-to-do family. Her father was a man with a strong sense of power and will to command. Elizabeth was privately educated. She was incapacitated for nearly a decade after 1838 as a result of a childhood spinal injury and lung ailment. She was rescued from ill-health and life under an oppressive father by the poet Robert Browning, who married her in 1846. Her first publication was *Battle of Marathon* (1820). In 1826 her *An Essay on Mind and Other Poems* was published anonymously. Her translation of *Prometheus Bound*, by the Greek dramatist Aeschylus, appeared in 1833 and was highly regarded. Five years later, in *The Seraphim and Other Poems*, she expressed Christian sentiments in the form of classical Greek tragedy. She continued writing, however, and in 1844 produced a volume of poems including "The Cry of the Children" and "Lady Geraldine's Courtship".

In 1845 the poet Robert Browning began to write to Elizabeth to praise her poetry. Their romance, which was immortalized in 1930 in the play *The Barretts of Wimpole Street*, by Rudolf Besier, was bitterly opposed by her father. In 1846, however, the couple eloped and settled in Florence, Italy, where Elizabeth regained her health and bore a son at age 43.

Her *Sonnets from the Portuguese*, dedicated to her husband and written in secret before her marriage, was published in 1850. Critics generally consider the *Sonnets*, one of the most widely known collections of love lyrics in English, to be her best work. The *Sonnets* draw on a broad classical education, but the doubts and triumphs of a forbidden passion have the force of genuine feeling and show the victory of love over emotional death. This experience is often conveyed in original and powerful imagery, as in "Sonnet 24". Here, free at last from the suffocating inertia of Victorian propriety, Elizabeth Browning suggests that the cruel knife of worldly criticism now lies shut in the enfolding warmth of love's hand. Mutual passion has triumphed over social constraint, and a woman has asserted her personal freedom in love. She expressed her intense sympathy with the struggle for the unification of Italy in the collections of poems *Casa Guidi Windows* (1848-1851) and *Poems Before Congress* (1860). In her longest and most ambitious work, *Aurora Leigh* (1856), Mrs. Browning created a work which recent criticism has resurrected as a central document of Victorian feminism, a woman writer's powerful claim to establish her independent identity through her work. *Aurora Leigh* is a didactic, romantic poem in blank verse, in which she defends a woman's right to intellectual freedom and discusses issues of gender, class and the relation of art to politics.

5.5.2 "How Do I Love Thee?"

How do I love thee? Let me count the ways.
I love thee to the depth and breadth and height
My soul can reach, when feeling out of sight
For the ends of Being and ideal Grace.
I love thee to the level of everyday's
Most quiet need, by sun and candlelight.
I love thee freely, as men strive for Right;
I love thee purely, as they turn from Praise.
I love thee with the passion put to use
In my old griefs, and with my childhood's faith.
I love thee with a love I seemed to lose
With my lost saints — I love thee with the breath,
Smiles, tears, of all my life — and, if God choose,
I shall but love thee better after death.

Study Questions

1. How many different ways does the speaker love her beloved, according to this poem?
2. What images does the poet use to strengthen the theme of love in this poem?
3. This sonnet is probably the most-quoted love poem in the English language. What

qualities, both in its content and its style, make "How Do I Love Thee" memorable?

5.6 Charlotte Brontë

5.6.1 About the Author

Charlotte Brontë (1816-1855) was born at Thornton, Bradford in Yorkshire, the daughter of an Anglican minister. When she was a small child, Charlotte and her three sisters were sent to a school for clergymen's daughters. The eldest two died there due to the poor and unhealthy conditions. This experience inspired the later portrayal of Lowood School in the novel *Jane Eyre*. As she grew up, Charlotte first worked as a teacher, and then as a governess. During the following years at Howarth, Charlotte, Emily and Anne, along with their brother Branwell, had a great deal of freedom to explore the surrounding countryside, to read widely, and to create their own stories. In 1842, Charlotte and Emily went to Brussels to complete their studies. There Charlotte fell in love with a married teacher. This passionate yet hopeless love left its marks in almost all her works.

In 1845 the three sisters published a book of *Poems* at their own expense. But it received little attention. Then the three sisters turned to novel writing. Charlotte's first novel *The Professor* was rejected by the publisher. But her second one, *Jane Eyre*, won immediate success when it appeared in 1847. This success was followed up by tragedy, however. Branwell, the only boy in the family, died in September 1848. Emily died of consumption that same year, and Anne the following summer. Left lonely in the world, Charlotte continued writing. Her next important novel *Shirley*, a work about the industrial troubles between the mill-owners and machine-breakers in Yorkshire came out in 1849. Another novel *Villette* appeared in 1853. In 1854 she married Mr. Nicholls, her father's curate, a sincere but narrow-minded man. She was happy in the marriage, but died within a few months, worn out by the unremitting physical and moral strain of forty years.

Charlotte Brontë is a writer of realism combined with romanticism. On the one hand, she presents a vivid realistic picture of the English society by exposing the cruelty, hypocrisy and other evils of the upper classes, and by showing the misery and suffering of the poor; on the other hand, her writings are marked by an intensity of vision and of passion. Her works are all about the struggle of an individual consciousness towards self-realization, about some lonely and neglected young women with a fierce longing for love, understanding and a full happy life. So, whatever weakness her work may have, the vividness of her subjective narration, the intensely achieved characterization, and the most truthful presentation of the economical, moral, social life of the time — all this renders her works a never dying popularity.

5.6.2 An Excerpt from Chapter 23 of *Jane Eyre*

A splendid, Midsummer shone over England: skies so pure, suns so radiant as were then seen in long succession, seldom favor, even singly, our wave-girt land[1]. It was as if a band of Italian days had come from the South, like a flock of glorious passenger birds, and lighted to rest them on the cliffs of Albion[2]. The hay was all got in; the fields round Thornfield were green and shorn; the roads white and baked; the trees were in their dark prime: hedge and wood, full-leaved and deeply tinted, contrasted well with the sunny hue of the cleared meadows between.

On Midsummer-eve[3], Adèle[4], weary with gathering wild strawberries in Hay-Lane half the day, had gone to bed with the sun. I watched her drop asleep, and when I left her I sought the garden.

It was now the sweetest hour of the twenty-four: — "Day its fervid fires had wasted,"[5] and dew fell cool on panting plain and scorched[6] summit. Where the sun had gone down in simple state — pure of the pomp of clouds — spread a solemn purple, burning with the light of red jewel and furnace flame at one point, on one hill-peak, and extending high and wide, soft and still softer, over half heaven. The east had its own charm of fine, deep blue, and its own modest gem, a rising and solitary star: soon it would boast the moon; but she was yet beneath the horizon.

I walked awhile on the pavement; but a subtle, well-known scent — that of a cigar — stole from some window; I saw the library casement open a hand-breath; I knew I might be watched thence; so I went apart into the orchard. No nook in the grounds more sheltered and more Eden-like; it was full of trees, it bloomed with flowers: a very high wall shut it out from the court, on one side; on the other, a beech avenue screened it from the lawn. At the bottom was a sunk fence; its sole separation from lonely fields: a winding walk, bordered with laurels and terminating in a giant horse-chestnut, circled at the base by a seat, led down to the fence. Here one could wander unseen. While such honey-dew fell, such silence reigned, such gloaming gathered, I felt as if I could haunt such shade for ever: but in threading the flower and fruit-parterres at the upper part of the enclosure, enticed there by the light the now-rising moon casts on this more open quarter, my step is stayed — not by sound, not by sight, but once more by a warning fragrance.

Sweet-briar and southernwood, jasmine, pink, and rose have long been yielding their evening sacrifice of incense: this new scent is neither of shrub nor flower; it is — I know it well — it is Mr. Rochester's cigar. I look round and I listen. I see trees laden with ripening fruit. I hear a nightingale warbling[7] in a wood half a mile off; no moving form is visible, no coming step audible; but that perfume increases: I must flee. I make for the wicket leading to the shrubbery, and I see Mr. Rochester entering. I step aside into the ivy recess; he will not stay long: he will soon return whence he came, and if I sit still he will never see me.

But no — eventide is as pleasant to him as to me, and this antique garden as attractive; and he strolls on, now lifting the gooseberry-tree branches to look at the fruit, large as plums, with which they are laden; now taking a ripe cherry from the wall; now stooping towards a knot of flowers, either to inhale their fragrance or to admire the dew-beads on their petals. A great moth goes humming by me; it alights on a plant at Mr. Rochester's foot: he sees it, and bends to examine it.

"Now, he has his back towards me," thought I, "and he is occupied too; perhaps, if I walk softly, I can slip away unnoticed."

I trod on an edging of turf that the crackle of the pebbly gravel might not betray me: he was standing among the beds at a yard or two distant from where I had to pass; the moth apparently engaged him[8]. "I shall get by very well," I meditated. As I crossed his shadow, thrown long over the garden by the moon, not yet risen high, he said quietly without turning: —

"Jane, come and look at this fellow."

I had made no noise: he had not eyes behind — could his shadow feel? I started at first, and then I approached him.

"Look at his wings," said he, "he reminds me rather of a West Indian insect; one does not often see so large and gay a night-rover in England: there! he is flown."

The moth roamed away; I was sheepishly retreating also; but Mr. Rochester followed me; and when we reached the wicket, he said: —

"Turn back: on so lovely a night it is a shame to sit in the house; and surely no one can wish to go to bed while sunset is thus at meeting with moonrise."

It is one of my faults, that though my tongue is sometimes prompt enough at an answer, there are times when it sadly fails me in framing an excuse; and always the lapse[9] occurs at some crisis, when a facile word or plausible pretext is specially wanted to get me out of painful embarrassment. I did not like to walk at this hour alone with Mr. Rochester in the shadowy orchard; but I could not find a reason to allege for leaving him. I followed with lagging step, and thoughts busily bent on discovering a means of extrication[10]; but he himself looked so composed and so grave also, I became ashamed of feeling any confusion: the evil — if evil existent or prospective there was — seemed to lie with me only; his mind was unconscious and quiet.

"Jane," he recommenced, as we entered the laurel walk, and slowly strayed down in the direction of the sunk fence and the horse-chestnut, "Thornfield is a pleasant place in summer, is it not?"

"Yes, sir."

"You must have become in some degree attached to the house, — you, who have an eye for natural beauties, and a good deal of the organ of Adhesiveness[11]?"

"I am attached to it, indeed."

"And, though I don't comprehend how it is, I perceive you have acquired a degree of regard for that foolish little child Adèle, too; and even for simple dame Fairfax[12]?"

"Yes, sir; in different ways, I have an affection for both."

"And would be sorry to part with them?"

"Yes."

"Pity!" he said, and sighed and paused. "It is always the way of events in this life, " he continued presently: "no sooner have you got settled in a pleasant resting-place, than a voice calls out to you to rise and move on, for the hour of repose is expired."

"Must I move on, sir?" I asked. "Must I leave Thornfield?"

"I believe you must, Jane. I am sorry, Janet, but I believe indeed you must."

This was a blow: but I did not let it prostrate me.

"Well, sir, I shall be ready when the order to march comes."

"It is come now — I must give it to-night."

"Then you are going to be married, sir?"

"Ex-act-ly — pre-cise-ly: with your usual acuteness, you have hit the nail straight on the head[13]."

"Soon, sir?"

"Very soon, my — that is, Miss Eyre: and you'll remember, Jane, the first time I, or Rumour, plainly intimated to you that it was my intention to put my old bachelor's neck into the sacred noose, to enter into the holy estate of matrimony — to take Miss Ingram to my bosom, in short, (she's an extensive armful: but that is not to the point — one can't have too much of such a very excellent thing as my beautiful Blanche): well, as I was saying — listen to me, Jane! You're not turning your head to look after more moths, are you? That was only a lady-clock, child, 'flying away home.' I wish to remind you that it was you who first said to me, with that discretion I respect in you — with that foresight, prudence, and humility which befit your responsible and dependent position — that in case I married Miss Ingram, both you and little Adèle had better trot forthwith[14]. I pass over the sort of slur conveyed in this suggestion on the character of my beloved; indeed, when you are far away, Janet, I'll try to forget it: I shall notice only its wisdom; which is such that I have made it my law of action. Adèle must go to school; and you, Miss Eyre, must get a new situation."

"Yes, sir, I will advertise immediately: and meantime, I suppose — " I was going to say, "I suppose I may stay here, till I find another shelter to betake myself to:" but I stopped, feeling it would not do to risk a long sentence, for my voice was not quite under command.

"In about a month I hope to be a bridegroom," continued Mr. Rochester; "and in the interim, I shall myself look out for employment and an asylum for you."

"Thank you, sir; I am sorry to give — "

"Oh, no need to apologize! I consider that when a dependant does her duty as well as you have done yours, she has a sort of claim upon her employer for any little assistance he can conveniently render her; indeed I have already, through my future mother-in-law, heard of a place that I think will suit: it is to undertake the education of the five daughters of Mrs. Dionysius O'Gall of Bitternutt Lodge, Connaught, Ireland. You'll like Ireland, I think: they're such warm-hearted people there, they say."

"It is a long way off, sir."

"No matter — a girl of your sense will not object to the voyage or the distance."

"Not the voyage, but the distance: and then the sea is a barrier — "

"From what, Jane?"

"From England; and from Thornfield: and — "

"Well?"

"From you, sir."

I said this almost involuntarily; and with as little sanction of free will, my tears gushed out. I did not cry so as to be heard, however; I avoided sobbing. The thought of Mrs. O'Gall and Bitternutt Lodge struck cold to my heart; and colder the thought of all the brine and foam, destined, as it seemed, to rush between me and the master, at whose side I now walked; and coldest the remembrance of the wider ocean — wealth, caste, custom intervened between me and what I naturally and inevitably loved.

"It is a long way," I again said.

"It is, to be sure; and when you get to Bitternutt Lodge, Connaught, Ireland, I shall never see you again, Jane: that's morally certain. I never go over to Ireland, not having myself much of a fancy for the country. We have been good friends, Jane, have we not?"

"Yes, sir."

"And when friends are on the eve of separation, they like to spend the little time that remains to them close to each other. Come — we'll talk over the voyage and the parting quietly, half an hour or so, while the stars enter into their shining life up in heaven yonder: here is the chestnut tree; here is the bench at its old roots. Come, we will sit there in peace tonight, though we should never more be destined to sit there together." He seated me and himself.

"It is a long way to Ireland, Jane, and I am sorry to send my little friend on such weary travels: but if I can't do better, how is it to be helped? Are you anything akin to me, do you think, Jane?"

I could risk no sort of answer by this time, my heart was full.

"Because," he said, "I sometimes have a queer feeling with regard to you — especially when you are near me, as now: it is as if I had a string somewhere under my left ribs, tightly and inextricably knotted to a similar string situated in the corresponding quarter of your little frame. And if that boisterous channel, and two hundred miles or so of land come broad between us, I am afraid that cord of communion will be snapt; and then I've a nervous notion I should take to bleeding inwardly. As for you, — you'd forget me."

"That I never should, sir: you know — " impossible to proceed.

"Jane, do you hear that nightingale singing in the wood? — Listen!"

In listening, I sobbed convulsively; for I could repress what I endured no longer: I was obliged to yield; and I was shaken from head to foot with acute distress. When I did speak, it was only to express an impetuous wish that I had never been born, or never come to Thornfield.

"Because you are sorry to leave it?"

The vehemence of emotion, stirred by grief and love within me, was claiming mastery, and struggling for full sway; and asserting a right to predominate: to overcome, to live, rise and reign at last; yes, — and to speak.

"I grieve to leave Thornfield: I love Thornfield: — I love it, because I have lived in it a full and delightful life, — momentarily at least. I have not been trampled on[15]. I have not been petrified. I have not been buried with inferior minds, and excluded from every glimpse of communion with what is bright, and energetic, and high. I have talked, face to face, with what I reverence; with what I delight in, — with an original, a vigorous, an expanded mind. I have known you, Mr. Rochester; and it strikes me with terror and anguish to feel I absolutely must be torn from you forever. I see the necessity of departure; and it is like looking on the necessity of death."

"Where do you see the necessity?" he asked, suddenly.

"Where? You, sir, have placed it before me."

"In what shape?"

"In the shape of Miss Ingram; a noble and beautiful woman, — your bride."

"My bride! What bride? I have no bride!"

"But you will have."

"Yes; — I will! — I will!" He set his teeth.

"Then I must go: — you have said it yourself."

"No: you must stay! I swear it — and the oath shall be kept."

"I tell you I must go!" I retorted, roused to something like passion. "Do you think I can stay to become nothing to you? Do you think I am an automaton? — a machine without feelings? and can bear to have my morsel of bread snatched from my lips, and my drop of living water dashed from my cup? Do you think, because I am poor, obscure, plain, and little, I am soulless and heartless? — You think wrong! — I have as much soul as you, — and full as much heart! And if God had gifted me with some beauty, and much wealth, I should have made it as hard for you to leave me, as it is now for me to leave you. I am not talking to you now through the medium of custom, conventionalities, nor even of mortal flesh: — it is my spirit that addresses your spirit;

just as if both had passed through the grave, and we stood at God's feet, equal, — as we are!"

"As we are!" repeated Mr. Rochester — "so," he added, enclosing me in his arms, gathering me to his breast, pressing his lips on my lips: "so, Jane!"

"Yes, so, sir," I rejoined: "and yet not so; for you are a married man — or as good as a married man, and wed to one inferior to you — to one with whom you have no sympathy — whom I do not believe you truly love; for I have seen and heard you sneer at her. I would scorn such a union; therefore I am better than you — let me go!"

"Where, Jane? To Ireland?"

"Yes — to Ireland. I have spoken my mind, and can go anywhere now."

"Jane, be still; don't struggle so, like a wild, frantic bird that is rending its own plumage in its desperation."

"I am no bird; and no net ensnares me: I am a free human being with an independent will; which I now exert to leave you."

Another effort set me at liberty, and I stood erect before him.

"And your will shall decide your destiny," he said: "I offer you my hand, my heart, and a share of all my possessions."

"You play a farce, which I merely laugh at."

"I ask you to pass through life at my side — to be my second self, and best earthly companion."

"For that fate you have already made your choice, and must abide by it."

"Jane, be still a few moments; you are over-excited: I will be still too."

A waft of wind came sweeping down the laurel-walk, and trembled through the boughs of the chestnut: it wandered away — away — to an indefinite distance — it died. The nightingale's song was then the only voice of the hour: in listening to it, I again wept. Mr. Rochester sat quiet, looking at me gently and seriously. Some time passed before he spoke; he at last said: —

"Come to my side, Jane, and let us explain, and understand one another."

"I will never again come to your side: I am torn away now, and cannot return."

"But, Jane, I summon you as my wife: it is you only I intend to marry."

I was silent: I thought he mocked me.

"Come, Jane — come hither."

"Your bride stands between us."

He rose, and with a stride reached me.

"My bride is here," he said, again drawing me to him, "because my equal is here, and my likeness. Jane, will you marry me?"

Still I did not answer; and still I writhed myself from his grasp: for I was still incredulous.

"Do you doubt me, Jane?"

"Entirely."

"You have no faith in me?"

"Not a whit."

"Am I a liar in your eyes?" he asked passionately. "Little sceptic, you shall be convinced. What love have I for Miss Ingram? None: and that you know. What love has she for me? None: as I have taken pains to prove: I caused a rumour to reach her that my fortune was not a third of what was supposed, and after that I presented myself to see the result: it was coldness both from her and her mother. I would not — I could not — marry Miss Ingram. You — you strange — you almost unearthly thing! — I love as my own flesh. You — poor and obscure, and small and plain as you are — I entreat to accept me as a husband."

"What, me!" I ejaculated: beginning in his earnestness — and especially in his incivility — to credit his sincerity; "me, who have not a friend in the world but you — if you are my friend: not a shilling but what you have given me?"

"You, Jane, I must have you for my own — entirely my own. Will you be mine? Say yes, quickly."

"Mr. Rochester, let me look at your face, turn to the moonlight."

"Why?"

"Because I want to read your countenance; turn!"

"There: you will find it scarcely more legible than a crumpled, scratched page. Read on: only make haste, for I suffer."

His face was very much agitated and very much flushed, and there were strong workings in the features, and strange gleams in the eyes.

"Oh, Jane, you torture me!" he exclaimed. "With that searching and yet faithful and generous look, you torture me!"

"How can I do that? If you are true, and your offer real, my only feeling to you must be gratitude and devotion — they cannot torture."

"Gratitude!" he ejaculated; and added wildly — "Jane, accept me quickly. Say, Edward — give me my name — Edward, I will marry you."

"Are you in earnest? — Do you truly love me? — Do you sincerely wish me to be your wife?"

"I do; and if an oath is necessary to satisfy you, I swear it."

"Then, sir, I will marry you."

"Edward — my little wife!"

"Dear Edward!"

"Come to me — come to me entirely now," said he; and added, in his deepest tone, speaking in my ear as his cheek was laid on mine, "Make my happiness — I will make yours."

"God, pardon me!" he subjoined ere long; "and man, meddle not with me: I have her, and I will hold her."

"There is no one to meddle, sir. I have no kindred to interfere."

"No — that is the best of it," he said. And if I had loved him less I should have thought his accent and look of exultation savage: but, sitting by him, roused from the nightmare of parting — called to the paradise of union — I thought only of the bliss given me to drink in so abundant a flow. Again and again he said, "Are you happy, Jane?" And again and again I answered, "Yes." After which he murmured, "It will atone — it will atone. Have I not found her friendless, and cold, and comfortless? Will I not guard, and cherish, and solace her? Is there not love in my heart, and constancy in my resolves? It will expiate at God's tribunal. I know my Maker sanctions[16] what I do. For the world's judgment — I wash my hands thereof. For man's opinion — I defy it."

But what had befallen the night? The moon was not yet set, and we were all in shadow: I could scarcely see my master's face, near as I was. And what ailed the chestnut tree? It writhed and groaned; while wind roared in the laurel walk, and came sweeping over us.

"We must go in," said Mr. Rochester: "the weather changes. I could have sat with thee till morning, Jane."

"And so," thought I, "could I with you." I should have said so, perhaps, but a livid, vivid spark leapt out of a cloud at which I was looking, and there was a crack, a crash, and a close rattling peal; and I thought only of hiding my dazzled eyes against Mr. Rochester's shoulder.

The rain rushed down. He hurried me up the walk, through the grounds, and into the house; but we were quite wet before we could pass the threshold. He was taking off my shawl in the hall, and shaking the water out of my loosened hair, when Mrs. Fairfax emerged from her room. I did not observe her at first, nor did Mr. Rochester. The lamp was lit. The clock was on the stroke of twelve.

"Hasten to take off your wet things," said he; "and before you go, good-night — good-night, my darling!"

He kissed me repeatedly. When I looked up, on leaving his arms, there stood the widow, pale, grave, and amazed. I only smiled at her, and ran upstairs. "Explanation will do for another time," thought I. Still, when I reached my chamber, I felt a pang at the idea she should even temporarily misconstrue what she had seen. But joy soon effaced every other feeling; and loud as the wind blew, near and deep as the thunder crashed, fierce and frequent as the lightning gleamed, cataract-like as the rain fell during a storm of two hours' duration, I experienced no fear, and little awe. Mr. Rochester came thrice to my door in the course of it, to ask if I was safe and tranquil: and that was comfort, that was strength for anything.

Before I left my bed in the morning, little Adèle came running in to tell me that the great horse-chestnut at the bottom of the orchard had been struck by lightning in the night, and half of it split away.

Notes
1. **wave-girt land**: land surrounded by the waves; here referring to England.
2. **Albion**: old name for Great Britain.
3. **Midsummer-eve**: June 24 celebrated as the feast of the nativity of John, the Baptist.
4. **Adèle**: Adèle Varens, Jane's pupil.
5. **"Day its fervid fires had wasted"**: The line comes from Thomas Campbell's poem *The Turkish Lady*, in which the fifth and sixth lines go like this: "Day her sultry fires had wasted, /Calm and sweet the moonlight rose."
6. **scorched**: burnt.
7. **warble**: to sing in a melodious voice.
8. **engaged him**: attracted his attention.
9. **the lapse**: a period of time when one is unable to speak.
10. **extrication**: freeing oneself from a difficult situation.
11. **the organ of Adhesiveness**: the ability to quickly attach to something or somebody.
12. **dame Fairfax**: Alice Fairfax, Rochester's housekeeper at Thornfield Hall.
13. **hit the nail straight on the head**: to speak of something exactly to the point.
14. **trot forthwith**: to leave at once.
15. **be trampled on**: be treated cruelly or harshly.
16. **sanction**: to officially accept or allow something.

Study Questions
1. Why is it significant that the events of this chapter take place on Midsummer eve?
2. How does the orchard initially appear to Jane?
3. Why does Jane have difficulty in believing Rochester's declaration of love?
4. What might the storm and the splitting of the chestnut tree foreshadow?

Essay Topics
1. Explain the multiple ironies of Rochester's conversation with Jane in Chapter 23. What is Brontë's purpose here? What dramatic techniques does she employ?
2. At one point Jane says, "Do you think because I am plain and poor I have no soul?" What does she mean by that? Do people make this assumption today?

5.7 Emily Brontë

5.7.1 About the Author

Emily Brontë (1818-1848) was born at Thornton in Yorkshire, the fifth of six children of Patrick and Maria Brontë. When she was two years old, the family moved to Haworth, where her father had been appointed the vicar. In 1821, shortly after Emily's

 third birthday, her mother died of cancer. In 1824, Emily and her three elder sisters were sent to a school for daughters of impoverished clergymen. The conditions of the school were harsh and an epidemic soon broke out, taking the lives of her two eldest sisters. During the following years at Howarth, Emily had a great deal of freedom to explore the surrounding countryside. The lonely purple moors became one of the most important shaping forces in her life. And her father's bookshelf offered her a variety of reading. She was a reserved, courageous woman with a commanding will and manner. In 1835, Emily went to the Roe Head School where Charlotte was then teaching. Emily managed to stay only three months before she became very sick and had to go home. Emily found a teaching job at Law Hill School in September 1838. But her health broke down under the stress and she returned home again around April 1839. Then in 1842, Emily accompanied her sister Charlotte to Brussels, Belgium, for a year to study languages. During this time she impressed the professor as having a finer, more powerful mind than her sister.

Emily began writing poems at an early age and published twenty-one of them, together with poems by Anne and Charlotte, in 1846 in a slim volume titled *Poems*. In her poetry, Emily achieves a remarkable effect by the energy and sincerity, and often by the music, with which she portrays her stoicism, independence, and compassion. The major part of *Wuthering Heights* seems to have been written between the Autumns of 1845 and 1846; it was published in December 1847. It did not gain immediate success as Charlotte's *Jane Eyre*, but it has acclaimed later fame as one of the most intense novels written in the English language. In September 1848, Emily had caught cold at her brother's funeral and died of tuberculosis after an illness of about three months.

Wuthering Heights is Emily's only novel and is generally considered one of the most original works. In many aspects, it is unique and has no counterparts in mode as well as in manner of writing. In the aspect of vitalized, animated nature, Emily proves an even better artist than her elder sister in landscape painting. The typical Yorkshire characters, settings, dialect and the primitive, uncultivated, dark, naked aspects of life there can easily be found in this unique novel. And the novel is also remarkable for its simple, naked statement of violent emotions such as Catherine's dying farewell to Heathcliff. Unlike the works of her two sisters, Emily's *Wuthering Heights* shows no remarkable conventional influence in either idea or form. Readers are especially struck by the apparent absence of social morality in her novel. The reading of the novel makes us contemplate, without evasion, some of the most powerful primal human motives, engaged — against a wild, free, stormy background — in ferocious conflict. It will not be easy for us to find an answer, but the challenge is tempting.

5.7.2 An Excerpt from *Wuthering Heights*

Chapter 15

Another week over — and I[1] am so many days nearer health, and spring! I have now heard all my neighbor's[2] history, at different sittings,[3] as the housekeeper[4] could spare time from more important occupations. I'll continue it in her own words, only a little condensed. She is, on the whole, a very fair narrator, and I don't think I could improve her style.

In the evening, she said, the evening of my visit to the Heights, I knew, as well as if I saw him, that Mr. Heathcliff was about the place; and I shunned going out, because I still carried his letter[5] in my pocket, and didn't want to be threatened or teased any more. I had made up my mind not to give it till my master went somewhere, as I could not guess how its receipt would affect Catherine. The consequence was, that it did not reach her before the lapse of three days. The fourth was Sunday, and I brought it into her room after the family were gone to church. There was a manservant left to keep the house with me, and we generally made a practice of locking the doors during the hours of service; but on that occasion the weather was so warm and pleasant that I set them wide open, and, to fulfill my engagement,[6] as I knew who would be coming, I told my companion that the mistress wished very much for some oranges, and he must run over to the village and get a few, to be paid for on the morrow. He departed, and I went up-stairs.

Mrs. Linton sat in a loose white dress, with a light shawl over her shoulders, in the recess of the open window, as usual. Her thick, long hair had been partly removed at the beginning of her illness, and now she wore it simply combed in its natural tresses over her temples and neck. Her appearance was altered, as I had told Heathcliff; but when she was calm, there seemed unearthly beauty in the change. The flash of her eyes had been succeeded by a dreamy and melancholy softness; they no longer gave the impression of looking at the objects around her: they appeared always to gaze beyond, and far beyond — you would have said out of this world. Then, the paleness of her face — its haggard aspect having vanished as she recovered flesh — and the peculiar expression arising from her mental state, though painfully suggestive of their causes, added to the touching interest which she awakened; and — invariably to me, I know, and to any person who saw her, I should think — refuted more tangible proofs of convalescence, and stamped her as one doomed to decay.

A book lay spread on the sill before her, and the scarcely perceptible wind fluttered its leaves at intervals. I believe Linton had laid it there: for she never endeavored to divert herself with reading, or occupation of any kind, and he would spend many an hour in trying to entice her attention to some subject which had formerly been her amusement. She was conscious of his aim, and in her better moods endured his efforts placidly, only showing their uselessness by now and then suppressing a wearied sigh, and checking him at last with the saddest of smiles and kisses. At other times, she would turn petulantly away, and hide her face in her hands, or even push him off angrily; and then he took care to let her alone, for he was certain of doing no good.

Gimmerton chapel[7] bells were still ringing; and the full, mellow flow of the beck in the valley came soothingly on the ear. It was a sweet substitute for the yet absent murmur of the summer foliage, which drowned that music about the Grange when the trees were in leaf. At Wuthering Heights it always sounded on quiet days following a great thaw or a season of steady rain. And of Wuthering Heights Catherine was thinking as she listened: that is, if she thought or listened at all; but she had the vague, distant look I mentioned before, which expressed no recognition of material things either by ear or eye.

"There's a letter for you, Mrs. Linton, " I said, gently inserting it in one hand that rested on her knee. "You must read it immediately, because it wants an answer. Shall I break the seal?" "Yes, " she answered, without altering the direction of her eyes. I opened it — it was very short. "Now, " I continued, "read it." She drew away her hand, and let it fall. I replaced it in her lap, and stood waiting till it should please her to glance down; but that movement was so long delayed that at last I resumed — "Must I read it, ma'am? It is from Mr. Heathcliff."

There was a start and a troubled gleam of recollection, and a struggle to arrange her ideas. She lifted the letter, and seemed to peruse it; and when she came to the signature she sighed: yet still I found she had not gathered its import, for, upon my desiring to hear her reply, she merely pointed to the name, and gazed at me with mournful and questioning eagerness.

"Well, he wishes to see you, " said I, guessing her need of an interpreter. "He's in the garden by this time, and impatient to know what answer I shall bring."

As I spoke, I observed a large dog lying on the sunny grass beneath raise its ears as if about to bark, and then smoothing them back, announce, by a wag of the tail, that some one approached whom it did not consider a stranger. Mrs. Linton bent forward, and listened breathlessly. The minute after a step traversed the hall; the open house was too tempting for Heathcliff to resist walking in: most likely he supposed that I was inclined to shirk my promise, and so resolved to trust to his own audacity. With straining eagerness Catherine gazed towards the entrance of her chamber. He did not hit the right room[8] directly; she motioned me to admit him; but he found it out, ere[9] I could reach the door, and in a stride or two was at her side, and had her grasped in his arms.

He neither spoke, nor loosed his hold some five minutes, during which period he bestowed more kisses than ever he gave in his life before, I dare say; but then my mistress had kissed him first, and I plainly saw that he could hardly bear, for downright agony, to look into her face! The same conviction had stricken him as me, from the instant he beheld her, that there was no prospect of ultimate recovery there — she was fated, sure to die.

"O, Cathy! Oh, my life! How can I bear it?" was the first sentence he uttered, in a tone that did not seek to disguise his despair.

And now he stared at her so earnestly that I thought the very intensity of his gaze would bring tears into his eyes; but they burned with anguish, they did not melt. [10]

"What now?" said Catherine, leaning back, and returning his look with a suddenly clouded brow[11]— her humor was a mere vane for constantly varying caprices. "You and Edgar have broken my heart, Heathcliff! And you both come to bewail the deed to me, as if you were the people to be pitied! I shall not pity you, not I. You have killed me — thriven on it, I think. How strong you are! How many years do you mean to live after I am gone?'

Heathcliff had knelt on one knee to embrace her; he attempted to rise, but she seized his hair, and kept him down.

"I wish I could hold you, " she continued, bitterly, "till we were both dead! I shouldn't care what you suffered. I care nothing for your sufferings. Why shouldn't you suffer? I do! Will you forget me — will you be happy when I am in the earth? Will you say twenty years hence, 'That's the grave of Catherine Earnshaw. I loved her long ago, and was wretched to lose her; but it is past. I've loved many others since — my children are dearer to me than she was, and, at death, I shall not rejoice that I am going to her, I shall be sorry that I must leave them!' Will you say so, Heathcliff?"

"Don't torture me till I'm as mad as yourself, " cried he, wrenching his head free, and grinding his teeth.

The two, to a cool spectator, made a strange and fearful picture. Well might Catherine deem that heaven would be a land of exile to her, unless, with her mortal body, she cast away her mortal character also. Her present countenance had a wild vindictiveness in its white cheek, and a bloodless lip, and scintillating eye; and she retained, in her closed fingers, a portion of the locks she had been grasping. As to her companion, while raising himself with one hand, he had taken her arm with the other; and so inadequate was his stock of gentleness to the requirements of her condition, that on his letting go, I saw four distinct impressions left blue in the colorless skin.

"Are you possessed with a devil, " he pursued, savagely, "to talk in that manner to me, when you are dying? Do you reflect that all those words will be branded in my memory, and eating deeper eternally, after you have left me? You know you lie to say I have killed you; and, Catherine, you know that I could as soon as forget you, as my existence![12] Is it not sufficient for your infernal selfishness, that while you are at peace I shall writhe in the torments of hell?"

"I shall not be at peace," moaned Catherine, recalled to a sense of physical weakness by the violent, unequal throbbing of her heart, which beat visibly, and audibly, under this excess of agitation.

She said nothing further till the paroxysm was over; then she continued, more kindly —

"I'm not wishing you greater torment than I have, Heathcliff. I only wish us never to be parted — and should a word of mine distress you hereafter, think I feel the same distress underground, and for my own sake, forgive me! Come here and kneel down again! You never harmed me in your life. Nay, if you nurse anger,[13] that will be worse to remember than my harsh words! Won't you come here again? Do!"

Heathcliff went to the back of her chair, and leant over, but not so far as to let her see his face, which was livid with emotion. She bent round to look at him; he would not permit it; turning abruptly, he walked to the fireplace, where he stood, silent, with his back towards us.

Mrs. Linton's glance followed him suspiciously: every movement woke a new sentiment in her. After a pause, and a prolonged gaze, she resumed, addressing me in accents of indignant disappointment.

"Oh, you see, Nelly! He would not relent a moment to keep me out of the grave! *That* is how I'm loved! Well, never mind! That is not *my* Heathcliff. I shall love mine yet; and take him with me — he's in my soul. And," added she, musingly, "the thing that irks me most is this shattered prison, after all. I'm tired, tired of being closed here. I'm wearying to escape into that glorious world, and to be always there; not seeing it dimly through tears, and yearning for it through the walls of an aching heart; but really with it, and in it. Nelly, you think you are better and more fortunate than I; in full health and strength — you are sorry for me — very soon that will be altered. I shall be sorry for *you*. I shall be incomparably beyond and above you all. I *wonder* he won't be near me!" She went on to herself. "I thought he wished it. Heathcliff, dear! You should not be sullen now. Do come to me, Heathcliff."

In her eagerness she rose, and supported herself on the arm of the chair. At that earnest appeal, he turned to her, looking absolutely desperate. His eyes wide, and wet, at last, flashed fiercely on her; his breast heaved convulsively. An instant they held asunder;[14] and then how they met I hardly saw, but Catherine made a spring, and he caught her, and they were locked in an embrace from which I thought my mistress would never be released alive. In fact, to my eyes, she seemed directly insensible. He flung himself into the nearest seat, and on my approaching hurriedly to ascertain if she had fainted, he gnashed at me, and foamed like a mad dog, and gathered her to him with greedy jealousy. I did not feel as if I were in the company of a creature of my own species; it appeared that he would not understand, though I spoke to him; so, I stood off, and held my tongue, in great perplexity.

A movement of Catherine's relieved me a little presently: she put up her hand to clasp his neck, and bring her cheek to his, as he held her; while he, in return, covering her with frantic caresses, said wildly —

"You teach me now how cruel you've been — cruel and false. *Why* did you despise me? *Why* did you betray your own heart, Cathy? I have not one word of comfort — you deserve this. You have killed yourself.[15] Yes, you may kiss me, and cry; and wring out my kisses and tears. They'll blight you — they'll damn you. You loved me — then what *right* have you to leave me? What right — answer me — for the poor fancy you felt for Linton? Because misery, and degradation, and death, and nothing that god or Satan could inflict would have parted us, *you*, of your own will, did it. I have not broken your heart — *you* have broken it — and in breaking it, you have broken mine. So much the worse for me, that I am strong. Do I want to live? What kind of living will it be when you — oh, God! would *you* like to live with your soul[16] in the grave?'

"Let me alone. Let me alone," sobbed Catherine. "If I've done wrong, I'm dying for it. It is enough! You left me too; but I won't upbraid you! I forgive you. Forgive me!"

"It is hard to forgive, and to look at those eyes, and feel those wasted hands," he answered. "Kiss me again; and don't let me see your eyes! I forgive what you have done to me. I love *my* murderer — but *yours*! How can I?"

They were silent — their faces against each other, and washed by each other's tears. At least, I suppose the weeping was on both sides; as it seemed Heathcliff *could* weep on a great occasion like this.

I grew very uncomfortable, meanwhile; for the afternoon wore fast away, the man whom I had sent off returned from his errand, and I could distinguish, by the shine of the westering[17] sun up the valley, a concourse thickening outside Gimmerton chapel porch.

"Service is over," I announced. "My master will be here in half an hour."

Heathcliff groaned a curse, and strained Catherine closer — she never moved.

Ere long I perceived a group of the servants passing up the road towards the kitchen wing. Mr. Linton was not far behind; he opened the gate himself, and sauntered slowly up, probably enjoying the lovely afternoon that breathed as soft as summer.

"Now he is here," I exclaimed. "For Heaven's sake, hurry down! You'll not meet any one on the front stairs. Do be quick; and stay among the trees till he is fairly in."

"I must go, Cathy," said Heathcliff, seeking to extricate himself from his companion's arms. "But, if I live, I'll see you again before you are asleep. I won't stay five yards from your window."

"You must not go!" she answered, holding him as firmly as her strength allowed. "You shall not, I tell you."

"For one hour," he pleaded earnestly.

"Not for one minute," she replied.

"I must — Linton will be up immediately," persisted the alarmed intruder.

He would have risen, and unfixed her fingers by the act — she clung fast, gasping; there was mad resolution in her face.

"No!" she shrieked. "Oh, don't, don't go. It is the last time! Edgar will not hurt us. Heathcliff, I shall die! I shall die!"

"Damn the fool! There he is," cried Heathcliff, sinking back into his seat. "Hush, my darling! Hush, hush, Catherine! I'll stay. If he shot me so, I'd expire[18] with a blessing on my lips."

And there they were fast again. I heard my master mounting the stairs — the cold sweat ran from my forehead; I was horrified.

"Are you going to listen to her ravings?' I said, passionately. "She does not know what she says. Will you ruin her, because she has not wit to help herself? Get up! You could be free instantly. That is the most diabolical deed that ever you did. We are all done for — master, mistress, and servant."

I wrung my hands, and cried out; and Mr. Linton hastened his step at the noise. In the midst of my agitation, I was sincerely glad to observe that Catherine's arms had fallen relaxed, and her head hung down.

"She's fainted, or dead," I thought: "so much the better. Far better that she should be dead, than lingering a burden and a misery-maker to all about her."

Edgar sprang to his unbidden guest, blanched with astonishment and rage. What he meant to do I cannot tell; however, the other stopped all demonstrations, at once, by placing the lifeless- looking form in his arms.

"Look there!" he said. "Unless you be a fiend, help her first — then you shall speak to me!"

He walked into the parlor, and sat down. Mr. Linton summoned me, and with great difficulty, and after resorting to many means, we managed to restore her to sensation; but she was all bewildered; she sighed, and moaned, and knew nobody. Edgar, in his anxiety for her, forgot her hated friend. I did not. I went, at the earliest opportunity, and besought him to depart; affirming that Catherine was better, and he should hear from me in the morning how she passed the night.

"I shall not refuse to go out of doors," he answered; "but I shall stay in the garden: and, Nelly, mind you keep your word tomorrow. I shall be under those larch-trees. Mind! or I pay another visit, whether Linton be in or not."

He sent a rapid glance through the half-open door of the chamber, and, ascertaining that what I stated was apparently true, delivered the house of his luckless presence.

Notes

1. **I**: here referring to Mr. Lockwood, the new tenant of Thrushcross Grange (Heathcliff is his landlord).

2. **neighbor**: here referring to Mr. Heathcliff.
3. **at different sittings**: on different talks.
4. **the housekeeper**: here referring to Nelly Dean, a servant with the Earnshaws and the Lintons for all her life. She is also one of the main narrators of the novel, and she tells the following part of the story to Mr. Lockwood.
5. **his letter**: a letter by Heathcliff who asked Nelly Dean to pass it to Catherine.
6. **to fulfill my engagement**: that is, to pass the letter and to arrange the meeting between Heathcliff and Catherine.
7. **Gimmerton chapel**: a small church near the Thrushcross Grange.
8. **hit the right room**: find the room where Catherine was reclining.
9. **ere**: before.
10. **they did not melt**: implies that his eyes did not shed any tears.
11. **clouded brow**: gloomy and sorrowful expression.
12. **I could as soon as forget you, as my existence**: I could not forget you just like that I could not forget my own existence.
13. **nurse anger**: be angry all the time.
14. **held asunder**: stood wide apart from each other.
15. **You have killed yourself**: referring to Catherine's marriage to Linton, which destroyed her life.
16. **soul**: here referring to Catherine.
17. **westering**: going west.
18. **expire**: die.

Study Questions

1. Who is telling the story in this Chapter?
2. What do you think about Heathcliff, and his relationship with Catherine?
3. What does Heathcliff mean when he says, "I love my murderer, but yours! How can I"?
4. What are the key elements in the interaction between Catherine and Heathcliff?
5. How does this chapter explore the notion of romantic love?
6. How is Nelly behaving in this chapter? Do you think this is typical of her?

Essay Topics

1. Discuss the novel's narrative structure. Are the novel's narrators trustworthy? Why or why not? With particular reference to Nelly's story, consider what might be gained from reading between the lines of the narration. What roles do the personalities of the narrators play in the way that the story is told?
2. What role does social class and class ambiguity play in *Wuthering Heights*? To what extent is Heathcliff's social position responsible for the misery and conflict so

persistent in the book?

5.8 Matthew Arnold

5.8.1 About the Author

Matthew Arnold (1822-1888) was born in Middlesex, southeast of England. He was educated first at Rugby School, where his father was headmaster, and then at Balliol College, University of Oxford. He was elected to a fellowship at Oriel College in 1845. But soon he gave up his job at Oxford. After a period of teaching the classics at Rugby, Arnold served as an inspector of schools from 1851 to 1886. In 1857, he was elected to the professorship of poetry at Oxford, which he held for ten years. Arnold visited the Continent repeatedly in the interests of education and journeyed twice to the United States as a lecturer, in 1883 and 1886.

Arnold started his literary career as a poet. His first volume of verse *The Strayed Reveller and Other Poems* appeared in 1849. His poetical influence increased with the publication in 1853 of a collection of poems under his own name. An elevated, meditative, and elegiac tone is characteristic of Arnold's poetry. Most of Arnold's poetic production is beautiful, often formally impressive, yet he found it difficult to forge an industrial voice, perhaps because he found it difficult to come to terms with the Victorian world. In the "Memorial Verses" written after Wordsworth's death in 1850, "the freshness of the early world" is found to be staled by the adult's "time-ridden consciousness." In his greatest poem, *Dover Beach*, dealing with the slow ebb of religious faith, we have no sense of anguished personal involvement. The poem is not about how he lost his faith, but about what it is like to live in an age in which faith is decaying.

Matthew Arnold wrote almost no poetry after the age of forty, turning to the great prose works such as *Culture and Anarchy* which made him one of the great commentators on Victorian commercial civilization. During his later years he wrote many critical essays. As a critic, Arnold defended culture against scientific materialism. He believed that literature shaped culture, and argued for England to become sensitized to art and to accept high standards of literary judgment. His essays and lectures brought a broad and humane critical intelligence to bear on the discussion of literature, social questions and issues of religious belief.

5.8.2 "Dover Beach"[1]

> The sea is calm tonight.
> The tide is full, the moon lies fair

Upon the straits[2]— on the French coast the light
Gleams and is gone; the cliffs of England stand,
Glimmering and vast, out in the tranquil bay.
Come to the window, sweet is the night air!
Only, from the long line of spray
Where the sea meets the moon-blanched[3] land,
Listen! you hear the grating roar[4]
Of pebbles which the waves draw back, and fling,
At their return, up the high strand,[5]
Begin, and cease, and then again begin,
With tremulous cadence slow, and bring
The eternal note of sadness in.

Sophocles[6] long ago
Heard it on the Aegean,[7] and it brought
Into his mind the turbid[8] ebb and flow
Of human misery; we
Find also in the sound a thought,
Hearing it by this distant northern sea.

The Sea of Faith
Was once, too, at the full, and round earth's shore
Lay like the folds of a bright girdle furled.[9]
But now I only hear
Its melancholy, long, withdrawing roar,
Retreating, to the breath
Of the night wind, down the vast edges drear
And naked shingles[10] of the world.

Ah, love, let us be true
To one another! for the world, which seems
To lie before us like a land of dreams,
So various, so beautiful, so new,
Hath really neither joy, nor love, nor light,
Nor certitude, nor peace, nor help for pain;
And we are here as on a darkling[11] plain
Swept with confused alarms of struggle and flight,
Where ignorant armies[12] clash by night.

Notes

1. The poem is written in irregular metrical form and rhyme scheme.
2. **the straits**: referring to the Strait of Dover, between England and France.
3. **moon-blanched**: become white in the moon light.
4. **the grating roar**: the rubbing pebbles give forth a rumbling sound. Cf. Wordsworth's "It Is a Beauteous Evening": "listen! the mighty Being is awake, /And doth with his eternal motion make/A sound like thunder — everlastingly."
5. **the high strand**: upper part of a coastline, perhaps what lies just above the tide-marks.
6. **Sophocles**: (ca. 496-405 B. C.) a Greek tragic dramatist, author of *Oedipus* and *Antigone*.
7. **Aegean**: the Aegean Sea, the name used by the Greeks and Romans for that part of the Mediterranean Sea between Asia Minor and Greece.
8. **turbid**: confused.
9. **like the folds of a bright girdle furled**: At high tide the water encircles the shore like the folds of bright clothing which have been compressed.
10. **shingles**: beach gravel composed of water-worn stones or pebbles.
11. **darkling**: lying in darkness.
12. **ignorant armies**: Some scholars think that it might refer to the revolution of 1848 or a reference to the siege of Rome by the French in 1849.

Study Questions

1. Describe the mood of the opening lines of the poem. Where and why does the mood shift?
2. What metaphor does Arnold use to describe Victorian "Faith"? To what kinds of faith may he refer?
3. How would you characterize the central concern of the poem?
4. How are the themes of the poem reflected in the arrangement of stanzas?
5. What is the speaker's assessment of the world? How do the sounds of the last stanza reinforce its meaning?

Essay Topics

1. What does Arnold mean by the "Sea of Faith"? Why does he say it was once full but is now withdrawing?
2. Do you think the view of human life presented in *Dover Beach* is applicable to today's world? Why or why not?

5.9 Gerard Manley Hopkins

5.9.1 About the Author

Hopkins (1844-1889) was born into a middle-class family of Welsh ancestry. His father was an insurance agent. He received his education first at Highgate School, then at Oxford. While studying classics at Oxford, he involved himself in the Oxford Movement. In 1866, following the example of Newman, he converted to Roman Catholicism, and in 1868 he decided to enter the priesthood. Yet, Oxford gave him the chance to have Walter Pater as his tutor, thus converting himself to the  cult of art. It was also at Oxford that he forged the friendship with Robert Bridges which would be of importance in his development as a poet. In 1882 Hopkins became a teacher at Mount St. Mary's College, Sheffield, and Stoneyhurst College, Lancashire, from where he progressed to professor of Greek at University College Dublin, though remaining a priest. During his lifetime he wrote a fairly small body of poetry and some prose works; but he published none of his poems. It was only through the efforts of his friend, Bridges, that his collected verse was published in 1918.

Hopkins wrote poems between 1875 and 1889. The themes of his poetry concern the relationship of man to God and the problem of man's suffering in a world created by God. His deeply moving poems are the last "dark" sonnets; for here the ruptured syntax, the inversions and the sound patterning answer a violence of spiritual conflict between faith and doubt as intense as any in English poetry. These poems are powerful statements of love and loss, of suffering and un-fulfillment, reflecting the contradictory feelings between his desire for an outlet for his art and his painful awareness of his priestly vocation.

Hopkins was also a great nature poet. The striking quality of his poetry lay in its energy which resulted from his close observation of and his excitement about the natural world. Hopkins could feel nature's beauty upon his pulses, and there was a reciprocal relationship between him and nature. Poems like *Spring*, *The Starlight Night*, *The Sea and the Skylark*, *The Windhover* and *Pied Beauty* are very remarkable nature poems, which communicate the excitement and individuality most immediately.

Hopkins was an important technical innovator in poetry writing. His experiment in meter resulted in "Sprung Rhythm" which allowed for the use in a line of verse of "either monosyllabic stressed feet or of stressed feet with any number of weak or slack syllables." In Hopkins' opinion, this "Sprung Rhythm" could achieve a flexibility rarely found in conventional meter. Hopkins also made full use of resources of language and imagery in his poetry writing. He forced the syntax to fit his thought by omitting the articles, pronouns, by breaking up combinations of words or by creating puns. His visional imagination was also powerful; consequently images play an important part in his poetry.

Hopkins' unconventional rhythm and syntax made his poetry seem very modern, but his concern with the imagination's shaping of the natural and religious world put him in the Victorian tradition.

5.9.2 "The Windhover"[1]

TO CHRIST OUR LORD

I caught this morning morning's minion,[2] king-
   dom of daylight's dauphin,[3] dapple-dawn-drawn Falcon, in his riding
   Of the rolling level underneath him steady air, and striding
High there, how he rung upon the rein of a wimpling wing[4]
In his ecstasy! then off, off forth on swing,
   As a skate's heel sweeps smooth on a bow-bend: the hurl and gliding
   Rebuffed the big wind. My heart in hiding
Stirred for a bird, — the achieve of, the mastery of the thing!

Brute beauty and valor and act, oh, air, pride, plume, here
   Buckle![5] AND[6] the fire that breaks from thee then, a billion
Times told lovelier, more dangerous, O my chevalier!

   No wonder of it: sheer plod makes plough down sillion[7]
Shine, and blue-bleak embers, ah my dear,
   Fall, gall[8] themselves, and gash gold-vermillion.

Notes

1. This poem is a sonnet. The octet (1st 8 lines) focuses on the bird in flight; the sestet (last 6 lines) moralizes. "Windhover" is a falcon or kestrel, which can hover in the wind by vibrating its wings, glide sideways, and dart for prey.
2. **minion**: darling.
3. **dauphin**: heir (literally, the title of the eldest son of the King of France); the word carries overtones of chivalry and splendor.
4. **how he rung upon the rein of a wimpling wing**: There is an implied comparison to a horse circling around its trainer at the end of a long rein. wimpling: rippling.
5. **Buckle**: The verb can be read as imperative or indicative. All three meanings of "buckle" are relevant: to prepare for action, to fasten together, to collapse.
6. **AND**: Hopkins emphasizes the "AND" to draw attention from the admiration of the bird and to the sense of Christ behind it which that admiration brings. A movement from appreciation of the life of nature to a religious sense of the God reflected in

nature is found in very many of Hopkins' poems.
7. **sillion**: The ridge between two furrows of a plowed field. Hopkins uses this archaic word perhaps to suggest an overtone from "silica" (the mineral which in the form of gleaming particles of quartz often makes dull rocks shine).
8. **gall**: break the surface of.

Study Questions

1. How does the speaker describe the falcon?
2. Why does the bird strike him as the crown prince ("dauphin") of the kingdom?
3. What does the speaker feel when he sees the bird riding like a horse in the sky?
4. What images does Hopkins use in this poem? Are they appropriate to the themes of the poem?
5. What does Hopkins believe about the presence of God in the natural world?
6. What does the octet (the first 8 lines) of this poem focus on?
7. How does the sestet (the final six lines) complete the poem's meaning?

5.10 Thomas Hardy

5.10.1 About the Author

Thomas Hardy (1840-1928), the son of a stonemason, was born near Dorchester, the area that later became the famous "Wessex" in many of his novels. When he was 8 years old, he went to the local school. At 16, he was apprenticed to a local architect. Six years later he went to London to work for a famous architect. In his spare time, he studied widely: language, literature, history, philosophy and art, and he even won two prizes for essays on architectural subjects. In 1870 Hardy met Emma Gifford in Cornwall. They fell in love and married four years later.

Hardy never took architecture as his desired profession. What he was interested was poetry. But he could not make a living by writing poetry. So he turned to write novels. His two novels, *Under the Greenwood Tree* (1872) and *Far from the Madding Crowd* (1874) came out with great success. So he gave up architecture for writing. In the following twenty-three years he produced over ten local-colored novels. In 1896 when he was tired of those hostile criticisms against his last two novels: *Tess of the D'Urbervilles* (1891) and *Jude the Obscure* (1896), Hardy returned to his first love — poetry writing. Of the eight volumes by Hardy — 918 poems in all — the most famous is *The Dynasts*, a long epic-drama about the Napoleonic Wars.

Living at the turn of the century, Hardy is often regarded as a transitional writer. In him we see the influence from both the past and the modern. In his novels, there is an apparent nostalgic touch in his description of the simple and beautiful though primitive rural life, which was gradually declining and disappearing as England marched into an industrial country. With those traditional characters he is always sympathetic. On the other hand, the immense impact of scientific discoveries and modern philosophic thoughts upon the man is quite obvious, too. He also believed that man's fate is pre-determinedly tragic, driven by a combined force of nature and culture. This pessimistic view of life predominates most of Hardy's later works and earns him a reputation as a naturalistic writer.

Hardy is a great painter of nature. In his hand, nature assumes the form of life and becomes a most powerful, forbidding force with its own life and will. His heroes and heroines, those unfortunate young men and women in their desperate struggle for personal fulfillment and happiness, are all vividly and realistically depicted. They all seem to possess a kind of exquisitely sensuous beauty. They are not only individual cases but also of universal truth. Their plight is not just their own; it applies to any one, any age. Finally, all the works of Hardy are noted for the rustic dialect and a poetic flavor which fits well into their perfectly designed architectural structures. They are the product of a conscientious artist.

5.10.2 "The Man He Killed"

> Had he and I but met
>   By some old ancient inn,
> We should have set us down to wet
>   Right many a nipperkin[1]!
>
> But ranged as infantry,
>   And staring face to face,
> I shot at him as he at me,
>   And killed him in his place.
>
> I shot him dead because —
>   Because he was my foe,
> Just so — my foe of course he was;
>   That's clear enough; although
>
> He thought he'd 'list[2], perhaps,
>   Off-hand like — just as I —
> Was out of work — had sold his traps —
>   No other reason why.

Yes; quaint and curious war is!
　　You shoot a fellow down
You'd treat if met where any bar is,
　　Or help to half-a-crown³.

Notes

1. **nipperkin**: small glass for ale, beer or wine.
2. **'list**: enlist (in the military).
3. **half-a-crown**: coin.

Study Questions

1. What reason does the speaker give for the shooting?
2. In what way does the speaker compare the dead man to himself?
3. Who should be blamed for the killing?
4. What is Hardy's attitude toward war?

5.10.3　An Excerpt from Chapter 35 of *Tess of the d'Urbervilles*

　　Her narrative ended¹; even its re-assertions and secondary explanations were done. Tess's voice throughout had hardly risen higher than its opening tone; there had been no exculpatory phrase of any kind, and she had not wept.

　　But the complexion even of external things seemed to suffer transmutation² as her announcement progressed. The fire in the grate looked impish — demoniacally funny, as if it did not care in the least about her strait. The fender grinned idly, as if it too did not care. The light from the water-bottle was merely engaged in a chromatic problem³. All material objects around announced their irresponsibility with terrible iteration. And yet nothing had changed since the moments when he had been kissing her; or rather, nothing in the substance of things. But the essence of things had changed.⁴

　　When she ceased the auricular impressions from their previous endearments seemed to hustle away into the corner of their brains, repeating themselves as echoes from a time of supremely purblind foolishness⁵.

　　Clare performed the irrelevant act of stirring the fire; the intelligence had not even yet got to the bottom of him⁶. After stirring the embers he rose to his feet; all the force of her disclosure had imparted itself now. His face had withered. In the strenuousness of his concentration he treadled fitfully on the floor. He could not, by any contrivance, think closely enough; that was the meaning of his vague movement. When he spoke it was in the most inadequate, commonplace voice of the many varied tones she had heard from him.

"Tess!"

"Yes, dearest."

"Am I to believe this? From your manner I am to take it as true. O you cannot be out of your mind! You ought to be! Yet you are not... My wife, my Tess — nothing in you warrants such a supposition as that?"

"I am not out of my mind," she said.

"And yet — " He looked vacantly at her, to resume with dazed senses: "Why didn't you tell me before? Ah, yes, you would have told me, in a way — but I hindered you, I remember!"

These and other of his words were nothing but the perfunctory babble of the surface while the depths remained paralyzed. He turned away, and bent over a chair. Tess followed him to the middle of the room where he was, and stood there staring at him with eyes that did not weep. Presently she slid down upon her knees beside his foot, and from this position she crouched in a heap.

"In the name of our love, forgive me!" she whispered with a dry mouth. "I have forgiven you for the same!"

And, as he did not answer, she said again —

"Forgive me as you are forgiven! I forgive you, Angel."

"You — yes, you do."

"But you do not forgive me?"

"O Tess, forgiveness does not apply to the case! You were one person; now you are another. My God — how can forgiveness meet such a grotesque — prestidigitation[7] as that!"

He paused, contemplating this definition; then suddenly broke into horrible laughter — as unnatural and ghastly as a laugh in hell.

"Don't — don't! It kills me quite, that!" she shrieked. "O have mercy upon me — have mercy!"

He did not answer; and, sickly white, she jumped up.

"Angel, Angel! what do you mean by that laugh?" she cried out. "Do you know what this is to me?"

He shook his head.

"I have been hoping, longing, praying, to make you happy! I have thought what joy it will be to do it, what an unworthy wife I shall be if I do not! That's what I have felt, Angel!"

"I know that."

"I thought, Angel, that you loved me — me, my very self! If it is I you do love, O how can it be that you look and speak so? It frightens me! Having begun to love you, I love you for ever — in all changes, in all disgraces, because you are yourself. I ask no more. Then how can you, O my own husband, stop loving me?"

"I repeat, the woman I have been loving is not you."

"But who?"

"Another woman in your shape."

She perceived in his words the realization of her own apprehensive foreboding in former times. He looked upon her as a species of imposter; a guilty woman in the guise of an innocent one. Terror was upon her white face as she saw it; her cheek was flaccid[8], and her mouth had almost the aspect of a round little hole. The horrible sense of his view of her so deadened her that she staggered; and he stepped forward, thinking she was going to fall.

"Sit down, sit down, " he said gently. "You are ill; and it is natural that you should be."

She did sit down, without knowing where she was, that strained look still upon her face, and her eyes such as to make his flesh creep.

"I don't belong to you any more, then; do I, Angel?" she asked helplessly. "It is not me, but another woman like me that he loved, he says."

The image raised caused her to take pity upon herself as one who was ill-used. Her eyes filled as she regarded her position further; she turned round and burst into a flood of self-sympathetic tears.

Clare was relieved at this change, for the effect on her of what had happened was beginning to be a trouble to him only less than the woe of the disclosure itself. He waited patiently, apathetically, till the violence of her grief had worn itself out, and her rush of weeping had lessened to a catching gasp at intervals.

"Angel, " she said suddenly, in her natural tones, the insane, dry voice of terror having left her now. "Angel, am I too wicked for you and me to live together?"

"I have not been able to think what we can do."

"I shan't ask you to let me live with you, Angel, because I have no right to! I shall not write to mother and sisters to say we be married, as I said I would do; and I shan't finish the good-hussif[9] I cut out and meant to make while we were in lodgings."

"Shan't you?"

"No, I shan't do anything, unless you order me to; and if you go away from me I shall not follow 'ee; and if you never speak to me any more I shall not ask why, unless you tell me I may."

"And if I order you to do anything?"

"I will obey you like your wretched slave, even if it is to lie down and die."

"You are very good. But it strikes me that there is a want of harmony between your present mood of self-sacrifice and your past mood of self-preservation."

These were the first words of antagonism. To fling elaborate sarcasms at Tess, however, was much like flinging them at a dog or cat. The charms of their subtlety passed by her unappreciated, and she only received them as inimical sounds which meant that anger ruled. She remained mute, not knowing that he was smothering his affection for her. She hardly observed that a tear descended slowly upon his cheek, a tear so large that it magnified the pores of the skin over which it rolled, like the object lens of a microscope. Meanwhile re-illumination as to the terrible and total change that her confession had wrought in his life, in his universe, returned to him, and he tried desperately to advance among the new conditions in which he stood. Some consequent action was necessary; yet what?

"Tess," he said, as gently as he could speak, "I cannot stay — in this room — just now. I will walk out a little way."

He quietly left the room, and the two glasses of wine that he had poured out for their supper — one for her, one for him — remained on the table untasted. This was what their Agape[10] had come to. At tea, two or three hours earlier, they had, in the freakishness of affection, drunk from one cup.

The closing of the door behind him, gently as it had been pulled to, roused Tess from her stupor. He was gone; she could not stay. Hastily flinging her cloak around her she opened the door and followed, putting out the candles as if she were never coming back. The rain was over and the night was now clear.

She was soon close at his heels, for Clare walked slowly and without purpose. His form beside her light gray figure looked black, sinister, and forbidding, and she felt as sarcasm the touch of the jewels of which she had been momentarily so proud. Clare turned at hearing her footsteps, but his recognition of her presence seemed to make no difference to him, and he went on over the five yawning arches of the great bridge in front of the house.

The cow and horse tracks in the road were full of water, and rain having been enough to charge them, but not enough to wash them away. Across these minute pools the reflected stars flitted in a quick transit as she passed; she would not have known they were shining overhead if she had not seen them there — the vastest things of the universe imaged in objects so mean.[11]

The place to which they had traveled today was in the same valley as Talbothays, but some miles lower down the river; and the surroundings being open she kept easily in sight of him. Away from the house the road wound through the meads, and along these she followed Clare without any attempt to come up with him or to attract him, but with dumb and vacant fidelity.

At last, however, her listless walk brought her up alongside him, and still he said nothing. The cruelty of fooled honesty is often great after enlightenment, and it was mighty in Clare now. The outdoor air had apparently taken away from him all tendency to act on impulse; she knew that he saw her without irradiation — in all her bareness;

Chapter 5　The Victorian Period

that Time was chanting his satiric psalm at her then —
 Behold, when thy face is made bare, he that loved thee shall hate;
 Thy face shall be no more fair at the fall of thy fate
 For thy life shall fall as a leaf and be shed as the rain;
 And the veil of thine head shall be grief, and the crown shall be pain. [12]

He was still intently thinking, and her companionship had now insufficient power to break or divert the strain of thought. What a weak thing her presence must have become to him! She could not help addressing Clare.

"What have I done — what have I done! I have not told of anything that interferes with or belies my love for you. You don't think I planned it, do you? It is in your own mind what you are angry at, Angel; it is not in me. O, it is not in me, and I am not that deceitful woman you think me!"

"H'm — well. Not deceitful, my wife; but not the same. No, not the same. But do not make me reproach you. I have sworn that I will not; and I will do everything to avoid it."

But she went on pleading in her distraction; and perhaps said things that would have been better left to silence.

"Angel! — Angel! I was a child — a child when it happened! I knew nothing of men."

"You were more sinned against than sinning[13], that I admit."

"Then will you not forgive me?"

"I do forgive you, but forgiveness is not all."

"And love me?"

To this question he did not answer.

"O Angel — my mother says that it sometimes happens so! — she knows several cases where they were worse than I, and the husband has not minded it much — has got over it at least. And yet the woman had not loved him as I do you!"

"Don't, Tess; don't argue. Different societies, different manners. You almost make me say you are an unapprehending peasant woman, who have never been initiated into the proportions of social things[14]. You don't know what you say."

"I am only a peasant by position, not by nature!"

She spoke with an impulse to anger, but it went as it came.

"So much the worse for you. I think that parson[15] who unearthed your pedigree would have done better if he had held his tongue. I cannot help associating your decline as a family with this other fact — of your want of firmness. Decrepit families imply decrepit wills, decrepit conduct. Heaven, why did you give me a handle for despising you more by informing me of your descent! Here was I thinking you a new-sprung child of nature; there were you, the belated seedling of an effete aristocracy[16]!"

"Lots of families are as bad as mine in that! Retty's family were once large landowners, and so were Dairyman Billett's. And the Debbyhouses, who now are carters, were once the De Bayeux family. You find such as I everywhere; 'tis a feature of our county[17], and I can't help it."

"So much the worse for the county."

She took these reproaches in their bulk simply, not in their particulars; he did not love her as he had loved her hitherto, and to all else she was indifferent.

They wandered on again in silence. It was said afterwards that a cottager of Wellbridge, who went out late that night for a doctor, met two lovers in the pastures, walking very slowly, without converse, one behind the other, as in a funeral procession, and the glimpse that he obtained of their faces seemed to denote that they were anxious and sad. Returning later, he passed them again in the same field, progressing just as slowly, and as regardless of the hour and of the cheerless night as before. It was only on account of his preoccupation with his own affairs, and the illness in his house, that he did not bear in mind the curious incident, which, however, he recalled a long while after.

During the interval of the cottager's going and coming, she had said to her husband —

"I don't see how I can help being the cause of much misery to you all your life. The river is down there. I can put an end to myself in it. I am not afraid."

"I don't wish to add murder to my other follies[18]," he said.

"I will leave something to show that I did it myself — on account of my shame. They will not blame you then."

"Don't speak so absurdly — I wish not to hear it. It is nonsense to have such thoughts in this kind of case, which is rather one for satirical laughter than for tragedy. You don't in the least understand the quality of the mishap. It would be viewed in the light of a joke by nine-tenths of the world if it were known. Please oblige me by returning to the house, and going to bed."

"I will," said she dutifully.

They had rambled round by a road which led to the well-known ruins of the Cistercian abbey[19] behind the mill, the latter having, in centuries past, been attached to the monastic establishment. The mill still worked on, food being a perennial necessity; the abbey had perished, creeds being transient. One continually sees the ministration of the temporary outlasting the ministration of the eternal[20]. Their walk having been circuitous they were still not far from the house, and in obeying his direction she only had to reach the large stone bridge across the main river, and follow the road for a few yards. When she got back everything remained as she had left it, the fire being still burning. She did not stay downstairs for more than a minute, but proceeded to her chamber, whither the luggage had been taken. Here she sat down on the edge of the bed, looking blankly around, and presently began to undress. In removing the light towards the bedstead its rays fell upon the tester of white dimity[21]; something was hanging beneath it, and she lifted the candle to see what it was. A bough of mistletoe[22]. Angel had put it there; she knew that in an instant. This was the explanation of that mysterious parcel which it had been so difficult to pack and bring; whose contents he would not explain to her, saying that time would soon show her the purpose thereof. In his zest and his gaiety he had hung it there. How foolish and inopportune that mistletoe looked now.

Having nothing more to fear, having scarce anything to hope, for that he would relent there seemed no promise whatever, she lay down dully. When sorrow ceases to be speculative sleep sees her opportunity. Among so many happier moods which forbid repose this was a mood which welcomed it, and in a few minutes the lonely Tess forgot existence, surrounded by the aromatic stillness of the chamber that had once, possibly, been the bride-chamber of her own ancestry.

Notes

1. **Her narrative ended**: Tess confessed her affair with Aleck to Angel.
2. **transmutation**: the change of one situation into another.
3. **a chromatic problem**: that is, a problem about color.
4. **And yet nothing had changed... But the essence of things had changed**: the sentences imply that things around Tess are still the same but they have made quite a different impression on her now.
5. **a time of supremely purblind foolishness**: a time of extremely blind foolishness, which refers to their early passionate love.
6. **the intelligence had not even yet got to the bottom of him**: Tess's confession stuns him so much that he is unable to recover from his normal wit.
7. **prestidigitation**: sleight of hand or any artful trick. The word used here to display Clare's feeling that Tess's confession has completely changed herself as if the case of a prestidigitation.
8. **flaccid**: yielding to pressure readily or without resistance, or lacking firmness.
9. **good-hussif**: (Dial.) bag holding needle and thread.
10. **Agape**: (Greek) love-feast, as held by the early Christians.
11. **objects so mean**: referring to those pools of water in the road.
12. **Behold, when thy face... shall be pain**: quoted from a chorus in Swinburne's *Atalanta in Calydon*.
13. **You were more sinned against than sinning**: Cf. a man more sinned than sinning (*King Lear*, III, 2).
14. **who have never been initiated into the proportions of social things**: who have never been taught the knowledge of social relationship between different ranks.
15. **that parson**: Parson Tringham, who discovers Tess's kindred with the noble

D'Urbervilles.

16. **an effete aristocracy**: an aristocracy who decays so much that he is unable in fertility.
17. **'tis a feature of our county**: It is a feature of our Dorsetshire, where there had been a great number of French descendents.
18. **my other follies**: referring to Angel's love for and marriage to Tess.
19. **the Cistercian abbey**: referring to an abbey in Dorsetshire, which was built by members of a monastic order founded by St. Robert of Molesme in 1098 at Citeaux, France, under an austere Benedictine rule.
20. **the ministration of the temporary outlasting the ministration of the eternal**: material things outlasting the spiritual things, such as religion.
21. **the tester of white dimity**: canopy with white stripes (dimity: stout cotton cloth, with raised pattern, often used for bed-hangings).
22. **mistletoe**: a green shrub with small white berries, which was traditionally believed to bring good luck and fertility. Angel's hanging some over the bed was a light-hearted gesture of paganism.

Study Questions
1. What effect does Tess's confession have on Angel?
2. Why is Angel unable to forgive Tess when she just bestowed the gift of forgiveness on him?
3. Why does Tess submit to Angel's anger and take no action to win him back?
4. What moral differences between men and women in the Victorian period, does this chapter reflect?

Essay Topics
1. Discuss the character of Tess. To what extent is she a helpless victim?
2. How does Angel change in the novel?

Chapter 6   The Modern Period

6.1   An Introduction

In the second half of the 19th century and the early decades of the 20th century, both natural and social sciences in Europe had enormously advanced. Their rapid development led to great gains in material wealth. But when capitalism came into its monopoly stage, the sharpened contradictions between socialized production and the private ownership caused frequent economic depressions and mass unemployment. The gap between the rich and the poor were further deepened. To crown it all, the catastrophic First World War tremendously weakened the British Empire and brought about great sufferings to its people as well. The postwar economic dislocation and spiritual disillusion produced a profound impact upon the British people, who came to see the prevalent wretchedness in capitalism. The Second World War marked the last stage of the disintegration of the British Empire. Britain suffered heavy losses in the war: thousands of people were killed; the economy was ruined; and almost all its former colonies were lost. The once sun-never-set empire finally collapsed.

All these radical changes gave rise to all kinds of philosophical ideas in Western Europe. In the mid-19th century, Karl Marx and Friedrich Engels put forward the theory of scientific socialism, which not only provides a guiding principle for the working people, but also inspires them to make dauntless fights for their own emancipation. Darwin's theory of evolution exerted a strong influence over the people, causing many to lose their religious faith. The social Darwinism, under the cover of "survival of the fittest", vehemently advocated colonialism or jingoism. Einstein's theory of relativity provided entirely new ideas to the concepts of time and space. Freud's analytical psychology had drastically altered our conception of human nature. Arthur Schopenhauer, a pessimistic philosopher, started a rebellion against rationalism, stressing the importance of will and intuition. Having inherited the basic principles from Schopenhauer, Friedrich Nietzsche went further against rationalism by advocating the doctrines of power and superman and completely rejecting the Christian morality. Based on the major ideas of his predecessors, Henry Bergson established his irrational philosophy, which put emphasis on creation, intuition, irrationality and unconsciousness. The irrational philosophers exerted immense influence upon the major modernist writers in Britain.

Modernism rose out of skepticism and disillusion of capitalism. The appalling shock of the First World War severely destroyed people's faith in the Victorian values; and the rise of the irrational philosophy and new science greatly incited writers to make new explorations on human natures and human relationships.

The French symbolism, appearing in the late 19th century, heralded modernism. After the First World War, all kinds of literary trends of modernism appeared: expressionism, surrealism, futurism, Dadaism, imagism and streams of consciousness. Towards the 1920s, these trends converged into a mighty torrent of modernist movement, which swept across the whole Europe and America. The major figures that were associated with this movement were Kafka, Picasso, Pound, Webern, Eliot, Joyce and Virginia Woolf. Modernism was somewhat curbed in the 1930s. But after the Second World War, a variety of modernism, or post-modernism, like existentialist literature, theater of absurd, new novels and black humor, rose with the spur of the existentialist idea that "the world was absurd, and the human life was an agony".

Modernism takes the irrational philosophy and the theory of psycho-analysis as its theoretical base. The major themes of the modernist literature are the distorted, alienated and ill relationships between man and nature, man and society, man and man, and man and himself. The modernist writers concentrate more on the private than on the public, more on the subjective than on the objective. They are mainly concerned with the inner being of an individual. Therefore, they pay more attention to the psychic time than the chronological one. In their writings, the past, the present and the future are mingled together and exist at the same time in the consciousness of an individual.

Modernism is, in many aspects, a reaction against realism. It rejects rationalism, which is the theoretical base of realism; it excludes from its major concern the external, objective, material world, which is the only creative source of realism; by advocating a free experimentation on new forms and new techniques in literary creation. It casts away almost all the traditional elements in literature such as story, plot, character, chronological narration, etc., which are essential to realism. As a result, the works created by the modernist writers are often labeled as anti-novel, anti-poetry and anti-drama.

The 20th century has witnessed a great achievement in English poetry. In the early years of this century, Thomas Hardy and the war poets of the younger generation were important realistic poets. Hardy expressed his strong sympathies for the suffering poor and his bitter disgusts at the social evils in his poetry as in his novels. The soldiers-poets of the First World War revealed the appalling brutality of the war in the most realistic way. The early poems of Pound and Eliot and Yeats's matured poetry marked the rise of "modern poetry", which was, in some sense, a revolution against the conventional ideas and forms of the Victorian poetry. The modernist poets fought against the romantic fuzziness and self-indulged emotionalism, advocating new ideas in poetry-writing such as to use the language of common speech, to create new rhythms as the expression of a new mood, to allow absolute freedom in choosing subjects, and to use hard, clear and precise images in poems.

The 1930s witnessed great economic depressions, mass unemployment, and the rise of the Nazis. Facing such a severe situation, most of the young intellects started to turn to the left. Therefore the period was known as "the red thirties". A group of young poets during this period expressed in their poetry a radical political enthusiasm and a strong protest against fascism.

With the coming of the 1950s, there was a return of realistic poetry again. By advocating reason, moral discipline and traditional forms, a new generation of poets started "The Movement", which explicitly rejected the modernist influence. There was no significant poetic movement in the 1960s. A multiplicity of choices opened to both the poet and the reader. Poets gradually moved into more individual styles.

The realistic novels in the early 20th century were the continuation of the Victorian tradition; yet its exposing and criticizing power against capitalist evils had been somewhat weakened both in width and depth. The outstanding realistic novelists of this period were John Galsworthy, H. G. Wells and Arnold Bennett. The three trilogies of Galsworthy's Forsyte novels are masterpieces of critical realism in the early 20th century, which revealed the corrupted capitalist world. In his novels of social satire, H. G. Wells made realistic studies of the aspirations and frustrations of the "Little Man"; whereas Bennett presented a vivid picture of the English life in the industrial Midlands in his best novels.

Realism was, to a certain extent, eclipsed by the rapid rise of modernism in the 1920s. But with the strong swing of leftism in the 1930s, novelists began to turn their attention to the urgent social problems. They also enriched the traditional ways of creation by adopting some of the modernist techniques. However, the realistic novels of this period were more or less touched by a pessimistic mood, pre-occupied with the theme of man's loneliness, and shaped in different forms: social satires by Aldous Huxley (*Brave New World*, 1932) and George Orwell (*Nineteen Eighty-Four*, 1949); comic satires on the English upper class by Evelyn Waugh (*A Handful of Dust*, 1934); and Catholic novels by Graham Greene (*The Power and the Glory*, 1940). Another important aspect of realistic novels in this period is the fact that there rose a few working-class writers, who gave a direct portray of the working-people's poverty and sufferings, by singing highly the heroic struggles against capitalism waged by the working class. Among this group, the Scottish writer Lewis Grassic Gibbon was the most outstanding. His Trilogy: *Sunset Song* (1932), *Cloud Howe* (1933), and *Grey Granite* (1934) presented the social changes and the working-people's life on farms, in towns and cities through the personal experience of Chris Guthrie.

In the mid-1950s and early 1960s, there appeared a group of young novelists and playwrights with lower-middle-class or working-class background, who were known as "the Angry Young Men". They demonstrated a particular disillusion over the depressing situation in Britain and launched a bitter protest against the outmoded social and political values in their society. Kingsley Amis, John Wain, John Braine and Alan Sillitoe were the major novelists in this group. Amis was the first to start the attack on middle-class privileges and power in his novel *Lucky Jim* (1954). Both Braine and Sillitoe came from working-class families. They portrayed unadorned working-class life in their novels with great freshness and vigor of the working-class language.

Having been merged and interpenetrated with modernism in the past several decades, the realistic novel of the 1960s and 1970s appeared in a new face with a richer, more vigorous and more diversified style.

The first three decades of this century were golden years of the modernist novel. In stimulating the technical innovations of novel creation, the theory of the Freudian and Jungian psycho-analysis played a particularly important role. With the notion that multiple levels of consciousness existed simultaneously in the human mind, that one's present was the sum of his past, present and future, and that the whole truth about human beings existed in the unique, isolated, and private world of each individual. Writers like Dorothy Richardson, James Joyce and Virginia Woolf concentrated all their efforts on digging into the human consciousness. They had created unprecedented stream-of-consciousness novels such as *Pilgrimage* (1915-1938) by Richardson, *Ulysses* (1922) by Joyce, and *Mrs. Dalloway* (1925) by Woolf. One of the remarkable features of their writings was their continuous experimentation on new and sophisticated techniques in novel writing, which made tremendous impacts on the creation of both realistic and modernist novels in the 20th century. James Joyce is the most outstanding stream-of-consciousness novelist; in *Ulysses*, his encyclopedia-like masterpiece, Joyce presents a fantastic picture of the disjointed, illogical, illusory, and mental-emotional life of Leopold Bloom, who becomes the symbol of everyman in the post-World-War-I Europe.

In the works of E. M. Forster and D. H. Lawrence, old traditions were still there, but their subject matter about human relationships and their symbolic or psychological presentations of the novel were entirely modern. Forster's masterpiece, *A Passage to India* (1924), was a novel of decidedly symbolist aspirations, in which the author set up, within a realistic story, a fable of moral significance that implied a highly mystical, symbolic view of life, death, human relationship, and the relationship of man with the infinite universe. D. H. Lawrence was regarded as revolutionary as Joyce in novel writing; but unlike Joyce, he was not concerned with technical innovations; his interest lay in the tracing of the psychological development of his characters and in his energetic criticism of the dehumanizing effect of the capitalist industrialization on human nature. He believed that life impulse was the primacy of man's instinct, and that any conscious repression of such an impulse would cause distortion or perversion of the individual's personality. In his best novels like *The Rainbow* (1915) and *Women in Love* (1920), Lawrence made a bold psychological exploration of various human relationships, especially those between men and women, with a great frankness. Lawrence claimed

Chapter 6 The Modern Period

that the alienation of the human relationships and the perversion of human nature in the modern society were caused by the desires for power and money, by the shams and frauds of middle-class life, and, above all, by the whole capitalist mechanical civilization, which turned men into inhuman machines.

Modernist novels came to a decline in the 1930s, though Joyce and Woolf continued their experiments. After the Second World War, modernism had another upsurge with the rise of existentialism, but it was reflected mainly in drama.

The most celebrated dramatists in the last decade of the 19th century were Oscar Wilde and George Bernard Shaw, who, in a sense, pioneered the modern drama, though they did not make so many innovations in techniques and forms as modernist poets or novelists. Wilde expressed a satirical and bitter attitude towards the upper-class people by revealing their corruption, their snobbery, and their hypocrisy in his plays, especially in his masterpiece — *The Importance of Being Earnest* (1895). Shaw was a more important figure in drama than Wilde. He is considered to be the best-known English dramatist since Shakespeare. His works were examples of the plays that were inspired by social criticism. John Galsworthy carried on this tradition of social criticism in his plays. By dramatizing social and ethical problems, Galsworthy made considerable achievements in his plays. *The Silver Box* (1906) and *Strife* (1910) were such examples, in which Galsworthy presented not only realistic pictures of social injustice, but also the workers' heroic struggles against their employers.

With their joint efforts, the Irish playwrights like W. B. Yeats, Lady Gregory, and J. M. Synge brought about the Irish National Theater Movement in the early 20th century, thus starting an Irish dramatic revival. Yeats, a prominent poet of this century, was the leader of this movement. He was a verse playwright who desired to restore lyrical drama to popularity. With the heroic portrayal of spiritual truth as his main concern, Yeats wrote a number of verse plays, introducing Irish myths and folk legends; but the plot in his plays was seldom very dramatic. As a result, none of his plays was among the best of his poetical achievement. J. M. Synge was the most gifted dramatist of the movement. By adopting the vivid figurative language of the Irish peasantry, Synge brought vigor, ironic humor and dramatic pathos to the Irish stage. His most popular play is the comedy, *The Playboy of the Western World* (1907). Another original and distinguished artist that the Abbey Theater produced was Sean O'Casey, who dealt in his work with political and social themes of the Irish Nationalist Movement, and with the suffering of the Irish townspeople. By combining "richness" with "reality", O'Casey presented an urban drama of Dublin slum life to the Irish audience in plays like *Juno and the Paycock* (1925), and *The Plough and the Stars* (1926).

The 1930s witnessed a revival of poetic drama in England. One of the early experimenters was T. S. Eliot who regarded drama as the best medium of poetry. Eliot wrote several verse plays and made a considerable success. *Murder in the Cathedral*

(1935), with its purely dramatic power, remains the most popular of his verse plays, in spite of its primarily religious purpose. After Eliot, Christopher Fry had gained considerable success in poetic drama. His exuberant though poetically commonplace verse drama, *The Lady's Not for Burning* (1948), attracted delighted audience.

The English dramatic revolution came in the 1950s under various European and American influences. This revolution developed in two directions: the working-class drama and the Theater of Absurd.

The working-class drama was started by a group of young writers from the lower-middle class, or working class, who presented a new type of plays which expressed a mood of restlessness, anger and frustration, a spirit of rebelliousness, and a strong emotional protest against the existing social institutions. John Osborne was the man who started the first change in drama by presenting his play, *Look Back in Anger* (1956). In a fresh, unadorned working-class language, the play angrily, violently and unrelentingly condemned the contemporary social evils. With an entirely new sense of reality, Osborne brought vitality to the English theater and became known as the first "Angry Young Man".

The most original playwright of the Theater of Absurd is Samuel Beckett, who wrote about human beings living a meaningless life in an alien, decaying world. His first play, *Waiting for Godot* (1955), is regarded as the most famous and influential play of the Theater of Absurd.

6.2 George Bernard Shaw

6.2.1 About the Author

George Bernard Shaw (1856-1950) was born in Dublin, Ireland, of English parentage. With an unhappy childhood, he did not do well at school but showed much interest in literature. He left school at the age of 14 and started to work in a land-agent's office. His job was to collect rents in the local districts. Through his work he came to know the poor people's miserable life. This experience surely enriched his understanding of the society and the sufferings of the people.

In 1876, Shaw gave up his job and went to London, where he devoted much of his time to self-education by widely reading in the libraries. Between 1879 and 1883, he wrote 5 novels, but none of them brought him profit or fame. Later Shaw came under the influence of Henry George and William Morris and took an interest in socialist theories. In 1884 Shaw joined the Fabian Society. Together with his fellow Fabians, he regarded the establishment of socialism as the final goal. But on how to achieve it, he differed greatly from the Marxists. He was against the means of violent revolution or armed struggle in achieving the goal of socialism; he also had a distrust of the uneducated working class in fighting against capitalists. He held that only those superior intellects could have the ability to shoulder this task.

In a period of ten years from 1885, Shaw served as a critic of music and drama for a number of magazines and newspapers. His criticism was witty, biting and often brilliant. Shaw was strongly against the credo of "art for art's sake" held by those decadent aesthetic artists. Shaw held that art should serve social purposes by reflecting human life, revealing social contradictions and educating the common people.

His career as a dramatist began in 1892, when his first play *Widowers' Houses* (1892) was put on by the Independent Theater Society. Following this success, his wonderful plays came out one after another. In his long dramatic career, Shaw wrote more than 50 plays, touching upon a variety of subjects. His early plays were mainly concerned with social problems and directed towards the criticism of the contemporary social, economic, moral and religious evils. *Widowers' Houses* and *Mrs. Warren's Profession* (1893) can be regarded as the typical representatives of Shaw's early plays. Shaw wrote quite a few history plays, in which he kept an eye on contemporary society. The important plays of this group are *Caesar and Cleopatra* (1898) and *St. Joan* (1923). Shaw also produced several plays, exploring his idea of "Life Force", the power that would create superior beings to be equal to God and to solve all the social, moral and metaphysical problems of human society. The typical examples of this group are *Man and Superman* (1903) and *Back to Methuselah* (1921).

6.2.2 An Excerpt from *Pygmalion*

ACT IV

The Wimpole Street laboratory, Midnight. Nobody in the room. The clock on the mantelpiece strikes twelve. The fire is not alight: it is a summer night.

Presently Higgins[1] and Pickering[2] are heard on the stars.

HIGGINS [*calling down to Pickering*] I say, Pick: lock up, will you? I shant[3] be going out again.

PICKERING Right. Can Mrs. Pearce go to bed? We dont[4] want anything more, do we?

HIGGINS Lord, no!

ELIZA *opens the door and is seen on the lighted landing in all the finery in which she has just won HIGGINS'S bet for him. She comes to the hearth, and switches on the electric lights there. She is tired: her pallor[5] contrasts strongly with her dark eyes and hair; and her expression is almost tragic. She takes off her cloak;*

puts her fan and gloves on the piano; and sits down on the bench, brooding and silent. HIGGINS, *in evening dress, with overcoat and hat, comes in, carrying a smoking jacket which he has picked up downstairs. He takes off the hat and overcoat, throws them carelessly on the newspaper stand, disposes of his coat in the same way, puts on the smoking jacket, and throws himself wearily into the easy-chair at the hearth.* PICKERING, *similarly attired, comes in. He also takes off his hat and overcoat, and is about to throw them on* HIGGINS'S *when he hesitates.*

PICKERING I say: Mrs Pearce[6] will row if we leave these things lying about in the drawing room.

HIGGINS Oh, chuck them over the bannisters into the hall. She'll find them there in the morning and put them away all right. She'll think we were drunk.

PICKERING We are, slightly. Are there any letters?

HIGGINS I didn't look. [PICKERING *takes the overcoats and hats and goes down stairs.* HIGGINS *begins half singing half yawning an air from* La Fanciulla del Golden West[7]. *Suddenly he stops and exclaims*] I wonder where the devil my slippers are!

ELIZA *looks at him darkly, then rises suddenly and leaves the room.*

HIGGINS *yawns again, and resumes his song.*

PICKERING *returns, with the contents of the letter-box in his hand.*

PICKERING Only circulars[8], and this coroneted billet-doux[9] for you. [*He throws the circulars into the fender, and posts himself on the hearthrug, with his back to the grate.*]

HIGGINS [*glancing at the billet-doux*] Money-lender. [*He throws the letter after the circulars.*]

ELIZA *returns with a pair of large down-at-heel slippers. She places them on the carpet before* HIGGINS, *and sits as before without a word.*

HIGGINS [*yawning again*] Oh Lord! What an evening! What a crew! What a silly tomfoolery[10]! [*He raises his shoe to unlace it, and catches sight of the slippers. He stops unlacing and looks at them as if they had appeared there of their own accord.*] Oh! they're there, are they?

PICKERING [*stretching himself*] Well, I feel a bit tired. It's been a long day. The garden party, a dinner party, and the reception! Rather too much of a good thing. But you've won your bet, Higgins. Eliza did the trick, and something to spare, eh?

HIGGINS [*fervently*] Thank God it's over!

ELIZA *flinches violently; but they take no notice of her; and she recovers herself and sits stonily as before.*

PICKERING Were you nervous at the garden party? *I was.* Eliza didn't seem a bit nervous.

HIGGINS Oh, she wasnt nervous. I knew she'd be all right. No, it's the strain of putting the job through all these months that has told on me. It was interesting enough at first, while we were at the phonetics; but after that I got deadly sick of it. If I hadnt backed myself to do it I should have chucked the whole thing up two months ago. It was a silly notion: the whole thing has been a bore.

PICKERING Oh come! the garden party was frightfully exciting. My heart began beating like anything.

HIGGINS Yes, for the first three minutes. But when I saw we were going to win hands down, I felt like a bear in a cage, hanging about doing nothing. The dinner was worse: sitting gorging there for over an hour, with nobody but a damned fool of a fashionable woman to talk to! I tell you, Pickering, never again for me. No more artificial duchess. The whole thing has been simple purgatory[11].

PICKERING Youve never been broken in properly to the social routine. [*Strolling over to the piano*] I rather enjoy dipping into it occasionally myself, it makes me feel young again. Anyhow, it was a great success, an immense success. I was quite frightened once or twice because Eliza was doing it so well. You see, lots of the real people cant do it at all: theyre such fools that they think style comes by nature to people in their position; and so they never learn. Theres always something professional about doing a thing superlatively well.

HIGGINS Yes, thats what drives me mad: the silly people dont know their own silly business. [*Rising*] However, it's over and done with; and now I can go to bed at last without dreading tomorrow.

ELIZA'S *beauty becomes murderous.*

PICKERING I think I shall turn in too. Still, it's been a great occasion: a triumph for you. Goodnight. [*He goes.*]

HIGGINS [*following him*] Good-night. [*Over his shoulder, at the door*] Put out the lights, Eliza, and tell Mrs Pearce not to make coffee for me in the morning. I'll take tea. [*He goes out.*]

ELIZA *tries to control herself and feel indifferent as she rises and walks across to the hearth to switch off the lights. By the time she gets there she is on the point of screaming. She sits down in* HIGGINS'S *chair and holds on hard to the arms. Finally she gives way and flings herself furiously on the floor raging.*

HIGGINS [*in despairing wrath outside*] What the devil have I done with my slippers? [*He appears at the door.*]

ELIZA [*snatching up the slippers, and hurling them at him one after the other with all her force*] There are your slippers. And there. Take your slippers, and may you never have a day's luck with them!

HIGGINS [*astounded*] What on earth — ! [*He comes to her.*] Whats the matter? Get up. [*He pulls her up.*] Anything wrong?

ELIZA [*breathless*] Nothing wrong — with you. Ive won your bet for you, havnt I? Thats enough for you. I dont matter, I suppose.

HIGGINS You won my bet! You! Presumptuous[12] insect! I won it. What did you throw those slippers at me for?

ELIZA Because I wanted to smash your face. I'd like to kill you, you selfish brute. Why didnt you leave me where you picked me out of — in the gutter? You thank God it's all over, and that now you can throw me back again there, do you? [*She crisps her fingers*[13] *frantically.*]

HIGGINS [*looking at her in cool wonder*] The creature is nervous, after all.

ELIZA [*gives a suffocated scream of fury, and instinctively darts her nails at his face!!*]

HIGGINS [*catching her wrists*] Ah! would you? Claws in, you cat. How dare you shew your temper to me? Sit down and be quiet. [*He throws her roughly into the easy-chair.*]

ELIZA [*crushed by superior strength and weight*] Whats to become of me? Whats to become of me?

HIGGINS How the devil do I know whats to become of you? What does it matter what becomes of you?

ELIZA You dont care. I know you dont care. You wouldnt care if I was dead. I'm nothing to you — not so much as them slippers.

HIGGINS [*thundering*] Those slippers.

ELIZA [*with bitter submission*] Those slippers. I didnt think it made any difference now.

A pause. ELIZA *hopeless and crushed.* HIGGINS *a little uneasy.*

HIGGINS [*in his loftiest manner*] Why have you begun going on like this? May I ask whether you complain of your treatment here?

ELIZA No.

HIGGINS Has anybody behaved badly to you? Colonel Pickering? Mrs Pearce? Any of the servants?

ELIZA No.

HIGGINS I presume you dont pretend that I have treated you badly.

ELIZA No.

HIGGINS I am glad to hear it. [*He moderates his tone.*] Perhaps youre tired after the strain of the day. Will you have a glass of champagne? [*He moves towards the door.*]

ELIZA No. [*Recollecting her manners*] Thank you.

HIGGINS [*good-humored again*] This has been coming on you for some days. I suppose it was natural for you to be anxious about the garden party. But thats all over now. [*He pats her kindly on the shoulder. She writhes.*] Theres nothing more to worry about.

ELIZA   No. Nothing more for you to worry about. [*She suddenly rises and gets away from him by going to the piano bench, where she sits and hides her face.*]   Oh God! I wish I was dead.

HIGGINS   [*staring after her in sincere surprise*]   Why? In heaven's name, why? [*Reasonably, going to her*]   Listen to me, Eliza. All this irritation is purely subjective.

ELIZA   I dont understand. I'm too ignorant.

HIGGINS   It's only imagination. Low spirits and nothing else. Nobody's hurting you. Nothing's wrong. You go to bed like a good girl and sleep it off[14]. Have a little cry and say your prayers; that will make you comfortable.

ELIZA   I heard your prayers. "Thank God it's all over!"

HIGGINS   [*impatiently*]   Well, dont you thank God it's all over? Now you are free and can do what you like.

ELIZA   [*pulling herself together in desperation*]   What am I fit for? What have you left me fit for? Where am I to go? What am I to do? Whats to become of me?

HIGGINS   [*enlightened, but not at all impressed*]   Oh, thats whats worrying you, is it? [*He thrusts his hands into his pockets, and walks about in his usual manner, rattling the contents of his pockets, as if condescending to a trivial subject out of pure kindness.*]   I shouldnt bother about it if I were you. I should imagine you wont have much difficulty in settling yourself somewhere or other, though I hadnt quite realized that you were going away. [*She looks quickly at him: he does not look at her, but examines the dessert stand on the piano and decides that he will eat an apple.*]   You might marry, you know. [*He bites a large piece out of the apple, and munches[15] it noisily.*]   You see, Eliza, all men are not confirmed old bachelors like me and the Colonel. Most men are the marrying sort (poor devils!); and youre not bad-looking; it's quite a pleasure to look at you sometimes — not now, of course, because youre crying and looking as ugly as the very devil; but when youre all right and quite yourself, youre what I should call attractive. That is, to the people in the marrying line, you understand. You go to bed and have a good nice rest; and then get up and look at yourself in the glass; and you wont feel so cheap.

ELIZA *again looks at him, speechless, and does not stir.*

The look is quite lost on him: he eats his apple with a dreamy expression of happiness, as it is quite a good one.

HIGGINS   [*a genial afterthought occurring to him*]   I dare say my mother could find some chap or other who would do very well.

ELIZA   We were above that at the corner of Tottenham Court Road.

HIGGINS   [*waking up*]   What do you mean?

ELIZA   I sold flowers. I didnt sell myself. Now youve made a lady of me I'm not fit to sell anything else. I wish youd left me where you found me.

HIGGINS [*slinging the core of the apple decisively into the grate*] Tosh, Eliza. Dont you insult human relations by dragging all this cant[16] about buying and selling into it. You neednt marry the fellow if you dont like him.

ELIZA What else am I to do?

HIGGINS Oh, lots of things. What about your old idea of a florist's shop? Pickering could set you up in one: he has lots of money. [*Chuckling*] He'll have to pay for all those togs you have been wearing today; and that, with the hire of the jewellery, will make a big hole in two hundred pounds. Why, six months ago you would have thought it the millennium to have a flower shop of your own. Come! youll be all right. I must clear off to bed: I'm devilish sleepy. By the way, I came down for something; I forget what it was.

ELIZA Your slippers.

HIGGINS Oh yes, of course. You shied them at me. [*He picks them up, and is going out when she rises and speaks to him.*]

ELIZA Before you go, sir —

HIGGINS [*dropping the slippers in his surprise at her calling him Sir*] Eh?

ELIZA Do my clothes belong to me or to Colonel Pickering?

HIGGINS [*coming back into the room as if her question were the very climax of unreason*] What the devil use would they be to Pickering?

ELIZA He might want them for the next girl you pick up to experiment on.

HIGGINS [*shocked and hurt*] Is that the way you feel towards us?

ELIZA I dont want to hear anything more about that. All I want to know is whether anything belongs to me. My own clothes were burnt.

HIGGINS But what does it matter? Why need you start bothering about that in the middle of the night?

ELIZA I want to know what I may take away with me. I dont want to be accused of stealing.

HIGGINS [*now deeply wounded*] Stealing! You shouldnt have said that, Eliza. That shews a want of feeling.

ELIZA I'm sorry. I'm only a common ignorant girl; and in my station I have to be careful. There cant be any feelings between the like of you and the like of me. Please will you tell me what belongs to me and what doesn't?

HIGGINS [*very sulky*] You may take the whole damned houseful if you like. Except the jewels. Theyre hired. Will that satisfy you? [*He turns on his heel and is about to go in extreme dudgeon*[17].]

ELIZA [*drinking in his emotion like nectar*[18], *and nagging him to provoke a further supply*] Stop, please. [*She takes off her jewels.*] Will you take these to your room and keep them safe? I dont want to run the risk of their being missing.

HIGGINS [*furious*] Hand them over. [*She puts them into his hands.*] If these belonged to me instead of to the jeweler, I'd ram them down your ungrateful throat. [*He perfunctorily thrusts them into his pockets, unconsciously decorating himself with the protruding ends of the chains.*]

ELIZA [*taking a ring off*] This ring isnt the jeweler's: it's the one you bought me in Brighton. I dont want it now. [HIGGINS *dashes the ring violently into the fireplace, and turns on her so threateningly that she crouches over the piano with her hands over her face, and exclaims*] Dont you hit me.

HIGGINS Hit you! You infamous creature, how dare you accuse me of such a thing? It is you who have hit me. You have wounded me to the heart.

ELIZA [*thrilling with hidden joy*] I'm glad. I've got a little of my own back, anyhow.

HIGGINS [*with dignity, in his finest professional style*] You have caused me to lose my temper: a thing that has hardly ever happened to me before. I prefer to say nothing more tonight. I am going to bed.

ELIZA [*pertly*] You'd better leave a note for Mrs Pearce about the coffee; for she wont be told by me.

HIGGINS [*formally*] Damn Mrs Pearce; and damn the coffee; and damn you; and [*wildly*] damn my own folly in having lavished my hard-earned knowledge and the treasure of my regard and intimacy on a heartless guttersnipe. [*He goes out with impressive decorum, and spoils it by slamming the door savagely.*]

ELIZA *goes down on her knees on the hearthrug to look for the ring. When she finds it she considers for a moment what to do with it. Finally she flings it down on the desert stand and goes upstairs in a tearing rage.*

Notes

1. **Higgins**: Henry Higgins, a professor of phonetics.
2. **Pickering**: Colonel Pickering, the author of *Spoken Sanskrit*, who is a match for Higgins in his passion for phonetics.
3. **shant**: shan't.
4. **dont**: don't.
5. **pallor**: unhealthy paleness of the skin or face.
6. **Mrs Pearce**: Higgins' housekeeper and representative mother figure in his bachelor establishment at the Wimpole Street laboratory.
7. **La Fanciulla del Golden West**: *The Girl of the Golden West*, opera by Italian composer Giacomo Puccini (1858-1924).
8. **circular**: a printed letter, notice or advertisement sent to a large number of people.
9. **coroneted billet-doux**: a love letter decorated with a small crown.
10. **tomfoolery**: foolish behavior or act.

11. **purgatory**: any place or situation of suffering.
12. **presumptuous**: too bold or self-confident; acting without the necessary authority.
13. **crisps her fingers**: clenches her fingers into fists.
14. **sleep it off**: to recover from something by sleeping.
15. **munch**: to eat with a strong movement of the jaw, especially by making a noise.
16. **cant**: hollow words and borrowed phrases, repeated without thought.
17. **dudgeon**: in a state of bad temper or anger caused by hurt feelings.
18. **nectar**: (in ancient Greek and Roman literature) the drink of the gods; any sweet and good tasting drink.

Study Questions

1. Higgins says to Eliza: "Now you are free and can do what you like." Is that true? In what ways is Eliza NOT free?
2. What does Eliza say to "shock and hurt" Higgins? Is there a symbolic meaning to Eliza's returning to Higgins the ring he gave her? What do you think the ring meant to Higgins when he gave it to her? What did it mean to Eliza?
3. What are the personality changes resulting from the treatments given in the main character Eliza Doolittle?

Essay Topics

1. Discuss the characterization of and the relationship between Eliza Doolittle and Professor Henry Higgins. In your opinion, is Shaw a feminist? If so, can you tell any reasons why?
2. Discuss the symbolic meaning of the title (the legend of Pygmalion and Galatea). In what way is this meaning linked to the theme of the play?

6.3 Alfred Edward Housman

6.3.1 About the Author

A. E. Housman (1859-1936) was born into a middle-class family in Worcestershire. He was educated first at Bromsgrove and then at Oxford where he studied classics. During

his student days at Oxford he formed his important relationship with Moses J. Jackson, which was to color his later life and some of his poems. After working in the Patent Office for some years, his contributions to classical journals earned him a professorship at London University, and later at Cambridge.

As a youth Housman visited Shropshire, which impressed him so much that he used the place to symbolize a pastoral mystery and enchantment in his first collection of poems, *A Shropshire Lad* (1896). This collection achieved for Housman wide and almost immediate fame as a poet. By projecting his disappointed emotion into the melodramatic figure of the Shropshire lad, who passed from inexperience to sorrow, from illusion to bitter disillusion, from content to regret, Housman expressed the profound frustration and futility of human life. His next collection *Last Poems* came out in 1922, suggesting finality, but *More Poems* was published posthumously in the year he died.

Housman was a pessimist, and his homosexuality was certainly an element in his pessimism. Again and again he spoke of lost love, love misunderstood, love ending in bitter separation, love ending in death or the wish for death in his poems. He held that Nature was heartless and witless, caring nothing for man, whose lot was to act out the tragedy of his brief life, to "endure an hour and see injustice done". His favorite themes are inconstancy of man and woman, the transience of human joys and sorrows, the inevitable and unending oblivion of death.

Housman was essentially a classical poet with a romantic temperament. His poetry is simple and direct in manner, precise and condensed in language, lucid and cadenced in rhythm, and ironic and cynical in tone. His verses are highly finished, but they seem to stand outside the current of modern poetry. His characteristic fault is a slipping off into sentimentality. Though he has been widely read, he cannot be regarded as a major poet because of his narrow range and thematic repetitiveness.

6.3.2 "When I Was One-and-Twenty"

When I was one-and-twenty
　　I heard a wise man say,
'Give crowns and pounds and guineas[1]
　　But not your heart away;
Give pearls away and rubies
　　But keep your fancy free.'[2]
But I was one-and-twenty,
　　No use to talk to me.

When I was one-and-twenty
　　I heard him say again,
'The heart out of the bosom
　　Was never given in vain;
'Tis paid with sighs a plenty
　　And sold for endless rue[3].'
And I am two-and-twenty,
　　And oh, 'tis true, 'tis true.

Notes

1. **crowns and pounds and guineas**: denominations of money.
2. **keep your fancy free**: stay free of the power of love.
3. **rue**: sorrow, remorse.

Study Questions

1. According to the first stanza, what should a person not give away? What is the speaker's reaction to this advice?
2. According to the second stanza, what is the price that is paid for one's heart? What is the speaker's reaction to the advice in the second stanza?
3. What happens in the speaker's life in the time between the two stanzas? Explain how we know this from the poem.
4. In what ways would the impact of the poem be different if the speaker were much older in the second stanza?
5. What does the poem imply about the relationship between the old and the young?

6.4 John Galsworthy

6.4.1 About the Author

John Galsworthy (1867-1933) was born into an upper-middle-class family. He was educated first at Harrow and then at Oxford. Later he was trained to be a lawyer, but he did not like it. So after practicing the law for a short time, he turned to literature. Galsworthy published his first book, *From the Four Winds*, in 1897. In 1905 he married Ada, the divorced wife of his cousin, whose unhappy life of her first marriage aroused his deep sympathy. These experiences were reflected in *The Man of Property* (1906), which, together with his first play, *The Silver Box* (1906), established him as a prominent novelist and playwright in the public mind. Other novels and plays followed, but it was not until after the First World War that he completed *The Forsyte Saga*, his first trilogy: *The Man of Property*, *In Chancery* (1920) and *To Let* (1921). His second Forsyte trilogy, *A Modern Comedy*, appeared in 1929, and the third, *End of the Chapter*, posthumously in 1934.

Galsworthy was essentially a bourgeois liberal, a reformist. Throughout his life, he was preoccupied with the social injustice in his time. He regarded human life as a struggle between the rich and the poor. And his sympathy always went out to the suffering poor. In his works, the two classes often appear in contrast: a dull, parasitic and inhuman class of the rich, which is against any kind of change; and an oppressed, but rebellious and unyielding class of the poor, which is bent on reforming things. He battled for many liberal causes, from women's suffrage to the abolition of censorship. He was also a moralist and a critic whose primary aim as a writer was not to create a new society but to criticize the existing one, though his final aim was to keep a balance between the rich and the poor. His works were designed to help improve the status quo; there was no suggestion in them that society should be radically and painfully reconstructed if social enemies were to be reconciled and social ills remedied.

Galsworthy was a conventional writer, having inherited the fine traditions of the great Victorian novelists such as Dickens and Thackeray. He was also influenced by the continental novelists; he admired Maupassant for the vigor, economy and clarity of writing, Turgenev for the wisdom and naturalness, and Tolstoy for the depth of insight and the breadth of character drawing. He thought that he himself had learned more about the essentials of style from them than from any other writers. Technically, he was more traditional than adventurous, focusing on plot development and character portrayal. With an objective observation and a naturalistic description, Galsworthy had tried his best to make an impartial presentation of the social life in a documentary precision. By emphasizing the critical element in his writing, he dauntlessly laid bare the true features of the good and the evil of the bourgeois society. He was also successful in his attempt to present satire and humor in his writing. He wrote in a clear and unpretentious style with a clear and straightforward language.

6.4.2 An Excerpt from Chapter 13 of *The Man of Property*

"One mockturtle,[1] clear; one oxtail; two glasses of port."

In the upper room at French's,[2] where a Forsyte could still get heavy English food, James and his son were sitting down to lunch.

Of all eating-places James liked best to come here; there was something unpretentious, well-flavored, and filling about it, and though he had been to a certain extent corrupted by the necessity for being fashionable, and the trend of habits keeping pace with an income that *would* increase, he still hankered[3] in quiet City[4] moments after the tasty fleshpots of his earlier days. Here you were served by hairy English waiters in aprons; there was sawdust on the floor, and three round gilt looking-glasses hung just above the line of sight. They had only recently done away with the cubicles,[5] too, in which you could have your chop, prime chump, with a floury potato, without seeing your neighbors, like a gentleman.

He tucked the top corner of his napkin behind the third button of his waistcoat, a practice he had been obliged to abandon years ago in the West End.[6] He felt that he should relish his soup — the entire morning had been given to winding up the estate of an old friend.

After filling his mouth with household bread, stale, he at once began: "How are you going down to Robin Hill? You going to take Irene? You'd better take her. I should think there'll be a lot that'll want seeing to."

Without looking up, Soames answered: "She won't go."

"Won't go? What's the meaning of that? She's going to live in the house, isn't she?"

Soames made no reply.

"I don't know what's coming to women nowadays," mumbled James; "I never used to have any trouble with them. She's had too much liberty. She's spoiled — "

Soames lifted his eyes: "I won't have anything said against her," he said unexpectedly.

The silence was only broken now by the supping of James's soup.

The waiter brought the two glasses of port, but Soames stopped him.

"That's not the way to serve port," he said; "take them away, and bring the bottle."

Rousing himself from his reverie over the soup, James took one of his rapid shifting surveys of surrounding facts.

"Your mother's in bed," he said; "you can have the carriage to take you down. I should think Irene'd like the drive. This young Bosinney'll be there, I suppose, to show you over?"

Soames nodded.

"I should like to go and see for myself what sort of a job he's made finishing off," pursued James. "I'll just drive round and pick you both up."

"I am going down by train," replied Soames. "If you like to drive round and see, Irene might go with you, I can't tell."

He signed to the waiter to bring the bill, which James paid.

They parted at St. Paul's, Soames branching off to the station, James taking his omnibus westwards.

He had secured the corner seat next the conductor, where his long legs made it difficult for anyone to get in, and at all who passed him he looked resentfully, as if they had no business to be using up his air.

He intended to take an opportunity this afternoon of speaking to Irene. A word in time saved nine; and now that she was going to live in the country there was a chance for her to turn over a new leaf! He could see that Soames wouldn't stand very much more of her goings on![7]

It did not occur to him to define what he meant by her 'goings on'; the expression was wide, vague, and suited to a Forsyte. And James had more than his common share of courage after lunch.

On reaching home, he ordered out the barouche,[8] with special instructions that the groom was to go too. He wished to be kind to her, and to give her every chance.

When the door of No. 62 was opened he could distinctly hear her singing, and said so at once, to prevent any chance of being denied entrance.

Yes, Mrs. Soames was in, but the maid did not know if she was seeing people.

James, moving with the rapidity that ever astonished the observers of his long figure and absorbed expression, went forthwith into the drawing-room without permitting this to be ascertained. He found Irene seated at the piano with her hands arrested on the keys, evidently listening to the voices in the hall. She greeted him without smiling.

"Your mother-in-law's in bed," he began, hoping at once to enlist her sympathy. "I've got the carriage here. Now, be a good girl, and put on your hat and come with me for a drive. It'll do you good!"

Irene looked at him as though about to refuse, but, seeming to change her mind, went upstairs, and came down again with her hat on.

"Where are you going to take me?" she asked.

"We'll just go down to Robin Hill," said James, spluttering out his words very quick; "the horses want exercise, and I should like to see what they've been doing down there."

Irene hung back, but again changed her mind, and went out to the carriage, James brooding over her closely, to make quite sure.

It was not before he had got her more than half way that he began: "Soames is very fond of you — he won't have anything said against you; why don't you show him more affection?"

Irene flushed, and said in a low voice: "I can't show what I haven't got."

James looked at her sharply; he felt that now he had her in his own carriage, with his own horses and servants, he was really in command of the situation. She could not put him off;[9] nor would she make a scene[10] in public.

"I can't think what you're about," he said. "He's a very good husband!"

Irene's answer was so low as to be almost inaudible among the sounds of traffic. He caught the words: "You are not married to him!"

"What's that got to do with it? He's given you everything you want. He's always ready to take you anywhere, and now he's built you this house in the country. It's not as if you had anything of your own."

"No."

Again James looked at her; he could not make out the expression on her face. She looked almost as if she were going to cry, and yet —

"I'm sure," he muttered hastily, "we've all tried to be kind to you."

Irene's lips quivered; to his dismay James saw a tear steal down her cheek. He felt a choke rise in his own throat.

"We're all fond of you," he said, "if you'd only" — he was going to say, "behave yourself," but changed it to — "if you'd only be more of a wife to him."

Irene did not answer, and James, too, ceased speaking. There was something in her silence which disconcerted him; it was not the silence of obstinacy, rather that of acquiescence in all that he could find to say. And yet he felt as if he had not had the last word. He could not understand this.

He was unable, however, to long keep silence.

"I suppose that young Bosinney," he said, "will be getting married to June now?"

Irene's face changed. "I don't know," she said; "you should ask *her*."

"Does she write to you?"

"No."

"How's that?" said James. "I thought you and she were such great friends."

Irene turned on him. "Again" she said, "you should ask *her*!"

"Well," flustered James, frightened by her look, "it's very odd that I can't get a plain answer to a plain question, but there it is."

He sat ruminating over his rebuff, and burst out at last:

"Well, I've warned you. You won't look ahead. Soames, he doesn't say much, but I can see he won't stand a great deal more of this sort of thing. You'll have nobody but yourself to blame, and, what's more, you'll get no sympathy from anybody."

Irene bent her head with a little smiling bow. "I am very much obliged to you."

James did not know what on earth to answer.

The bright hot morning had changed slowly to a gray, oppressive afternoon; a heavy bank of clouds, with the yellow tinge of coming thunder, had risen in the south, and was creeping up. The branches of the trees drooped motionless across the road without the smallest stir of foliage. A faint odor of glue from the heated horses clung in the thick air; the coachman and groom, rigid and unbending, exchanged stealthy murmurs on the box, without ever turning their heads.

To James's great relief they reached the house at last; the silence and impenetrability of this woman by his side, whom he had always thought so soft and mild, alarmed him.

The carriage put them down at the door, and they entered.

The hall was cool, and so still that it was like passing into a tomb; a shudder ran down James's spine. He quickly lifted the heavy leather curtains between the columns into the inner court.

He could not restrain an exclamation of approval.

The decoration was really in excellent taste. The dull ruby tiles that extended from the foot of the walls to the verge of a circular clump of tall iris plants, surrounding in turn a sunken basin of white marble filled with water, were obviously of the best quality. He admired extremely the purple leather curtains drawn along one entire side, framing a huge white-tiled stove. The central partitions of the skylight had been slid back, and the warm air from outside penetrated into the very house.

He stood, his hands behind him, his head bent back on his high, narrow shoulders, spying the tracery on the columns and the pattern of the frieze which ran round the ivory-colored walls under the gallery. Evidently, no pains had been spared. It was quite the house of a gentleman. He went up to the curtains, and, having discovered how they were worked, drew them asunder and disclosed the picture-gallery, ending in a great window taking up the whole end of the room. It had a black oak floor, and its walls, again, were of ivory white. He went on throwing open doors, and peeping in. Everything was in apple-pie order, ready for immediate occupation.

He turned round at last to speak to Irene, and saw her standing over in the garden entrance, with her husband and Bosinney.

Though not remarkable for sensibility, James felt at once that something was wrong. He went up to them, and, vaguely alarmed, ignorant of the nature of the trouble, made an attempt to smooth things over.

"How are you, Mr. Bosinney?" he said, holding out his hand. "You've been spending money pretty freely down here, I should say!"

Soames turned his back, and walked away. James looked from Bosinney's frowning face to Irene's, and, in his agitation, spoke his thoughts aloud: "Well, I can't tell what's the matter. Nobody tells me anything!" And, making off after his son, he heard Bosinney's short laugh, and his "well, thank God! You look so — " Most unfortunately he lost the rest.

What had happened? He glanced back. Irene was very close to the architect, and her face not like the face he knew of her. He hastened up to his son.

Soames was pacing the picture-gallery.

"What's the matter?" said James. "What's all this?" Soames looked at him with his supercilious[11] calm unbroken, but James knew well enough that he was violently angry.

"Our friend," he said, "has exceeded his instructions again, that's all. So much the worse for him this time."

He turned round and walked back towards the door. James followed hurriedly, edging himself in front. He saw Irene take her finger from before her lips, heard her say something in her ordinary voice, and began to speak before he reached them:

"There's a storm coming on. We'd better get home. We can't take you, I suppose, Mr. Bosinney? No, I suppose not. Then, good-bye!" He held out his hand. Bosinney did not take it, but, turning with a laugh, said:

"Good-bye, Mr. Forsyte. Don't get caught in the storm!" and walked away.

"Well," began James, "I don't know — "

But the sight of Irene's face stopped him. Taking hold of his daughter-in-law by the elbow, he escorted her towards the carriage. He felt certain, quite certain, they had been making some appointment or other....

Nothing in this world is more sure to upset a Forsyte than the discovery that something on which he has stipulated to spend a certain sum has cost more. And this is reasonable, for upon the accuracy of his estimates the whole policy of his life is ordered. If he cannot rely on definite values of property, his compass is amiss; he is adrift upon bitter waters without a helm.

After writing to Bosinney in the terms that have already been chronicled, Soames had dismissed the cost of the house from his mind. He believed that he had made the matter of the final cost so very plain that the possibility of its being again exceeded had really never entered his head. On hearing from Bosinney that his limit of twelve thousand pounds would be exceeded by something like four hundred, he had grown white with anger. His original estimate of the cost of the house completed had been ten thousand pounds, and he had often blamed himself severely for allowing himself to be led into repeated excesses. Over this last expenditure, however, Bosinney had put himself completely in the wrong. How on earth a fellow could make such an ass of himself Soames could not conceive; but he had done so, and all the rancor[12] and hidden jealousy that had been burning against him for so long was now focused in rage at this crowning piece of extravagance. The attitude of the confident and friendly husband was gone. To preserve property — his wife — he had assumed it, to preserve property of another kind he lost it now.

"Ah!" he had said to Bosinney when he could speak, "and I suppose you're perfectly contented with yourself. But I may as well tell you that you've altogether mistaken your man!"

What he meant by those words he did not quite know at the time, but after dinner he looked up the correspondence between himself and Bosinney to make quite sure. There could be no two opinions about it — the fellow had made himself liable for[13] that extra four hundred, or, at all events, for three hundred and fifty of it, and he would have to make it good.

He was looking at his wife's face when he came to this conclusion. Seated in her usual seat on the sofa, she was altering the lace on a collar. She had not once spoken to him all the evening.

He went up to the mantelpiece, and contemplating his face in the mirror said: "Your friend The Buccaneer had made a fool of himself; he will have to pay for it!"

She looked at him scornfully, and answered: "I don't know what you are talking about!"

"You soon will. A mere trifle, quite beneath your contempt — four hundred pounds."

"Do you mean that you are going to make him pay that towards this hateful house?"

"I do."

"And you know he's got nothing?"

"Yes."

"Then you are meaner than I thought you."

Soames turned from the mirror, and unconsciously taking a china cup from the mantelpiece, clasped his hands around it, as though praying. He saw her bosom rise and fall, her eyes darkening with anger, and taking no notice of the taunt,[14] he asked quietly:

"Are you carrying on a flirtation with Bosinney?"

"No, I am not!"

Her eyes met his, and he looked away. He neither believed nor disbelieved her, but he knew that he had made a mistake in asking; he never had known, never would know, what she was thinking. The sight of her inscrutable[15] face, the thought of all the hundreds of evenings he had seen her sitting there like that, soft and passive, but so unreadable, unknown, enraged him beyond measure.

"I believe you are made of stone," he said, clenching his fingers so hard that he broke the fragile cup. The pieces fell into the grate. And Irene smiled.

"You seem to forget," she said, "that cup is not!"[16]

Soames gripped her arm. "A good beating," he said, "is the only thing that would bring you to your senses," but turning on his heel, he left the room.

Notes

1. **mockturtle**: made to imitate turtle soup.
2. **at French's**: at the French restaurant.
3. **hankered**: had a strong desire.
4. **City**: the oldest part of London, now the commercial and financial center.
5. **cubicles**: a small part of a room that is separated from the rest of the room so that you cannot be seen by other people.
6. **the West End**: the western part of central London where there are large shops, theaters, expensive hotels, etc.
7. **goings-on**: (colloq) behavior.
8. **barouche**: a four-wheeled carriage with a driver's seat high in front, two double seats inside facing each other, and a folding top over the back seat.
9. **put him off**: hinder, distract him.
10. **make a scene**: give an emotional outburst.
11. **supercilious**: showing contemptuous indifference.
12. **rancor**: deep and long-lasting feeling of bitterness; spitefulness.
13. **liable for**: responsible according to law.
14. **taunt**: remark intended to hurt somebody's feelings.
15. **inscrutable**: mysterious, that cannot be understood.
16. **"that cup is not"**: It means the cup is not made of stone.

Study Questions

1. What is happening between Soames (the husband) and Irene (the wife)?
2. What does James try to do by taking Irene down to Robin Hill?
3. Why does Soames become so angry with Bosinney, the architect?
4. There is a fight between husband and wife at the end of the chapter. Who do you think has won the fight? Why?
5. According to your understanding, why does Irene feel unhappy all the time while her husband tries to do everything for her?

6.5 William Butler Yeats

6.5.1 About the Author

William Butler Yeats (1865-1939) was born into an Anglo-Irish Protestant family in Dublin. His childhood was largely spent between school in London and his mother's native county of Sligo, where old Irish way of life and folklore were still very strong. After high school, Yeats entered the School of Art in Dublin where he met many artists and writers who encouraged him to be a poet. With a strong passion for Celtic legends, he read Irish poetry and the Gaelic sagas in translation. His youth was spent during the high tide of the Irish Nationalist Movement led by Parnell. Yeats met Lady Gregory and John Synge in 1896. With the common cultural ideals of reviving the Irish literature, they organized the Irish National Dramatic Society and opened the Abbey Theater in 1904. Yeats served as its director and wrote more than 20 plays for the theater. In 1923, he was awarded Nobel Prize for literature.

Yeats is considered to be one of the greatest poets in the English language; and his poetic achievement stands at the center of modern literature. He had a very long poetic career, stretching from the 1880s to the 1930s, and had experienced a slow and painful change in his poetic creation, starting in the romantic tradition and finishing as a matured modernist poet. Generally, his poetic career can be divided into three periods according to the contents and style of his poetry.

As a young man, Yeats began his poetic career in the romantic tradition. The major themes are usually Celtic legends, local folktales, or stories of the heroic age in Irish history. Many of his early poems have a dreamy quality, expressing melancholy, passive and self-indulgent feelings. But in a number of poems, Yeats has achieved suggestive patterns of meaning by a careful counterpointing of contrasting ideas or images like human and fairy, natural and artificial, domestic and wild, and ephemeral and permanent. The overall style of his early poetry is very delicate with natural imagery and musical beauty.

The first two decades of the 20th century were a period of transition to Yeats, during which his attitude towards politics, life and poetry had experienced a great change. His disgust at the bourgeois philistinism soured his political optimism, leaving him a disillusioned patriotic sentiment. His long-cherished but hopeless love for Gonne brought him only suffering and bitterness. Gradually, Yeats turned from the traditional poetry to a modernist one. Ideologically, he responded to Nietzsche's works with great excitement; artistically, he came under the influence of French Symbolism and John Donne's metaphysical poetry; and poetically, he accepted the modernist ideas in poetry writing advocated by Ezra Pound and T. S. Eliot. He began to write with realistic and concrete themes on a variety of subjects, exploring the profound and complicated human problems, such as life, love, politics and religion. The new vigor of his verse is reflected in the precise and concrete imagery, the strong passion, and the active verb forms. His style is both simple and rich, colloquial and formal, with a quality of metaphysical wit and symbolic vision, which indicates that Yeats has already been on his way to modernist poetry.

Yeats reached the last stage of his poetic creation when he was over fifty. The scorn so pervasive before was gone; but the loss of youth and the waste of life made him feel more bitter and more disillusioned. He yearned to move away from the sensual world of growth and change, and to enter the timeless, eternal world of art and intellect. Yeats came to realize that eternal beauty could only live in the realm of art. His concern has turned to the great subjects of dichotomy, such as, youth and age, love and war, vigor and wisdom, body and soul, and life and art. This dichotomy has brought constant tensions in his works and revealed the human predicament. In this last period, Yeats has developed a tough, complex and symbolical style.

6.5.2 "The Lake Isle of Innisfree[1]"

I will arise and go now, and go to Innisfree,
And a small cabin build there, of clay and wattles[2] made:
Nine bean-rows will I have there, a hive for the honeybee,
And live alone in the bee-loud glade[3].

And I shall have some peace there, for peace comes dropping slow,
Dropping from the veils of the morning to where the cricket sings;
There midnight's all a glimmer, and noon a purple glow,
And evening full of the linnet's wings[4].

> I will arise and go now, for always night and day
> I hear lake water lapping with low sounds by the shore;
> While I stand on the roadway, or on the pavements gray,
> I hear it in the deep heart's core[5].

Notes

1. The poem was written in 1893. Tired of the life of his day, Yeats sought to escape into an ideal "fairy land" where he could live calmly as a hermit and enjoy the beauty of nature. The poem consists of three quatrains of iambic pentameter, with each stanza rhymed *abab*. Innisfree is an inlet in the lake in Irish legends. Here the author is referring to a place for hermitage.
2. **wattles**: stakes interwoven with twigs or branches.
3. **the bee-loud glade**: an open place in the wood where bees buzz loudly.
4. **full of the linnet's wings**: Here it refers to the fact that lots of linnets fly here and there. **linnet**: a small brown singing bird.
5. **in the deep heart's core**: at the bottom of my heart.

Study Questions

1. Contrast the speaker's present location with the place that beckons him. What is the emotional effect of this contrast?
2. Instead of actually going to Innisfree, what is the speaker doing in the poem? How does hearing something "in the deep heart's core" differ from hearing it with one's ears?
3. How does Yeats use sound images to heighten the emotional effect of the poem?

6.5.3 "Down by the Salley Gardens[1]"

Down by the salley[2] gardens my love and I did meet;
She passed the salley gardens with little snow-white feet.
She bid me take love easy, as the leaves grow on the tree;
But I, being young and foolish, with her would not agree.

In a field by the river my love and I did stand,
And on my leaning shoulder she laid her snow-white hand.
She bid me take life easy, as the grass grows on the weirs[3];
But I was young and foolish, and now am full of tears.

Notes

1. Originally entitled "An Old Song Resung", with Yeats's footnote: "This is an attempt to reconstruct an old song from three lines imperfectly remembered by an old peasant

woman in the village of Ballysodare, Sligo, who often sings them to herself."
2. **salley**: a variant of "sallow", a species of willow tree.
3. **weirs**: walls or barriers across a river to control the flow of water.

Study Questions

1. What is the speaker's attitude towards love? Do you think it right or wrong? Why?
2. What did the lady tell the speaker in the second stanza?
3. Why didn't the speaker listen to the lady's advice?
4. What can you learn from this poem?

6.5.4 "The Second Coming[1]"

Turning and turning in the widening gyre[2]
The falcon cannot hear the falconer;
Things fall apart; the center cannot hold;
Mere anarchy is loosed upon the world,
The blood-dimmed tide is loosed, and everywhere
The ceremony of innocence is drowned;
The best lack all conviction, while the worst
Are full of passionate intensity.[3]

Surely some revelation[4] is at hand;
Surely the Second Coming is at hand.
The Second Coming! Hardly are those words out
When a vast image out of *Spiritus Mundi*[5]
Troubles my sight: somewhere in sands of the desert
A shape with lion body and the head of a man,[6]
A gaze blank and pitiless as the sun,
Is moving its slow thighs, while all about it
Reel shadows of the indignant desert birds.
The darkness drops again; but now I know
That twenty centuries[7] of stony sleep
Were vexed to nightmare by a rocking cradle,[8]
And what rough beast, its hour come round at last,
Slouches towards Bethlehem to be born?

Notes

1. This poem expresses Yeats's sense of the dissolution of the civilization of his time, the end of one cycle of history and the approach of another. The birth of Christ brought to an end the cycle that had lasted from what Yeats called the "Babylonian

mathematical starlight" (2000 B. C.) to the dissolution of Creco-Roman culture. "What if the irrational return?" Yeats asked in his prose work *A Vision*. "What if the circle begin again?" He speculates that "we may be about to accept the most implacable authority the world has known."

2. **gyre**: circular or spiral form or motion, which Yeats uses as the symbol for the winding up and winding down of circles of history (Yeats pronounced it with a hard g).

3. **The blood-dimmed tide... full of passionate intensity**: These four lines refer to the Russian Revolution of 1917, seen as a portent, but later Yeats accepted the poem as an unconscious prophecy of the rise of Fascism also. Speaking in 1924, Yeats declared: "It is impossible not to ask oneself to what great task of the nations we have been summoned in this transformed world where there is so much that is obscure and terrible." "**The ceremony of innocence**" suggests Yeats's view of ritual as the basis of civilized living. Cf. the last stanza of "A Prayer for My Daughter."

4. **revelation**: disclosure; in Christian teaching, God's unfolding of His will to the human race.

5. *Spiritus Mundi*: the Spirit or Soul of the Universe, with which all individual souls are connected through the "Great Memory," which Yeats held to be a universal subconscious in which the human race preserves its past memories. It is thus a source of symbolic images for the poet.

6. **A shape with lion body and the head of a man**: referring to the sphinx.

7. **twenty centuries**: Yeats's cycles each lasted two thousand years.

8. **cradle**: the cradle of the infant Christ.

Study Questions

1. What religious event does the Second Coming refer to?
2. The poem begins with the image of a falcon flying out of control. Yeats is using this image to suggest the situation of the modern world. In what ways do you think the modern world is like the distant, circling falcon?
3. What is the significance of the poem's mention of the Sphinx myth?
4. What kind of creature suggested by Yeats seems to be coming? Does this creature seem to be positive or negative?
5. What country or area of the world seems to be the setting for the creature's arrival?
6. How long has the creature been sleeping? Is there any significance to this number?

6.6 T. S. Eliot

6.6.1 About the Author

T. S. Eliot (1888-1965) was born at St. Louis, Missouri, USA. He was first educated at Smith Academy in his hometown and then at Harvard. Later he studied literature and philosophy in France, Germany and at Oxford, England. He took interest in Elizabethan literature, the Italian Renaissance and Indian mystical philosophy of Buddhism. He was also attracted by the French symbolist poetry.

Eliot got married and settled down in London in 1915. After a year or two of teaching, he began to write. His first important poem, "The Love Song of J. Alfred Prufrock", appeared in 1915. From 1917 to 1919, he served as the assistant editor of *The Egoist*, a magazine advocating Imagism. In 1922 he became the editor of *The Criterion*, which was one of the two most influential literary reviews of this century. Eliot's most famous poem, *The Waste Land*, appeared in the first number of *The Criterion*. In 1927, Eliot took English citizenship and became a devout member of the Anglican Church. In his later career, Eliot busied himself with different kinds of literary work such as writing, editing, publishing and lecturing. He won various awards, including the Nobel Prize and the Order of Merit in 1948.

Eliot had a long poetic career, which was generally divided into two periods: the early one from 1915 to 1925, and the later one from 1927 onward. In his early period, Eliot produced a fairly large number of poems, which were mainly collected in *Poems 1909-1925* (1925). He also published *Prufrock and Other Observations* (1917), *The Waste Land* (1922) and two other small volumes of poetry. As a young man with bitter disillusionment and with boldness in the handling of language, Eliot had explored in his early poetry various aspects of decay of culture in the modern Western world, expressing a sense of the disintegration of life. Most of his early poems are about a state of mind. There is little "action" in a physical sense; the action is totally psychological. The poems are dominated by the dark horror of an earthly hell.

The Waste Land is a poem concerned with the spiritual breakup of a modern civilization in which human life has lost its meaning, significance and purpose. The poem has developed a whole set of historical, cultural and religious themes; but it is often regarded as being primarily a reflection of the 20th-century people's disillusionment and frustration in a sterile and futile society.

In his later period, Eliot produced only two major volumes of poetic works, *Ash Wednesday* (1930) and *Four Quartets* (1944), both clearly reflect his allegiance to the Church of England. *The Four Quartets*, based on the Christian dogmas of incarnation and resurrection, is concerned with the quest for the immortal element, the stillness within time or history. Man, disillusioned and hopeless in his early poetry, now finds reconciliation in God. Thus, *the Four Quartets* is characterized by a philosophical and emotional calm quite in contrast to the despair and suffering of the early works.

T. S. Eliot was one of the important verse dramatists in the first half of the 20th century. Besides some fragmentary pieces, Eliot had written in his life time five full-length plays: *Murder in the Cathedral* (1935), *The Family Reunion* (1939), *The Cocktail Party* (1950), *The Confidential Clerk* (1954), and *The Elder Statesman* (1959). All the plays have something to do with Christian themes. Eliot's major achievement in play writing has been the creation of a verse drama in the 20th century to express the ideas and actions of modern society with new accents of the contemporary speech.

T. S. Eliot was also an important prose writer. During his literary career, he wrote a large number of essays, articles and book reviews. His essays are mainly concerned with cultural, social, religious, as well as literary issues. In his famous essay, *Tradition and Individual Talent*, Eliot put great emphasis on the importance of tradition both in creative writing and in criticism. In presenting his doctrine of impersonality, Eliot argued that a poet's mind should remain "inert" and "neutral" towards his subject matter, keeping a gulf between the man who suffers and the mind which creates. It is not inappropriate to say that Eliot, as a critic, may have occupied today a position of distinction and influence equal in importance to his position as a poet.

6.6.2 "The Love Song of J. Alfred Prufrock[1]"

> *S' io credessi che mia risposta fosse*
> *a persona che mai tornasse al mondo,*
> *questa fiamma staria senza piu scosse.*
> *Ma per cio che giammai di questo fondo*
> *non torno vivo alcun, s' i' odo il vero,*
> *senza tema d' infamia ti rispondo.* [2]
>
> Let us go then, you and I,
> When the evening is spread out[3] against the sky
> Like a patient etherized upon a table[4];
> Let us go, through certain half-deserted streets,
> The muttering retreats
> Of restless nights in one-night cheap hotels
> And saw dust restaurants with oyster shells:
> Streets that follow like a tedious argument
> Of insidious intent
> To lead you to an overwhelming question...
> Oh, do not ask, "What is it?"
> Let us go and make our visit.
>
> In the room the women come and go

Talking of Michelangelo.[5]

The yellow fog[6] that rubs its back upon the windowpanes,
The yellow smoke that rubs its muzzle on the windowpanes
Licked its tongue into the corners of the evening,
Lingered upon the pools that stand in drains,
Let fall upon its back the soot that falls from chimneys,
Slipped by the terrace, made a sudden leap,
And seeing that it was a soft October night,
Curled once about the house, and fell asleep.

And indeed there will be time[7]
For the yellow smoke that slides along the street,
Rubbing its back upon the windowpanes;
There will be time, there will be time
To prepare a face to meet the faces that you meet;
There will be time to murder and create,
And time for all the works and days of hands[8]
That lift and drop a question on your plate;
Time for you and time for me,
And time yet for a hundred indecisions,
And for a hundred visions and revisions,
Before the taking of a toast and tea.

In the room the women come and go
Talking of Michelangelo.

And indeed there will be time
To wonder, "Do I dare?" and, "Do I dare?"
Time to turn back and descend the stair,
With a bald spot in the middle of my hair —
(They will say: "How his hair is growing thin!")
My morning coat, my collar mounting firmly to the chin,
My necktie rich and modest, but asserted by a simple pin —
(They will say: "But how his arms and legs are thin!")
Do I dare
Disturb the universe?
In a minute there is time
For decisions and revisions which a minute will reverse.

For I have known them all already, known them all —
Have known the evenings, mornings, afternoons,
I have measured out my life with coffee spoons;
I know the voices dying with a dying fall[9]
Beneath the music from a farther room.
    So how should I presume?

And I have known the eyes already, known them all —
The eyes that fix you in a formulated phrase,
And when I am formulated, sprawling on a pin[10],
When I am pinned and wriggling on the wall,
Then how should I begin
To spit out all the butt-ends[11] of my days and ways?
    And how should I presume?

And I have known the arms already, known them all —
Arms that are braceleted and white and bare[12]
(But in the lamplight, downed with light brown hair!)
Is it perfume from a dress
That makes me so digress?
Arms that lie along a table, or wrap about a shawl.
    And should I then presume?
    And how should I begin?

*   *   *

Shall I say, I have gone at dusk through narrow streets
And watched the smoke that rises from the pipes
Of lonely men in shirt-sleeves, leaning out of windows?
...
I should have been a pair of ragged claws[13]
Scuttling across the floors of silent seas.

*   *   *

And the afternoon, the evening, sleeps so peacefully!
Smoothed by long fingers,
Asleep... tired... or it malingers,
Stretched on the floor, here beside you and me.
Should I, after tea and cakes and ices,
Have the strength to force the moment to its crisis?
But though I have wept and fasted, wept and prayed,

Though I have seen my head (grown slightly bald) brought in upon a platter[14],
I am no prophet — and here's no great matter;
I have seen the moment of my greatness flicker,
And I have seen the eternal Footman[15] hold my coat, and snicker,
And in short, I was afraid.

And would it have been worth it, after all,
After the cups, the marmalade, the tea,
Among the porcelain, among some talk of you and me,
Would it have been worth while,
To have bitten off the matter with a smile,
To have squeezed the universe into a ball[16]
To roll it toward some overwhelming question,
To say: "I am Lazarus,[17] come from the dead,
Come back to tell you all, I shall tell you all" —
If one, settling a pillow by her head,
    Should say: "That is not what I meant at all.
    That is not it, at all."

And would it have been worth it, after all,
Would it have been worth while,
After the sunsets and the dooryards and the sprinkled streets,
After the novels, after the teacups, after the skirts that trail along the floor —
And this, and so much more? —
It is impossible to say just what I mean!
But as if a magic lantern threw the nerves in patterns on a screen:
Would it have been worth while
If one, settling a pillow or throwing off a shawl,
And turning toward the window, should say:
    "That is not it at all,
    That is not what I meant, at all."
  * * *
No! I am not Prince Hamlet[18], nor was meant to be;
Am an attendant lord[19], one that will do
To swell a progress[20], start a scene or two,

Advise the prince; no doubt, an easy tool,
Deferential, glad to be of use,
Politic, cautious, and meticulous;
Full of high sentence[21], but a bit obtuse[22];
At times, indeed, almost ridiculous —
Almost, at times, the Fool[23].

I grow old... I grow old...
I shall wear the bottoms of my trousers rolled.

Shall I part my hair behind?[24] Do I dare to eat a peach?
I shall wear white flannel trousers, and walk upon the beach.
I have heard the mermaids singing, each to each.

I do not think that they will sing to me.

I have seen them riding seaward on the waves
Combing the white hair of the waves blown back
When the wind blows the water white and black.

We have lingered in the chambers of the sea
By sea-girls wreathed with seaweed red and brown
Till human voices wake us, and we drown.

Notes

1. A dramatic monologue in which the speaker builds up a mood of social futility and inadequacy through the thoughts and images which haunt his consciousness and by means of the symbolic landscape in which he moves. The title implies an ironic contrast between the romantic suggestions of "love song" and the dully prosaic name, "J. Alfred Prufrock."
2. ***Epigraph***: These lines are taken from Dante's "Inferno", and are spoken by the character of Count Guido da Montefelltro. Dante meets the punished Guido in the Eighth chasm of Hell. Guido explains that he is speaking freely to Dante only because he believes Dante is one of the dead who could never return to earth to report what he says. Translated from the original Italian, the lines are as follows: "If I thought that my reply would be to someone who would ever return to earth, this flame would remain without further movement; but as no one has ever returned alive from this gulf, if what I hear is true, I can answer you with no fear of infamy."

3. **spread out**: This metaphor occurs many times in Bergson's *Time and Free Will* (1910), the work which Eliot, while in Harvard, quoted from most frequently in his writings about Bergson.
4. **Like a patient etherized upon a table**: Here the evening is compared to a patient who is etherized on an operation table. A contrast is perhaps implied between "ether" as the free sky and the word's medical connotations — helplessness, disease, the elimination of consciousness and personality.
5. **In the room the women come and go/Talking of Michelangelo**: Jules Laforgue, a French symbolist, wrote: "In the room the women come and go/Talking of the masters of the Sienne school." Eliot parodies Laforgue but creates a realistic scene of intellectual gossip, setting off as a kind of chorus. **Michelangelo**: great Italian sculptor, painter and poet.
6. **fog**: According to Eliot, the smoke from the factories of his hometown St. Louis.
7. **And indeed there will be time**: Cf. "Had we but world enough and time," from Andrew Marvell's "To His Coy Mistress". The speaker of the poem argues to his "coy mistress" that they could take their time in courtship games only if they were immortal; ironically, Prufrock deludes himself into thinking there will be time to court his lady.
8. **works and days of hands**: "Works and Days" is a poem about the farming year by Greek poet Hesiod (8th century BC). Eliot's contrast is between useful farm labor and the futile "works and days of hands" engaged in meaningless social gesturing.
9. **dying fall**: In Shakespeare's *Twelfth Night*, the lovesick Duke Orsino asks for an encore of moody piece of music: "That strain again! It had a dying fall" (1.1.4).
10. **sprawling on a pin**: Insect specimens are pinned into place for scientific study. Prufrock feels as though he is being brutally analyzed in a similar manner.
11. **butt-ends**: the ends of smoked cigarettes.
12. **Arms that are braceleted and white and bare**: Cf. "A bracelet of bright hair about the bone" in John Donne's "The Relic". Eliot admires the line in his essay "The Metaphysical Poets" (1921).
13. **a pair of ragged claws**: Self-pitying remark that he would have been better as a crab at the bottom of the ocean. Cf. *Hamlet* (2.2.205-206). Hamlet mocks the unwitting and aging Polonius, saying that Polonius could become young like Hamlet only if he somehow went back in time: "for you yourself, sir, should be old as I am, if, like a crab, you could go backward."
14. **Though I have seen my head (grown slightly bald) brought in upon a platter**: Matthew 14:3-11, Mark 6:17-29 in the Bible; the death of John the Baptist. King Herod was enamored of a dancing girl named Salome. He offered her a gift of anything she wanted in his kingdom. Salome's mother told her to request the head of John the Baptist on a silver platter. Herod complied. Prufrock's observation of his "(grown

slightly bald)" head parodies the event and gives it the flavor of mock-heroism found throughout the poem.

15. **eternal Footman**: Death.
16. **To have squeezed the universe into a ball**: Cf. Andrew Marvell "To His Coy Mistress" (41-44): "Let us roll all our strength and all/Our sweetness up into one ball,/And tear our pleasures with rough strife/Through the iron gates of life." The imagery is suggestive of phallic penetration of the hymen.
17. **Lazarus**: Another Biblical story. In Luke 16:19-31, Lazarus is a beggar associated with a rich man named Dives in a parable. After they died Lazarus went to Heaven while Dives went to Hell. Dives wanted to warn his brothers about Hell and asked Abraham if Lazarus could be sent back to tell them. Abraham refused, saying: "if they hear not Moses and the prophets, neither will they be persuaded, though one rose from the dead."
18. **Prince Hamlet**: Shakespeare's most famous character, from Hamlet. *Hamlet*, like Prufrock, is indecisive and anxious about future consequences. Prufrock echoes Hamlet's famous "to be or not to be" (3.1.66) at the end of this line ("nor was meant to be"), a line that is about wondering whether it is worth existing ("to exist or not to exist") and couches itself in the passive tense ("to be").
19. **attendant lord**: Prufrock, having an inferiority complex, stating that he will never be a main character with a purpose, like Hamlet, but rather an "attendant lord" (in this case Polonius), a mere auxiliary character who may slightly move the plot.
20. **To swell a progress**: An Elizabethan state journey made by a royal or noble person. Elizabethan plays sometimes showed full-blown "progresses" crossing the stage.
21. **full of high sentence**: sententiousness, in the habit of saying or writing things in a short and witty manner.
22. **obtuse**: dull witted.
23. **Fool**: Standard character in Elizabethan drama, such as a court jester who entertains the nobility and speaks wise nonsense (the Fool in *King Lear* is perhaps the best example).
24. **I shall wear the bottoms of my trousers rolled./Shall I part my hair behind**? At the time, both styles were considered bohemian; the middle-aged Prufrock pathetically wonders if he can reverse his aging by embracing such youthful fashions.

Study Questions

1. What social class does Prufrock belong to? How does Prufrock respond to the attitudes and values of his class?
2. What does the description of the city streets tell you about the mind of the speaker?
3. When Prufrock starts talking about the "bald spot" in the middle of his head, what do you think he is worrying about?

4. When Prufrock starts talking about having known all the evenings already, what kind of a life do you think he has led?
5. Why do you think Prufrock keeps repeating that there will be enough time?

Essay Topics

1. What is the effect of the Biblical allusions in the poem?
2. What types of images show that people are dehumanized in modern life, and suggest that inanimate objects are alive?

6.7 James Joyce

6.7.1 About the Author

James Joyce (1882-1941) was born into a Catholic family in Dublin. When he was young, his family was quite well-off; but gradually it became impoverished. Joyce got his education at Catholic schools where he received very strict religious training. During his school days, Joyce passed through a phase of religious enthusiasm; but he finally rejected the Catholic Church and started a rebellion against the narrowness and bigotry of the bourgeois philistines in Dublin. When he studied modern languages at Dublin's University College, he read a lot of books forbidden by the Catholic Church. Influenced by Ibsen, Joyce finally decided to take the literary mission as his career. He refused to take any part in the nationalist activities of his fellow students. After his graduation, Joyce left Ireland for the continent. He lived and worked in France, Italy and Switzerland for the rest of his life except a few brief trips back to Ireland; for Joyce regarded exile as the only way to preserve his integrity and to enable him to recreate the life in Dublin truthfully, completely and objectively in his writings.

Joyce is not a commercial writer. In his life time, he wrote altogether three novels, a collection of short stories, two volumes of poetry, and one play. The novels and short stories are regarded as his great works, all of which have the same setting: Ireland, especially Dublin, and the same subject: the Irish people and their life.

The stories in *Dubliners* (1914) have an artistic unity given by Joyce who intended to write a chapter of the moral history of his country under four of its aspects: childhood, adolescence, maturity and public life. Joyce published his first novel *The Portrait of the Artist as a Young Man* in 1916. The novel can be read as a naturalistic account of the hero's bitter experiences and his final artistic and spiritual liberation. *Ulysses* (1922), Joyce's masterpiece, has become a prime example of modernism in literature. It is such an uncommon novel that there arises the question whether it can be termed as a "novel" at all; for it seems to lack almost all the essential qualities of the novel in a traditional sense: there is virtually no story, no plot, almost no action, and little characterization in the usual sense. Broadly speaking, *Ulysses* gives an account of man's life during one day (16 June, 1904) in Dublin. In *Ulysses*, Joyce intends to present a microcosm of the whole human life by providing an instance of how a single event contains all the events of its kind, and how history is recapitulated in the happenings of one day. With complete objectivity and minute details of man's everyday routines and his psychic processes, Joyce illustrates a symbolic picture of all human history, which is simultaneously tragic and comic, heroic and cowardly, magnificent and dreary. Joyce spent 17 years working on his last important book, *Finnegans Wake* (1939). In this encyclopaedic work, Joyce ambitiously attempted to pack the whole history of mankind into one night's dream. In the dream experience, there is no self-conscious logic, no orderly associations, no established values, no limits of time or space; all the past, present and future are mingled and float freely in the mind. Thus, *Finnegans Wake* is regarded as the most original experiment ever made in the novel form, and also the most difficult book to read.

James Joyce is one of the most prominent literary figures of the 20th century. As a great artistic genius, Joyce has created a body of work worthy of comparison with the other masterpieces of English literature. In Joyce's opinion, the artist, who wants to reach the highest stage and to gain the insights necessary for the creation of dramatic art, should rise to the position of a god-like objectivity; he should have the complete conscious control over the creative process and depersonalize his own emotion in the artistic creation. He should appear as an omniscient author and present unspoken materials directly from the psyche of the characters. This literary approach to the presentation of psychological aspects of characters is usually termed as "stream of consciousness". Another remarkable feature of Joyce's writings is his style. His own style is a straightforward one; subtlety, economy and exactness are his standards. But when he tries to render the so-called stream of consciousness, the style changes: incomplete, rapid, broken wording and fragmentary sentences are the typical features, which reflect the shifting, flirting, disorderly flow of thoughts in the major characters' mind.

6.7.2 "Araby[1]" from *Dubliners*

North Richmond Street[2], being blind[3], was a quiet street except at the hour when the Christian Brothers' School set the boys free[4]. An uninhabited house of two storeys stood at the blind end, detached from its neighbors in a square ground. The other houses of the street, conscious of decent lives within them, gazed at one another with brown[5] imperturbable faces.

The former tenant of our house, a priest, had died in the back drawing-room. Air, musty from having been long enclosed, hung in all the rooms, and the waste room behind the kitchen was littered with old useless papers. Among these I found a few paper-covered books, the pages of which were curled and damp: *The Abbot*, by Walter Scott, *The Devout Communicant*, and *The Memoirs of Vidocq*[6]. I liked the last best because its leaves were yellow. The wild garden behind the house contained a central apple-tree and a few straggling bushes, under one of which I found the late tenant's rusty bicycle-pump. He had been a very charitable priest; in his will he had left all his money to institutions and the furniture of his house to his sister.

When the short days of winter came, dusk fell before we had well eaten our dinners. When we met in the street the houses had grown somber. The space of sky above us was the color of ever-changing violet and towards it the lamps of the street lifted their feeble lanterns. The cold air stung us and we played till our bodies glowed. Our shouts echoed in the silent street. The career of our play brought us through the dark muddy lanes behind the houses, where we ran the gantlet[7] of the rough tribes from the cottages, to the back doors of the dark dripping gardens where odors arose from the ashpits, to the dark odorous stables where a coachman smoothed and combed the horse or shook music from the buckled harness. When we returned to the street, light from the kitchen windows had filled the areas. If my uncle was seen turning the corner, we hid in the shadow[8] until we had seen him safely housed. Or if Mangan's sister[9] came out on the doorstep to call her brother in to his tea, we watched her from our shadow peer up and down the street. We waited to see whether she would remain or go in and, if she remained, we left our shadow and walked up to Mangan's steps resignedly. She was waiting for us, her figure defined by the light from the half-opened door. Her brother always teased her before he obeyed, and I stood by the railings looking at her. Her dress swung as she moved her body, and the soft rope of her hair tossed from side to side.

Every morning I lay on the floor in the front parlor watching her door. The blind was pulled down to within an inch of the sash so that I could not be seen. When she came out on the doorstep my heart leaped. I ran to the hall, seized my books and followed her. I kept her brown figure always in my eye and, when we came near the point at which our ways diverged, I quickened my pace and passed her. This happened morning after morning. I had never spoken to her, except for a few casual words, and yet her name was like a summons to all my foolish blood.

Her image accompanied me even in places the most hostile to romance. On Saturday evenings when my aunt went marketing I had togo to carry some of the parcels. We walked through the flaring streets, jostled by drunken men and bargaining women, amid the curses of laborers, the shrill litanies of shop-boys who stood on guard by the barrels of pigs' cheeks, the nasal chanting of street-singers, who sang a *come-all-you* about O'Donovan Rossa[10], or a ballad about the troubles in our native land. These noises converged in a single sensation of life for me: I imagined that I bore my chalice safely through a throng of foes. Her name sprang to my lips at moments in strange prayers and praises which I myself did not understand. My eyes were often full of tears (I could not tell why) and at times a flood from my heart seemed to pour itself out into my bosom. I thought little of the future. I did not know whether I would ever speak to her or not or, if I spoke to her, how I could tell her of my confused adoration. But my body was like a harp and her words and gestures were like fingers running upon the wires.

One evening I went into the back drawing-room in which the priest had died. It was a dark rainy evening and there was no sound in the house. Through one of the broken panes I heard the rain impinge upon the earth, the fine incessant needles of water playing in the sodden beds. Some distant lamp or lighted window gleamed below me. I was thankful that I could see so little. All my senses seemed to desire to veil themselves and, feeling that I was about to slip from them, I pressed the palms of my hands together until they trembled, murmuring: "*O love! O love!*" many times.

At last she spoke to me[11]. When she addressed the first words to me, I was so confused that I did not know what to answer. She asked me was I going to *Araby*. I forgot whether I answered yes or no. It would be a splendid bazaar; she said she would love to go.

— And why can't you? I asked.

While she spoke she turned a silver bracelet round and round her wrist. She could not go, she said, because there would be a retreat[12] that week in her convent. Her brother and two other boys were fighting for their caps, and I was alone at the railings. She held one of the spikes, bowing her head towards me. The light from the lamp opposite our door caught the white curve of her neck, lit up her hair that rested there and, falling, lit up the hand upon the railing. It fell over one side of her dress and caught the white border of a petticoat, just visible as she stood at ease.

— It's well for you, she said.

— If I go, I said, I will bring you something.

What innumerable follies laid waste my waking and sleeping thoughts after that evening! I wished to annihilate the tedious intervening days. I chafed against the work of school. At night in my bedroom and by day in the classroom her image came between me and the page I strove to read. The syllables of the word *Araby* were called to me through the silence in which my soul luxuriated and cast an Eastern enchantment over me. I asked for leave to go to the bazaar on Saturday night. My aunt was surprised, and hoped it was not some Freemason affair[13]. I answered few questions in class. I watched my master's face pass from amiability to sternness; he hoped I was not beginning to idle. I could not call my wandering thoughts together. I had hardly any patience with the serious work of life which, now that it stood between me and my desire, seemed to me child's play, ugly monotonous child's play.

On Saturday morning I reminded my uncle that I wished to go to the bazaar in the evening. He was fussing at the hallstand, looking for the hat-brush, and answered me curtly:

— Yes, boy, I know.

As he was in the hall I could not go into the front parlor and lie at the window. I felt the house in bad humor and walked slowly towards the school. The air was pitilessly raw and already my heart misgave me.

When I came home to dinner my uncle had not yet been home. Still it was early. I sat staring at the clock for some time and, when its ticking began to irritate me, I left the room. I mounted the staircase and gained the upper part of the house. The high cold empty gloomy rooms liberated me and I went from room to room singing. From the front window I saw my companions playing below in the street. Their cries reached me weakened and indistinct and, leaning my forehead against the cool glass, I looked over at the dark house where she lived. I may have stood there for an hour, seeing nothing but the brown-clad figure cast by my imagination, touched discreetly by the lamplight at the curved neck, at the hand upon the railings and at the border below the dress.

When I came downstairs again I found Mrs. Mercer sitting at the fire. She was an old garrulous woman, a pawnbroker's widow, who collected used stamps for some pious purpose. I had to endure the gossip of the tea-table. The meal was prolonged beyond an hour and still my uncle did not come. Mrs. Mercer stood up to go: she was sorry she couldn't wait any longer, but it was after eight o'clock and she did not like to be out late, as the night air was bad for her. When she had gone I began to walk up and down the room, clenching my fists. My aunt said:

— I'm afraid you may put off your bazaar for this night of Our Lord.

At nine o'clock I heard my uncle's latchkey in the hall door. I heard him talking to himself and heard the hallstand rocking when it had received the weight of his overcoat. I could interpret these signs. When he was midway through his dinner I asked him to give me the money to go to the bazaar. He had forgotten.

— The people are in bed and after their first sleep now, he said.

I did not smile. My aunt said to him energetically:

— Can't you give him the money and let him go? You've kept him late enough as it is.

My uncle said he was very sorry he had forgotten. He said he believed in the old saying: "All work and no play makes Jack a dull boy." He asked me where I was going and, when I told him a second time, he asked me did I know *The Arab's Farewell to his Steed*[14]. When I left the kitchen he was about to recite the opening lines of the piece to my aunt.

I held a florin[15] tightly in my hand as I strode down Buckingham Street towards the station. The sight of the streets thronged with buyers and glaring with gas recalled to me the purpose of my journey. I took my seat in a third-class carriage of a deserted train. After an intolerable delay the train moved out of the station slowly. It crept onward among ruinous houses and over the twinkling river. At Westland Row Station a crowd of people pressed to the carriage doors; but the porters moved them back, saying that it was a special train for the bazaar. I remained alone in the bare carriage. In a few minutes, the train drew up beside an improvised wooden platform. I passed out onto the road and saw by the lighted dial of a clock that it was ten minutes to ten. In front of me was a large building which displayed the magical name.

I could not find any sixpenny entrance and, fearing that the bazaar would be closed, I passed in quickly through a turnstile, handing a shilling to a weary-looking man. I found myself in a big hall girded at half its height by a gallery. Nearly all the stalls were closed and the greater part of the hall was in darkness. I recognized a silence like that which pervades a church after a service. I walked into the center of the bazaar timidly. A few people were gathered about the stalls which were still open. Before a curtain, over which the words *Café Chantant*[16] were written in colored lamps, two men were counting money on a salver[17]. I listened to the fall of the coins.

Remembering with difficulty why I had come I went over to one of the stalls and examined porcelain vases and flowered tea-sets. At the door of the stall a young lady was talking and laughing with two young gentlemen. I remarked their English accents and listened vaguely to their conversation.

— O, I never said such a thing!

— O, but you did!

— O, but I didn't!

— Didn't she say that?

— Yes. I heard her.

— O, there's a... fib!

Observing me, the young lady came over and asked me did I wish to buy anything. The tone of her voice was not encouraging; she seemed to have spoken to me out of a sense of duty. I looked humbly at the great jars that stood like eastern guards at either side of the dark entrance to the stall and murmured:

— No, thank you.

The young lady changed the position of one of the vases and went back to the two young men. They began to talk of the same subject. Once or twice the young lady glanced at me over her shoulder.

I lingered before her stall, though I knew my stay was useless, to make my interest in her wares seem the more real. Then I turned away slowly and walked down the middle of the bazaar. I allowed the two pennies to fall against the sixpence in my pocket. I heard a voice call from one end of the gallery that the light was out. The upper part of the hall was now completely dark.

Gazing up into the darkness I saw myself as a creature driven and derided by vanity; and my eyes burned with anguish and anger.

Chapter 6 The Modern Period

Notes

1. **Araby**: a term used to express the romantic view of the east that had been popular since Napoleon's triumph over Egypt. Of course, the story is about Romantic Irony, for the unnamed boy has a romantic view of the world.
2. **North Richmond Street**: In 1894, little Jimmy Joyce was 12, and lived at 17 North Richmond Street.
3. **being blind**: referring to the street being dead end. But this also describes the condition of the boy's relation to reality.
4. **set the boys free**: Joyce uses this neat phrase to suggest that religion has imprisoned the boys.
5. **brown**: the most frequently used color in Dubliners. We note how quickly Joyce has been able to set a nearly hopeless and discouraged mood. In Stephen Hero, Joyce writes: "... one of those brown brick houses which seem the very incarnation of Irish paralysis."
6. *The Abbot*, **by Walter Scott**, *The Devout Communicant*, **and** *The Memoirs of Vidocq*: a historical tale, a manual of religious instruction, and the recollections of a French adventure, respectively.
7. **gantlet**: an archaic spelling of "gauntlet".
8. **shadow**: Note the repetition of "shadow" (three times) in this paragraph. The people of Dublin are not living, but ghosts; the boys, who are very much alive, are surrounded by shades of people.
9. **Mangan's sister**: Here Joyce makes the connection with the popular, but sentimental and romantic 19th century Irish poet, James Clarence Mangan (1803-1849). Mangan was himself fond of writing about "Araby", and even though he knew no Arabic he claimed that some of his poems were translations from Arabic. Joyce's use of "Mangan" is one of the strongest supports for the theme of romanticism in the story, while at the same time it serves to strengthen previous instances of hypocrisy and false sentiment.
10. *come-all-you* **about O'Donovan Rossa**: a street ballad, so called from its opening words. This one was about the 19th-century Irish nationalist Jeremiah Donovan, popularly known as O'Donovan Rossa.
11. **she spoke to me**: Here is a good example of an important modernist technique: "Show, do not tell."
12. **a retreat**: a period of seclusion from ordinary activities devoted to religious exercises.
13. **Freemason affair**: international secret service society, also called the Free and Accepted Masons. His aunt shares her church's distrust of the Freemansons.
14. *The Arab's Farewell to his Steed*: a popular 19th-century poem, which tells about an

253

Arab boy who sells for gold coins the thing that he loves the most in the world, his horse, however, as the horse is being led away the boy changes his mind and rushes after the man to return to money and reclaim his love.

15. **a florin**: a former two-shilling coin. It was a considerable amount of money for this boy. The florin originated in Florence during the Renaissance and had a likeness of the Virgin Mary on one side and that of St. John the Baptist on the other.
16. *Café Chantant*: a French coffee house where musical entertainment is provided.
17. **a salver**: a tray, usually used for serving food.

Study Questions

1. What kind of conflict does the boy experience in the story between him and his environment, or between him and the adults?
2. How does the boy describe his feelings for Mangan's sister?
3. Why does the boy want to go to the bazaar?
4. Why does he arrive so late?
5. What is the role of the boy's uncle in the story? What values and attitudes does he represent?

Essay Topics

1. What do you think the boy has learned?
2. Why does the bazaar become a negative experience for the boy? What do you think the experience teaches him about dreams as opposed to reality?

6.8 D. H. Lawrence

6.8.1 About the Author

D. H. Lawrence (1885-1930) was born at a mining village in Nottinghamshire. His father was a coal miner with little education; but his mother, once a school teacher, was from a somewhat higher class, who came to think that she had married beneath her and desired to have her sons well educated so as to help them escape from the life of coal miners. The conflict between the earthy, coarse, energetic but often drunken father and the refined, strong-willed and up-climbing mother is vividly presented in his autobiographical novel, *Sons and Lovers* (1913).

Lawrence is one of the greatest English novelists of the 20th century, and, perhaps, the greatest from a working-class family. During his life-long literary career, he had written more than ten novels, several volumes of short stories and a large number of poems. *The Rainbow* (1915) and *Women in Love* (1920) are generally regarded as his masterpieces. Symbolism and complex narrative are employed richly in these works. In the novels of his later period, such as *Aaron's Rod* (1922), *Kangaroo* (1923), and *The Plumed Serpent* (1926), Lawrence deals more extensively with themes of power, dominance and leadership. However, in *Lady Chatterley's Lover* (1928), Lawrence has returned to his early subjects and background of Nottioghamshire. By presenting an old romantic story about a dissatisfied aristocratic lady who deserts her half-man, half-machine husband to find love with a man of nature, Lawrence not only condemns the civilized world of mechanism that distorts all natural relationships between men and women, but also advocates a return to nature.

Lawrence turns his eyes outward to human society in his short stories. He is not only telling a story, but also using them to expose the bankruptcy of the mechanical civilization and to find an answer to it. Irony, humor and wit are the characteristic features of many of the stories. *St. Mawr*, *The Daughter of the Vicar*, *The Horse Dealer's Daughter*, *The Captain's Doll*, *The Prussian Officer*, and *The Virgin and the Gypsy* are generally considered to be Lawrence's best known stories.

Lawrence began his poetry writing very early and wrote quite a large number of poems in his whole career. His poems fall roughly into three categories — satirical and comic poems, poems about human relationships and emotions, and poems about nature. Lawrence does not care much about the conventional metrical rules; what he tries to do in poetry is to catch the instant life of the immediate present. In several of his best animal poems, Lawrence reveals the sheer unknowable otherness of the non-human life.

Lawrence's artistic tendency is mainly realism, which combines dramatic scenes with an authoritative commentary. And the realistic feature is most obviously seen in its detailed portraiture. With the working-class simplicity and directness, Lawrence can summon up all the physical attributes associated with the common daily objects. In presenting the psycho-logical aspects of his characters, Lawrence makes use of poetic imagination and symbolism in his writing. By using sets of natural images as poetic symbols to embody the emotional states of the characters and to illustrate human situations, Lawrence endows the traditional realism with a fresh psychological meaning. Through a combination of traditional realism and the innovating elements of symbolism and poetic imagination, Lawrence has managed to bring out the subtle ebb and flow of his characters' subconscious life.

6.8.2 An Excerpt from Chapter 10 of *Sons and Lovers*

When he was twenty-three years old Paul sent in a landscape to the winter exhibition at Nottingham Castle. Miss Jordan had taken a good deal of interest in him, had invited him to her house, where he met other artists. He was beginning to grow ambitious.

One morning the postman came just as he was washing in the scullery[1]. Suddenly he heard a wild noise from his mother. Rushing into the kitchen, he found her standing on

the hearthrug wildly waving a letter and crying "Hurrah!" as if she had gone mad. He was shocked and frightened.

"Why, mother!" he exclaimed.

She flew to him, flung her arms round him for a moment, then waved the letter, crying:

"Hurrah, my boy! I knew we should do it!"

He was afraid of her — the small, severe woman with graying hair suddenly bursting out in such frenzy. The postman came running back, afraid something had happened. They saw his tipped cap over the short curtains. Mrs. Morel rushed to the door.

"His picture's got first prize, Fred," she cried, "and is sold for twenty guineas."

"My word, that's something like!" said the young postman, whom they had known all his life.

"And Major Moreton has bought it!" she cried.

"It looks like meanin' something, that does, Mrs. Morel," said the postman, his blue eyes bright. He was glad to have brought such a lucky letter. Mrs. Morel went indoors and sat down, trembling. Paul was afraid lest she might have misread the letter, and might be disappointed after all. He scrutinized[2] it once, twice. Yes, he became convinced it was true. Then he sat down, his heart beating with joy.

"Mother!" he exclaimed.

"Didn't I *say* we should do it!" she said, pretending she was not crying.

He took the kettle off the fire and mashed the tea.

"You didn't think, mother — " he began tentatively.

"No, my son — not so much — but I expected a good deal."

"But not so much," he said.

"No — no — but I knew we should do it."

And then she recovered her composure, apparently at least. He sat with his shirt turned back, showing his young throat almost like a girl's, and the towel in his hand, his hair sticking up wet.

"Twenty guineas, mother! That's just what you wanted to buy Arthur out. Now you needn't borrow any. It'll just do."

"Indeed, I shan't take it all," she said.

"But why?"

"Because I shan't."

"Well — you have twelve pounds, I'll have nine."

They cavilled[3] about sharing the twenty guineas. She wanted to take only the five pounds she needed. He would not hear of it. So they got over the stress of emotion by quarreling.

Morel came home at night from the pit, saying:

"They tell me Paul's got first prize for his picture, and sold it to Lord Henry Bentley for fifty pound."

"Oh, what stories people do tell!" she cried.

"Ha!" he answered. "I said I wor sure it wor a lie. But they said tha'd told Fred Hodgkisson."

"As if I would tell him such stuff!"

"Ha!" assented the miner.

But he was disappointed nevertheless.

"It's true he has got the first prize," said Mrs. Morel.

The miner sat heavily in his chair.

"Has he, beguy!" he exclaimed.

He stared across the room fixedly.

"But as for fifty pounds — such nonsense!" she was silent awhile. "Major Moreton bought it for twenty guineas, that's true."

"Twenty guineas! Tha niver says!" exclaimed Morel.

"Yes, and it was worth it."

"Ay!" he said. "I don't misdoubt it. But twenty guineas for a bit of a paintin' as he knocked off[4] in an hour or two!"

He was silent with conceit of his son. Mrs. Morel sniffed, as if it were nothing.

"And when does he handle th' money?" asked the collier.

"That I couldn't tell you. When the picture is sent home, I suppose."

There was silence. Morel stared at the sugar-basin instead of eating his dinner. His black arm, with the hand all gnarled with work, lay on the table. His wife pretended not to see him rub the back of his hand across his eyes, nor the smear in the coal-dust on his black face.

"Yes, an' that other lad 'ud 'a done as much if they hadna ha' killed 'im,"[5] he said quietly.

The thought of William went through Mrs. Morel like a cold blade. It left her feeling she was tired, and wanted rest.

Paul was invited to dinner at Mr. Jordan's. Afterwards he said:

"Mother, I want an evening suit."

"Yes, I was afraid you would," she said. She was glad. There was a moment or two of silence. "There's that one of William's," she continued, "that I know cost four pounds ten and which he'd only worn three times."

"Should you like me to wear it, mother?" he asked.

"Yes, I think it would fit you — at least the coat. The trousers would want shortening."

He went upstairs and put on the coat and vest. Coming down, he looked strange in a flannel collar and a flannel shirt-front, with an evening coat and vest. It was rather large.

"The tailor can make it right," she said, smoothing her hand over his shoulder. "It's beautiful stuff. I never could find in my heart to let your father wear the trousers, and very glad I am now."

And as she smoothed her hand over the silk collar she thought of her eldest son. But this son was living enough inside the clothes. She passed her hand down his back to feel him. He was alive and hers. The other was dead.

He went out to dinner several times in his evening suit that had been William's. Each time his mother's heart was firm with pride and joy. He was started now. The studs[6] she and the children had bought for William were in his shirt-front; he wore one of William's dress shirts. But he had an elegant figure. His face was rough, but warm-looking and rather pleasing. He did not look particularly a gentleman, but she thought he looked quite a man.

He told her everything that took place, everything that was said. It was as if she had been there. And he was dying to introduce her to these new friends who had dinner at seven-thirty in the evening.

"Go along with you[7]!" she said. "What do they want to know me for?"

"They do!" he cried indignantly. "If they want to know me — and they say they do — then they want to know you, because you are quite as clever as I am."

"Go along with you, child!" she laughed.

But she began to spare her hands. They, too, were work-gnarled now. The skin was shiny with so much hot water, the knuckles rather swollen. But she began to be careful to keep them out of soda. She regretted what they had been — so small and exquisite. And when Annie insisted on her having more stylish blouses to suit her age, she submitted. She even went so far as to allow a black velvet bow to be placed on her hair. Then she sniffed in her sarcastic manner, and was sure she looked a sight. But she looked a lady[8], Paul declared, as much as Mrs. Major Moreton, and far, far nicer. The family was coming on[9]. Only Morel remained unchanged, or rather, lapsed[10] slowly.

Paul and his mother now had long discussions about life. Religion was fading into the background. He had shoveled away all the beliefs that would hamper him, had cleared the ground, and come more or less to the bedrock of belief that one should feel inside oneself for right and wrong, and should have the patience to gradually realize one's God. Now life interested him more.

"You know," he said to his mother, "I don't want to belong to the well-to-do middle class. I like my common people best. I belong to the common people."

"But if anyone else said so, my son, wouldn't you be in a tear. You know you consider yourself equal to any gentleman."

"In myself," he answered, "not in my class or my education or my manners. But in myself I am."

"Very well, then. Then why talk about the common people?"

"Because — the difference between people isn't in their class, but in themselves. Only from the middle classes one gets ideas, and from the common people — life itself, warmth. You feel their hates and loves."

"It's all very well, my boy. But, then, why don't you go and talk to your father's pals?"

"But they're rather different."

"Not at all. They're the common people. After all, whom do you mix with now — among the common people? Those that exchange ideas, like the middle classes. The rest don't interest you."

"But — there's the life — "

"I don't believe there's a lot more life from Miriam than you could get from any educated girl — say Miss Moreton. It is you who are snobbish about class."

She frankly wanted him to climb into the middle class, a thing not very difficult, she knew. And she wanted him in the end to marry a lady.

Now she began to combat him in his restless fretting. He still kept up his connexion with Miriam, could neither break free nor go the whole length of engagement. And this indecision seemed to bleed him of his energy. Moreover, his mother suspected him of an unrecognized leaning towards Clara, and, since the latter was a married woman, she wished he would fall in love with one of the girls in a better station of life. But he was stupid, and would refuse to love or even to admire a girl much, just because she was his social superior.

"My boy," said his mother to him, "all your cleverness, your breaking away from old things, and taking life in your own hands, doesn't seem to bring you much happiness."

"What is happiness!" he cried. "It's nothing to me! How am I to be happy?"

The plump[11] question disturbed her.

"That's for you to judge, my lad. But if you could meet some good woman who would make you happy — and you began to think of settling your life — when you have the means — so that you could work without all this fretting — it would be much better for you."

He frowned. His mother caught him on the raw[12] of his wound of Miriam. He pushed the tumbled hair off his forehead, his eyes full of pain and fire.

"You mean easy, mother," he cried. "That's a woman's whole doctrine for life — ease of soul and physical comfort. And I do despise it."

"Oh, do you!" replied his mother. "And do you call yours a divine discontent?"

"Yes. I don't care about its divinity. But damn your happiness! So long as life's full, it doesn't matter whether it's happy or not. I'm afraid your happiness would bore me."

"You never give it a chance," she said. Then suddenly all her passion of grief over him broke out. "But it does matter!" she cried. "And you ought to be happy, you ought to try to be happy, to live to be happy. How could I bear to think your life wouldn't be a happy one!"

"Your own's been bad enough, mater, but it hasn't left you so much worse off than the folk who've been happier. I reckon you've done well. And I am the same. Aren't I well enough off?"

"You're not, my son. Battle — battle — and suffer. It's about all you do, as far as I can see."

"But why not, my dear? I tell you it's the best — "

"It isn't. And one ought to be happy, one ought."

By this time Mrs. Morel was trembling violently. Struggles of this kind often took place between her and her son, when she seemed to fight for his very life against his own will to die. He took her in his arms. She was ill and pitiful.

"Never mind, Little," he murmured. "So long as you don't feel life's paltry and a miserable business, the rest doesn't matter, happiness or unhappiness."

She pressed him to her.

"But I want you to be happy," she said pathetically.

"Eh, my dear — say rather you want me to live."

Mrs. Morel felt as if her heart would break for him. At this rate[13] she knew he would not live. He had that poignant carelessness about himself, his own suffering, his own life, which is a form of slow suicide. It almost broke her heart. With all the passion of her strong nature she hated Miriam for having in this subtle way undermined[14] his joy. It did not matter to her that Miriam could not help it. Miriam did it[15], and she hated her.

Notes

1. **scullery**: a room next to the kitchen, especially in a large old house, where cleaning jobs are done.
2. **scrutinize**: to carefully examine.
3. **cavil**: to make unnecessary complaints about someone or something.
4. **knocked off**: finished rapidly.
5. **an' that other lad 'ud 'a done as much if they hadna ha' killed 'im**: (local dialect) and that other boy (William) would have done just as well, if they had not killed him.
6. **stud**: a small thing for fastening a shirt or collar that consists of two rounds, flat pieces of metal joined together by a bar.
7. **Go along with you**: (informal) It is used to say that you do not believe what someone is saying to you.
8. **looked a lady**: had the appearance of a lady.

9. **The family was coming on**: The family was improving or making progress, especially in education or health.
10. **lapse**: fail to keep his position as if disappearing.
11. **plump**: unqualified, direct.
12. **caught him on the raw**: said something that upset him.
13. **At this rate**: If this state continues.
14. **undermined**: gradually destroyed.
15. **Miriam did it**: Miriam undermined his joy.

Study Questions

1. What makes Mrs. Morel so excited?
2. How does the father feel about the good news?
3. Why does Mrs. Morel want her son to get happiness?
4. Why does Paul want only life, not happiness?
5. How does Mrs. Morel know that Paul would not live under the present condition? Whom does she blame for causing all this? Why?
6. What are Mrs. Morel's hopes and dreams? What is her character like?

Essay Topics

1. What influences contributed to the failure of Mrs. Morel's marriage?
2. Discuss how Mrs. Morel helps and hurts Paul.

6.9 William Golding

6.9.1 About the Author

William Golding (1911-1993) was born in Cornwall, son of a schoolmaster. He was educated at Malborough Grammar School and Oxford. His parents intended to bring him up as a scientist, but Golding developed an interest in literature and chose writing as his career. During the Second World War, he served as a naval officer, taking part in a number of combat operations. His wartime experiences played a large part in formulating his view of life. After the war, Golding devoted himself to teaching and writing.

In 1954, Golding published his first novel, *Lord of the Flies*, which was soon recognized as a major work of art. It tells about the story of a group of English schoolboys being evacuated by air to a place of safety during a nuclear war in the near future. Their plane crashes and the boys are stranded on an uninhabited tropical island. At first, the boys are able to maintain themselves, but soon most of them relapse into a form of primitive savagery, throwing away nearly all the sanctions of civilization. Thematically, the novel primarily deals with the innate evil and original sin in man. After his initial success, Golding went on writing and turned out five more novels: *The Inheritors* (1955), *Pincher Martin* (1956), *Free Fall* (1959), *The Spire* (1964), and *Darkness Visible* (1979).

Golding is a genuinely serious writer who holds a strong pessimistic view towards human nature, regarding man as inherently savage and violent, which reflects the mood of the postwar years. He thinks that modern civilization, the institutions and order imposed from without, is fragile and temporary, but that man's irrationality and innate evil are strong and enduring. Thus, his primary aim in his novel is to reveal this evil as a destructive force in man, which operates counter to the forces of reason and civilization.

Golding's fame has been in part due to his inventiveness in realistic fantasy, his richness in biblical symbolism, and his disposition to use the novel form as a fable. His novels are all in one way or another fables. By creating a mythology of his own, he has bridged a gap between the allegory of the past and the realistic fiction of the present. The structure of his novels is well organized and the narration is under heavy control. His prose is easy, smooth, but strenuous and compact, with a style rich in imagination, powerful in drama, and subtle in literary and mythic overtones.

6.9.2 An Excerpt from Chapter 9 of *Lord of the Flies*

Long before Ralph and Piggy came up with Jack's lot, they could hear the party. There was a stretch of grass in a place where the palms left a wide band of turf[1] between the forest and the shore. Just one step down from the edge of the turf was the white, blown sand of above high water, warm, dry, trodden. Below that again was a rock that stretched away towards the lagoon. Beyond was a short stretch of sand and then the edge of the water. A fire burned on the rock and fat dripped from the roasting pig-meat into the invisible flames. All the boys of the island, except Piggy, Ralph, Simon, and the two tending the pig, were grouped on the turf. They were laughing, singing, lying,

squatting, or standing on the grass, holding food in their hands. But to judge by the greasy faces, the meat-eating was almost done; and some held coconut shells in their hands and were drinking from them. Before the party had started a great log had been dragged into the center of the lawn and Jack, painted and garlanded[2], sat there like an idol. There were piles of meat on green leaves near him, and fruit, and coconut shells full of drink.

Piggy and Ralph came to the edge of the grassy platform and the boys, as they noticed them, fell silent one by one till only the boy next to Jack was talking. Then the silence intruded even there and Jack turned where he sat. For a time he looked at them and the crackle of the fire was the loudest noise over the bourdon of the reef. Ralph looked away; and Sam, thinking that Ralph had turned to him accusingly, put down his gnawed bone with a nervous giggle. Ralph took an uncertain step, pointed to a palm tree, and whispered something inaudible to Piggy; and they both giggled like Sam. Lifting his feet high out of the sand, Ralph started to stroll past. Piggy tried to whistle.

At this moment the boys who were cooking at the fire suddenly hauled off a great chunk of meat and ran with it towards the grass. They bumped Piggy who was burnt, and yelled and danced. Immediately, Ralph and the crowd of boys were united and relieved by a storm of laughter. Piggy once more was the center of social derision so that everyone felt cheerful and normal.

Jack stood up and waved his spear.

"Take them some meat."

The boys with the spit gave Ralph and Piggy each a succulent[3] chunk. They took the gift, dribbling, so they stood and ate beneath a sky of thunderous brass that rang with the storm coming.

Jack waved his spear again.

"Has everybody eaten as much as they want?"

There was still food left, sizzling on the wooden spits, heaped on the green platter. Betrayed by his stomach, Piggy threw a picked bone down on the beach and stooped for more.

Jack spoke again, impatiently.

"Has everybody eaten as much as they want?"

His tone conveyed a warning, given out of the pride of ownership, and the boys ate faster while there was still time. Seeing there was no immediate likelihood of a pause, Jack rose from the log that was his throne and sauntered to the edge of the grass. He looked down from behind his paint at Ralph and Piggy. They moved a little further off over the sand and Ralph watched the fire as he ate. He noticed without understanding, how the flames were visible now against the dull light. Evening was come, not with calm beauty but with the threat of violence.

Jack spoke.

"Give me a drink."

Henry brought him a shell and he drank, watching Piggy and Ralph over the jagged rim. Power lay in the brown swell of his forearms: authority sat on his shoulder and chattered in his ear like an ape.

"All sit down."

The boys ranged themselves in rows on the grass before him but Ralph and Piggy stayed a foot lower, standing on the soft sand. Jack ignored them for the moment, turned his mask down to the seated boys and pointed at them with the spear.

"Who is going to join my tribe?"

Ralph made a sudden movement that became a stumble. Some of the boys turned towards him.

"I gave you food," said Jack, "and my hunters will protect you from the beast. Who will join my tribe?"

"I'm chief," said Ralph, "because you chose me. And we were going to keep the fire going. Now you run after food — "

"You ran yourself!" shouted Jack. "Look at that bone in your hands!"

Ralph went crimson.

"I said you were hunters. That was your job."

Jack ignored him again.

"Who'll join my tribe and have fun?"

"I'm chief," said Ralph tremulously. "And what about the fire? And I've got the conch — "

"You haven't got it with you," said Jack, sneering. "You left it behind, See, clever? And the conch doesn't count at this end of the island — "

All at once the thunder struck. Instead of the dull boom there was a point of impact in the explosion.

"The conch counts here too," said Ralph, "and all over the island."

"What are you going to do about it then?"

Ralph examined the ranks of boys. There was no help in them and he looked away, confused and sweating. Piggy whispered.

"The fire — rescue."

"Who'll join my tribe?"

"I will."

"Me."

"I will."

"I'll blow the conch," said Ralph breathlessly, "and call an assembly."

"We shan't hear it."

Piggy touched Ralph's wrist.

"Come away. There's going to be trouble. And we've had our meat."

There was a blink of bright light beyond the forest and the thunder exploded again so that a littlun started to whine.[4] Big drops of rain fell among them making individual sounds when they struck.

"Going to be a storm," said Ralph, "and you'll have rain like when we dropped here. Who's clever now? Where are your shelters? What are you going to do about that?"

The hunters were looking uneasily at the sky, flinching from the stroke of the drops. A wave of restlessness set the boys swaying and moving aimlessly. The flickering light became brighter and the blows of the thunder were only just bearable. The littluns began to run about, screaming.

Jack leapt on to the sand.

"Do our dance! Come on! Dance!"

He ran stumbling through the thick sand to the open space of rock beyond the fire. Between the flashes of lightning the air was dark and terrible; and the boys followed him, clamorously. Roger became the pig, grunting and charging at Jack, who sidestepped. The hunters took their spears, the cooks took spits, and the rest clubs of firewood. A circling movement developed and a chant. While Roger mimed the terror of the pig, the littluns ran and jumped on the outside of the circle. Piggy and Ralph, under the threat of the sky, found themselves eager to take a place in this demented[5] but partly secure society. They were glad to touch the brown backs of the fence that hemmed in the terror and made it governable.

"*Kill the beast! Cut his throat! Spill his blood!*"

The movement became regular while the chant lost its first superficial excitement and began to beat like a steady pulse. Roger ceased to be a pig and became a hunter, so that the center of the ring yawned emptily. Some of the littluns started a ring on their own; and the complementary circles went round and round as though repetition would achieve safety of itself. There was the throb and stamp of a single organism.

The dark sky was shattered by a blue-white scar. An instant later the noise was on them like the blow of a gigantic whip. The chant rose a tone in agony.

"*Kill the beast! Cut his throat! Spill his blood!*"

Now out of the terror rose another desire, thick, urgent, blind.

"*Kill the beast! Cut his throat! Spill his blood!*"

Again the blue-white scar jagged above them and the sulfurous explosion beat down. The littluns screamed and blundered about, fleeing from the edge of the forest, and one of them broke the ring of biguns in his terror.

"Him! Him!"

The circle became a horseshoe. A thing was crawling out of the forest. It came darkly, uncertainly. The shrill screaming that rose before the beast was like a pain. The beast stumbled into the horseshoe.

"*Kill the beast! Cut his throat! Spill his blood!*"

The blue-white scar was constant, the noise unendurable. Simon was crying out something about a dead man on a hill.

"*Kill the beast! Cut his throat! Spill his blood! Do him in!*"

The sticks fell and the mouth of the new circle crunched and screamed. The beast was on its knees in the center, its arms folded over its face. It was crying out against the abominable noise something about a body on the hill. The beast struggled forward, broke the ring and fell over the steep edge of the rock to the sand by the water. At once the crowd surged after it, poured down the rock, leapt on to the beast, screamed, struck, bit, tore. There were no words and no movements but the tearing of teeth and claws.

Then the clouds opened and let down the rain like a waterfall. The water bounded from the mountain-top, tore leaves and branches from the trees, poured like a cold shower over the struggling heap on the sand. Presently the heap broke up and figures staggered away. Only the beast lay still, a few yards from the sea. Even in the rain they could see how small a beast it was; and already its blood was staining the sand.

Now a great wind blew the rain sideways, cascading the water from the forest trees. On the mountain-top the parachute filled and moved; the figure slid, rose to its feet, spun, swayed down through a vastness of wet air and trod with ungainly[6] feet the tops of the high trees; falling, still falling, it sank towards the beach and the boys rushed screaming into the darkness. The parachute took the figure forward, furrowing the lagoon, and bumped it over the reef and out to sea.

Notes
1. **turf**: a surface that is made up of soil and a thick covering of grass.
2. **garland**: to put one or more circle of flowers, leaves on someone.
3. **succulent**: juicy and delicious.
4. **whine**: to complain (too much) in an unnecessarily sad voice.
5. **demented**: mad; of unbalanced mind.
6. **ungainly**: not look graceful; awkward in movement; clumsy.

Study Questions
1. How do Jack's leadership style and personality differ from Ralph's?
2. What chant do the boys sing as they dance?
3. Who emerges from the jungle with the secret of the beast?
4. Under what circumstances did Simon die?

Essay Topics
1. Where does Golding think evil comes from?
2. In what way is Lord of the Flies a novel about power?

6.10 Samuel Beckett

6.10.1 About the Author

Beckett (1906-1989) was born into a prosperous Protestant family in Dublin. He was sent off at the age of 14 to attend the legendary Portora Royal School. In 1923 he began his study of French and Italian at Trinity College, Dublin. Upon his graduation, he went to teach English at a French university in Paris. In 1930, he returned to Trinity College as a lecturer in French, but gave it up after a year's teaching. He went again to the continent, wandering about for some years. In the course of his journeys, he came into contact with many tramps and wanderers, and these acquaintances would later translate into some of his finest characters. He finally settled down in Paris in 1937. During World War Ⅱ, Beckett joined the French Resistance Movement, fighting against the Nazi Germany. The arrest of some of his close fellow fighters in 1942 obliged him to move away to a remote part of the country. He returned to Paris after the war.

Beckett began his literary career in his early twenties, while teaching English in Paris. He wrote poetry, stories, novels, plays, and critical essays. His first novel, *Murphy*, appeared in 1938. It deals with the philosophical problem of the relation of mind and body. His next novel *Watt* (1944) is a symbolic story set in Ireland. During an incredibly creative period, Beckett produced in French a trilogy of novels under the titles of *Molloy*, *Malone Dies* and *The Unnamable* (1951-1953). These novels, together with his later one *How It Is* (1961), have made him a fairly important and original novelist.

Beckett wrote the play *Waiting for Godot*, which, with its successful production in Paris in 1953 and in London in 1955, made Beckett a famous writer. Over the next two decades, Beckett produced some twenty or so works for the theatre, radio, TV and the cinema. Among them the more important ones are: *End Game* (1958), *Krapp's Last Tape* (1959), *Happy Days* (1962), *The Last Ones* (1972), and some radio and TV plays such as *All that Fall* (1957), *Embers* (1959), *Cascando* (1964), *Breath* (1969), and *Not I* (1973). In his later years, his writing became very brief and highly abstracted in words with condensed ideas. Beckett was awarded the Nobel Prize for literature in 1969. He died in December, 1989.

Perhaps the most famous play written by Beckett is *Waiting for Godot*. The heroes of the play are two tramps, Vladimir and Estragon, who spend consecutive evenings waiting for somebody called Godot on a country road. While waiting, the two men occupy themselves with all kinds of trivial things or empty talks: they tell jokes, abuse each other, recall their past, wonder what they are doing, contemplate suicide, compare themselves to the two thieves who were crucified beside Christ, and so on. Two other characters, Pozzo and Lucky, come along as master and slave. Pozzo abuses and ill-treats Lucky, who is tethered at the end of a rope. Godot sends word that he will not come that day but will surely come the next. In Act Ⅱ the two tramps still wait at the same place. The two visitors appear again, Pozzo now blind and Lucky dumb. With difficulties, they pass on. Then the boy comes with the same message as yesterday. Then the two tramps declare their intention of leaving, but they still go on their waiting. Thematically, Beckett explores and examines man's life by taking away the illusory charms and by reducing him to the essential base. By so doing, he tries to make his audience see the negative side of man's life — a meaningless, hopeless and painful progress towards death. He concludes that man cannot find his true identity, cannot attain his real self, nor can he escape the hellish suffering and boredom; the only thing man can do is wait and pass time with meaningless trivial things or empty talks till death finally relieves him of the burden of life.

Under the influence of Existentialism, Beckett has developed a very pessimistic view towards life and human society. He regards human existence as a very brief, unimportant event in an indifferent universe, a "flash of light between the darkness of the womb and of the tomb." Actually, Beckett is the prophet of negation and sterility. He holds out no hope to humanity in an alien and decaying world. His vision to man's entire life is a torment, a hell, an incomprehensible nullity enveloped by colorful patterns which, in essence, are composed of absurd and futile activities.

Beckett is an atheist, and his atheism springs from the scars left from a Christian belief once deeply felt. With rich religious images and symbols, Beckett presents in his works strong Christian nihilism, which shows his bitter rejection and blasphemy against his early beliefs. A typical example of this kind is the famous line about God from his play, *End Game*, "The dirty dog, he doesn't even exist!" which best reflects his grudge against God. Artistically, Beckett has come under the strong influence of James Joyce. His works, which parody the unsympathetic world and man's wretched lot, derive obviously from Joyce. If Joyce is concerned with portraying the richness and variety of life, Beckett is preoccupied with rendering the human impotence and nihilistic vacuum of life.

6.10.2　An excerpt from Act Ⅰ of *Waiting for Godot*

Estragon, sitting on a low mound, is trying to take off his boot. He pulls at it with both hands, panting. He gives up, exhausted, rests, tries again. As before.

Enter Vladimir.

ESTRAGON: (*giving up again.*) Nothing to be done.

VLADIMIR: (*advancing with short, stiff strides, legs wide apart.*) I'm beginning to come round to that opinion. All my life I've tried to put it from me, saying, Vladimir, be reasonable you haven't yet tried every thing. And I resumed the struggle. (*He broods, musing on the struggle, Turning to Estragon.*) So there you are again.

ESTRAGON: Am I?

VLADIMIR: I'm glad to see you back. I thought you were gone forever.

ESTRAGON: Me too.

VLADIMIR: Together again at last! We'll have to celebrate this. But how? (*He reflects.*) Get up till I embrace you.

Chapter 6 The Modern Period

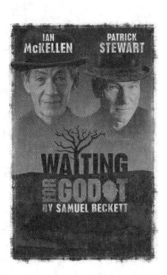

ESTRAGON: (*irritably.*) Not now, not now.

VLADIMIR: (*hurt, coldly.*) May one enquire where His Highness spent the night?

ESTRAGON: In a ditch.

VLADIMIR: (*admiringly.*) A ditch! Where?

ESTRAGON: (*without gesture.*) Over there.

VLADIMIR: And they didn't beat you?

ESTRAGON: Beat me? Certainly they beat me.

VLADIMIR: The same lot as usual?

ESTRAGON: The same? I don't know.

VLADIMIR: When I think of it... all these years... but for me... where would you be...? (*Decisively.*) You'd be nothing more than a little heap of bones at the present minute, no doubt about it.

ESTRAGON: And what of it?

VLADIMIR: (*gloomily.*) It's too much for one man. (*Pause. Cheerfully.*) On the other hand what's the good of losing heart now, that's what I say. We should have thought of it a million years ago, in the nineties.[1]

ESTRAGON: Ah stop blathering and help me off with this bloody thing.

VLADIMIR: Hand in hand from the top of the Eiffel Tower, among the first. We were presentable in those days. Now it's too late. They wouldn't even let us up. (*Estragon tears at his boot.*) What are you doing?

ESTRAGON: Taking off my boot. Did that never happen to you?

VLADIMIR: Boots must be taken off every day, I'm tired telling you that. Why don't you listen to me?

ESTRAGON: (*feebly.*) Help me!

VLADIMIR: It hurts?

ESTRAGON: Hurts! He wants to know if it hurts!

VLADIMIR: (*angrily.*) No one ever suffers but you. I don't count. I'd like to hear what you'd say if you had what I have.

ESTRAGON: It hurts?

VLADIMIR: Hurts! He wants to know if it hurts!

ESTRAGON: (*pointing.*) You might button it all the same.

VLADIMIR: (*stooping.*) True. (*He buttons his fly.*) Never neglect the little things of life.

ESTRAGON: What do you expect, you always wait till the last moment.

VLADIMIR: (*amusingly.*) The last moment... (*He meditates.*) Hope deferred[2] maketh the something sick, who said that?

ESTRAGON: Why don't you help me?

VLADIMIR: Sometimes I feel it coming all the same. Then I go all queer. (*He takes off his hat, peers inside it, feels about inside it, shakes it, puts it on again.*) How shall I say? Relieved and at the same time... (*he searches for the word*)... appalled. (*With emphasis.*) AP-PALLED. (*He takes off his hat again, peers inside it.*) Funny. (*He knocks on the crown as though to dislodge a foreign body, peers into it again, puts it on again.*) Nothing to be done. (*Estragon with a supreme effort succeeds in pulling off his boot. He looks inside it, feels about inside it, turns it upside down, shakes it, looks on the ground to see if anything has fallen out, finds nothing, feels inside it again, staring sightlessly before him.*) Well?

ESTRAGON: Nothing.

VLADIMIR: Show.

ESTRAGON: There's nothing to show.

VLADIMIR: Try and put it on again.

ESTRAGON: (*examining his foot.*) I'll air it for a bit.

VLADIMIR: There's man all over for you, blaming on his boots the faults of his feet. (*He takes off his hat again, peers inside it, feels about inside it, knocks on the crown, blows into it, puts it on again.*) This is getting alarming. (*Silence. Vladimir deep in thought, Estragon pulling at his toes.*) One of the thieves was saved. (*Pause.*) It's a reasonable percentage. (*Pause.*) Gogo.

ESTRAGON: What?

VLADIMIR: Suppose we repented.

ESTRAGON: Repented what?

VLADIMIR: Oh... (*He reflects.*) We wouldn't have to go into the details.

ESTRAGON: Our being born?

(*Vladimir breaks into a hearty laugh which he immediately stifles, his hand pressed to his pubis, his face contorted.*)

VLADIMIR: One daren't even laugh any more.

ESTRAGON: Dreadful privation.

VLADIMIR: Merely smile. (*He smiles suddenly from ear to ear, keeps smiling, ceases as suddenly.*) It's not the same thing. Nothing to be done. (*Pause.*) Gogo.

ESTRAGON: (*irritably.*) What is it?

VLADIMIR: Did you ever read the Bible?

ESTRAGON: The Bible... (*He reflects.*) I must have taken a look at it.

VLADIMIR: Do you remember the Gospels?

ESTRAGON: I remember the maps of the Holy Land. Colored they were. Very pretty. The Dead Sea was pale blue. The very look of it made me thirsty. That's where we'll go, I used to say, that's where we'll go for our honeymoon. We'll swim. We'll be happy.

VLADIMIR: You should have been a poet.

ESTRAGON: I was. (*Gesture towards his rags.*) Isn't that obvious. (*Silence.*)
VLADIMIR: Where was I... How's your foot?
ESTRAGON: Swelling visibly.
VLADIMIR: Ah yes, the two thieves. Do you remember the story?
ESTRAGON: No.
VLADIMIR: Shall I tell it to you?
ESTRAGON: No.
VLADIMIR: It'll pass the time. (*Pause.*) Two thieves, crucified at the same time as our Savior. One —
ESTRAGON: Our what?
VLADIMIR: Our Savior. Two thieves. One is supposed to have been saved and the other... (*he searches for the contrary of saved*)... damned.
ESTRAGON: Saved from what?
VLADIMIR: Hell.
ESTRAGON: I'm going. (*He does not move.*)
VLADIMIR: And yet... (*pause*)... how is It — this is not boring you I hope-how is it that of the four Evangelists[3] only one speaks of a thief being saved. The four of them were there — or thereabouts — and only one speaks of a thief being saved. (*Pause.*) Come on, Gogo, return the ball,[4] can't you, once in a way?
ESTRAGON: (*with exaggerated enthusiasm.*) I find this really most extraordinarily interesting.
VLADIMIR: One out of four. Of the other three two don't mention any thieves at all and the third says that both of them abused him.
ESTRAGON: Who?
VLADIMIR: What?
ESTRAGON: What's all this about? Abused who?
VLADIMIR: The Savior.
ESTRAGON: Why?
VLADIMIR: Because he wouldn't save them.
ESTRAGON: From hell?
VLADIMIR: Imbecile! From death.
ESTRAGON: I thought you said hell.
VLADIMIR: From death, from death.
ESTRAGON: Well what of it?
VLADIMIR: Then the two of them must have been damned.
ESTRAGON: And why not?
VLADIMIR: But one of the four says that one of the two was saved.
ESTRAGON: Well? They don't agree, and that's all there is to it.
VLADIMIR: But all four were there. And only one speaks of a thief being saved. Why

believe him rather than the others?

ESTRAGON: Who believes him?

VLADIMIR: Everybody. It's the only version they know.

ESTRAGON: People are bloody ignorant apes.

(He rises painfully, goes limping to extreme left, halts, gazes into distance off with his hand screening his eyes, turns, goes to extreme right, gazes into distance, Vladimir watches him, then goes and picks up the boot, peers into it, drops it hastily.)

VLADIMIR: Pah! *(He spits. Estragon moves to center, halts with his back to auditorium.)*

ESTRAGON: Charming spot. *(He turns, advances to front, halts facing auditorium.)* Inspiring prospects. *(He turns to Vladimir.)* Let's go.

VLADIMIR: We can't.

ESTRAGON: Why not?

VLADIMIR: We're waiting for Godot.

ESTRAGON: *(despairingly.)* Ah! *(Pause.)* You're sure it was here?

VLADIMIR: What?

ESTRAGON: That we were to wait.

VLADIMIR: He said by the tree. *(They look at the tree.)* Do you see any others?

ESTRAGON: What is it?

VLADIMIR: I don't know. A willow.

ESTRAGON: Where are the leaves?

VLADIMIR: It must be dead.

ESTRAGON: No more weeping.

VLADIMIR: Or perhaps it's not the season.

ESTRAGON: Looks to me more like a bush.

VLADIMIR: A shrub.

ESTRAGON: A bush.

VLADIMIR: A —. What are you insinuating? That we've come to the wrong place?

ESTRAGON: He should be here.

VLADIMIR: He didn't say for sure he'd come.

ESTRAGON: And if he doesn't come?

VLADIMIR: We'll come back tomorrow.

ESTRAGON: And then the day after tomorrow.

VLADIMIR: Possibly.

ESTRAGON: And so on.

VLADIMIR: The point is —

ESTRAGON: Until he comes.

VLADIMIR: You're merciless.

ESTRAGON: We came here yesterday.
VLADIMIR: Ah no, there you're mistaken.
ESTRAGON: What did we do yesterday?
VLADIMIR: What did we do yesterday?
ESTRAGON: Yes.
VLADIMIR: Why... (*Angrily.*) Nothing is certain when you're about.
ESTRAGON: In my opinion we were here.
VLADIMIR: (*looking round.*) You recognize the place?
ESTRAGON: I didn't say that.
VLADIMIR: Well?
ESTRAGON: That makes no difference.
VLADIMIR: All the same... that tree... (*turning towards the auditorium*) that bog...
ESTRAGON: You're sure it was this evening?
VLADIMIR: What?
ESTRAGON: That we were to wait.
VLADIMIR: He said Saturday. (*Pause.*) I think.
ESTRAGON: You think.
VLADIMIR: I must have made a note of it. (*He fumbles in his pockets, bursting with miscellaneous rubbish.*)
ESTRAGON: (*very insidious.*) But what Saturday? And is it Saturday? Is it not rather Sunday? (*Pause.*) Or Monday? (*Pause.*) Or Friday?
VLADIMIR: (*looking wildly about him, as though the date was inscribed in the landscape.*) It's not possible!
ESTRAGON: Or Thursday?
VLADIMIR: What'll we do?
ESTRAGON: If he came yesterday and we weren't here you may be sure he won't come again today.
VLADIMIR: But you say we were here yesterday.
ESTRAGON: I may be mistaken. (*Pause.*) Let's stop talking for a minute, do you mind?
VLADIMIR: (*feebly.*) All right. (*Estragon sits down on the mound. Vladimir paces agitatedly to and fro, halting from time to time to gaze into distance off. Estragon falls asleep. Vladimir halts before Estragon.*) Gogo!... Gogo!... GOGO! (*Estragon wakes with a start.*)
ESTRAGON: (*restored to the horror of his situation.*) I was asleep! (*Despairingly.*) Why will you never let me sleep?
VLADIMIR: I felt lonely.
ESTRAGON: I had a dream.
VLADIMIR: Don't tell me!

ESTRAGON: I dreamt that —

VLADIMIR: DON'T TELL ME!

ESTRAGON: (*gesture towards the universe.*) This one is enough for you? (*Silence.*) It's not nice of you, Didi. Who am I to tell my private nightmares to if I can't tell them to you?

VLADIMIR: Let them remain private. You know I can't bear that.

ESTRAGON: (*coldly.*) There are times when I wonder if it wouldn't be better for us to part.

VLADIMIR: You wouldn't go far.

ESTRAGON: That would be too bad, really too bad. (*Pause.*) Wouldn't it, Didi, be really too bad? (*Pause.*) When you think of the beauty of the way. (*Pause.*) And the goodness of the wayfarers. (*Pause. Wheedling.*) Wouldn't it, Didi?

VLADIMIR: Calm yourself.

ESTRAGON: (*voluptuously.*) Calm... calm... The English say calm. (*Pause.*) You know the story of the Englishman in the brothel?

VLADIMIR: Yes.

ESTRAGON: Tell it to me.

VLADIMIR: Ah stop it!

ESTRAGON: An Englishman having drunk a little more than usual goes to a brothel. The bawd asks him if he wants a fair one, a dark one, or a red-haired one. Go on.

VLADIMIR: STOP IT!

(*Exit Vladimir hurriedly. Estragon gets up and follows him as far as the limit of the stage. Gestures of Estragon like those of a spectator encouraging a pugilist. Enter Vladimir. He brushes past Estragon, crosses the stage with bowed head. Estragon takes a step towards him, halts.*)

ESTRAGON: (*gently.*) You wanted to speak to me? (*Silence. Estragon takes a step forward.*) You had something to say to me? (*Silence. Another step forward.*) Didi...

VLADIMIR: (*without turning.*) I've nothing to say to you.

ESTRAGON: (*step forward.*) You're angry? (*Silence. Step forward.*) Forgive me. (*Silence, Step forward. Estragon lays his hand on Vladimir's shoulder.*) Come Didi. (*Silence.*) Give me your hand. (*Vladimir half turns.*) Embrace me! (*Vladimir stiffens.*) Don't be stubborn! (Vladimir softens. They embrace. Estragon recoils.) You stink of garlic!

VLADIMIR: It's for the kidneys. (*Silence. Estragon looks attentively at the tree.*) What do we do now?

ESTRAGON: Wait.

VLADIMIR: Yes, but while waiting.

ESTRAGON: What about hanging ourselves?

VLADIMIR: Hmm. It'd give us an erection!

ESTRAGON: (*highly excited.*) An erection!

VLADIMIR: With all that follows, Where it falls mandrakes grow. That's why they shriek when you pull them up. Did you not know that?

ESTRAGON: Let's hang ourselves immediately!

VLADIMIR: From a bough? (*They go towards the tree.*) I wouldn't trust it.

ESTRAGON: We can always try.

VLADIMIR: Go ahead.

ESTRAGON: After you.

VLADIMIR: No no, you first.

ESTRAGON: Why me?

VLADIMIR: You're lighter than I am.

ESTRAGON: Just so!

VLADIMIR: I don't understand.

ESTRAGON: Use your intelligence, can't you? (*Vladimir uses his intelligence.*)

VLADIMIR: (*finally.*) I remain in the dark.

ESTRAGON: This is how it is. (*He reflects.*) The bough... the bough... (*Angrily.*) Use your head, can't you?

VLADIMIR: You're my only hope.

ESTRAGON: (*with effort.*) Gogo light — bough not break — Gogo dead. Didi heavy — bough break — Didi alone. Whereas —

VLADIMIR: I hadn't thought of that.

ESTRAGON: If it hangs you it'll hang anything.

VLADIMIR: But am I heavier than you?

ESTRAGON: So you tell me. I don't know. There's an even chance. Or nearly.

VLADIMIR: Well? What do we do?

ESTRAGON: Don't let's do anything. It's safer.

VLADIMIR: Let's wait and see what he says.

ESTRAGON: Who?

VLADIMIR: Godot.

ESTRAGON: Good idea.

Notes

1. **We should have thought of it a million years ago, in the nineties**: According to the context, Vladimir is saying that they should have committed suicide long ago.
2. **Hope deferred**: Hope delayed.
3. **the four Evangelists**: referring to the four of Jesus Christ's disciples who wrote the four Gospels. They were St. Matthew, St. Mark, St. Luke, and St. John.
4. **return the ball**: answer me.

Study Questions

1. How are Estragon and Vladimir alike? How are they different?
2. What is the barrier between the decision to act and action itself in *Waiting for Godot*?
3. Why do Estragon and Vladimir want to kill themselves?
4. What is the value of life in *Waiting for Godot*?
5. "Nothing to be done" is repeated two times in this section. In each case, who says it and why?
6. What is the worst kind of suffering we see in *Waiting for Godot*?
7. Soon after the play opens, Vladimir and Estragon discuss the theme of two thieves on the cross. What biblical story does this theme refer to?
8. Vladimir and Estragon are said to have complementary characters. What seem to be their complementary personal characteristics? In your opinion, does Beckett want them to represent themselves as individuals or do they stand for the entire humanity?
9. What are the main characteristics of the stage convention known as the Theatre of the Absurd? How are they shown in the play?

Essay topics

1. Discuss the body/soul relationship in terms of Estragon and Vladimir's relationship.
2. Discuss Beckett's attitude toward hope in the play. Are there any real signs of hope?

6.11 Dylan Thomas

6.11.1 About the Author

Dylan Thomas (1914-1953) was born in Swansea, South Wales. He was educated at the local grammar school. From early childhood, Thomas was exposed to English literature. After working for a time as a newspaper reporter, Thomas was "discovered" as a poet in 1933 through a poetry contest in a popular newspaper. When he published his first volume of poetry, Eighteen Poems, in 1934, Thomas was only 19. The book was widely noticed and enthusiastically reviewed by the critics. His early career was rounded off with two more books: *Twenty-Five Poems* (1936) and *The Map of Love*, which includes poems and prose writings.

In 1939, Thomas moved to London to work for BBC, writing and performing radio broadcasts. The physical and psychic havoc of World War II deeply affected Thomas, a conscious objector, and shaped his third volume of poetry, *Deaths and Entrances* (1946), which contains many of Thomas' most famous work. Thomas also wrote prose work. His best-known prose work was *Portrait of the Artist as a Young Dog* (1940), a collection of semi-autobiographical short stories, which stylistically and thematically bears comparison to Joyce's *Dubliners* and *Portrait of the Artist as a Young Man*. His radio play *Under Milk Wood*, first broadcast by BBC and later transferred to the stage, became extremely popular and was published in 1954.

Thomas is a bold and original poet, probably the greatest lyric poet of his generation. His major poetic themes are limited but elemental — birth, childhood, sex and death. And death casts its shadow on almost every poem. One of Thomas's outstanding merits is his rich vocabulary, his sensual appreciation of words, and his intense persuasive idioms. His style is very much of his own: a fast-moving tide of images, fractured syntax and personal symbology. His tone is usually grave and depressing, but the sound is rich in music.

6.11.2 "Do Not Go Gentle into That Good Night"

Do not go gentle into that good night,
Old age should burn and rave at close of day;
Rage, rage against the dying of the light.

Though wise men at their end know dark is right,
Because their words had forked no lightning they
Do not go gentle into that good night.

Good men, the last wave by, crying how bright
Their frail deeds might have danced in a green bay,
Rage, rage against the dying of the light.

Wild men who caught and sang the sun in flight,
And learn, too late, they grieved it on its way,
Do not go gentle into that good night.

Grave men, near death, who see with blinding sight
Blind eyes could blaze like meteors and be gay,
Rage, rage against the dying of the light.

And you, my father, there on the sad height,
Curse, bless, me now with your fierce tears, I pray
Do not go gentle into that good night.
Rage, rage against the dying of the light.

Study Questions

1. Who is the speaker of this poem?
2. What do wise men know? What do they do in spite of this knowledge, and why?
3. How would you interpret the words *good night* and *the dying of the light*? What might dark and light symbolize in the poem?

Essay Topics

1. Describe the emotional impact of the poem and the view of life and death it expresses.
2. Which poet, Eliot or Thomas, touches you more? Explain.

6.12 Ted Hughes

6.12.1 About the Author

Ted Hughes (1930-1998) was born in Mytholmroyd, Yorkshire and educated at Mexborough Grammar School and Cambridge where he first studied English and then archaeology and anthropology. In 1956, Hughes married Sylvia Plath, an American poet, whom he met at Cambridge. Then they lived in the United States for some years. Their marriage was fruitful to both of them, but in 1962 Hughes separated from Plath, who committed suicide in 1963.

Hughes began writing poems when he was only fifteen. He published his first collection of poems, *Hawk in the Rain* in 1957. His second book of poems, *Lupercal*, appeared in 1960. These two volumes of poetry established him as a prominent poet of nature and animal in the 1960s. In this period Hughes also wrote poems for children. In the later period of his poetic career, Hughes published six more volumes of poems: *Wodwo* (1967), *Crow* (1970), *Season Songs* (1974), *Gaudete* (1977), *Cave Birds* (1978) and *Remains of Elmet* (1979). Hughes also wrote short stories, plays for radio and stage, and some very fine critical essays in which he went straight to the heart of the matter, conveying somewhat single-minded critical insights with enthusiasm and power. In 1985, Ted Hughes was honored with the title of the Poet Laureate of the United Kingdom.

Hughes is a poet writing in the romantic tradition. He prefers to express an individual insight rather than present conventional values of the society. In poetry writing, he thinks a good poem is an organism, "an assembly of living parts moved by a single spirit". To write a good poem is to capture a spirit, or in his words, "to capture a wild animal". To achieve this, Hughes makes use of freer poetic forms, relies less on strict metrical schemes, and is more inclined towards an arrogant tone and an exaggerated diction. His images are usually simple, vivid but grim with a stark, hard-edged quality; his rhythms are bold, strong and rapid, with heavy stresses and obtrusive alliterations, producing an effect of urgent violence and primitive strength; his language, colloquial and varied, tends to move from comic levity and violence to grotesque surrealism. By mixing the Biblical and classical mythology with sharply topical allusions to motor-car accidents, pollutions, mechanized wars and nuclear devastations, Hughes creates a body of poetic myth that stands for the black and violent experiences of modern man. It is undeniable that Hughes is a talented poet with great gifts of imagination and originality of expression.

6.12.2 "Hawk Roosting[1]"

I sit in the top of the wood, my eyes closed.
Inaction, no falsifying dream
Between my hooked head and hooked feet:
Or in sleep rehearse perfect kills and eat.

The convenience of the high trees!
The air's buoyancy[2] and the sun's ray
Are of advantage to me;
And the earth's face upward for my inspection.

My feet are locked upon the rough bark.
It took the whole of Creation
To produce my foot, my each feather:
Now I hold Creation in my foot

Or fly up, and revolve it all slowly —
I kill where I please because it is all mine.
There is no sophistry[3] in my body:
My manners are tearing off heads —
The allotment of death.
For the one path of my flight is direct
Through the bones of the living.
No arguments assert my right:

The sun is behind me.
Nothing has changed since I began.
My eye has permitted no change.
I am going to keep things like this.

Notes

1. This poem is the monologue of a hawk sitting in the top of a wood. Hughes said he had in mid the personality of someone like Hitler, so the poem can be read as an insight into fascist psychology. roosting: a bird sitting comfortably through the night, perhaps sleeping.
2. **buoyancy**: the ability to float, either on water or (metaphorically) in the air.
3. **sophistry**: false but clever and believable reasoning or argument.

Study Questions

1. Who is the speaker? What traits make him seem human? Inhuman?
2. Describe the speaker's image of himself and of the world. How valid do you find his view of life?
3. Describe the emotional effect of the poem — is it amusing, frightening, moving or something else altogether? Explain how Hughes creates that effect?
4. What does the poet's view of nature seem to be? Do you think the poem also portrays an aspect of human nature? Explain.

6.13 Seamus Heaney

6.13.1 About the Author

Seamus Heaney (1939-) was born in County Derry, Northern Ireland. Heaney was the eldest of nine children, and he grew up on his father's farm. He attended local schools, earned a degree in English with first-class honors from Queen's University, Belfast, and then took a teacher's certificate in English at St. Joseph's College. After one year as a secondary school teacher, Heaney returned to St. Joseph's College to serve as a lecturer for three years. Here he began to write, joining a poetry workshop with Derek Mahon, Michael Longley, and others under the guidance of Philip Hobsbaum. In 1965 he met and married Marie Devlin. They had three children.

Heaney became a lecturer at Queen's University in 1966. Partly to escape the violence of Belfast, he gave up his work and moved to the Irish republic in 1972, working at a teacher training college in Dublin. Since 1981 he has spent part of each year teaching at Harvard University, where he is a Professor of Rhetoric and Oratory. Between the years 1989 and 1994 he held Professorship of Poetry at Oxford.

His poetry often deals with "the local" — that is Ireland, and particularly Northern Ireland. His first two collections, *Death of a Naturalist* (1966) and *Door into the Dark* (1969), largely written before the renewed outbreak of the so-called "Troubles" in 1968, show Heaney alerting his audience to the violent history of colonization on his native ground, but preoccupied also by the rhythms of life in a rural setting remembered from his childhood. With *Wintering Out* (1972), Heaney sought to find historical and mythic analogies for the plight in which the minority found itself. In *Field Work* (1979) the political debate is out in the open in a more resonant and Yeatsian way than hitherto; with *Station Island* (1984), written after the deaths of the hunger-strikers and the so-called "dirty protests" in prisons, Heaney more openly ponders the relevance of his poetry in time of violence and polarization.

Heaney's two most recent volumes of poetry, *The Spirit Level* (1996) and *Electric Light* (2001), have seen him turning away from immediate political issues to consider further ideas with visionary and allegorical views. Besides poetry, he also writes critical essays and does translations. His verse translation of *Beowulf* (1999) from Old English is highly praised.

Extremely evocative yet clear and direct, balanced between the personal and the topical, Heaney's carefully crafted poetry has been praised for its powerful imagery, meaningful content, musical phrasing, and compelling rhythms. The development of his poetry has often manifested a canny and clear-eyed responsiveness to changing patterns of violence and peace-seeking across the last thirty years of the twentieth century. Widely recognized as Ireland's greatest poet since William Butler Yeats, Heaney was awarded the 1995 Nobel Prize in Literature.

6.13.2　"Follower"

My father worked with a horse plough,
His shoulders globed[1] like a full sail strung
Between the shafts and the furrow.
The horse strained at his clicking tongue[2].

An expert. He would set the wing
And fit the bright steel-pointed sock.
The sod rolled over without breaking.
At the headrig, with a single pluck

Of reins, the sweating team[3] turned round
And back into the land. His eye
Narrowed and angled at the ground,
Mapping the furrow exactly.

I stumbled in his hob-nailed[4] wake,
Fell sometimes on the polished sod;

Sometimes he rode me on his back
Dipping and rising to his plod.

I wanted to grow up and plough,
To close one eye, stiffen my arm.
All I ever did was follow
In his broad shadow round the farm.

I was a nuisance, tripping, falling,
Yapping always. But today
It is my father who keeps stumbling
Behind me, and will not go away.

Notes

1. **globed**: formed into a ball-like shape.
2. **clicking tongue**: making a short hard sound with the tongue, especially in order to get someone's attention.
3. **the sweating team**: here referring to the ploughing man and horses together.
4. **hob-nailed**: marked by the short, hard-headed nails used as studs in shoes.

Study Questions

1. What images does the speaker use to describe his father working in the field?
2. What did the speaker do while his father worked? What did he want to do when he grew up?
3. What does the speaker say about his father today?
4. What does the last sentence of the poem mean? What might the "stumbling" father who "will not go away" symbolize?
5. In what way can the past be both a gift and a burden?

Appendix Ⅰ Sample Test Paper

Ⅰ. **Multiple Choice** (1 × 20 = 20%):

Directions: *In this part, there are 20 statements or questions; in each of them, there are four choices marked by A, B, C and D. Choose the ONE answer that is most suitable to the statement or question.*

1. It's Chaucer alone who, for the first time in English literature, presented to us a comprehensive realistic picture of the English society in his masterpiece _____.
    A. *The Canterbury Tales.*   B. *The Legend of Good Women.*
    C. *Troilus and Criseyde.*   D. *The Book of the Duchess.*

2. Which of the following historical events does not directly help to stimulate the rising of the Renaissance Movement?
    A. The rediscovery of ancient Greek and Roman culture.
    B. The new discoveries in geography and astrology.
    C. The English Bourgeois Revolution.
    D. The religious reformation and the economic expansion.

3. In the English Renaissance period, _____ was regarded as the "Poet's Poet".
    A. Philip Sidney   B. Edmund Spenser
    C. Thomas Wyatt   D. Christopher Marlowe

4. Which of the following statements best illustrates the theme of Shakespeare's Sonnet 18?
    A. The speaker meditates on man's morality.
    B. The speaker satirizes human vanity.
    C. The speaker eulogizes the power of artistic creation.
    D. The speaker tells one of his dream visions.

5. Milton's *Paradise Lost* is actually a story taken from _____.
    A. Greek Mythology   B. Roman legend
    C. The Old Testament   D. The New Testament

6. In *The Pilgrim's Progress*, John Bunyan describes the Vanity Fair in a _____ tone.
    A. delightful   B. solemn
    C. sentimental   D. satirical

7. Daniel Defoe describes _____ as a typical English middle-class man of the 18th century, the very prototype of the empire builder or the pioneer colonist.
    A. Tom Jones   B. Gulliver
    C. Moll Flanders   D. Robinson Crusoe

8. In which of the following works can you find the proper names "Lilliput," "Brobdingnag," "Houyhnhnm" and "Yahoo"?

A. *The Pilgrim's Progress*   B. *Gulliver's Travels*
C. *Moll Flanders*   D. *Joseph Andrews*

9. Which of the following is not a typical feature of Samuel Johnson's language style?

A. His sentences are long and well structured.
B. His sentences are interwoven with parallel phrases.
C. He tends to use informal and colloquial words.
D. His sentences are complicated, but his thoughts are clearly expressed.

10. As a literary figure, Sophia Western appears in Henry Fielding's _____.

A. *Tom Jones*   B. *Amelia*
C. *Joseph Andrews*   D. *Jonathan Wild the Great*

11. In a sense, we can say that Romanticism designates a literary and philosophical theory which tends to see the _____ as the very center of all life and all experience.

A. individual   B. society
C. family   D. country life

12. _____ defines poetry as "the spontaneous overflow of powerful feelings, which originates in emotion recollected in tranquility."

A. William Blake   B. William Wordsworth
C. Samuel Taylor Coleridge   D. John Keats

13. The lines "It was a miracle of rare device, / A sunny pleasure dome with caves of ice" are found in _____.

A. Samuel Taylor Coleridge's "Kubla Khan"
B. William Wordsworth's "I Wandered Lonely as a Cloud"
C. John Keats's "Ode to Autumn"
D. Percy Bysshe Shelly's "Ode to the West Wind"

14. After reading the first chapter of *Pride and Prejudice*, we may come to know that Mrs. Bennet is a woman of _____.

A. simple character and quick wit
B. simple character and poor understanding
C. intricate character and quick wit
D. intricate character and poor understanding

15. "My Last Duchess" is a poem that best exemplifies Robert Browning's _____.

A. sensitive ear for the sounds of the English language
B. excellent choice of words
C. mastering of the metrical devices
D. use of the dramatic monologue

16. A typical feature of the English _____ literature is that writers became social and moral critics, exposing all kinds of social evils.
   A. Medieval   B. Romantic
   C. Victorian   D. Modern

17. In Hardy's *Tess of d'Urbervilles*, the heroine's tragic ending is due to _____.
   A. her weak character   B. her ambition
   C. Angel Clare's selfishness   D. a hostile society

18. Dickens takes the French Revolution as the background of his novel _____.
   A. *Great Expectations*   B. *A Tale of Two Cities*
   C. *Bleak House*   D. *Oliver Twist*

19. Among the great writers of the modern period, _____ might be the greatest in radical experimentation of technical innovations in novel writing.
   A. Joseph Conrad   B. James Joyce
   C. D. H. Lawrence   D. T. S. Eliot

20. *The Rainbow* and _____ are generally regarded as D. H. Lawrence's masterpieces.
   A. *Women in Love*   B. *Sons and Lovers*
   C. *Lady Chatterley's Lover*   D. *The Plumed Serpent*

II. Define the literary terms listed below (10 × 2 = 20%):

1. Humanism

2. Neoclassicism

III. Reading comprehension (5 × 4 = 20%):

Directions: *Read each of the following quotations carefully and then try to give brief answers to the questions.*

1. ... "Nor lose possession of that fair thou ow'st;
Nor shall Death brag thou wand'rest in his shade,
So long as men can breathe or eyes can see,
So long lives this, and this gives life to thee."

Questions:
1) Identify the poem and the poet.
2) What does "thou wand'rest in his shade" mean?

3) What idea do the last two lines in the quotation express?

2. "Ye Muses, then, whoever ye are, who love to sing battles, and principally thou who whilom didst recount the slaughter in those fields where Hudibras and Trulla fought, if thou wert not starved with thy friend Butler, assist me on this great occasion." (Henry Fielding: *Tom Jones*)

Questions:
1) What does the word "Muse" mean?
2) What is the tone of the author?
3) What kind of writing style does the author use here? And what kind of effect can this style achieve?

3. "She thanked men — good! but thanked
Somehow — I know not how — as if she ranked
My gift of a nine-hundred-years-old name
With anybody's gift."

Questions:
1) Identify the poem and the poet.
2) What kind of tone does the speaker use here?
3) What idea does the quoted passage express?

4. "And when I am formulated, sprawling on a pin,
When I am pinned and wriggling on the wall,
Then how should I begin
To spit out all the butt-ends of my days and ways."

Questions:
1) Identify the poem and the poet.
2) What does the phrase "butt-ends" mean?
3) What idea does the quoted passage express?

IV. **Give brief answers to the following questions** ($10 \times 2 = 20\%$):

Directions: *In this part you are given 2 questions. You are asked to give only a brief answer, explaining what you know about it. You should use no more than 100 words for each answer, and you should, therefore, concentrate on those essential points.*

Appendix I   Sample Test Paper

1. In his novel *Tom Jones*, Henry Fielding created two major male characters, Tom and Blifill. What differences are there between the two characters?

2. Dickens's *Great Expectation* is a novel about "expectations," that is, dreams people have cherished in life. What is Pip's "expectation" or dream and what is the result?

V. **Topic Discussion** (20 points in all):

Directions: *In this part you are asked to write a short essay on the given topic. You should write no more than 150 words on the topic. Therefore, you should concentrate on those important points. Try your best to be logical in your essay and keep your writing clear and tidy.*

Jane Austen makes use of letters in her novel writing. What are the important functions do letters play in *Pride and Prejudice*?

Keys

Ⅰ. **Multiple Choice** (1 × 20 = 20%):
   1-5 ACBCC   6-10 DDBCA   11-15 ABABD   16-20 CDBBA

Ⅱ. **Define the literary terms listed below** (10 × 2 = 20%):
   1. Humanism
   Broadly, this term suggests any attitude that tends to exalt the human element or stress the importance of human interests, as opposed to the supernatural, divine elements — or as opposed to the grosser, animal elements. In a more specific sense, humanism suggests a devotion to those studies supposed to promote human culture most effectively — in particular, those dealing with the life, thought, language, and literature of ancient Greece and Rome. In literary history the most important use of the term is to designate the revival of classical culture that accompanied the Renaissance.

   2. Neoclassicism
   The term mainly applies to the classical tendency that dominated English literature during the last decades of the seventeenth century and the first half of the eighteenth century. It was, at least in part, the result of a reaction against the fires of passion, which had blazed in the late Renaissance, especially in the Metaphysical poetry. It found its artistic models in the classical literature of the ancient Greek and Roman writers like Homer, Virgil, Horace, Ovid, etc. and in the contemporary French writers such as Voltaire and Diderot. In literary creation, it emphasized the classical artistic ideals of order, logic, proportion, restrained emotion, accuracy, good taste and decorum. It had a lasting wholesome influence upon literature of the coming generations in its clarifying and chastening effect upon English prose style and in its establishing in English literature the importance of certain classical graces, such as order, good form, unified structure, clarity, conciseness, and restraint. Poetic techniques as developed by Pope, too, had become a permanent heritage.

Ⅲ. **Reading comprehension** (5 × 4 = 20%):
   1.
   1) Shakespeare: Sonnet 18 "Shall I Compare Thee to a Summer's Day?"
   2) You live in his influence. (That is, you are under death's power, or controlled by death.)
   3) So long as men can stay alive, so long as this poem lives, it gives you eternal life. (This ending part of the poem provides a major "turning" in the sonnet and answers the question raised earlier: a nice summer's day is usually transient, but the beauty in

poetry is eternal.)

2.

1) Goddess of poetry.

2) Satirical.

3) By presenting the trivial event of a fight between Molly and the villagers as if it were a grand heroic war, Fielding uses a mock-epic style, imitating the way Homer narrated about battles in the epic *Iliad*. By such imitation, Fielding is able to reveal the discrepancy between the triviality of the real event and the grand epic style of narration, thus making the event much funnier and the satire much keener.

3.

1) Robert Browning: "My Last Duchess".

2) Haughty and sarcastic.

3) The Duke was displeased because she regarded the title of Duchess, which he gave her and which has a history of nine hundred years, to be of the same value as the gift given to her by some insignificant persons.

4.

1) T. S. Eliot: "The Love Song of J. Alfred Prufrock."

2) The ends of cigarettes, meaning trivial things here.

3) Here, Prufrock's inability to do anything against the society he is in is made strikingly clear by using a sharp comparison. Prufrock imagines himself as a kind of insect pinned on the wall and struggling in vain to get free. This image vividly shows Prufrock's current predicament.

Ⅳ. **Give brief answers to the following questions** (10 ×2 =20%):

1.

A. Tom is impulsive, imprudent, and erring but being frank, honest, and good-natured, he is basically a good man. In contrast, Blifill, who seems to be a moral example, is essentially a scheming hypocrite.

B. The contrast highlights criticism of the moral degeneracy, the immorality and hypocrisy behind the mask of honorable living and high-sounding moral principles of the aristocratic-bourgeois society in the 18th-century England.

2.

A. Pip's great expectation or dream is to grow up to be a rich gentleman and marry his princess, Estella.

B. But it turns out that the person who pays for his education is Magwitch, a convict whom he once helped in the past, and Estella, his long dreamed-of princess, is no one but the daughter of Magwitch and a criminal woman.

C. The revelation of the truth of the source of his money and of the identities of Magwitch and Estella, and the realization of the drastic changes in himself, leave him disheartened and disillusioned.

Ⅴ. **Topic Discussion** (20 points in all):

A. Letters are used to reveal characters, as in the case of Mr. Collins and of Lydia (her letter telling of her elopement).

B. Letters are used to speed up the development of the plot and avoid the description of the unimportant events, as in the case of Jane Bennet (who wrote from London to tell her sufferings after the separation between her and Bingley). The correspondence between the Bennets and the Gardeners after Lydia's elopement plays the same function.

C. Letters are also used to reinforce the theme of the story. For instance, Darcy's letter explains many points of misunderstanding and brings the success of the love story much closer. Mrs. Gardiner's letter in response to Elizabeth's inquiry reveals Darcy's nobility in bringing about Lydia's marriage and his modesty instead of his early pride, which makes Elizabeth realize that she has fallen in love with Darcy.

Appendix II A Brief Introduction to the Study of Literature

The aim of this guide is to provide the students with some general background knowledge and specific comments on individual works so that they can get a better understanding of *An Introductory Course Book of English and American Literatures*. Most of the students majoring in English find the first step in literature study difficult. In order to help the students overcome the initial difficulties, we would like to offer some basic things in understanding literature here.

I. Three Uses of the Language

1.1 Practical Use of the Language

Language has different uses. The commonest use of language is to communicate information. That is the practical use of the language. The practical use of the language is to narrow down the meaning of the words, to confine the words to one meaning at a time, to choose one single, exact meaning and throw the rest away. The following dialogue is a typical example of the practical use of the language.

Mr. Smith is asking the policeman the way to Fleet Street in London.
"Excuse me, Sir. Can you tell me the way to Fleet Street?"
"Yes, Sir. Go straightforward, turn left at the first cross, then turn right at the next, and you'll find Fleet Street."
"Thank you very much."
"It's a pleasure, Sir."

Generally you would make practical use of the language to keep a diary, to write letters, history books, science textbooks, etc.

The purest form of the practical language is the scientific language. The scientist intends to write with a language in which every word would have one meaning only, and for every meaning there would be only one word. Since the ordinary language does not fulfill these conditions, he has invented one like this: $SO_2 + H_2O = H_2SO_3$.

The word sulfurous, if it occurred in poetry, might have all kinds of connotations: fire, smoke, brimstone, hell, and damnation. But H_2SO_3 means one thing and one thing only: sulfurous acid.

In literature, you can also find that language is used to pass information, or to communicate with each other. Especially the dialogues in literary works would just play this function. For instance, in the first chapter of *Pride and Prejudice*, there is such a dialogue between Mr. and Mrs. Bennets.

"*What is his name?*"

"*Bingley.*"

"*Is he married or single?*"

"*Oh! Single, my dear, to be sure! A single man of large fortune; four or five thousand a year. What a fine thing for our girls!*"

"*How so? How can it affect them?*"

"*My dear Mr. Bennet,*" *replied his wife,* "*how can you be so tiresome! You must know that I am thinking of his marrying one of them.*"

"*Is that his design in settling here?*"

"*Design! Nonsense, how can you talk so! But it is very likely that he may fall in love with one of them, and therefore you must visit him as soon as he comes.*"

1.2 Hortatory Use of the Language

A second use of the language is as an instrument of persuasion. For instance, here is an advertisement:

"*At* 60 *miles an hour the loudest noise in the new Rolls-Royce comes from the electric clock.*"

Other advertisements like:

"*The world smiles with reader's digest*" (Reader's Digest)
"*Melts in your mouth, not in your hand.*" —M&M chocolates

Besides advertisements, this kind of use of the language can also be found in propaganda bulletins, sermons, and political speeches.

1.3 Literary Use of the Language

The literary use of the language is not primarily to communicate information or to make somebody believe something that novels and stories and plays and poems are written. These exist to bring us a sense and a perception of life, to widen and sharpen our contacts with existence, and our understanding of life. That is the literary use of the language. The literary use of the language is to make full use of the words, to take the advantage of the word's connotations and to enrich the meaning of the words, to reinforce the meaning, the ambiguity and multiplicity of meanings. There are several special features of the literary language.

1.3.1 Make Full Use of the Word's Connotation

The average word has two parts of meanings: denotation and connotation. The basic meaning of the word, i.e. the dictionary meaning of the word, is called denotation. Beyond its denotations a word may also have connotations.

The connotation is what the word suggests beyond what it expresses; it is the overtones of meaning. It is acquired by its past history and association. Take the word "home" for example:

The denotation of the word is a place where one lives.

The connotation of the word suggests security, love, comfort and family.

So people say: "East, west, home is best."

The words "childlike" and "childish" both mean characteristics of a child, but "childlike" suggests meekness, innocence, and wide-eyed wonder; "childish" suggests pettiness, willfulness, immaturity, shallow thoughts, and inconstancy.

The connotation is very important to the author, for it is one of the means by which he can concentrate or enrich his meaning— say more in fewer words.

1.3.2 Saying One Thing, Meaning Another

The following is a dialogue between two students:

A: *Well, you're a pretty sight! Got slightly wet, didn't you?*

B: *Wet? I'm drowned! It's raining cats and dogs outside, and my raincoat's just like a sieve!*

From the dialogue, we can see that it is not a pretty sight but a wretched sight. And student B did not get slightly wet but very wet. Of cause he did not get drowned but only got drenched; and it was not raining cats and dogs but water. The raincoat is not like a sieve at all.

1.3.3 Saying Most in the Fewest Words

For example, when comparing Ben Jonson with Shakespeare, Dryden says: "Shakespeare was the Homer... Jonson was the Virgil; I admire him, but I love Shakespeare."

1.3.4 Figurative Use of the Language

Figurative language affords us imaginative pleasure. It is a way of bringing additional imagery into literary work, a way of making the abstract concrete. (For further illustrations and examples, please refer to the elements of poetry in Part III of this introduction)

1.3.5 Multidimensional Language

Literature is written in a special form of language. Besides denotative dimension, you may also have intellectual dimension of the language; the sensuous, emotional, and imaginative dimensions. For instance, in the poem, "Spring", Shakespeare paints a wonderful picture of spring with a variety of images, which make the reader see (the colors of flowers), feel (the warmth of spring), touch (the beauty of the season), and hear (the songs of birds).

Literature can convey information, carry instruction or persuasion, but the predominant function is to communicate experience. It is not to tell about experience; rather it is to allow the reader, through imagination, to participate the experience, to live more fully, deeply, richly the experience of life with greater awareness; by broadening the experience, it will make us acquainted with a wide range of experience; by deepening our experience, it will make us feel more poignantly and more understandingly the everyday experiences.

II. Fiction

2.1 What Is Fiction?

The word fiction refers to any narrative, in prose or verse, that is wholly or in part the product of the imagination. Rooted in the oral storytelling tradition, fiction has to do with the invented accounts of the deeds and fates of people, most of them likewise invented. Whatever its apparent factual content, fiction is finally a structured imitation of life and is not to be confused with a literal transcription of life itself. Fiction entertains, and also explores what has been grandly called "the human condition." Generally speaking, fiction includes romances, stories, novels, and other imaginative writings.

2.2 Elements of Fiction

In learning to read fiction well, we must understand something about its technique. One useful way to approach the techniques of fiction is to describe its basic elements or characteristics: theme, plot and structure, character, setting, point of view, style and language, and irony. We will discuss each element separately to highlight its special features. We should be aware that all the elements of a story work together to convey feelings and embody meaning. Consequently, we must relate our analysis of any one fictional element—theme or character, for example—to the other elements and to the work as a whole.

2.2.1 Theme

The theme is the central idea or statement about life that unifies and controls the total work. The theme in literature, whether it takes the form of a brief and meaningful insight or a comprehensive vision of life, is the author's way of communicating and sharing ideas, perceptions, and feelings with his readers or, as is often the case, of exploring with them the puzzling questions of human existence, most of which do not provide neat, tidy, or universally acceptable answers.

Appendix II   A Brief Introduction to the Study of Literature

Identifying the theme

(a) It is important to avoid confusing a work's theme with its subject or situation.

(b) We must be as certain as we can that our statement of theme does the work full justice.

(c) The test of any theme we may propose is whether it is fully and completely supported by the work's other elements.

(d) The title an author gives the work often suggests a particular focus or emphasis for the reader's attention.

Analyzing the theme

(a) Does the work have a theme? Is it stated or implied?

(b) What generalization(s) or statement(s) about life or human experience does the work make?

(c) What elements of the work contribute most heavily to the formulation of the theme?

(d) Does the theme emerge organically and naturally, or does the author seem to force the theme upon the work?

(e) What is the value or significance of the work's theme? Is it topical or universal in its application?

2.2.2 Plot and Structure

The plot, the action in fiction, is the arrangement of events that make up a story. A story's plot keeps us turning pages: we read to find out what will happen next. But for a plot to be effective, it must include a sequence of incidents that bear a significant causal relationship to each other. Causality is an important feature of realistic fictional plots: it simply means that one thing happens because of something else.

Many fictional plots turn on a conflict, or struggle between opposing forces, which is usually resolved by the end of the story. Typical fictional plots begin with an exposition that provides background information we need to make sense of the action, describes the setting, and introduces the major characters; these plots develop a series of complications of the conflict that lead to a crisis or moment of great tension. The conflict may reach a climax or turning point, a moment of greatest tension that fixes the outcome; then, the action falls off as the plot's complications are sorted out and resolved (the resolution).

A story's structure can be examined in relation to its plot. If the plot is the sequence of unfolding action, structure is the design or form of the completed action. In examining the plot, we are concerned with causality, with how one action leads into or ties in with another. In examining structure, we look for patterns, that is, the shape of the content that the story as a whole possesses. The plot directs us to the story in motion, structure to the story at rest. The plot and structure together reveal the aspects of the story's artistic design.

Structure is important in fiction for a number of reasons. It satisfies our need for order, for proportion, for arrangement. A story's symmetry or balance of details may please us, as may its alternation of moments of tension and relaxation. Structure is important for another reason: it provides a clue to a story's meaning.

Analyzing the plot

(a) What are the conflicts on which the plot turns? Are they external, internal, or some combination of the two?

(b) What are the chief episodes or incidents that make up the plot? Is its development strictly chronological, or is the chronology rearranged in some way?

(c) Compare the plot's beginning and end. What essential changes have taken place?

(d) Describe the plot in terms of its exposition, complication, crisis, falling action, and resolution.

(e) Is the plot unified? Do the individual episodes logically relate to one another?

(f) Is the ending appropriate to and consistent with the rest of the plot?

(g) Is the plot plausible? What role, if any, do chance and coincidence play?

2.2.3 Character

Characters are imaginary people that writers create in stories. If one reason we read stories is to find out what happens (to see how the plot works out), an equally compelling reason is to follow the fortunes of the characters. The plot and characters, in fact, are inseparable; we are often less concerned with "what happened" than with "what happened to him or her." When we examine characters in literary analysis, we are concerned essentially with three separate, but closely connected, activities. We are concerned, first of all, with being able to establish the personalities of the characters themselves and to identify their intellectual, emotional, and moral qualities. Second, we are concerned with the techniques an author uses to create and develop characters. Third, we are concerned with whether the characters are credible and convincing.

The major, or central, character of the plot is the protagonist; his opponent, the character against whom the protagonist struggles or contends, is the antagonist.

To describe the relative degree to which fictional characters are developed by their creators, critics usually distinguish between what are referred to as *flat* and *round characters*. *Flat characters* are those who embody or represent a single characteristic, trait, or idea, or at most a very limited number of such qualities. *Flat characters* are also referred to as *type characters*, as *one-dimensional characters*, or, when they are distorted to create humor, as *caricatures*.

Round characters are just the opposite. They embody a number of qualities and traits, and are complex multi-dimensional characters of considerable intellectual and emotional depth. Most importantly, they have the capacity to grow and change.

Characters in fiction can also be distinguished on the basis of whether they demonstrate the capacity to develop or change as the result of their experiences. *Dynamic characters* exhibit a capacity to change; *static characters* do not.

Methods of characterization

In presenting and establishing character, an author has two basic methods or techniques at his disposal. One method is telling, which relies on exposition and direct commentary by the author. The other method is the indirect, dramatic method of showing, which involves the author's stepping aside, as it were, to allow the characters to reveal themselves directly through their dialogue and their actions.

Direct methods of revealing character—characterization by telling—include the following.

(a) Characterization through the use of names.
(b) Characterization through appearance.
(c) Characterization by the author.
(d) Characterization through dialogue.
(e) Characterization through action.

Analyzing characters

(a) Who is the protagonist of the work and who (or what) is the antagonist? Describe the major traits and qualities of each.

(b) What is the function of the work's minor characters?

(c) Identify the characters in terms of whether they are flat or round, dynamic or static.

(d) What methods does the author employ to establish and reveal the characters? Are the methods primarily of showing or telling?

(e) Are the actions of the characters properly motivated and consistent?

(f) Are the characters of the work finally credible and interesting?

2.2.4 Setting

Setting is a term that, in its broadest sense, encompasses both the physical locale that frames the action and the time of day or year, the climatic conditions, and the historical period during which the action takes place.

Functions of the setting

The setting in fiction is called upon to perform a number of specific functions.

Among them are the following:

(a) Setting as a background for action.

(b) Setting as an antagonist.

(c) Setting as a means of creating appropriate atmosphere.

(d) Setting as a means of revealing the character.

(e) Setting as a means of reinforcing the theme.

Analyzing the setting

(a) What is the work's setting in space and time?

(b) How does the author go about establishing the setting? Does the author want the reader to see or feel the setting; or does the author want the reader to both see and feel it? What details of the setting does the author isolate and describe?

(c) Is the setting important? If so, what is its function? Is it used to reveal, reinforce, or influence the characters, the plot, or the theme?

(d) Is the setting an appropriate one?

2.2.5 Point of View

A story must have a storyteller: a narrative voice, real or implied, that presents the story to the reader. When we talk about the narrative voice, we are talking about the point of view, the method of narration that determines the position, or angle of vision from which the story is told.

Commonly used points of view

① Third-person point of view omniscient

With the third-person point of view omniscient, an "all-knowing" narrator firmly imposes his presence between the reader and the story, and retains complete control over the narrative. The great advantage of the third-person point of view omniscient is the flexibility it gives its "all-knowing" narrator, who can direct the reader's attention and control the sources of information.

② Third-person point of view limited

With the third-person point of view limited, the narrator limits his ability to penetrate the minds of characters by selecting a single character to act as the center of revelation. In other words, the narrator assumes only partial insight into one of the characters in the story, restricting his or her information to what the character sees, hears, feels, and thinks.

③ First-person point of view

The use of the first-person point of view places still another restriction on the voice that tells the story. It goes one step further by having that focal character address the reader directly, without an intermediary. This character refers to himself or herself as "I" in the story and addresses the reader as "you," either explicitly or by implication. Among the advantages of the first-person point of view is the sense of immediacy, credibility, and psychological realism that autobiographical storytelling always carries with it. No other point of view, in fact, is more effective in its capacity for eliciting the reader's direct intellectual and emotional involvement in the teller and the tale.

④ Dramatic point of view

In the dramatic, or objective, point of view the story is told ostensibly by no one. The narrator disappears completely and the story is allowed to present itself dramatically through action and dialogue. With the disappearance of the narrator, telling is replaced by showing, and the illusion is created that the reader is a direct and immediate witness to an unfolding drama.

Analyzing the point of view

(a) What is the point of view; who talks to the reader? Is the point of view consistent throughout the work or does it shift in some way?

(b) Where does the narrator stand in relation to the work? Where does the reader stand?

(c) To what sources of knowledge or information does the point of view give the reader access? What sources of knowledge or information does it serve to conceal?

(d) If the work is told from the point of view of one of the characters, is the narrator reliable? Does his or her personality, character, or intellect affect an ability to interpret the events or the other characters correctly?

(e) Given the author's purposes, is the chosen point of view an appropriate and effective one?

(f) How would the work be different if told from another point of view?

2.2.6　Tone

The tone of a work of fiction might be defined as how the story gets told. What are the properties of the voice and telling style of the author or the author's chosen narrator? Is the story told in a neutral, straightforward manner or humorously? Is the narrator calm and reflective or anxious or excited? Is the address colloquial—that is, casual and true to actual conversational speech—or formal? What does the diction, or word-choice, tell us? We answer these kinds of questions automatically as we read, and they shape our response significantly.

2.2.7　Language and Style

When we talk about an author's words and the characteristic way he uses the resources of language to achieve certain effects, we are talking about style. In its most general sense, style consists of diction (the individual words an author chooses) and syntax (the arrangement of those words), as well as such devices as rhythm and sound, allusion, ambiguity, irony, paradox, and the figurative language. Each writer's style is unique. It constitutes his "signature" in a way that sets his work apart.

Diction

Although words are usually meaningful only in the context of other words, stylistic analysis begins with the attempt to identify and understand the type and quality of the individual words that comprise an author's basic vocabulary. The analysis of diction includes the following considerations: the denotative meaning of words, as opposed to their connotative meaning; their degree of concreteness or abstractness; their degree of allusiveness; the parts of speech they represent; their length and construction; the level of usage they reflect (standard or nonstandard; formal, informal, or colloquial); the imagery they contain; the figurative devices (simile, metaphor, personification, etc,) they embody; their rhythm and sound patterns (alliteration, assonance, consonance, onomatopoeia). In studying diction, we also need to pay close attention to the use of repetition.

Syntax

When we examine style at the level of syntax, we are attempting to analyze the ways the author arranges words into phrases, clauses, and finally whole sentences to achieve particular effects. Sentences can be examined in terms of their length—whether they are short, spare, and economical or long and involved; in terms of their form—whether they are simple, compound, or complex; and in terms of their construction—whether they are loose (sentences that follow the normal subject-verb-object pattern, stating their main idea near the beginning in the form of an independent clause), periodic (sentences that deliberately withhold or suspend the completion of the main idea until the end of the sentence), or balanced (sentences in which two similar or antithetical ideas are balanced).

Each type of sentences will have a slightly different effect on the reader. Long, complicated sentences slow down and retard the pace of a narrative, whereas short, simple sentences hasten it. Loose sentences, because they follow the normal, predictable patterns of speech, tend to appear more natural and less contrived than either periodic or balanced sentences, particularly when they are used in the creation of dialogue. Moreover, the deliberate arrangement of words within individual sentences or groups of sentences can result in patterns of rhythm and sound that establish or reinforce feelings and emotions.

2.2.8 Irony

Irony may appear in fiction in three ways: in the work's language, in its incidents, or

Appendix II   A Brief Introduction to the Study of Literature

in its point of view. But in whatever forms it emerges, irony always involves a contrast or discrepancy between one thing and another. The contrast may be between what is said and what is meant or between what happens and what is expected to happen.

In verbal irony, for example, we say the opposite of what we mean. When someone says "That was a brilliant remark" and we know that it was anything but brilliant, we understand the speaker's ironic intention. In such relatively simple instances there is usually no problem in perceiving irony. In more complex instances, however, the designation of an action or a remark as ironic can be much more complicated.

Besides verbal irony, fiction makes use of irony of circumstance (sometimes called irony of situation). Writers sometimes create discrepancies between what seems to be and what is. Irony of circumstance or situation also refers to occasions when an individual expects one thing to occur only to discover that the opposite happens. Although verbal irony and irony of circumstance are the prevalent forms irony assumes in fiction, two others deserve mention: dramatic irony and ironic vision. More typical of plays than stories, dramatic irony is the discrepancy between what characters know and what readers know. Writers sometimes direct our responses by letting us see things that their characters do not. Some writers exploit the discrepancy between what readers and characters know to establish an ironic vision in a work. An ironic vision is established in a work as an overall tone that suggests how a writer views his or her characters and subject.

2.2.9 Symbol

A symbol, according to Webster's Dictionary, is "something that stands for or suggests something else by reason of relationship, association, convention, or accidental resemblance, a visible sign of something invisible." In literature, however, symbols—in the form of words, images, objects, settings, events and characters—are often used deliberately to suggest and reinforce meaning, to provide enrichment by enlarging and clarifying the experience of the work, and to help organize and unify the whole.

Traditional symbols are those whose associations are the common property of a society or culture and are so widely recognized and accepted that they can be said to be almost universal. The symbolic associations that generally accompany the forest and the sea, the moon and the sun, night and day, the colors—black, white and red, and the seasons of the year are examples of traditional symbols.

Original symbols are those whose associations are neither immediate nor traditional; instead, they derive their meanings, largely if not exclusively, from the context of the work in which they are used. Perhaps the most famous example of an original symbol is Melville's white whale, Moby Dick.

2.3 Guidelines for Reading

The following guidelines to reading stories highlight essential approaches, offering advice about how to read stories, and suggest both a method and a context for reading fiction.

(1) Read through the story for enjoyment. Savor its suspense, its humor, its language—whatever engages you, whatever distinguishes the work. If you have time, jot down a few responses to what you've read, perhaps a couple of questions. Think about your experience of the story, of how it affects you as you read.

(2) Establish the fictional type of the story. Consider how the story's typical features guide your reading and direct your understanding.

(3) Read the story a second time. During this reading concentrate on the structure of its plot and on its characters. Evaluate the characters, and examine how the writer creates whatever impression of them you have. Consider the techniques of characterization that he or she employs. During this reading also, center on the subject and tentative theme of the work, thinking about its ideas and values.

(4) Consider the story from the standpoint of the elements of fiction: plot and character, structure and setting, language and style, theme, and point of view. Be aware that certain of these elements may be more noticeable and more important in a given story. Moreover, in considering these elements, remember that the story is an integral work—that any analysis you make of its aspects should be done with a view of the whole in mind.

(5) Throughout your reading, try to be open to the work, however strange, different, or difficult it may at first seem. Relate it to your knowledge of literature and language and to your experience of life.

Ⅲ. Poetry

3.1 Types of Poetry

Poetry can be classified as narrative or lyric. Narrative poems stress action, and lyrics song. Each of these types has numerous subdivisions: narrative poetry includes the epic, romance, and ballad; lyric poetry includes the elegy and epigraph, sonnet and sestina, aubade and villanelle. Moreover, each major type of poetry adheres to different conventions. *Narrative poems*, for example, tell stories and describe actions; *lyric poems* combine speech and song to express feelings in varying degrees of verbal music.

3.2 Narrative Poetry

3.2.1 Epic

Epics are long narrative poems that record the adventures of a hero whose exploits are important to the history of a nation. Typically they chronicle the origins of a civilization and embody its central beliefs and values. Epics tend to be larger than life as they recount heroic deeds enacted in vast landscapes. The style of epic is as grand as the action; the conventions require that the epic be formal, complex, and serious—suitable to its important subjects.

3.2.2 Ballad

Ballads, which are less ambitious than epics, are perhaps the most popular form of narrative poetry. Originally ballads were meant to be sung or recited. Folk ballads (or popular ballads as they are sometimes called) were passed on orally, only to be written down much later. In addition to folk ballads of unknown authorship, there are also literary ballads of known authorship. One example is "La Belle Dame sans Merci" by John Keats. Literary ballads imitate the folk ballad by adhering to its basic conventions—repeated lines and stanzas in a refrain, swift action with occasional surprise endings, extraordinary events evoked in direct, simple language, and scant characterization—but are more polished stylistically and more self-conscious in their use of poetic techniques.

3.2.3 Romance

The romance is another type of narrative poem, in which adventure is a central feature. The plots of romances tend to be complex, with surprising and even magical actions common. The chief characters are human beings, though they often confront monsters, dragons, and disguised animals in a world that does not adhere consistently to the laws of nature, as we know them. The romance in short deals with the marvelous— with, for example, St. George slaying a dragon in a magical forest. Popular during the Middle Ages and Renaissance, the romance as a poetic genre has fallen from favor. Nevertheless, some of its chief characteristics have found expression in popular fictional types such as the western, the adventure story, and the romantic love story.

3.3 Lyric Poetry

In lyric poetry, however, story is subordinated to song, and action to emotion. We can define lyrics as subjective poems, often brief, that express the feelings and thoughts of a single speaker (who may or may not represent the poet). The lyric is more a poetic manner than a form; it is more variable and less subject to strict convention than narrative poetry.

Lyric poetry is typically characterized by brevity, melody, and emotional intensity. The music of lyrics makes them memorable, and their brevity contributes to the intensity of their emotional expression. Originally designed to be sung to a musical accompaniment (the word *lyric* derives from the Greek *lyre*), lyrics have been the predominant type of poetry in the West for several hundred years. The tones, moods, and voices of lyric poems are variable and as complexly intertwined as human feelings, thoughts, and imagination. Generally considered the most compressed poetic type, lyrics typically express much in little.

The major forms of lyrics are:

Epigram

The epigram is a brief witty poem that is often satirical, such as Alexander Pope's "On the Collar of a Dog."

Elegy

The elegy is a lament for the dead, such as Thomas Gray's "Elegy Written in a Country Churchyard."

Ode

The ode is a long stately poem in stanzas of varied length, meter, and form. An example of the ode is John Keats's "Ode to a Nightingale."

Aubade

The aubade is a love lyric expressing complaint that dawn means the speaker must part from his lover. An example of the aubade is represented by John Donne's "The Sun Rising."

Sonnet

The sonnet condenses into fourteen lines an expression of emotion or an articulation of idea according to one of two basic patterns: the *Italian* (or *Petrarchan*) and the *English* (or *Shakespearean*). An Italian sonnet is composed of an eight-line octave and a six-line sestet. A Shakespearean sonnet is composed of three four-line quatrains and a concluding two-line couplet. The thoughts and feelings expressed in each sonnet form typically follow the divisions suggested by their structural patterns. Thus an Italian sonnet may state a problem in the octave and present a solution in its sestet. A Shakespearean sonnet will usually introduce a subject in the first quatrain, expand and develop it in the second and third quatrains, and conclude something about it in its final couplet.

3.4 Elements of Poetry

The elements of a poem include a *speaker* whose voice we hear in it; its *diction* or selection of words; its *syntax* or the order of those words; its *imagery* or details of sight, sound, taste, smell, and touch; its *figures of speech* or non-literal ways of expressing one thing in terms of another, such as symbol and metaphors; its *sound effects*, especially rhyme, assonance, and alliteration; its *rhythm and meter* or the pattern of accents we hear in the poem's words, phrases, lines, and sentences; and its *structure* or formal pattern of organization. All the elements of a poem work together harmoniously

Appendix II A Brief Introduction to the Study of Literature

to convey feelings and embody meaning. We will consider them, however, individually, to sharpen our perception of what each element contributes.

3.4.1 Voice: Speaker and Tone

When we read or hear a poem, we hear a speaker's voice. It is this voice that conveys the poem's *tone*, its implied attitude toward its subject. Tone is an abstraction we make from the details of a poem's language: the use of meter and rhyme (or lack of them); the inclusion of certain kinds of details and exclusion of other kinds; particular choices of words and sentence patterns, of imagery and figurative language. In listening to a poem's language, in hearing the voice of its speaker, we catch its tone and feelings and ultimately its meaning. The range of tone we find in poems is as various and complex as the range of voices and attitudes we discern in everyday experience. The more important and persistent is the *ironic tone* of voice.

3.4.2 Diction

At their most successful, poems include "the best words in the best order," as Samuel Taylor Coleridge has said. In reading any poem it is necessary to know what the words mean, but it is equally important to understand what the words imply or suggest. The *denotation* or dictionary meaning of *dictator*, for example, is "a person exercising absolute power, especially one who assumes absolute control without the free consent of the people." But *dictator* also carries additional *connotations* or associations both personal and public. Beyond its dictionary meaning, *dictator* may suggest repressive force and tyrannical oppression; it may call up images of bloodbath, purges, executions; it may trigger associations that prompt us to think of Hitler, for example, or Mussolini. The same kind of associative resonance occurs with a word like *vacation*, the connotations of which far outstrip its dictionary definition: "a period of suspension of work, study, or other activity.' Because poets often hint indirectly at more than their words directly state, it is necessary to develop the habit of considering the connotations of words as well as their denotations. Often for both poets and readers the "best words" are those that do the most work; they convey feelings and indirectly imply ideas rather than state them outright. Poets choose a particular word because it suggests what they want to suggest. Its appropriateness is a function of both its denotation and its connotation.

3.4.3 Imagery

An *image* is a concrete representation of a sense impression, a feeling, or an idea. Images appeal to one or more of our senses or more precisely, they trigger our imaginative reenactment of sense experience by rendering feelings and thoughts in concrete details related directly to our physical apprehension of the world. Images may be visual (something seen), aural (something heard), tactile (something felt), olfactory (something smelled), or gustatory (something tasted).

Poetry, characteristically, is grounded in the concrete and the specific—in details that appeal to our senses, for it is through our senses that we perceive the world. We see daylight break and fade; we hear dogs bark and children laugh; we feel the sting of a bitterly cold wind; we smell the heavy aroma of perfume; we taste (as well as smell and feel) the ice cream or pizza we may enjoy eating. Poetry includes such concrete details and thereby triggers our memories, stimulates our feelings, and enjoins our response.

3.4.4 Figures of Speech: Simile and Metaphor

Rhetoricians have catalogued more than 250 different *figures of speech*, expressions or ways of using words in a non-literal sense. They include *hyperbole* or exaggeration ("I'll die if I miss that game"); understatement ("Being flayed alive is somewhat painful"); *synecdoche* or using a part to signify the whole ("Lend me a hand"); *metonymy* or substituting an attribute of a thing for the thing itself ("step on the gas"); *personification*, endowing inanimate objects or abstract concepts with animate characteristics or qualities ("the lettuce was lonely without tomatoes and cucumbers for company"). We will not go on to name and illustrate the others but instead will concentrate on two specially important for poetry (and for the other literary genres as well): simile and metaphor.

The heart of both these figures is comparison—the making of connections between normally unrelated things, seeing one thing in terms of another. Robert Frost suggests that metaphor is central to poetry, and that, essentially, poetry is a way of "saying one thing and meaning another, saying one thing in terms of another."

Although both figures involve comparisons between unlike things, *simile* establishes the comparison explicitly with the words *like* or *as*. *Metaphor*, on the other hand, employs no such explicit verbal clue. The comparison is *implied* in such a way that the figurative term is substituted for or identified with the literal one. "My daughter dances like an angel" is a simile; "my daughter is an angel" is a metaphor. In this example the difference involves more than the word *like*: the simile is more restricted in its comparative suggestion than is the metaphor. That is, the daughter's angelic attributes are more extensive in the unspecified and unrestricted metaphor. In the simile, however, she only dances like an angel. (There's no suggestion that she possesses other angelic qualities)

3.4.5 Symbolism

A *symbol* is any object or action that means more than itself, any object or action that represents something beyond itself. A rose, for example, can represent beauty or love or transience. A tree may represent a family's roots and branches. A soaring bird might stand for freedom. Light might symbolize hope or knowledge or life. These and other familiar symbols may represent different, even opposite things, depending on how they are deployed in a particular poem. Natural symbols like light and darkness, fire and water can stand for contradictory things. Water, for example, which typically symbolizes life (rain, fertility, food, life) can also stand for death (tempests, hurricanes, floods). And fire, which often indicates destruction, can represent purgation or purification. The meaning of any symbol, whether an object, an action, or a gesture, is controlled by its context.

How then do we know if a poetic detail is symbolic? How do we decide whether to leap beyond the poem's literal factual detail into a symbolic interpretation? There are no simple answers to these questions. Like any interpretive connections we make in reading, the decision to view something as symbolic depends partly on our skill in reading and partly on whether the poetic context invites and rewards a symbolic reading. The following questions can guide our thinking about interpreting symbols:

A. Is the object, action, gesture, or event important to the poem? Is it described in detail? Does it occur repeatedly? Does it appear at a climactic moment in the poem?

B. Does the poem seem to warrant our granting its details more significance than their immediate literal meaning?

C. Does our symbolic reading make sense? Does it account for the literal details without either ignoring or distorting them?

Even in following such guidelines, there will be occasions when we are not certain that a poem is symbolic. And there will be times when, though we are fairly confident *that* certain details are symbolic, we are not confident about *what* they symbolize. Such uncertainty is due largely to the nature of interpretation, which is an art rather than a science. But these interpretive complications are also due to the differences in complexity and variability with which poets use symbols. The most complex symbols resist definitive and final explanation. We can circle around them, but we neither exhaust their significance nor define their meaning.

3.4.6 Syntax

From a Greek word meaning "to arrange together," *syntax* refers to the grammatical structure of words in sentences and the development of sentences in longer units throughout the poem. Poets use syntax as they use imagery, diction, structure, sound, and rhythm—to express meaning and convey feelings. A poem's syntax is an important element of its tone and a guide to a speaker's state of mind. Speakers who repeat themselves or who break off abruptly in the midst of a thought, for example, reveal something about how they feel.

3.4.7 Sound: Rhyme, Alliteration, and Assonance

The most familiar element of poetry is *rhyme*, which can be defined as the matching of final vowel and consonant sounds in two or more words. When the corresponding sounds occur at the ends of lines we have *end rhyme*; when they occur within lines we have *internal rhyme*.

For the reader rhyme is a pleasure, for the poet a challenge. Part of its pleasure for the reader is in anticipating and hearing a poem's echoing song. Part of its challenge for the poet is in rhyming naturally, without forcing the rhythm, the syntax, or the sense. When the challenge is met successfully, the poem is a pleasure to listen to; it sounds natural to the ear. An added bonus is that rhyme makes it easier to remember.

Besides rhyme, two other forms of sound play prevail in poetry: *alliteration* or the repetition of consonant sounds, especially at the beginning of words, and *assonance* or the repetition of vowel sounds. In his witty guide to poetic technique, *Rhyme's Reason*, John Hollander describes alliteration and assonance like this:

Assonance is the spirit of a rhyme,

A common vowel, hovering like a sigh

After its consonantal body dies....

...

Alliteration lightly links

Stressed syllables with common consonants.

Both alliteration and assonance are clearly audible in "Stopping by Woods," particularly in the third stanza:

He gives his harness bells a shake

To ask if there is some mistake.

The only other sound's the sweep

Of easy wind and downy flake.

Notice that the long *e* of "sw*ee*p" is echoed in "*ea*-sy" and "down-*y*," and that the *ow* of "d*ow*ny" echoes the same sound in "s*ou*nd's." These repetitions of sound accentuate the images the words embody, aural images (wind-blow and snow-fall), tactile images (the soft fluff of down and the feel of the gently blowing wind), and visual images (the white flakes of snow).

The alliterative *s*'s in "*s*ome," "*s*ound," and "*s*weep" are supported by the internal and terminal *s*'s: "Give*s*," "hi*s*," "harne*s*s bell*s*," and "i*s*," and also by mid-word *s*'s: "a*s*k," "mi*s*take," and "ea*s*y." There is a difference in the weight of these sounds; some are heavier than others— the two similar heavy *s*'s of "ea*s*y" and "hi*s*" contrast the lighter softer "*s*" in "harne*s*s" and "mi*s*take."

3.4.8 Rhythm and Meter

Rhythm is the pulse or beat we feel in a phrase of music or a line of poetry. Rhythm refers to the regular recurrence of the accent or stress in poems or songs. We derive our sense of rhythm from everyday life and from our experience with language and music. We

Appendix II A Brief Introduction to the Study of Literature

experience the rhythm of day and night, the seasonal rhythm of the year, the beat of our hearts, and the rise and fall of our chests as we breathe in and out.

Poets rely heavily on rhythm to express meaning and convey feelings. In "The Sun Rising" John Donne puts words together in a pattern of stressed and unstressed syllables:

Busy old FOOL, unRUly SUN
WHY DOST THOU THUS
Through WINdows, and through CURtains, CALL on US?

Donne uses four accents per line—even in the second more slowly paced short line. Later in the stanza, he retards the tempo further. Listen to the accents in the following lines:

LOVE, all aLIKE, no SEAson knows, nor CLIME,
Nor HOURS, DAYS, MONTHS, which ARE the RAGS of TIME.

The accents result partly from Donne's use of monosyllabic words and partly from pauses within the line (indicated by commas). Such pauses are called *caesuras* and are represented by a double slash (//). The final couplet of Donne's poem illustrates a common use of caesura—to split a line near its midpoint:

Shine here to us, // and thou art everywhere;
This bed thy center is, // these walls thy sphere.

Marking the accents as well, we get this:
SHINE HERE to US, // and THOU art EVeryWHERE;
THIS BED thy CENter IS, // THESE WALLS THY SPHERE.

Notice again how the monosyllabic diction and the balanced phrasing combine with the caesuras to slow the lines down. The stately rhythm enforces the speaker's dignified tone and serious point: "Here is everywhere; this room is a world in itself; it is all that matters to us."

In the following brief poem, you can readily hear and feel the contrasting pace and rhythms of the two lines:

The Span of Life (by Robert Frost)
The OLD DOG BARKS BACKward withOUT GETting UP.
I can reMEMber when HE was a PUP.

The first line is slower than the second. It is harder to pronounce and takes longer to say because Frost clusters the hard consonants, d, k and g sounds, in the first line, and because the first line contains seven stresses to the four accents of the second. Three of the seven stresses fall at the first part of the line, which gets it off to a slow start, whereas the accents of the second line are evenly spaced. The contrasting rhythms of the lines reinforce their contrasting images and sound effects. More importantly, however, the differences in the sounds and rhythms in the two lines echo the contrast of youth and age.

But we cannot proceed any further in this discussion of rhythm without introducing more precise terms to refer to the patterns of accents we hear in a poem. If rhythm is the pulse or beat we hear in the line, then we can define *meter* as the measure or patterned count of a poetic line. The meter is a count of the stresses we feel in the poem's rhythm. By convention the unit of a poetic meter in English is the foot, a unit of measure consisting of stressed and unstressed syllables. A poetic foot may be either *iambic* or *trochaic*, *anapestic* or *dactylic*. An iambic line is composed primarily of *iambs*, an *iamb* being defined as an unaccented syllable followed by an accented one as in the word "preVENT" or "conTAIN." Reversing the order of accented and unaccented syllables we get a trochee, which is an accented syllable followed by an unaccented one, as in "FOOTball" or "Liquor." We can represent an accented syllable by a ´ and an unaccented syllable by a ~: thus, prevent (~ ´), an iamb, and liquor (´ ~), a trochee. Because both iambic and trochaic feet contain two syllables per foot, they are called *duple* (or double) meters. These duple meters can be distinguished from *triple* meters (three-syllable meters) like anapestic and dactylic meters. An *anapest* (~ ~ ´) consists of two unaccented syllables followed by an accented one as in compreHEND or interVENE. A *dactyl* reverses the anapest, beginning with an accented syllable followed by two unaccented ones. DANgerous and CHEERfully are examples. So is the word ANapest.

Two additional points must be noted about poetic meters. First, anapestic (~ ~ ´) and iambic (~ ´) meters move from an unstressed syllable to a stressed one. For this reason they are called *rising* meters. (They "rise" to the stressed syllable) Lines in anapestic or iambic meter frequently end with a stressed syllable. Trochaic (´ ~) and dactylic (´ ~ ~) meters, on the other hand, are said to be *falling* meters because they begin with a stressed syllable and decline in pitch and emphasis. (Syllables at the ends of trochaic and dactylic lines are generally unstressed)

Here is a chart of the various meters and poetic feet.

	Foot	Meter	Example
Rising feet	iamb	iambic	prevent
	anapest	anapestic	comprehend
Falling feet	trochee	trochaic	football
	dactyl	dactylic	cheerfully
Substitute feet	spondee	spondaic	knick-knack
	pyrrhic	pyrrhic	(light) of the (world)

Duple meters: two syllables per foot: iambic and trochaic
Triple meters: three syllables per foot: anapestic and dactylic
Number of feet per line

| One foot | Monometer |
| Two feet | Dimeter |

Three feet	Trimeter
Four feet	Tetrameter
Five feet	Pentameter
Six feet	Hexameter
Seven feet	Heptameter
Eight feet	Octameter

IV. Drama

When we speak of a drama, we mean a story in dialogue performed by actors, on a stage, before an audience—in other words, a play. We also use the term drama in a more general sense to refer to the literary genre that encompasses all written plays and to the profession of writing, producing, and performing plays.

4.1 Elements of Drama

Every play unfolds a story through the dialogue and actions of its characters. An understanding of these four elements—story, dialogue, action, and character—is therefore crucial to the appreciation of drama.

4.1.1 Plot

The plot is the structure of a play's action. Although it encompasses what happens in a play, the plot is more than a sum of its incidents. The plot is the order of the incidents, their arrangement and form. Traditional plot structure has been described according to the following formula: *exposition*, presentation of background information necessary for the development of the plot; *rising action*, a set of conflicts and crises; *climax*, the play's most decisive crisis; *falling action*, a follow-up that moves toward the play's *resolution* or *denouement*.

By the arrangement of incidents, a dramatist may create suspense, evoke laughter, cause anxiety, or elicit surprise. Frequently surprise follows suspense—fulfilling our need to find out what will happen as we wait for a resolution of a play's action. Suspense is created by conflicts. Drama is essentially the development and resolution of conflicts.

Like a typical short story, the plot of nearly every play contains five structural elements: exposition, rising action, crisis, falling action, and resolution. The exposition provides essential background information, introduces the cast, begins the characterization, and initiates the action. The rising action introduces and develops the conflict. It commences when one or more of the main characters first become aware of an impending difficulty or when their relationships first begin to change. The crisis, or turning point of the play, occurs at the moment of peak emotional intensity and usually involves a decision, a decisive action, or an open conflict between the protagonist and antagonist. It is often called the *obligatory scene* because the audience demands to see such moments acted out on stage. As the consequences of the crisis accumulate, events develop a momentum of their own. Especially in tragedy, the falling action of the play results from the protagonist's loss of control and a final catastrophe often appears inevitable. In both tragedy and comedy, the resolution brings to an end the conflict that has been implicit (or explicit) since the play's opening scenes. When the curtain falls, the relationships among the characters have once more stabilized. The resolution merits special attention because it is the author's last chance to get the point across. Thus, it is not surprising that the resolution often contains a clear statement of the theme and a full revelation of character.

4.1.2 Character

If the plot is the skeletal framework of a play, the character is its vital center. Characters bring plays to life. First and last we attend to characters: to how they look and what their appearance tells us about them; to what they say and what their manner of saying expresses; to what they do and how their actions reveal who they are and what they represent. But even though the characters in plays are not real people, their human dimension is impossible to ignore since actors portray them, and their human qualities are perhaps their most engaging feature. It is, indeed, their human aspect that attracts us to the characters of drama, not their symbolic significance.

4.1.3 Dialogue

Drama is described by Ezra Pound as "persons moving about on a stage using words"—in short, people talking. Listening to their talk we hear identifiable, individual voices. In their presence we encounter persons, for dialogue inevitably brings us back to characters, drama's human center. And though dialogue in plays typically has three major functions—to advance the plot, to establish the setting (the time and place of the action), and to reveal the characters, its most important and consistent function is the revelation of characters.

Dramatic dialogue clearly and continuously builds toward its point, eliminating irrelevancies and unnecessary repetitions. Dramatic dialogue also includes sufficient background information to fix the time, place, and circumstance of the action firmly in the mind of the audience. The dialogue serves many simultaneous functions. It is used to provide necessary factual information, to reminisce, to characterize, to speculate, and to foreshadow. Such dialogue may take the form of discussion, argument, or inquiry. It may accompany and clarify actions or simply reveal attitudes and opinions.

4.1.4 Staging

By staging we have in mind the spectacle a play presents in performance, its visual detail. This includes such things as the positions of actors onstage, their nonverbal gestures and movements, the scenic background, the props and costumes, lighting and sound effects.

4.1.5 Theme

From the plot, characters, dialogue, and staging we derive a sense of the play's meaning or significance. An abstraction of this meaning is its central idea or theme. It is often helpful to try to express the theme of a play in a carefully worded sentence or two, but we should be aware, however, that any summary statement of a complex work of art is bound to be limited and limiting.

4.2 Comedy

Comedy is a light form of drama, which aims primarily to amuse and which ends happily. Since it strives to provoke smiles and laughter, both wit and humor are utilized. In general, the comic effect arises from recognition of some incongruity of speech, action, or character revelation, with the intricate plot. Viewed in another sense, comedy may be considered to deal with people in their human state, restrained and often made ridiculous by their limitations, faults, bodily functions, and animal nature. In Shakespeare's comedies, the playwright sang of youth, love and ideals of happiness. The heroes and heroines fight against destiny and mold their own fate according to their own free will. The general spirit of these comedies is optimism.

4.3 Tragedy

Tragedy is concerned with the harshness and apparent injustice of life. It usually recounts an important and causally related series of events in the life of a person of significance. The events would culminate in trials and catastrophes of a hero, who falls down from power and whose eventual death leads to the downfall of others. Often the hero's fall from happiness is due to a weakness in his character, a weakness such as the excessive pride of Faustus, the overweening ambition of Macbeth, or the uncontrolled jealousy of Othello, which brings self-destruction. The tragic action arouses feelings of awe in the audience, who often leave the theatre with a renewed sense of the seriousness and significance of human life. The word catharsis is often used to describe the audience's feelings. It means the purging from the mind of the feelings of pity and fear the play has aroused.

4.4 Guidelines for Reading a Play

(1) Read the opening stage directions carefully. Try to set the scene mentally. If a cast of characters is listed, spend a few minutes ascertaining the characters' relationships.

(2) Read the opening scene slowly, referring back to the cast of characters if you become confused about who is who. Read slowly and deliberately, noting details that may assume prominence later.

(3) Note places in the action where conflicts develop most intensely. Satisfy yourself that you understand the nature of the conflict—what causes it and how it might be resolved. Pinpoint the play's crisis and consider its implications.

(4) Decide what values the characters embody and believe in. Consider what they may represent. Examine their relationships with one another, attending especially to their effects on each other.

(5) Listen carefully to the play's dialogue. Notice what the characters say and how they say things. Try to hear their tones of voice; try to imagine the pace and tempo of the dialogue. Consider what the characters' speech reveals about them.

(6) Try staging parts of the play in your mind. Imagine where the actors would stand, how they would be dressed, how they would deliver their lines, and what nonverbal gestures they might make. Try to visualize the play's setting by attending to dialogue and stage directions. Notice the visual details of the play. Consider their dramatic function and their possible symbolic significance.

(7) Consider whether the play is a tragedy, comedy, or tragicomedy. If it is a comedy, is it satiric or romantic? Also consider the play's mood and tone.

(8) Try to sum up your sense of the play's central ideas. What point does it seem to make? What values emerge, what attitudes are taken toward these values, and where does the playwright seem to stand on the issues, attitudes, and ideas the play embodies?

Acknowledgments

Acknowledgments must be made to the following works, from which we have benefited a lot in the course of editing *An Introductory Course Book of English and American Literatures*.

Abrams, M. H., et al., eds. *The Norton Anthology of English Literature*. New York: Norton, 1986.

Barnard, Robert. *A Short History of English Literature*. 2nd edition. Oxford: Oxford University Press, 1994.

Bradbury, Malcolm. *The Modern British Novel*. Beijing: Foreign Language Teaching and Research Press, 2005.

Brooks, Cleanth. *Understanding Fiction*. Beijing: Foreign Language Teaching and Research Press, 2005.

Brooks, Cleanth. *Understanding Poetry*. Beijing: Foreign Language Teaching and Research Press, 2005.

Chen, Jia. *A History of English Literature*. 4 vols., Beijing: Commercial Press, 1986.

Chen, Jia. *Selected Readings in English Literature*. 3 vols., Beijing: Commercial Press, 1986.

Coote, Stephen. *The Penguin Short History of English Literature*. New York: Penguin Books Ltd. 1993.

Cronin, Richard. *Shelley's Poetic Thoughts*. London: The MacMillan Press Ltd. 1981.

Curran, Stuart (ed.). *The Cambridge Companion to British Romanticism*. Cambridge: Cambridge University Press, 1993.

Drabble, Margaret. *The Oxford Companion to English Literature*. 5th ed. rev. and updated. Oxford: Oxford University Press, 1995.

He, Qixin. *A History of English Drama*. Nanjing: Yilin Press, 1999.

Head, Dominic. *The Modernist Short Story — A Study in Theory and Practice*. Cambridge: Cambridge University Press, 1992.

Hou, Weirui. *A Comprehensive History of English Literature*. Shanghai: Shanghai Foreign Language Education Press, 1999.

Luo, Jingguo. *A New Anthology of English Literature*. 2 vols., Beijing: Beijing University Press, 1996.

Richetti, John (ed.). The Columbia History of the British Novel. Beijing: Foreign Language Teaching and Research Press, 2005.

Rogers, Pat. *An Outline of English Literature*. Oxford: Oxford University Press,

1998.

Rosenthal, M. L. *The Modern Poets — A Critical Introduction*. Beijing: Foreign Language Teaching and Research Press, 2004.

Wang, Zuoliang. *A History of English Literature*. Beijing: Commercial Press, 1996.

Zhang, Boxiang. *A Course Book of English Literature*. Wuhan: Wuhan University Press, 2005.

Zhang, Dingquan and Wu Gang. *A New Concise History of English Literature*. Shanghai: Shanghai Foreign Language Education Press, 2002.